COMMUNIST REGIMES IN EASTERN EUROPE

COMMUNIST REGIMES IN EASTERN EUROPE

Third edition

RICHARD F. STAAR

HOOVER INSTITUTION PRESS 1977
Stanford University, Stanford, California

Hoover Institution Publication 171

© 1967, 1971, 1977 by the Board of Trustees
  of the Leland Stanford Junior University
All rights reserved
International Standard Book Number: 0-8179-6711-7
Library of Congress Catalog Card Number: 77-72053
Printed in the United States of America
First edition published 1967, second edition 1971,
  third edition 1977

For Jadwiga, Monica, and Christina

Contents

List of Tables

CHARTS

Preface

This third edition has been undertaken in order to update my book, which appeared in earlier editions during December 1967 and April 1971; both of these editions are now out of print. The six years since the second edition was published have witnessed many changes in Eastern Europe. The revised book should continue to serve as an introduction to the source materials that are available for study of this complicated part of the world. Besides the changes in the text, the tables have been revised, and the bibliography has been updated.

The data, in large part, have been extracted from articles and books in the original East European languages. Albanian, Hungarian, and Romanian sources were used mostly in translation, as the footnotes indicate. Transcripts from monitoring by the U.S. Department of Commerce, Foreign Broadcast Information Service, proved most useful, as did *Situation Reports* and other materials from Radio Free Europe (abbreviated as RFE in the text). Central Intelligence Agency *Directories* helped with some of the identifications, especially for purposes of establishing interlocking directorates.

This book is organized into eleven chapters. The first eight treat individually the countries of Eastern Europe, now under communist rule. Each describes the governmental structure, including the constitutional framework and the electoral system; the ruling party, which is called variously a communist, socialist, or workers' movement; domestic policies; and foreign relations. The last three chapters incorporate an area-wide approach. They discuss military and economic integration through the Warsaw Treaty Organization and the Council for Mutual Economic Assistance, together with developments in intrabloc party relations.

Although errors in fact and interpretation remain my own, I wish to acknowledge with gratitude the reading of individual revised chapters by the following: Nicholas C. Pano (Albania), L. A. D. Dellin (Bulgaria), Zdenek Suda (Czechoslovakia), Eric Waldman (East Germany), Bennett Kovrig (Hungary), Witold S. Sworakowski (Poland), George Duca (Romania), Milorad M. Drachkovitch (Yugoslavia), and John J. Dziak (Warsaw Pact). In addition, I am grateful to the Research and Analysis Department of Radio Free Europe, which supplied me with data and information to update this edition.

Both staff members from the Readers' Services Department and certain of the area curators at the Hoover Institution, especially Nicholas Pappas, who served as my research assistant, were most helpful. Denver Shannon located some of the data on the Warsaw Pact. To all of them I owe a special debt of gratitude. The laborious typing of text, footnotes, and tables, as well as the computation of statistics, is the work of Nancy Dibble. The Earhart Foundation of Ann Arbor, Michigan, provided financial assistance to cover some of the research and typing, for which I am grateful. Finally I wish to thank the publications department, especially George Marotta and Mickey Hamilton as well as Betsy Brandt, who did the copy editing, for expediting arrangements to print this book.

RICHARD F. STAAR

Stanford University
January 1977

Chapter 1

People's Socialist Republic of Albania

Still a thorn in the flank of Yugoslavia, a shadow on a formerly Soviet sphere of influence, Albania provides a window into Europe for the Chinese communists. The region now known as the People's Republic of Albania, bordering on Yugoslavia and Greece as well as the Adriatic Sea, has an area of about 11,100 square miles and a population of approximately 2.4 million. Yet this small, poor, and unproductive land of mountaineers, no larger in area than the state of Maryland, plays a significant role in communist international politics. From the days of the Greek and Roman empires, when traders plied its coasts, until well into modern times, Albania remained aloof and detached from world affairs.[1] It was ruled by the Ottomans for nearly four hundred years, commencing in 1468 with the defeat of the Albanian national patriot Skanderbeg, who with his rugged mountain warriors had defended the country against the Turkish army for almost a quarter of a century.

Although the people of Albania have usually stood aside from affairs outside their borders, they found themselves overrun and engulfed by events of the Second World War. A little known school teacher and later self-appointed army general, Enver Hoxha, organized a clandestine group that became known as the National Liberation Front. As the Italians and Germans withdrew in 1944, Hoxha and his communist-dominated organization succeeded in liquidating most of the Albanian anticommunist organizations, such as the Nationalist Front (Balli Kombetar) and the Legality movement.[2]

---

1. For good historical introductions see Stavro Skendi (ed.), *Albania* (New York, 1956), pp. 1–30; and Nicholas C. Pano, *The People's Republic of Albania* (Baltimore, 1968), p. 13–43.

2. About fifteen thousand Albanians were executed and fifty thousand others imprisoned. *ACEN News*, No. 144 (January–February 1970), p. 26; and [Albania], *Twenty Years of Socialism in Albania* (Tirana, 1964), p. 12.

In the absence of any other effective opposition, Hoxha and his associates on 29 November 1944 established a new, revolutionary government at Tirana.[3] Up to this time they had been advised by Josip Broz-Tito's partisans in Yugoslavia. Although the Albanian communists could claim only 4 or 5 percent of the population as supporters, their spurious democratic front received 93.2 percent of the votes cast to elect a constituent assembly, which in January 1946 declared Albania a people's republic. The new dictatorial regime, supported by neighboring Yugoslavia, strengthened communist influence within the country not only through the physical liquidation of notable anticommunists but also by application of ruthless purges to its own ruling party.

Seemingly unimportant to the world, except for the Soviet Union, which was looking for a foothold on the Mediterranean, Albania began to move closer to Moscow. Afraid of impending annexation by his Yugoslav mentors, Hoxha severed relations in July 1948 with Tito.[4] He continued to maintain close ties with the USSR until Khrushchev's denunciation of the deceased Stalin, which led in 1961 to the public break. Left without a strong protector in Europe, Hoxha turned to the Chinese communists, who readily answered his request for assistance in the ideological dispute with the Soviet Union.

THE COMMUNIST PARTY OF ALBANIA

Sympathy for Marxist ideology among certain Albanians dates back to June– December 1924, the period of revolutionary government under Premier Bishop Fan Stylian Noli.[5] An earlier affinity for Russia became evident after Soviet communists revealed the secret treaty of London (1915), which provided for partition of Albania. Lenin was considered a hero by some in that country, since he allegedly saved it from partition. Five minutes of silence was observed by the Albanian parliament in tribute to the leader of the Bolshevik Revolution upon his death in January 1924. Although a communist party was not founded until 1941, Albanian communists and fellow travelers were supported by the Comintern in the late 1920s and 1930s while they continued to agitate as a minority group within their own country and from exile.

During the years 1924–1939, King Zog maintained an authoritarian regime. For twenty years no legal political parties existed in Albania except the fascist

---

3. Names and offices in this ten-man regime are listed by Free Europe Committee, Inc., *A Chronology of Events in Albania, 1944–1952* (New York, 1955), p. 1.

4. On the eve of the break with Tito, Stalin suggested that Yugoslavia absorb Albania. Milovan Djilas, *Conversations with Stalin* (New York, 1962), p. 143. Yugoslav aid to Albania before that time is discussed by Harry Hamm, *Albania: China's Beachhead in Europe* (London, 1963), p. 50.

5. An exile since December 1924, Noli died (1965) in the United States. An article in *Rabotnichesko delo*, 8 November 1976, published at Sofia, gives some details about communist activities in Albania during the 1920s and 1930s.

movement, which was organized after the 1939 Italian occupation. A communist party established itself secretly at Tirana in November 1941 under the supervision of two Yugoslav emissaries, Miladin Popovic and Dusan Mugosa, who advised the party until the end of the Second World War.[6]

The postwar system in Albania came into being without the assistance or presence of Soviet troops. Local communists organized and achieved power under the guidance of their Yugoslav mentors, who received directives from Tito. Leaders chosen by the Yugoslavs to head the party in Albania included the intellectual Enver Hoxha—the first and, as of this writing, the only head of the Albanian communist party—and the proletarian Koci Xoxe, who was executed in 1949 as an "enemy of the people."[7]

Organization. The structure of the party received sanction in 1948 at its first congress. A new name was also selected: the Albanian Party of Labor. The statute adopted at this congress based the organizational hierarchy on the principle of democratic centralism, wherein full and free discussion theoretically is permitted. After a unanimous or majority vote, the minority must submit to the majority. The 1950 constitution[8] of Albania had recognized the special status of the party, as does the current (1976) one. The Albanian Party of Labor is organized according to the country's territorial subdivisions, with a central apparatus in Tirana.

According to the party statute, the highest organ is the congress which meets every five years. This supreme body is made up of delegates nominally elected by district, regional, and city conferences. Its functions include ratification of reports submitted by the Central Committee and other main organs, review and amendment of the party program and statutes, determination of tactics regarding current policy, and election of members to the Central Committee. In practice, the principal roles of the congress remain those of giving the impression of democratic rule and providing an opportunity for deserving members to be elected as delegates.

The Central Committee, according to the statute, directs all party activities in periods between congresses. It supervises lower-ranking organizations, elects members to central organs, administers funds, and represents the movement in its relations with other communist parties and mass organizations in foreign countries. In reality the Central Committee has little authority and power, owing to its size and the fact that it is not in continuous session. The day-to-day functions of this Committee are delegated to the Politburo and the Secretariat,

---

6. Vladimir Dedijer, *Jugoslovensko-Albanski odnosi, 1939–1948* (Belgrade, 1949), p. 5.

7. Jani I. Dilo, *The Communist Party Leadership in Albania* (Washinton, D.C., 1961), pp. 7–8, provides names of others purged before and after Xoxe.

8. Article 21, as given in V. N. Durdenevskii (ed.), *Konstitutsii evropeiskikh stran narodnoi demokratii* (Moscow, 1954), p. 112.

both of which are composed of persons elected by the Central Committee from its own membership.

The real locus of power is the Politburo, the policy-formulating body of the party. At the end of 1976 it consisted of twelve full and five candidate members.[9] Through placement of these persons in top government offices and in the leadership of mass organizations, the Politburo can formulate policy that is certain to be carried out. The selection of Politburo members for the positions of premier and deputy premier represents a constant feature of policy, and this procedure assures continuity in power and control over the government. The system can be described as one of interlocking directorates, and it is still patterned directly after that of the USSR, despite the suspension of relations between the two countries as well as between their respective ruling parties.

Regardless of this basic pattern, the Albanian communists emulated the Chinese by temporarily assigning at least twelve high-ranking bureaucrats (including five Politburo members) to additional duties at the city or district level. An ''Open Letter,'' released by the Central Committee to all party members on 4 March 1966, admitted that a chasm existed between bureaucracy and masses.[10] Its dissemination probably reached the lowest organizational units, implementing the ideological and cultural revolution that had been inaugurated the previous month.

The lowest level in the party hierarchy is the basic unit, which corresponds to the primary party organization in the Communist Party of the Soviet Union. There are more than two thousand such units in factories, transport and construction centers, various institutions, and towns and villages. They can be formed only in places where at least three party members work, and they comprise a link between masses and governing party organs. Their functions include recruitment of new members, administration of local party affairs, and close surveillance over every group living in the community or work center. The basic unit acts as an arm of the police state, but it remains subordinate to local party committees which are formed successively at city, regional, and district levels.

Local committees meet once a month and are controlled by an executive agency, called the bureau, consisting of not more than eleven members. The bureau includes a first secretary plus two or more other secretaries, all of whom must be approved by the Central Committee. The first secretary is political boss over the committee and a trusted party member. Functions of local committees are to assure fulfillment of party directives, supervise implementation of these directives, administer party fiscal affairs, and approve enrollment of new members.

---

9. *Zeri i popullit,* 8 November 1976; and RFE, *Communist Party-Government Line-Up* (Munich, 17 November 1976), p. 1; hereafter cited as *Line-Up.*

10. *Neue Zuercher Zeitung,* 15 March 1966.

Membership and Composition.   The paucity of available information concerning the membership and social composition of the Albanian Party of Labor precludes more than a cursory and uncertain coverage of this subject. According to one author, who cites an official source, party membership in 1941 totaled about two hundred persons. Thirty-five years later the regime provided a figure of about 101,500 members, including 13,500 candidates for membership. (See table 1.)

TABLE 1

GROWTH OF THE ALBANIAN PARTY OF LABOR, 1941–1976

Year	Occasion	Membership
1941	. . . .	200
1943	. . . .	700
1944	. . . .	2,800
1948	. . . . First congress (November)	29,137
1952	. . . . Second congress (March–April).	44,418
1955	. . . . Third congress (May–June).	48,644
1961	. . . . Fourth congress (February)	ca. 53,000
1966	. . . . Fifth congress (November)	66,326
1969	. . . .	ca. 50,000
1971	. . . . Sixth congress (November)	86,985
1976	. . . . Seventh congress (November).	101,500

SOURCES: *Zeri i popullit*, 24 March 1954, as cited by Jani I. Dilo, *The Communist Party Leadership in Albania* (Washington, D.C., 1961), p. 10; Tirana radio, 1 November 1966; *Rruga e partise* (March 1969), p. 65; *Zeri i popullit*, 4 November 1971 and 3 November 1976.

Data concerning the social composition of the party are similarly of dubious validity. In 1952 the membership could be classified by origin as 74.1 percent from the poorer class (probably from rural areas for the most part), 22.2 percent from the middle class, and the remaining 3.7 percent formerly from the wealthy classes. In the words of one expert, written in 1955, "the Albanian Communist Party is fundamentally a party of poor peasants."[11] More recent statistics indicate that the proportion of industrial workers in the party had increased to 37.5 percent and the proportion of peasants on collective farms to 29 percent. The remaining 33.5 percent in late 1976 were probably for the most part government officials, intelligentsia, and members of the armed forces.

In recent years, there has been a concerted effort to bring more women into the party. Thus, in 1971 only 22 percent of the members were women, but in 1976 they made up 27 percent. Recruitment has been emphasized also among the younger segments of the population, and the overwhelming majority of those admitted to the party during 1971–1976 have been thirty or under.[12]

11. Skendi, *op. cit.* (in note 1 above), pp. 84–85.

12. *Zeri i popullit*, 2 November 1976.

The communist party of Albania resembles that of the Soviet Union in many ways besides organizational structure. Politics and activities of both have included widespread purges and internecine rivalry. In Albania, as in any other communist totalitarian state, the country is run by one man who heads the party. Numerous front organizations operate to implement policies of the party-government.

CONSTITUTION AND GOVERNMENT

The People's Socialist Republic of Albania currently functions under a fundamental law known as the 1976 constitution.[13] It is the third such document adopted since the power seizure by the communists and the ninth since Albanians won independence in 1912 from Turkey. Because the Albanian communists represented in effect an adjunct to the Yugoslav communist party, the first postwar constitution in March 1946 did not present much difficulty. Its verbiage strikes the reader as an almost direct translation from the then newly promulgated document in Yugoslavia which, in turn, was based on the 1936 "Stalin" constitution of the Soviet Union.

The major difference was that the Albanian constitution provided for a single legislative chamber known as the People's Assembly, whereas Yugoslavia, owing to its federal structure, had a legislature composed of two houses. Other distinctions included omission of any reference to political supremacy of the Albanian communist party, which already represented the locus of power. References to a regime monopoly over domestic trade and the socialist development of agriculture also were lacking. These deficiencies, however, came to be remedied in subsequent documents adopted in 1950 and 1976.

At the sixth congress of the Albanian Party of Labor in November 1971, it was announced that the 1950 constitution would be superseded by a new one. Almost four years later, approval for drafting a new basic law came at the eighth plenum of the Central Committee.[14] A constitutional commission of 51 leaders, elected by the People's Assembly the following month, included a majority of Central Committee members and Enver Hoxha as chairman.[15] In early 1976 a draft constitution of the People's Socialist Republic of Albania was made public so that it could be "widely discussed by the people before being approved by the People's Assembly."[16]

---

13. *Ibid.*, 29 December 1976, printed the full text of this new constitution.

14. *Ibid.*, 10 October 1975.

15. *Ibid.*, 18 November 1975.

16. Tirana radio, 21 January 1976, broadcast the draft which was three articles longer than the final version.

Principal Features of the 1976 Constitution. The new constitution begins with a lengthy preamble that praises the regime's political-social order and emphasizes the need for protecting as well as strengthening that order, "promoting the construction of the socialist society in order to then progress gradually into a communist society." The body of the document consists of three parts, as did that of the 1950 constitution. The first part, which deals with the social order, defines political and economic foundations of the state as well as rights and duties of citizens. The second treats governmental structure, which includes the People's Assembly, Council of Ministers, armed forces, people's councils, and judiciary. The third part describes the state seal and flag, confirms Tirana as the capital city, and details procedures for making constitutional amendments.

The People's Socialist Republic of Albania is defined as having all powers derived from and belonging to the working people, who rule through people's councils (i.e., organs of local government) and the People's Assembly or national legislature. These bodies are elected by citizens allegedly on the basis of a universal, equal, direct, and secret ballot. Social and economic measures are stressed in the 1976 constitution, as they are in corresponding documents of other communist-ruled countries. Control over natural resources and industry, as well as other means of production, remains in the hands of the state. Private property is guaranteed protection, but it can be limited in amount or expropriated if it is used to the detriment of the state. Rights and duties of citizens resemble those affirmed by the basic laws of other East European countries. In fact, the outside observer may be led to believe that the 1976 constitution includes Western democratic principles that guarantee certain inalienable rights vis-a-vis the state. In reality, however, the constitution is superseded by a dictatorship of the proletariat, or rather its vanguard, the communist party. Unrestricted authority of the state is upheld, and rights of citizens may be curtailed at any time.

According to the 1976 constitution, the 250-member People's Assembly is the highest and most important organ in the governmental structure (Article 66). The Assembly is "elected" every four years by all citizens eligible to vote. It ordinarily meets twice a year, and at these times deputies are expected to approve all items on the agenda. Since the party selects all Assembly candidates and presents them to voters on a single-slate ballot for election, the national legislature is merely a rubber stamp used to approve decisions made in advance by the party. Political rights, as they are known in Western democracies, are nonexistent. (See table 2 for official election returns.)

The People's Assembly elects fifteen of its members to form a legislative presidium, and powers are exercised between its sessions by this small group.[17] The presidium interprets and makes decisions concerning constitutionality of laws, ratifies international agreements, appoints and recalls diplomatic envoys,

---

17. The chairman of the People's Assembly presidium, his three deputies, and the secretary are identified in *Line-Up,* p. 1.

TABLE 2

OFFICIAL ALBANIAN ELECTION RETURNS, 1958–1974

Date	Registered voters	Votes for regime	Percent	Votes against regime
1 June 1958	780,061	779,935	99.80	126
3 June 1962	889,875	889,868	99.98	7
10 July 1966	978,161	978,154	99.99	3
20 September 1970	1,097,123	1,096,967	99.99	156
6 October 1974	1,248,530	1,248,528	99.99	2

SOURCES: ACEN, *Survey of Developments in the Captive Countries* (March–October 1958), p. 6, and (January–June 1962), p. 53; Tirana radio, 11 July 1966; *Zeri i popullit,* 22 September 1970, and 8 October 1974.

issues decrees, and promulgates legislation passed by the Assembly. It also creates governmental commissions, proclaims elections, and convenes the Assembly. Yet the presidium is said to be responsible to the Assembly which in theory may recall, replace, or dismiss any or all presidium members.

The Council of Ministers is considered the supreme executive and administrative organ; it is formally appointed by the People's Assembly. Powers assigned by the constitution to the Council of Ministers include supervision of all social, economic, and cultural activities. In reality, the premier, his deputies, and various ministers comprising the Council are selected by the party's Politburo.[18] Their main function is to ensure that all decisions by the latter are carried out.

Local government organs consist of people's councils at district, regional, and city levels. These councils are elected directly for terms of three years and exercise authority over administrative, economic, and cultural matters within their own geographic areas. They also maintain order, enforce state laws, and are supposed to uphold citizens' rights. Executive committees are elected by people's councils and exercise the above functions between meetings of the councils.

According to the 1976 constitution, the highest judicial organ is the Supreme Court. Judges are elected by secret ballot in the People's Assembly. Courts at lower levels are formed similarly by corresponding people's councils and, thus, allegedly represent the "will of the citizens."

The Office of the Prosecutor General is yet another agency that is supposedly controlled by the People's Assembly. It supervises implementation of laws by ministries, other administrative bodies, all public officials, and citizens.

18. Article 69 of the 1950 constitution had enumerated only ten ministries. Durdenevskii, *op. cit.* (in note 8 above), pp. 121–122. There existed, however, thirteen such offices in late 1976. *Line-Up*, p. 2, provides the names of incumbents.

The 1976 constitution shows little difference from or innovation in relation to its 1950 predecessor and merely reflects changes previously enacted (e.g., a 250-member limit in the People's Assembly) as well as emphasis on completion of socialist construction throughout the country.

Government.   The typical Soviet-style relationship between communist movement and government is well established in Albania. The constitution of 1976 recognizes the privileged and controlling position of the Albanian Party of Labor, as mentioned above. Enver Hoxha, as first secretary of the Central Committee, holds the top party position.[19] He effectively controls the government from this office, even though the titular head of state is the chairman of the Assembly presidium, Haxhi Lleshi. Table 3 lists Politburo members and indicates related positions they hold in government. Hoxha (b. 1908) and other party leaders in top positions are relatively old, so it is likely that some of these men will retire from the political scene in the near future.

If free elections were to be held in Albania, the communists probably would not poll a majority. Such elections cannot be expected, however, because the ruling party will not permit them.[20] Neither should one anticipate that Albania will supply strong enough indigenous leadership to bring the country out from under communist control, but some writers think the future is not without hope for recovering the country from the influence of Peking.

DOMESTIC AFFAIRS

Economic and social transformation has come slowly and only recently to Albania, owing to its historic isolation from the mainstream of European affairs. More than thirty years of communist rule, however, have brought greater changes than occurred during all the preceding four centuries of Ottoman domination and the sixty years of influence, to varying degrees, by European powers. Progress in modernization has been considerable, in relation to past backwardness, but it still leaves Albania far behind other states on the continent.

Tradition.   Despite the communist philosophy of subordinating individual to state through contrived mass uniformity, certain parts of the Albanian population apparently have changed little and cling to prewar ethnic customs. In rural areas clan or feudal relationships still persist and, as is usual in such sociological groupings, traditional norms can be altered only at a slow rate. Although the clan

---

19. In this post he is also commander-in-chief of the armed forces and chairman of the Defense Council, according to Article 89 of the 1976 constitution.

20. See articles by a German visitor, Rolf Italiaander, in *Christ und Welt,* 9, 16, and 30 January 1970, pp. 32, 28, and 26, respectively. His book is entitled *Albanien-Vorposten Chinas* (Munich, Delp, 1970), 282 pp.

TABLE 3

ALBANIA'S INTERLOCKING DIRECTORATE, 1976

Politburo	Year elected	National Secretariat	Council of Ministers	Other position
MEMBERS (12)				
Hoxha, Enver	1941	First Secretary		Chairman, Democratic Front
Alia, Ramiz	1961	Secretary		Deputy Chairman, Democratic Front
Carcani, Adil	1961		First Deputy premier	
Hazbiu, Kadri	1971		Internal Affairs minister	
Isai, Hekuran	1975	Secretary		
Kapo, Hysni	1946	Secretary		
Koleka, Spiro	1948			Chairman, Sino-Albanian Friendship Society
Marko, Rita	1956			Chairman, Trade Unions
Miska, Pali	1975		Deputy premier	
Myftiu, Manush	1956		Deputy premier	
Shehu, Mehmet	1948		Premier and Defense minister	
Toska, Haki	1961		Finance minister	
CANDIDATE MEMBERS (5)				
Cuko, Lenka	1976			First Secretary, Lushnje district
Gegprifti, Llambi	1975		Deputy defense minister	
Mihali, Qirjako	1975			First Secretary, Tirana district
Peristeri, Pilo	1952			Chairman, Party Control Commission
Stefani, Simon	1976	Secretary		

SOURCES: *Zeri i popullit*, 8 and 14 November 1976; Tirana radio, 29 December 1976.

may now call itself a village people's council, there is some question whether this is a fiction of communist terminology or genuine sovietization of organizational forms. While the past three decades have brought change in established mores and institutions, these differences cannot be attributed exclusively to the nature of government. To a certain extent, customs keep pace with the social phenomena that accompany the modernization of any traditional society. The communist regime, of course, has done its utmost to mold and adapt these changes according to the Stalinist model.

Before the Second World War, Albania essentially comprised a two-class society of large landowners and peasant farmers. The smaller groups of artisans, government employees, and teachers could be classified as the nucleus of a middle class, although their limited numbers rendered their influence insignificant. Under the present regime this basic social stratification still exists; only the occupations of the elite have changed. Party members immediately assumed the role formerly held by the *beys,* or landed aristocracy, to form what Milovan Djilas in neighboring Yugoslavia called the ''new class.''

Industrial progress and the rise of a government bureaucracy have fostered social mobility, and the Albanian ''new class'' (which is not recognized by communist definition) is increasing in size. Within this group, the rejection of tradition has been most pronounced. While in one sense this break is designed to lead, under state guidance, to the formation of the patterns of a Marxist utopia, in another sense it creates the basis for some political objectivity.

The migration of labor, under government control, from agrarian pursuits to city industrial complexes represents another significant factor in the gradual diminution of Albanian traditionalism. During 1976 two-thirds of the population still lived in rural areas and, therefore, was employed mostly in agriculture. While urbanization of transposed peasants under a communist regime might seem to represent a potential source of unrest within the country, in actual fact it has created few problems. The inequity of living conditions, totalitarian rule, long working hours, and low pay of the new industrial worker merely represent a continuation of the conditions of his former agrarian existence. Substitution of local party leadership for feudal clan elders remains the essential difference.

The party and government launched an ideological and cultural revolution during February 1966, in part patterned after the one taking place in Mainland China at that time. This movement in Albania was designed to accelerate the pace of modernization and inculcate Marxist values throughout the country. The campaign has been reintensified periodically and it continues as a permanent aspect of Albanian society, emphasizing ideological isolation from Western and revisionist cultural influences, antibureaucratism, and ideological indoctrination of the population.[21] The popular slogan, ''holding in one hand a pick and in the other a rifle,'' is still being repeated.

---

21. Nicholas C. Pano, ''The Albanian Cultural Revolution,'' *Problems of Communism* (July–August 1974), pp. 44–57.

Religion. Since communist regimes have been unable to eliminate religion, they first try to "nationalize" it as a compromise expedient to its control and as a step toward its eventual destruction.[22] In Albania this effort has been carried out with limited opposition owing to the division into sects of Moslem believers who comprise some 70 percent of the population. They are divided into Sunni, Bektashi, and other orders recognized by the regime as independent religious communities. The rest of the population, which is about 20 percent Eastern-rite Orthodox and 10 percent Roman Catholic, is insufficient numerically to register serious opposition. A temporary accord appeared in the 1950 constitution, which stated that freedom of religious practice would be guaranteed so long as churches did not utilize it as a political vehicle. Due to the basic intransigence of the Catholic Church vis-a-vis the tenets of communism, all ties with the Vatican were severed in August 1951 and a "National Albanian Catholic Church" was established.[23]

While the state could bring religious and even church officials under strict control, of necessity a more tolerant attitude had to be taken toward personal religious beliefs. Again, this represented expediency rather than relaxation of ideological imperatives. The principal tactic at first involved a subtle campaign to degrade religion to the level of superstition and slowly to eliminate places of worship. The thought seems to have been that, without the substance of organization and ceremony, the credence given to religious concepts would gradually become eroded.

After Hoxha's nine-hour speech at the November 1966 congress, the regime intensified its campaign to eliminate religion as an influence in Albanian public life. Places of worship were converted into "movie houses, garages, dance halls, stores. Over 2,000 mosques and churches underwent demolition. . . . The beautiful Turkish mosque in the center of Tirana, adjacent to the Venetian clock tower, is a museum today."[24]

By 1976 all places of worship had been closed. However, the regime has had to admit that religion still maintains a following among Albanians. In order to suppress religious life, the following article has been included in the 1976 constitution: "The state recognizes no religion and supports and carries out atheistic propaganda to implant the scientific materialistic world outlook in people" (Article 37). In its antireligious moves, the regime has gone so far as to order persons to change their names if they are of a religious origin.[25]

---

22. Kemel Vokopola, "Church and State in Albania," in U.S. Senate, Committee on the Judiciary, *The Church and State under Communism* (Washington, D.C., 1965), II, 33–47.

23. *L'Osservatore Romano,* 11 July 1967, reported that the last churches were closed by Red Guards, depriving 130,000 Catholics of public places in which to worship.

24. Italiaander, *op. cit.* (in note 20 above), 16 January 1970.

25. Tirana radio, 21 January 1976; *Zeri i popullit,* 29 February 1976.

Culture.   Literature, the theater, music and art are controlled by the party through various cultural organizations, such as the League of Writers and Artists, the Union of Albanian Women, and the Committee for Arts and Culture. Influenced by the Chinese communists, Albania in 1966 launched a cultural revolution of its own that called for production of a national and a socialist culture as well as selective rejection of the classics.

Intellectual revisionism of the type appearing in Poland, Hungary, or Czechoslovakia is almost nonexistent. While the controls of the Hoxha regime are more than adequate for suppressing any artistic deviation into nonconformity, it is probably the current scarcity of intellectuals rather than repression that accounts for the absence of substantial dissident sentiment after more than three decades of communist rule. However, cultural organizations and higher education have been undergoing an upheaval, with crackdowns on the "bourgeois-revisionist life style" among students and younger intellectuals.

Education.   The objectives of the Albanian educational system vary little from those pursued by any standard communist thought-control program: development of technical skills, popular acceptance of Marxist ideology, and formation of a politically reliable intellectual elite. As with certain of the other less-developed East European countries, initial emphasis has been on the creation of technical competence in vocational and engineering fields.[26] Each government ministry is responsible for such training through *teknikums* (vocational schools). Although a university had been established, until the end of 1961 most students were sent to the USSR and other neighboring East European states for a higher education.

Illiteracy represented the fundamental problem to be overcome by the communist government. By 1963 the prewar (1938) illiteracy rate of 90 percent reportedly had been all but eliminated in the population group up to age forty. According to a statement at the end of 1969 by the education minister at that time, some 287 out of every 1,000 Albanians were attending schools.[27] Claims by the regime regarding the effectiveness of its educational system are somewhat offset by frequent reforms. An elaborate description of one such reorganization, which appeared in the Albanian publication *Ylli,* noted that the new system would offer fresh incentive to the secondary-school graduate: a diploma qualifying him as a "worker."

Training in communist doctrine is conducted at all levels and within all schools. Adult education in such matters takes place through the medium of local party organizations. Outside observers indicate that the people have little interest

---

26. John I. Thomas, *Education for Communism: School and State in the People's Republic of Albania* (Stanford, Ca., 1969), 131 pp.

27. *Zeri i popullit,* 24 December 1969. The 1976 constitution guarantees eight years of school (Article 52).

in such efforts, and the benefits supposedly derived from the process are more than countered by day-to-day experiences of Stalinist communism in action.

An educational reform introduced in 1970 requires students to work one year in a factory or on a farm before entering high school. The new curriculum foresees 6½ months of study, another 2½ months of physical labor, and one month of military training each year. Corresponding figures for the thirteen thousand university students are seven, one, and two months. During 1976, the school system was revolutionized further under the direction of a new education minister, Tefta Cani.[28]

Security Controls.   By democratic standards, Albania is unquestionably a police state. Leaders maintain themselves in power through an all-pervasive and powerful security organization. Police effectiveness may have created a conviction among the people of the invincibility of the regime.[29] The hostility of the average Albanian toward the government, in whatever degree it may occur, stems from a basic dislike for the communist system and from the failure of the regime to fulfill its promises of "freedom, bread, and land."

It would be an error, however, to postulate that the communist nature of the regime per se is the only reason for this hostility. Albanians have a long tradition of dislike for central authority, particularly when it stems from an alien system. Control over popular disaffection and acts of protest, either passive or active, is vested with the police and security forces under the Interior ministry. These forces include a directorate of state security, called *Sigurimi,* or secret police; border guards; and regular uniformed police.

The secret police employ standard communist techniques of population control, such as personal documentation, surveillance, and censorship. Paid or unpaid informants remain the principal source of information on antistate activities or sentiments. There is no apparent organized resistance,[30] and most instances of arrest or liquidation seem to result not from anticommunist activities but from disagreement with the Hoxha regime.

During the spring of 1973, more than three years prior to the seventh party congress, a purge began in the cultural sphere; it spread to the defense establishment by mid-1974 and subsequently engulfed the economic bureaucracy of government. Two-thirds of all cabinet posts, one-third of the Politburo seats,

---

28. Tirana radio, 5 July 1976.

29. A United Nations survey indicated that some 80,000 persons of the then 1.7 million population were being held in concentration camps during 1945–1956 and that more than 16,000 had died there.

30. According to a transcript from an espionage trial, at least four organizations as late as 1950 opposed the communists: the Nationalist Front, the Legality movement, the Independent Bloc, and the Agrarian Party. Georges Fournial (preface), *Le Proces des Espions Parachutes en Albanie* (Paris, 1950), p. 23. See also the articles by Italiaander (in note 20 above).

and nearly half the Central Committee posts changed incumbents.[31] Reportedly some ten thousand of the affected bureaucrats have been exiled into rural areas. Few, if any, attempted to escape.

Border guards, primarily operating to protect frontiers against infiltration, also serve to prevent Albanians from clandestinely leaving the country. Ingress and egress across the mountain borders should not represent any substantial problem for the indigenous population, if they are so inclined, however. Regular police are charged with conventional tasks of keeping public order and safety. Close collaboration is maintained by the border guards with the directorate of state security and the uniformed police.

News.   Daily papers and other media of mass communication are state or party controlled. The official newspaper, *Zeri i popullit,* which is the Albanian communist party organ, and the democratic front's *Bashkimi* are used as political instruments. Tirana radio functions as the broadcasting equivalent.[32] Despite claims to the contrary, there seems to be no jamming of foreign broadcasts. One observer has attributed this more to the technical inability of the regime to effect jamming than to any disregard for the effect of transmissions from abroad. A single television broadcasting station operates in Albania. Citizens prosperous enough to purchase TV sets can also receive Italian and Yugoslav stations, whose broadcasts appear to be preferred to local programs.

ECONOMIC AND MILITARY AFFAIRS

By any standard, Albania is the least-developed country in Eastern Europe. Modernization and industrialization are long-range objectives of the government, with the principal emphasis on extraction of mineral resources, agriculture, and light manufactured goods. Under the communist regime substantial gains have been made in all economic areas, as selected figures in table 4 indicate. Although industrial production has expanded much more rapidly than agriculture, the difference remains relative.[33] Industrialization by Western standards has just begun, and agriculture and mining contribute the most to the national product.

Economic policies are formulated by the party Politburo, and specific production goals are established by the State Planning Commission. The latter

---

31. Louis Zanga, "Changes in Albanian Leadership Signify Struggle for Succession to Power," RFE, *Background Report,* 24 November 1975, p. 17; *Christian Science Monitor,* 19 May 1976; *Zeri i popullit,* 30 April, 8 and 14 November, 1976.

32. Pano, *op. cit.* (in note 1 above), p. xvi, gives figures on radio receivers and newspaper circulation.

33. Between 1970 and the end of 1975, industrial output reportedly increased by 52 percent whereas agricultural products grew by only 33 percent. *Zeri i popullit,* 12 November 1976.

TABLE 4

SELECTED ECONOMIC INDICATORS IN ALBANIA, 1950–1975

Commodity	Unit	1950	1955	1960	1970	1975
Electricity	million KWH	21.4	85.3	341.8	943.5	1,533
Petroleum	thousand metric tons	131.8	208.1	727.5	1,283.2	1,578
Coal	thousand metric tons	62.8	194.6	303.9	694.6	1,001
Cement	thousand metric tons	15.9	44.5	72.9	345.3	–
Bread	thousand metric tons	51.0	79.0	138.3	–	–
Sugar	thousand metric tons	0.5	7.1	13.3	7.6	–
Olive butter	metric tons	1,342.0	2,735.0	2,169.0	–	–
Fresh fish	metric tons	1,493.0	2,581.0	2,599.0	–	–
Cheese	metric tons	771.0	1,024.0	2,418.0	–	–
Sausage	metric tons	139.0	73.0	244.0	–	–

SOURCES: L. N. Tolkunov (ed.), *Sotsialisticheskii lager* (Moscow, 1962), pp. 41–42; Harilla Papajorgii, *The Development of Socialist Industry and Its Prospects in the People's Republic of Albania* (Tirana, 1964), p. 47; *Vjetari Statistikor 1971–1972* (Tirana, 1973), pp. 66, 68; *Zeri i popullit*, 20 and 23 October 1976.

NOTES: The 1965 statistical yearbook gives only value in leks and percentage increase over the 1938 base year. *Vjetari Statistikor 1965* (Tirana, 1965).

As of this writing, no meaningful economic data for 1975 are available. Figures in that column were given in percentage increase over 1970 and have been computed.

agency coordinates plans of national and local government, enterprises, cooperatives, and individual producers. All economic activity is state owned and operated, according to the 1976 constitution, and private property is forbidden (Article 16).

Albania joined the Council for Mutual Economic Assistance (CMEA). Since the break with Moscow in October 1961, however, it has not participated in Council activities or sent representatives to meetings. The USSR had been the principal trading partner of Albania from 1948 to 1961, accounting for more than half of all exports and imports. During this period a consistently adverse foreign-trade balance of payments had to be financed with Soviet and other East European loans. These credits reportedly amounted to more than 1.6 billion rubles, as table 5 shows. After the Albanian–Soviet rift, China assumed a major part of the trade formerly conducted by the USSR. In 1950 Tirana's deficit amounted to 779 million leks, but it has increased since then, amounting in 1955 to almost 1.5 billion and in 1960 surpassing that, dropping in 1970 to 1.3 billion, and in 1975 totaling just under 2.4 billion leks.[34] (See table 8.) The 1976 constitution specifically prohibits Albania from obtaining credits from foreign capitalist and revisionist monopolies or states (Article 28).

34. V. I. Zolotarev, *Vneshnyaya torgovlya sotsialisticheskikh stran* (Moscow, 1964), p. 141. [Albania], *Vjetari statistikor i Republikes Popullore te Shqiperise 1965* (Tirana, 1965), p. 313; hereafter cited as *Vjetari statistikor*. See also *Rruga i partise* (August 1976), p. 12.

TABLE 5

SINO-SOVIET BLOC CREDITS TO ALBANIA, 1945–1975
(In millions of rubles)

Country	Amount	Country	Amount
USSR	948	Poland	85
Czechoslovakia	222	Hungary	80
East Germany	152	Bulgaria	62
China	1,327		
Romania	92	Total	2,968

SOURCES: Ranko Banovic, *Posleratni razvoj privrede u Albaniji* (Belgrade, 1959), p. 14; Presseausschnitte und Radioberichte aus den Osteuropaeischen Laendern, *Albanien und seine "Protektoren"* (Munich, 17 August 1966), pp. 10–11; Moscow radio, 1 August 1976, which claimed that R 422 million had been cancelled from the total Soviet credits; CIA, *Handbook of Economic Statistics 1976* (Washington, D.C., September 1976), p. 71.

Industry. This sector of the Albanian economy comprises extraction of basic raw materials, processing industries, and food and textile plants, but little else. The government has stressed development of mining, petroleum, and building materials. Only limited attempts have been made to establish other heavy industries, due to a limited market within the country and a lack of technical expertise.

Albania's industrial policy can be divided chronologically into two basic phases. The years 1944–1947 involved the reconstruction of factories destroyed by war and the nationalization of the sources of production. From 1947 to the present the industrial sector has been guided by the original Stalinist model and a succession of economic plans. The earliest plans were drawn up on an annual basis, followed by a two-year plan for 1949–1950.

By 1951 sufficient progress had been made to allow for reasonable planning over five-year intervals. This first *pyatiletka* followed the Stalinist line of increasing heavy industrial output at the expense of agriculture and consumers' goods. With a great deal of Soviet technical aid, the objectives of this plan reportedly were reached. During the second five-year plan (1956–1960), industrial output again reportedly increased.[35] It has been asserted that before the break with Moscow a fifteen-year (1961–1975) perspective plan had been worked out to coordinate Albanian economic development with that of other East European countries.[36]

The third five-year plan (1961–1965) was proclaimed before completion as having been relatively successful, despite minor setbacks ensuing from the

35. The USSR claims to have delivered 93 percent of the equipment needed by Albania for petroleum and mining industries, about 90 percent of its trucks, more than 80 percent of its tractors, and 65 percent of its other agricultural machinery during this period. *Izvestiya,* 28 November 1976.

36. E. B. Valev, *Albaniya* (Moscow, 1960), pp. 30–31.

disagreement with the USSR. Official reports indicate that substantial economic difficulties, postulated by Western observers as resulting from the withdrawal of Soviet economic assistance, did not fully materialize, thanks primarily to the substitution of Chinese aid. One problem stemmed from the lack of spare parts for machinery of Soviet or East European origin. The Chinese, through extensive copying, were able either to provide necessary parts or to replace basic equipment.

Economic agreements with France, Italy, Austria, and Romania also led to significant (by Albanian standards) technical and material aid for Tirana's industrial efforts. The fourth five-year plan (1966–1970) goals reportedly were met and exceeded.[37] However, there are indications that industrial output from the fifth five-year plan (1971–1975) has been less satisfactory, judging by the removal from office during 1975–1976 of the heavy industry and mining minister (Koco Theodosi), the State Planning Commission chairman (Abdyl Kellezi), and the trade minister (Kico Kgjela).[38] An important factor in this lower rate of achievement has been Albania's basic problem with agricultural output. While attainment of current five-year plan goals will still leave the industrial sector far behind the rest of Eastern Europe, gains made, on a relative basis, serve as evidence that a communist regime can create economic progress through totalitarian means over a limited period of time. Announced targets for 1976–1980 appear in table 6.

Agriculture.   In common with many other East European countries, Albania suffers from the fact that agriculture has not kept pace with industrial development. While this can be attributed to a number of factors, it would appear that the difficulty lies essentially in the ideological foundation of Marxism. The millennium for the proletariat did not initially embrace the working peasantry. The Albanian or any other standard communist doctrine regarding collectivization fails to recognize the traditional independence of farmers and their attachment to the land.[39] A factory worker, having once been deprived of his traditional orientations, can in some instances be molded according to socialist form; the peasant, who has different psychological characteristics, is less likely to adapt.

The drive to collectivize the agrarian sector has gone through the customary cycles. Unlike revisionist policies in Poland and Yugoslavia, the immediate

---

37. Heavy industry increased twice as rapidly as production of consumers' goods. The goals for overall industrial production were reportedly attained in four years and seven months. Tirana radio, 10 August 1970.

38. *Zeri i popullit*, 5 June 1975, and 2 November 1976.

39. Article 23 of the 1976 constitution limits private propery to income from work and other lawful resources, dwellings, and "other objects serving to meet personal and family material and cultural needs."

TABLE 6

Sixth Five-Year Plan Targets, 1976–1980

Category	Increase, 1980 versus 1975 (percentages)
Industry	41 to 44
Agriculture	38 to 41
Investment total, including agricultural cooperatives	35 to 38
Transportation	30 to 32
Labor productivity	
industry	15 to 17
construction	12 to 13
Production cost reduction	
industry	8 to 10
construction	8 to 10
National income	38 to 40
Real per capita income	11 to 14

Source: *Zeri i popullit,* 10 November 1976, provides official plan directives approved by the seventh party congress; *ibid.,* 30 December 1976, gives a detailed report by State Planning Commission chairman Petro Dode.

objective in Albania had been full collectivization.[40] Hoxha reported to the party congress in February 1961 that 86 percent of all arable land had come into the possession of collective farms and that the peasantry had slowly begun to change its way of life by embracing a "new culture." No comparison was given of the levels of production achieved on this high percentage of the land and on the remaining 14 percent, which was still almost all independently owned at that time. A comprehensive book on Albania published in 1956 claimed that despite collectivization independent farmers working on less than 80 percent of the land raised some 94 percent of all agricultural products.[41] The years 1955–1957 seem to have been the time of greatest pressure by the regime, because collectivization increased to 57 percent during that period. By February 1967 complete socialization of agriculture had been achieved.[42]

Policies of soil reclamation and cultivation of marginal land have helped to raise agricultural production. Although programs for expanding the amount of arable land are limited by topography, a target date of 1970 was selected for increasing the area under cultivation by 89,000 hectares to a total of 540,000

---

40. For basic documents, see N. D. Kazantsev (ed.), *Osnovnye zakonodatelnye akty po agrarnym preobrazovaniyam v zarubezhnykh sotsialisticheskikh stranakh* (Moscow, 1958), 4th ed., pp. 5–60, on Albania.

41. Skendi, *op. cit.* (in note 1 above), p. 170.

42. L. V. Tyagunenko, *Development of the Albanian Economy* (Washington, D.C., 1961), p. 42. Translated from the Russian. The victory of collectivization is described in *Probleme ekonomike* (January–March 1967), pp. 83–87.

hectares. State farms seem to play a less significant role than collectives. They occupy 13.8 percent of all arable land, and concentrate on animal husbandry, olive growing, and seed production. The data in table 7 show the breakdown by type of farm in percentages. Food production during the latest five-year plan (1971–1975) lagged behind industrial output.[43] The regime had attempted to remedy the situation by procuring Chinese loans for agriculture, offering pension incentives to collective farmers, merging collective farms, and other means.

TABLE 7

DEVELOPMENT OF AGRICULTURE, 1955–1976

(In percentages)

Year	State farms	Collective farms	Private entrepreneurs
1955	7.3	13.4	79.3
1960	13.1	73.8	13.1
1965	17.5	72.9	9.6
1970	23.0	77.0	–
1975	22.0	78.0	–
1976	13.8	ca. 86.0	0.2*

SOURCES: *Vjetari statistikor 1963* (Tirana, 1963), p. 150; *ibid. 1966–67*, p. 76; [Albania], *Republika Popullore e Shqiperise ne jubileum e 30 vjetorit te themelimit te PPSh* (Tirana, 1971), p. 101; Tirana radio, 3 September 1975; *Zeri i popullit*, 11 November 1976.

NOTE: *These probably comprise small garden plots for growing vegetables.

Students of East European affairs have observed that communism does not appeal to the peasant and that, almost without exception, this element of the population is hostile to regime policies. Although this is unquestionably true, the very independence that engenders such hostility precludes any action in unison against the government. Consequently, it can be somewhat misleading to assume that the peasantry poses a substantial threat to any communist regime. The danger, if any, is indirect and stems from dissatisfaction created among more cohesive elements of the population when food is not in ample supply.

Labor.   Workers in Albania have been strictly regimented, and rigid labor legislation provides penalties for those who do not fulfill state norms or who fail to appear for work. The work force is controlled partly by a Labor Directorate and partly by trade unions, whose organization is divided into three basic sub-

43. By the end of 1980 the output of bread grains is supposed to increase by 55 percent compared with the 1975 totals, according to *Zeri i popullit*, 25 July 1976. An editorial already has claimed self-sufficiency. *Ibid.*, 7 January 1977.

elements, for (1) industrial workers; (2) administration, public health, and educational-cultural employees; and (3) agricultural laborers on state farms.[44]

Compulsory work, freezing of personnel in their jobs, and state control over mobility proceed along Stalinist lines. The principal difficulties involve a shortage of trained industrial workers and the lack of sufficient incentive to increase output. Stakhanovite and shock-worker methods have been copied from Soviet experience, but have met with greater resistance than in the USSR. Many Albanians still tend to regard factory work as unmanly, and only by intense indoctrination of the younger generation through contrived "youth action" programs is this belief slowly being dispelled.

Armed Forces.   The military in Albania is relatively insignificant by East European standards; it consists of approximately sixty thousand men, including internal security and border guards.[45] The Chinese have replaced the Soviets as advisors, although on a smaller scale. Also a politicization of the armed forces along Chinese lines has ensued in recent years. The 1974−1975 purge of the military high command seems to have stemmed from this politicization. Professional officers may have wanted to limit party influence among the troops and to downplay the Chinese people's war concepts. Firmer party control over the military was affirmed by the purge.

Departure of Soviet naval forces from the Valona base and Sasseno Island marked the end of Moscow's influence. One source has reported that the Albanians refused to allow the USSR to withdraw some of its submarines after the Tirana−Moscow break.[46] An armed engagement of limited scope allegedly took place between Soviet and Albanian military personnel. Subsequent negotiations resulted in the USSR's leaving four Class "W" submarines at Valona, along with support equipment. The Albanian armed forces pose little threat either to the North Atlantic Treaty Organization (NATO) or to Eastern Europe. In combination with internal security troops, they do comprise an effective element of control over the country.

FOREIGN AFFAIRS

While the postwar history of Albania's friendship and differences with the outside world has been shaded to a degree by overtones of political doctrine, there is little to indicate that ideological differences per se have predominantly influenced Albanian actions. As one expert has phrased it: "In the Communist

---

44. A party-government decision reduced the highest wages (more than 900 leks per month) from 4 to 25 percent, making the ratio between highest and lowest wages only two to one. *Zeri i popullit,* 2 April 1976.

45. International Institute for Strategic Studies, *The Military Balance 1976−1977* (London, September 1976), p. 27.

46. Eight submarines and a modern Soviet supply ship reportedly did leave Albania in June 1961. Hamm, *op. cit.* (in note 4 above), p. 23.

world, conflicts have to take an ideological form even when the real motives may be the interests of individuals or groups or the power politics of countries."[47]

Yugoslavia. Relations between Albania and Yugoslavia traditionally have been hostile, stemming from ethnic differences, territorial disputes, and the nature of Balkan politics. During the Second World War, common interests were generated by Axis occupation and the Marxist orientation of guerrilla groups in both countries. This collaboration became increasingly unilateral in favor of Belgrade: by 1947 it appeared that Tito's vision of Balkan unity involved less an independent federation of Balkan states and more a Greater Yugoslavia.[48] The link between Belgrade and Tirana paralleled the master–satellite relationship of the Soviet Union vis-a-vis the other countries of Eastern Europe. The political opportunity for a break came with the expulsion by the Cominform of the Yugoslav communist party. Beginning in July 1948, Moscow replaced Belgrade as the protector of Albania.

During the remaining years of Stalin's life, Tirana radio supplied a prominent voice in the Soviet-inspired campaign of East European vituperation against Yugoslavia. Traditional animosities and the existence of the Kosmet (Kosovo and Metohija) enclave, in which some 900,000 Albanians reside within Yugoslavia, made it easier for the Tirana regime to maintain that close cooperation with the Soviet Union was a necessity for preserving its independence. The USSR in turn benefited from the arrangement both through the propaganda advantage and access to a military base on the Adriatic.

After the death of Stalin and the subsequent modification in Soviet policy toward Yugoslavia, the advantages of close Albanian cooperation with the USSR became more economic than military. The attempt by Tito to influence the politics of Eastern Europe, coupled with the geographic proximity of Belgrade to Tirana, created a threat to the party leadership in Albania. This danger, while not necessarily directed at territorial integrity, remained sufficiently grave to cause concern for their personal security among Hoxha and his followers. It was apparent that, for them to remain in power, repressive methods of Stalinism had to be continued.

In recent years there has been détente between Albania and Yugoslavia, probably brought about by the threat of a possible Soviet invasion like the one in Czechoslovakia. Full diplomatic ties were reestablished in 1971, and cultural contacts (mostly between ethnic Albanians of both countries) subsequently increased in frequency. During 1975 this rapprochement reached its peak with the exchange of cordial messages, an increase in Yugoslav-Albanian trade, and the

---

47. Stavro Skendi, "Albania and the Sino-Soviet Conflict," *Foreign Affairs* (April 1962), p. 474.

48. Yet the ruling party's Central Committee reportedly met at Tirana in February 1948 to discuss incorporation of Albania by Yugoslavia. Skendi, *op. cit.* (in note 1 above), p. 24.

virtual absence of ideological attacks. However, early in 1976 a serious rift occurred between the two countries, resulting in a return to polemics and border incidents, which seem to stem from new unrest and Albanian irredentist activity in the Kosovo region of Yugoslavia.[49]

The Soviet-Albanian Rift. During a speech to a 1957 plenum of his Central Committee in defense of Stalin, Hoxha injected an ideological basis for the subsequent rift between Albania and the USSR. During the period 1957–1960 charges and countercharges of Marxist deviation were relatively subdued, being conducted on a rather esoteric level.[50] Soviet military and economic aid to Albania continued, but ties between Tirana and Peking were already forming. The Chinese embassy in Albania enlarged its staff; translations of articles from *Pravda* were gradually replaced with translations from *Jen-min jih-pao*, the principal Chinese communist daily newspaper.

In 1960 the extent of discord between Albania and the Soviet Union became more apparent to the Western world. The absence of Hoxha and Mehmet Shehu from the East European summit meeting at Bucharest, the purging in September of Politburo member Liri Belishova and Audit Commission chairman Koco Tashko from the Albanian communist party, and the ever increasing shrillness of the academic debate on "revisionism" indicated that a serious split had developed.[51] These events were compounded by a growing divergence of views between the USSR and Communist China.

Tirana did not receive an invitation to the twenty-second congress of the Soviet party in October 1961, an event of considerable significance for the international communist movement. At this congress, Khrushchev bitterly attacked the Albanian leadership. Chou En-lai, chief representative of the Chinese communists, departed from Moscow soon thereafter but not before indicating his support for Albania and his condemnation of certain USSR policies. It was alleged by Tirana that a Khrushchev-sponsored coup had attempted to overthrow the Hoxha regime. With words now reportedly translated into action, the split became irreconcilable. Albanians did not appear at the June 1969 international meeting of communist and workers' parties in Moscow or at any other Soviet-sponsored conference through the end of 1976.

While Albania is of little current economic or military value to the Soviet Union, the fact of its successful defiance, its position as an amplifier of internal discord within the communist bloc, and its use by the Chinese as an actual rather than a theoretical platform for influence throughout Eastern Europe do appear

---

49. About thirty young ethnic Albanians were jailed in Kosovo for planning a so-called national liberation movement. *Christian Science Monitor,* 9 March 1976.

50. Hamm, *op. cit.* (in note 4 above), pp. 11–23.

51. Dilo, *op. cit.* (in note 7 above), p. 8.

important. Tirana also has become the European gathering place for Maoist "Marxist-Leninist" party representatives from other parts of the world.[52]

Communist China.   With the disappearance of Moscow's influence, Peking assumed the role of protector over Albania. Initially, the ability of distant China to support a European protégé appeared questionable. The USSR may have felt that this might soon become obvious to Tirana and that an accord might again be reached. This has not happened, if for no other reason than China's surprisingly effective program of assistance. The aid from Peking, which amounted to loans of $125 million during 1961–1965, some $215 million in the period 1966–1970, and approximately $400 million during 1971–1975, does not approach the previous Soviet effort in quantity, but the impetus earlier given Tirana by Moscow seems to have created a base sufficient to make the Chinese support adequate. Peking is committed to supplying assistance for the construction of some thirty industrial projects throughout Albania in 1976–1980.

Attitude to the West.   Despite its hostility toward the United States, which is based to a large extent on ideology, the Tirana regime maintains varying degrees of diplomatic and economic relations with other Western powers. France, Austria, Italy, and the Scandinavian countries have become increasingly active in its foreign trade. Britain has indicated a willingness to resume diplomatic relations, subject to a compensation settlement for the damage sustained by two British warships that in 1946 struck mines in the Corfu Channel.[53]

Differences with Greece, stemming from the latter's claim to part of southern Albania (northern Epirus), the abduction into Albania of about 25,000 Greek nationals by the communist-insurgent "Democratic Army" at the termination of the civil war in Greece, and the support given Greek communists by Albania during this conflict are gradually being forgotten. Following establishment of informal trade agreements between the two countries (in 1966 and 1970) and the reestablishment of electronic communications, formal diplomatic relations were resumed in 1971 after more than three decades of *de jure* belligerency. This came about after the Greek government had withdrawn claims to northern Epirus. Subsequent changes in Athens have not affected this new relationship.

Albania was the only European country not to attend the Helsinki conference in July–August 1975; it charged that the conference represented a tool of the superpowers for achieving a condominium over Europe. It also stressed that peace could only come about in Europe after dissolution of the Warsaw Pact and NATO. Likewise, in early 1976 Tirana refused to attend the Balkan conference at Athens, although it expressed a willingness for bilateral relations. This stand

---

52. See individual profiles in R. F. Staar (ed.), *1977 Yearbook on International Communist Affairs* (Stanford, Ca., 1977), for activities of these groups.

53. Il Yung Chung, *Legal Problems Involved in the Corfu Channel Incident* (Geneva, 1959).

again reflected a suspicion that multinational gatherings are merely ploys of the two superpowers.

Other Countries.   Most probably due to the common tie provided by their Moslem backgrounds, Albania has maintained friendly relations with Algeria, Egypt, and Libya. Since the break with Moscow, contacts with Turkey also have improved markedly. There is some significance to the fact that several of the communist-ruled countries (while otherwise following the USSR) have maintained trade with Albania, although after 1961 they suspended diplomatic relations. That they have done so may mean that Moscow had second thoughts on the usefulness of a total economic blockade and even encouraged some of these countries to maintain commercial relations. They include Cuba, East Germany, North Korea, Romania, and Vietnam.[54] However, the adverse balance of payments continues, as shown on table 8.

TABLE 8

ALBANIA'S FOREIGN TRADE, 1955−1975
(In millions of leks)

Category		1955	1960	1965	1970	1975
Imports		2,141	4,054	4,260	5,450	9,646
Exports		650	2,441	3,050	4,150	7,275
	Deficits	−1,491	−1,613	−1,210	−1,300	−2,371

SOURCES: L. N. Tolkunov (ed.), *Sotsialisticheskii lager* (Moscow, 1962), p. 47; *Vjetari Statistikor 1965* (Tirana, 1965), p. 313; *Zeri i popullit,* 17 July 1969; *Rruga e partise* (August 1976), p. 12.
NOTES: The current official rate of exchange is five leks to one US dollar. The figures in the table reflect the old (pre-August 1965) rate of fifty leks to the dollar. All data have been calculated on this basis.
According to an editorial in the last source cited above, exports were 75 percent greater and imports 77 percent higher during 1971−1975 than they had been in the preceding five-year period. These data are not precisely comparable with those obtained from earlier sources.

The position of Albania vis-a-vis the United States has continued to be hostile, despite an improvement in Sino-American relations during the 1970s. Indications that Tirana would be disposed favorably toward some type of trade with the USA have not fully materialized. The United States continues to represent an important component in the Albanian world image of the superpowers in their alleged roles as Gog and Magog, of which Hoxha spoke at the most recent party congress.

Albania is a member of the United Nations, admitted in 1955 through the

---

54. Note, for example, the 1976−1980 trade and payments agreement signed with Romania. Tirana radio, 26 July 1976. Albania claims to have diplomatic relations with 74 states. *Zeri i popullit,* 2 November 1976.

device of a trade-off and an American voting abstention. Although it had not participated in Warsaw Pact matters since 1961, Albania's membership in this treaty organization was not formally dissolved until 13 September 1968, that is, after the Soviet invasion of Czechoslovakia.[55]

One school of thought contended that the verbal friction between the Soviet Union and Albania had evolved into a personal vendetta between Khrushchev and Hoxha. From this followed the conclusion that, with the passing of one or both of these leaders from the political scene, Tirana and Moscow might again be brought together. While this outcome is well within the realm of possiblity (Khrushchev was deposed in mid-October 1964), the events of the past several years[56] suggest that a rapprochement is likely only if it involves an advantage for the Albanian leadership that outweighs significantly what can be obtained from China.

---

55. Hoxha provided an explantion in his twenty-fifth anniversary speech, broadcast over Tirana radio on 28 November 1969. See also Peter R. Prifti, *Albania Since the Fall of Khrushchev* (Cambridge, Mass., June 1970), p. 35.

56. The current leader's position is strong because he has purged 13 of the 14 original resistance commanders, almost half of the 31 postwar Central Committee members (1944–1948), and 79 of the 109 deputies to the first National Assembly. Peter S. H. Tang, *The Twenty-second Congress of the Communist Party of the Soviet Union and Moscow-Tirana-Peking Relations* (Washington, D.C., 1962), p. 134, n. 3.

Louis Zanga, *op. cit.* (in note 31 above) gives developments during 1974 and 1975. In his report to the seventh party congress premier Mehmet Shehu named eight persons among those purged. They had been prominent in the armed forces, ideology, and economics. *Zeri i popullit,* 5 November 1976. See also Nicholas C. Pano, "Albania," in R. F. Staar (ed.), *1977 Yearbook on International Communist Affairs* (Stanford, Ca., 1977).

Chapter 2

People's Republic of Bulgaria

In a geographical sense, Bulgaria occupies a rather special position among the communist-ruled states of Eastern Europe. Anchored on the southern flank of this formerly monolithic belt, it remains unique in having just one other bloc neighbor (Romania to the north) and in bordering more than two nonbloc states (Turkey and Greece to the south, Yugoslavia to the west).[1] Also, the Bulgarians share with the East Germans the distinction of remaining under Soviet influence without being contiguous to the USSR.

Slightly smaller than New York State, Bulgaria encompasses 42,818 square miles within dimensions of roughly 250 by 150 miles. Significant topographical features include the Danubian tableland across the north, the Balkan mountains in the center, the Thracian plains to the south, and mountains in the southwest. The national language is Slavic but it shows the influence of Turkish and Greek. The population in 1976 numbered 8.7 million, of which roughly 5.1 million people were classified as urban (58.8 percent) and 3.6 million as rural.[2]

HISTORY

Over a period of 500 years Bulgaria remained under Turkish rule; with the decline of this rule came oppression, which seemed all the less tolerable because of new aspirations brought by the penetration of modern ideas from Western Europe.[3]

During the early nineteenth century a national awakening had begun to develop, based on the writings of a monk named Paissi of Hildender, who recalled heroic deeds of the past and inspired people to fight for spiritual and political

---

1. [Bulgaria], *Statisticheski godishnik na Narodna Republika Bulgariya 1975* (Sofia, 1976), p. 2.
2. Sofia radio, 7 January 1976; *Rabotnichesko delo*, 9 July 1976.
3. L. A. D. Dellin (ed.), *Bulgaria* (New York, 1957), pp. 6–7; henceforth, cited as Dellin, *Bulgaria*.

liberation. Bulgarians suffered setbacks in several minor revolts but finally in 1876 started a major and widespread uprising. It failed also and resulted in the massacre of about thirty thousand men, women, and children.

Yet this insurrection generated an international protest over Turkish atrocities, evoked considerable sympathy for Bulgarians, and eventually became one factor in Russia's taking up arms against Turkey. The following year a Tsarist army crossed the Danube and, joined by Bulgarian volunteers, defeated the Turks. The terms of peace, which were signed in 1878 at San Stefano near Constantinople, provided for an autonomous Bulgarian state encompassing most of Macedonia and having access to the Aegean. This, however, proved unacceptable to Great Britain and Austria-Hungary. When the terms were renegotiated that same year under the Treaty of Berlin, the country's proposed size was reduced by two-thirds. Additional territorial gains were achieved at Turkey's expense, however, in 1885 and again in 1912.

During World War I, Bulgaria entered into a secret alliance with the Central Powers and subsequently declared war against neighboring Serbia. Not being on the winning side cost the Bulgarians the loss of a part of Western Thrace to Greece and a part of the western frontier area to Yugoslavia.[4] When the Second World War broke out, Bulgaria repeated the same mistake and in 1941 it became an ally of Germany for the purpose of obtaining the territories envisaged at San Stefano. Initially things went well and, with the Germans, Bulgaria occupied parts of Greece and Yugoslavia to which it felt it held legitimate claim. By 1944 defeat appeared inevitable, and Bulgaria sought to break away from the alliance. Its plea for an armistice with the Western Powers was disregarded by the USSR which, although not then in a state of full belligerency with Bulgaria, proceeded to declare war and occupy the country. Under the terms of the armistice Bulgaria was forced to evacuate the territories it had gained from Greece and Yugoslavia.

The Tirnovo Constitution.   Both treaties of 1878 at San Stefano and Berlin provided for the convocation of a national assembly to elect a prince and institutionalize a future government. An initial draft of the Bulgarian constitution prepared by the temporary Tsarist governor and elaborated upon by a Russian professor of constitutional law, explicitly included the principles of a parliamentary monarchy. But the assembly, which was convened the following year at the ancient capital of Tirnovo, went even further:

> [It] adopted the principles of extreme liberalism with the framework of a parliamentary form of government. Parliament was to be unicameral, elected on the basis of universal suffrage, and controlling the executive. Ab-

---

4. For a useful summary of these events, see *ibid.*, pp. 16−17.

solute political and civil liberty was explicitly guaranteed. Thus, the pure and spontaneous democratism of the Bulgarian people gave them what was then referred to as "one of the most democratic constitutions in the world"[5]

During the sixty-five years of its existence, the Tirnovo constitution was frequently violated due to impulsive actions and personal ambitions. Probably some blame can be attributed to lack of experience and the general absence of a tradition of self-government. Nevertheless, this constitution represented one of the most advanced and democratic among the fundamental laws in the world at that time. It explicitly guaranteed broad political, civil, and social liberties. Significantly, "the Tirnovo constitution has remained the symbol of free government for all democratic Bulgarians."[6] Possibly with this in mind the communists, when they usurped power in the Second World War, disarmingly professed a return to its principles.

The 1947 Dimitrov Constitution. After the Fatherland Front[7] seized the government and the Red Army occupied Bulgaria in 1944, the communists methodically undertook to consolidate their rule. Initially holding only the ministries of Interior (police) and Justice, they conducted widespread purges and trials in order to eliminate all opposition. As their control became more nearly absolute, an attack was launched on the old Tirnovo constitution and "popular requests" were trumped up for a new one. In September 1946 the results of a plebiscite eliminated the monarchy and declared Bulgaria a republic.[8] The following month, elections were held for a Grand National Assembly (*Sobranje*) that would enact a new constitution. After the legislature convened, Georgi Dimitrov formed his government.

Since he had been so closely associated with it, the new fundamental law of the People's Republic of Bulgaria is commonly called the Dimitrov constitution. Dimitrov was born in 1882 of a working-class Protestant family; as a young man he became active through the trade unions in the "narrow" socialist movement and instrumental in its transformation (1919) into the Bulgarian Communist party. During the years 1920–1921 Dimitrov served as delegate to the second

---

5. *Ibid.*, p. 85.

6. *Ibid.*, pp. 86, 88–89, 118.

7. The Fatherland Front (*Otechestven Front*) was a communist-inspired coalition established secretly in 1942. The name is used currently for the umbrella front organization, which is quite different from the original movement. It now includes trade unions and the youth movement as collective members; communist party and the subordinate Bulgarian National Agrarian Union members; and also private citizens, who may join as individuals. Officers are listed in CIA, *Directory of Officials of the Bulgarian People's Republic* (Washington, D.C., September 1975), pp. 80–84.

8. Robert Lee Wolff, "Bulgaria," in Stephen D. Kertesz (ed.), *The Fate of East Central Europe* (Notre Dame, Ind., 1956), p. 282. King Simeon and his mother went into exile.

and third Comintern congresses at Moscow and subsequently as a member of the organization's executive committee.[9] In 1923 he fled Bulgaria after an unsuccesful coup. Ten years later, the Nazi government arrested him for alleged complicity in the Reichstag fire.

Through the intervention of the USSR, Dimitrov was released and deported to Moscow, where he became a Soviet citizen. From 1935 to 1943 he held the post of Comintern secretary-general. He initiated the Fatherland Front and returned to Bulgaria, still as a Soviet citizen, in November 1945 to become at various times chairman (later secretary-general) of the ruling party's Central Committee, Politburo chairman, and premier. Dimitrov went to the USSR for medical treatment at the beginning of 1949 and died in July of that year at a sanatorium near Moscow.[10]

Although the initial draft of the Dimitrov constitution, as it was prepared by an Assembly committee, looked like the Tirnovo document, it later underwent revision by a special group. When it was promulgated, the new basic law closely resembled the 1936 "Stalin constitution" of the USSR. It seems more than coincidental that, during the period between drafts, all legal opposition within the Assembly had been silenced. Moreover, the signing of a peace treaty eliminated further necessity for the Tirnovo facade. The new constitution received formal approval by the Assembly on 4 December 1947, the eleventh anniversary of the constitution named after Stalin.[11]

A successor document was adopted on 16 May 1971 to fit the new stage in the building of an advanced socialist society. It defines collective ownership of the means of production by the state or cooperatives; indicates that the regime can nationalize any and all industrial, trade, transport or credit facilities; affirms that ownership can not be detrimental to the public interest; and specifically mentions that private property is subject to compulsory restrictions and expropriation. Furthermore, Bulgaria is referred to as a socialist state, although it remains a people's republic, and the communist party is named as the leading force in society and the state. The document also guarantees ties with the socialist camp and fidelity to the Soviet Union.[12]

The constitution defines the unicameral National Assembly as the "supreme organ of the state power" and stipulates that its 400 members, who are elected to

9. He should not be confused with Dr. Georgi M. Dimitrov (nicknamed "Gemeto"), secretary-general of the Agrarian party, who resigned under communist pressure and was succeeded by Nikola Petkov (arrested and executed in September 1947). G. M. Dimitrov escaped from Bulgaria and died in the United States. See also Michael Padev, *Dimitrov Wastes no Bullets* (London, 1948).

10. Dellin, *Bulgaria,* pp. 390–391.

11. V. N. Durdenevskii, *Konstitutsii evropeiskikh stran narodnoi demokratii* (Moscow, 1954), pp. 5–26, gives the text in Russian.

12. For the new constitution, see [Bulgaria], *Konstitutsiia na Narodna Republika Bulgariya* (Sofia, 1971), p. 64; henceforth cited as *Constitution.*

five-year terms in constituencies that have equal numbers of inhabitants, shall meet three times annually as convened by the State Council.[13] The Assembly elects the State Council, Council of Ministers, Supreme Court, and Chief Prosecutor; amends the constitution; and performs a number of other legislative functions. The twenty-seven-member Council of State combines legislative and executive authority.[14] It exercises the prerogatives of a collective head of state by representing the country externally, legislating by decree, interpreting laws, and calling elections. In actual fact, however, these are not deliberative bodies; they merely serve to ratify communist party proposals.

The Council of Ministers is defined by the constitution as "the supreme executive and administrative organ of the state." After being reorganized in June 1976 following elections, it consisted of a chairman or premier, a first deputy premier, four deputy premiers, twenty-two ministers, and four heads of various committees.[15] The present State Council chairman, Todor Zhivkov, also serves as first secretary of the Bulgarian Communist Party. The current premier, Stanko Todorov, remains a member of the party Politburo.

Local government is administered by people's councils that are elected for 2½-year terms and are primarily responsible for the implementation of the economic, social, and cultural policies laid down by superior organs of the state. These councils, which are equivalent to soviets in the USSR, exist at the district and commune levels.

The judicial organ at the highest level is the Supreme Court, supported by three city, twenty-seven regional, and ninety-three district courts. Judges and lay assessors are generally elected by citizens, people's councils, or the National Assembly. The Chief Prosecutor wields exceptional power in controlling observance of the law by government organs and officials as well as citizens. He is charged specifically

> to attend to the prosecution and punishment of crimes which affect the state national, and economic interests of the People's Republic, and crimes and actions detrimental to the independence and state sovereignty of the country.[16]

The longest chapter in the constitution deals with guarantees covering a wide range of civil liberties and economic and social rights. As in the corresponding Soviet document, almost every desirable right is spelled out:[17] equality before

---

13. Articles 66–89, *ibid.*

14. Articles 90–97, *ibid.* Party leader Todor Zhivkov gave up the premiership in 1971 and became State Council chairman.

15. Articles 98–108, *ibid.;* the incumbents are listed in *Rabotnichesko delo,* 16 June 1976.

16. Dellin, *Bulgaria,* p. 94. In addition, the regime has mobilized "volunteer" units of workers to preserve social order.

17. Articles 34–65, *Constitution.*

the law; individual liberty; inviolability of domicile; and freedom of religion, speech, press, and assembly. There is the qualification, however, that these rights may be exercised only in the interests of the working people.

It would seem on the surface that the 1971 constitution provides Bulgaria with a democratically representative form of government. While the document does not adhere to the principle of separation of powers, it nevertheless suggests a theoretical degree of responsibility. Against the objection that it is strongly flavored with the dominance of state over individual, the communists argue that the state represents the people who elect the government and that guarantees of individual rights and liberties are abundantly enumerated.

Constitution and Government in Practice. Theory remains far removed from practice in Bulgaria, where the literal provisions of the constitution bear only faint resemblance to the actual operation of the government. The basic law amounts to little more than a facade behind which the ruling party wields tight control over all levers of national power. Hence, the constitution is merely an instrument that can be used or abused as need dictates. Bulgaria today is a dictatorship of the proletariat (i.e., of the communist party), and, in Lenin's definition, "a power limited by nothing, by no law, directly based on violence."[18]

In practice, the constitutional provisions for a representative government remain a farce, since only the views of the communist leadership become policy and law. Furthermore, only those persons who are ultimately approved by the party are allowed to participate in administering the government.[19] Assembly deputies are nominated in advance under party supervision and then elected without opposition. They convene a few times a year for periods of several days and rubber stamp proposals of the Assembly presidium, the Council of Ministers, or the ruling party's Central Committee. The same electoral process applies to the judiciary. In all cases, office holders who fail to adhere to the party line can be recalled. Despite the assertion of individual liberties and human rights in the basic law, it is obvious from many examples that freedom of speech, assembly, and press is permitted only when its exercise is consonant with communist policies. Deviation from the dictates and will of the party simply is not permitted.

THE COMMUNIST PARTY OF BULGARIA

Dimitur Blagoyev, who was born in Macedonia and educated in Russia, introduced communist ideas into Bulgaria toward the end of the nineteenth

---

18. Quoted by Dellin in *Bulgaria*, p. 95.

19. Admitted by implication in B. Spasov and A. Angelov, *Gosudarstvennoe pravo Narodnoi Respubliki Bolgarii* (Moscow, 1962), pp. 82–83.

century. The movement that received its inspiration at this time failed to grow during its early years owing to a split into "narrow" and "broad" groups. In addition to the absence of a substantial urban proletariat, peasants on their small holdings simply were not susceptible to easy organization. The "narrow" fraction advocated policies based on an industrialized economy, while the "broad" group felt, more realistically, that the almost wholly agrarian economy in Bulgaria would be unable to support the classical Marxist approach. The communist party did not play any role in the government until the end of the Second World War.[20]

After 1944, defeated Bulgaria appeared in the plans of the Soviet Union. The so-called Fatherland Front, including communists, left-wing agrarians, the Zveno group, and left-wing social democrats, came to power following the entry of the Red Army and a military coup, which resulted in the installation of Kimon Georghiev (Zveno) as premier. The new cabinet had four Zvenos, four communists,[21] four agrarians, two socialists, and two independents. Staliniza-tion took hold in Bulgaria with perhaps more aggressiveness than in any other East European country. Already in 1944 large numbers of persons who were considered threats to the regime were being tried as "fascists" or "traitors" and summarily executed.[22] Despite a renewal of this terror during 1945—1947, the main opposition party managed to hold one-third of the vote.

In a September 1946 broadcast to the Bulgarian people, communist party leader Georgi Dimitrov proclaimed:

> Bulgaria will be a people's republic, a factor for Slav unity and fraternity against any possible aggression. It will not grease the axle of any anti-Slav or anti-Soviet policy leading to enmity between the peoples. Bulgaria will be a people's republic which, together with other democratic and freedom-loving peoples, will represent a strong element of peace and democracy in the Balkans and Europe and not a tool for military adventures and aggressive wars.[23]

During a later speech, at the fifth congress of the Bulgarian Communist Party, Dimitrov stated that the foundation of the government involved collaboration and friendship with the Soviet Union and that Bulgaria belonged to the anti-imperialist camp.

---

20. The war period is covered in the Soviet version of the party history by L. Bidinskaya (ed.), *Istoriya Bolgarskoi Kommunisticheskoi Partii* (Moscow, 1960), pp. 345—383. See also Nissan Oren, *Bulgarian Communism* (New York, 1971).

21. The communists had only twenty-five thousand members at this time and, because of their weakness, were forced to establish a coalition regime. See the interview with Todor Zhivkov in *Le Monde*, 4 August 1976.

22. An official statement issued in March 1945 admitted to 2,138 executions, some 1,940 prison sentences of twenty years, and 1,689 sentences of ten to fifteen years. Stanley G. Evans, *A Short History of Bulgaria* (London, 1960), p. 189.

23. Quoted in *ibid.*, p. 184.

Along with the purges, Dimitrov created thirty trade unions, replaced the former police organization with his own militia, and appointed trusted individuals from his party to positions of authority. The general election held in November 1945 to choose members of the new National Assembly was anything but free. After the count the Fatherland Front had won 364 seats, as opposed to 101 for the noncommunist opposition. Of those in the Front, a total of 277 were communists, who thus held an absolute majority.

Dimitrov, despite some vacillation (especially in his views on a Balkan federation), supported the Moscow line in opposition to certain nationalists who felt that Bulgarian interests should come first. After he died in July 1949, Vulko Chervenkov assumed control of the party and promptly eliminated the nationalist group. The orthodox Bulgarian communists were so anxious to imitate the USSR that they found themselves making the same mistakes, long after the Soviets had taken a new approach and attempted to rectify their errors.

Purges within the party had been so thorough that they left few people of stature who were willing or able to offer any effective opposition to Moscow's directives. Stalin was suspicious of all Bulgarian communists who had spent the war inside their own country rather than in the USSR, the more so after Tito of Yugoslavia came into conflict with the Cominform. Traicho Kostov, who had been the most obvious successor to Dimitrov, ended on the gallows as a Titoist. Chervenkov soon became the little Stalin of Bulgaria.[24] During his six years of rule approximately 100,000 persons were purged from a communist party of about 460,000 members.

After the death of Stalin in 1953, the Chervenkov group would have preferred to continue its hard line, but it was held in check by the milder "new course" in the Soviet Union. Although Chervenkov remained loyal to his mentors in Moscow, realignments within the USSR between 1953 and 1956 resulted in the rise of Soviet leaders who were patrons of his opponents in the Bulgarian party and in the demise of those who had supported him. In accordance with the collective leadership philosophy, which was current in Moscow after Stalin's death, Chervenkov gave up the highest party position in 1954 but continued to hold office as premier and remained the dominant figure until 1956. The rise of Khrushchev in the USSR brought about promotion of Todor Zhivkov, and Chervenkov lost the premiership. Although he was gradually stripped of his

---

24. Having become an "unperson" in the 1960s, Chervenkov is not mentioned in a party history covering this period. P. Kostov, M. Trifonova, and M. St. Dimitrov (eds.), *Materiali po istoriya na Bulgarskata Komunisticheska Partiya, 1944–1960* (Sofia, 1961), pp. 87–98. It appears that only the party leader can identify an unperson by name. Todor Zhivkov, in his report to the eighth congress, stated that the "personality cult of Vulko Chervenkov" had led to "incorrect, anti-Leninist methods of work and leadership." [Bulgarian Communist Party], *Osmi Kongres: stenografski protokol* (Sofia, 1963), p. 125.

party position, his purge did not come until 1962 amid the familiar charges of excess and error during "the period of the personality cult."[25]

Soviet support had been essential in resolving the intense struggle among Bulgarian party factions. The departure of Chervenkov, plus previous purges, left Todor Zhivkov more fully in control. He had entered the Politburo in 1952, and had become first secretary in 1954 and additionally premier in 1962. His victory was assured when he obtained the support of a majority on the then nine-man Politburo and an enlarged Central Committee. (In 1962 the larger Committee had 101 full members and 67 nonvoting candidates. The party's eleventh congress, in March 1976, elected 154 members and 121 candidates.) The serious internal factionalism and infighting among Bulgarian party leaders left them susceptible to Soviet manipulation; hence, Bulgaria has been probably the most conservative of all East European states.

After a Central Committee plenum in December 1972, a series of measures were introduced to improve living conditions, and some progress has since been made. Zhivkov also took steps to reduce the use of terror and to bring the Interior ministry under closer control.

The current leaders around Zhivkov show a tendency toward continuity and unity. They are generally mediocre individuals who are willing to accede to the desires of Moscow. There are no groups or individuals of sufficient strength to suggest an independent course of action in the near future. As late as 1965, however, a plot was uncovered to overthrow the Bulgarian leadership. Of the ten men implicated, one committed suicide and the others were sentenced to prison terms.[26] About half of this group consisted of officers who had fought in guerrilla detachments inside Bulgaria during the war, and it may therefore have represented a more nationalist and independent way of thinking.

There has been no indication of disloyalty among the rank and file of the party, which in 1976 totaled 789,795 members and candidates, organized into 28,850 local units. This represents a net increase of more than 300,000 in membership since 1958, with bureaucrats and blue-collar workers accounting for most of the gain. Party members within the group who are under twenty-eight years of age had dropped from a high of 20 percent down to 15 percent in 1970, and admission of rural young people had practically ceased at that time. Women comprised in 1976 only 20 percent of the party membership.[27] The intelligentsia seems frustrated by controls, but the younger generation is apathetic toward

---

25. L. A. D. Dellin, "Bulgaria," in Stephen D. Kertesz (ed.), *East Central Europe and the World* (Notre Dame, Ind., 1962), pp. 169–196. Chervenkov's party membership was restored on 19 May 1969.

26. Sofia radio, 19 June 1965; cited in RFE report, "Sentences of Bulgarians in April Conspiracy," 24 June 1965.

27. Todor Zhivkov to the eleventh BCP congress, *Rabotnichesko delo*, 30 March 1976.

them; the family remains unreceptive to regime indoctrination; peasants are hostile to programs imposed by the government.

Party members and candidates constitute 9 percent of the country's population. In 1976 workers still maintained the largest bloc within the party (some 41.4 percent), although not an absolute majority, and this group claims the largest share of new members. The proportion of farmers in the party has declined to 23 percent. White-collar and intelligentsia membership is increasing and has reached 35.6 percent.[28] (See table 9.)

On the other hand, the Secretariat already concluded in 1970 that party organizations "show liberalism and little meticulous effort, underestimate the control and inspection of task fulfillment as basic methods of party leadership, and tolerate essential shortcomings in the training and education of cadres." The organizational, agitprop, and science and education departments were given either two or three months to submit to the Secretariat detailed plans for measures to correct these negative manifestations.[29]

TABLE 9

COMPOSITION OF THE BULGARIAN COMMUNIST PARTY, 1962–1976
(In numbers of members and percents of total)

Occupational class	November 1962 (eighth congress)	November 1966 (ninth congress)	April 1971 (tenth congress)	March 1976 (eleventh congress)
Workers	196,449 (37.2)	234,693 (38.4)	280,480 (40.1)	326,974 (41.4)
Peasants	169,601 (32.1)	178,464 (29.2)	182,563 (26.1)	181,655 (23.0)
White-collar workers and others	162,624 (30.7)	198,022 (32.4)	236,433 (33.8)	281,167 (35.6)
Total	528,674 (100.0)	611,179 (100.0)	699,476 (100.0)	789,796 (100.0)

SOURCES: *Rabotnichesko delo,* 6 November 1962; RFE report, "Zhivkov's Party Congress Report," 25 November 1966; RFE report, "The BCP Theses on the Party and Mass Organizations," 23 February 1976; *Rabotnichesko delo,* 30 March 1976.

Even though pressure may have eased against the noncommunist population since 1972, under the new policy, the machinery of the Interior ministry has been streamlined and its new head, Dimitar Stoyanov, controls only uniformed police and fire-department personnel. On the twenty-fifth anniversary of this organization, his predecessor described one aspect of security as follows: "In the same way as hundreds of institutes of the capitalist countries cultivate the bacilli of

28. RFE report, "BCP Theses on the Party and Mass Organizations," 23 February 1976. Many of these officials are among the 13.5 percent of employees who comprise the managerial-administrative apparatus in the economy. Belgrade radio, 18 August 1976: a commentary on the new Bulgarian law to eliminate inefficiency.

29. *Rabotnichesko delo,* 14 January 1970.

deadly diseases, so are the bacilli of ideological diversion cultivated in hundreds of institutes, radio and television companies, departments and publishing houses. Every day these bacilli penetrate our frontiers and look for a fertile soil."[30] Security provisions remain, and their enforcement varies with the policy in effect at any particular time.

The people realize this, and that is probably why they vote. In the elections of 30 May 1976, it was claimed that 99.93 percent of the adult population went to the polls. According to official figures, 99.92 percent of the qualified electorate cast ballots for candidates of the Fatherland Front. Despite the pressure to register an affirmative vote for the single candidate in each constituency, 780 persons voted against the regime, and the ballots of another 4,461 had probably been mutilated or left blank in protest, as they were judged to be invalid.[31] (See table 10.)

TABLE 10

Composition of the Bulgarian National Assembly, 1957–1976

| Party | Number of representatives | | | | |
	1957	1962	1966	1971	1976
Bulgarian Communist Party	160	197	280	266	272
Bulgarian Agrarian Union[a].	65	80	99	100	100
Nonparty.	28	44	37	34	28
Total.	253	321	416	400	400[b]

Sources: L. N. Tolkunov (ed.), *Sotsialisticheskii lager* (Moscow, 1962), p. 56; *Rabotnichesko delo*, 26 February 1962; Sofia radio, 28 February 1966; *Rabotnichesko delo*, 1 June 1976.

Notes: [a]The Bulgarian Agrarian Union (BAU), a separate political party in name only, is maintained by the communists as a control device in the villages because of its past importance and for external propaganda. It has 130,000 members, with about 85,000 of them working in agriculture. RFE, *Situation Report*, 8 December 1976, on the thirty-third BAU congress.

[b]All candidates, including those labeled "nonparty," run on the Fatherland Front ticket without any opposition. Nonparty includes also Komsomol members.

The influence of propaganda, apart from elections, permeates every field: education of adults and young people, trade unions, book publication and distribution, even dress and conduct. The regime attempts to mold completely the mind of every Bulgarian. Admittedly and openly

> the party is the guiding political force in socialist [Bulgarian] society. As for public opinion, on the one hand, the party plays a guiding role in the crea-
> tion of the conditions and forms which are necessary premises for the

30. Speech over Sofia radio, 15 September 1969. Since the beginning of 1970, a trend toward greater secrecy has developed and less documentary material is being published.

31. *Rabotnichesko delo*, 21 May 1976. See also the part on elections in Spasov and Angelov, *op. cit.* (in note 19 above), pp. 567–596.

normal and efficient functioning of public opinion; on the other, it is the
guiding subjective force in the formation of public opinion itself.[32]

According to an editorial in an official party publication: "Self-education
becomes the basic method of Marxist-Leninist training of the cadres [and]
depends most of all on the qualifications of the propagandist, who must have a
thorough knowledge of the subject he will teach."[33] The Central Committee has
called on Bulgarian women to treat friendship with the USSR as a sacred legacy
and "to watch over that friendship as over the apple of their eye, convey it to
their children with their mother's milk, and bequeath it from generation to
generation as the dearest heritage." Party leader Todor Zhivkov subsequently
stated that "Bulgaria and the Soviet Union will act as a single body, breathing
with the same lungs and nourished by the same blood stream."[34]

Zhivkov emphasized his personal allegiance to the USSR when he addressed
the thirtieth anniversary meeting to celebrate the seizure of power by the
Bulgarian communist party:

> Once, the great Lenin called the Bulgarian left wing socialists, "interna-
> tionalists in deeds." Several decades later Comrade Brezhnev defined the
> relations between Bulgaria and the Soviet Union as "socialist internation-
> alism in action." We are eternally proud of these two evaluations, because
> they define a straight and clear political line; the line of the BCP from the
> time of Dimitur Blagoyev, through the time of Georgi Dimitrov, up to our
> time. Years and decades will go by, new generations will grow, new leaders
> will lead our parties, countries and peoples, but the line of loyalty to
> Marxism-Leninism and proletarian internationalism, the line of Bulgarian-
> Soviet fraternity will continue to be bright and unchanging, marching
> forward and upwards through decades and through centuries.[35]

Although it may be difficult to identify the party's role in the government, it is
obvious from the interlocking directorate that all major plans, programs, and
policies of the regime originate with the party. (See table 11.) It retains control
over all important functions. Implementation of the communist program,
however, is another matter and has come up against several obstacles.

First of all, Bulgaria is a farming country with doubtful resources upon which
to base an industrialized economy. The emphasis on heavy industry has been

32. *Novo vreme* (January 1964), in RFE, *Bulgarian Press Survey,* 20 February 1964. Ten years
later, early in 1974, concern over ideology led to the establishment of a new Mass Information Media
Department within the BCP Secretariat.

33. *Partiyen zhivot* (December 1963).

34. Sofia radio, 5 March 1964; *Rabotnichesko delo,* 20 September 1973.

35. *Rabotnichesko delo,* 9 September 1974. Note also that since early 1973, ambassadors to the
USSR have held cabinet rank in the Bulgarian government.

supported by credits from the Soviet Union [36] and by capital extracted through forced collectivization of peasants. Considerable gains have been made in heavy industry, but production of consumers' goods and investment in agriculture have lagged behind. The results of this policy are visible, and the peasants have shown little desire to produce for the government. Even according to official data the number of cattle and sheep has not changed much in almost three decades. (See table 12). A tribute to personal initiative can be seen, however, since collectivized peasants with their "acre and a cow" private plots, occupying 9 percent of the arable land, in 1969 contributed 15.6 percent of the country's agricultural production. [37]

Second, the workers' indifference and lack of enthusiasm have made it necessary to decree harsh amendments to the labor codes. If an employee is absent without authorization during three consecutive days or for five days in any calendar year, he loses the standard increments of pay, all leave in excess of fourteen days, and all indemnities for invalidism or sickness and retirement. Work contracts must be signed for a specific period of time, and an employee is not allowed to break his contract without the consent of management. If he leaves without permission, he cannot be hired by another enterprise and remains subject to penalties for absence;[38] in addition, he must move out of government housing within one month.

Finally, poor discipline among the young is mentioned time after time, indicating a problem of major proportions. Party leaders enumerate the absence of conscience, bad upbringing, the lack of proper guidance at home and school, negative attitudes toward the state, formalism and banalities in lecture programs, inadequate Komsomol[39] curriculum and organization, the degenerate influence of bourgeois culture, the consumption of alcohol, decadent music, vulgarity in dances, and a desire for cars and travel outside Bulgaria as some of the reasons for juvenile delinquency.

Bulgarian leaders have committed the people to full support of the Soviet

---

36. *Narodna mladezh,* 11 May 1970, revealed that the total at that time amounted to 1.8 billion rubles. This included 530 million rubles granted in 1964 to have been used as capital investment during 1966–1970. Some of it may be repaid in the future with manganese, of which several hundred million tons in deposits have been discovered recently near Varna. Another loan of 500 million rubles was promised Bulgaria by the USSR for the 1971–1975 period. *Rabotnichesko delo,* 17 March 1969.

37. RFE, *Situation Report,* 30 April 1969. Previous restrictions on private plots were removed by Council of Ministers' decrees issued in July and August 1973, obviously in order to raise production.

38. *Darzhaven vestnik,* no. 34 (29 April 1969) published a decree that the name "construction troops" should be applied to penal work groups formerly called the Labor Service.

39. According to the national Komsomol secretary, there are about 12,000 "parasites" among the 1.3 million members of that youth organization. *Washington Post,* 11 May 1976. Todor Zhivkov in *World Marxist Review* (June 1976), p. 22, gave other criticisms.

TABLE 11

BULGARIAN PARTY-GOVERNMENT DIRECTORATE, 1976

Politburo	Secretariat	State Council	Council of Ministers	Other positions
FULL MEMBERS (9)	Doynov, Ognyan (41)			Chief, BCP Industry and Transport Department
Dragoycheva, Tsola (78)		Member		Chairman Bulgarian-Soviet Friendship Committee
Filipov, Grisha (57)	Secretary	Member		
Kubadinski, Pencho (58)		Member		Chairman, Fatherland Front
Lilov, Alexander (43)	Secretary	Member		
Mihailov, Ivan (79)		Member		Civil Defense Chief
	Pramov, Ivan (55)			Chairman, National Assembly Agriculture and Food Industries Committee
Todorov, Stanko (55)			Premier	
Tsolov, Tano (58)			First Deputy premier	
Velchev, Boris (62)	Secretary	Member		Chairman, State Defense Committee
Zhivkov, Todor (63)	First Secretary	Chairman		Chairman, National Assembly
	Bonev, Vladimir (59)			
	Dalbokov, Sava (57)			Deputy premier (supplies and state reserves)

TABLE 11 (Cont.)

BULGARIAN PARTY-GOVERNMENT DIRECTORATE, 1976

Politburo	Secretariat	State Council	Council of Ministers	Other positions
CANDIDATES (6)				
Dzhurov, Dobri (60)			National defense	
	Mishev, Misho (65)	Member		Chairman, Central Council of Trade Unions
Mladenov, Petar (40)			Foreign affairs	First Secretary, Varna BCP
Stoychev, Todor (56)		Member		
Takov, Peko (67)		Deputy chairman		Chairman, Council on Human Resources, Use and Development
Trichkov, Krastyu (53)			Deputy premier	Chairman, Committee on State and People's Control
Valcheva, Drazha, (45)				First Secretary, Plovdiv BCP
	Yordanov, Georgi (ca. 45)			First Secretary, Sofia BCP

SOURCES: CIA, *Directory of Officials of the Bulgarian People's Republic* (Washington, D.C., September 1975); RFE report, "The BCP Congress: Changes in the Politburo and Secretariat," 5 April 1976; *ibid.,* "The Central Committee After the 11th Party Congress," 16 June 1976, for ages given in parentheses; *ibid.,* "The New Bulgarian Government," 7 July 1976; RFE, *Line-up* (10 August 1976), pp. 3–5.

TABLE 12

LIVESTOCK NUMBERS, SELECTED YEARS, 1948–1976
(in thousands)

Livestock	1948	1961	1972	1973	1974	1975	1976
Cattle	1,783	1,452	1,379	1,441	1,454	1,554	1,656
(Cows)	(703)	(547)	(607)	(619)	(615)	(644)	(670)
Hogs	1,078	2,553	2,806	2,598	2,431	3,422	3,889
Sheep	9,266	9,333	10,127	9,920	9,765	9,791	10,020
Goats	720	246	318	301	285	299	–
Rabbits	128	470	350	288	292	345	–
Poultry	11,380	23,366	34,102	34,788	36,939	35,089	38,054

SOURCES: Eugene K. Keefe et al., *Area Handbook for Bulgaria* (Washington, D.C., 1974), p. 244; *Statisticheski godishnik 1974* (Sofia, 1974), p. 230; *Statistical Pocket Book 1976* (Sofia, 1976), pp. 55 and 94, for the years 1975 and 1976.

Union, with concomitant restrictions on freedom and initiative. Party authority is absolute within itself; it is supported completely by the proximity of USSR military power. It does not seem likely that the regime will be overthrown in the near future, although disenchantment with the leadership seems widespread even at middle party echelons. In view of the successful October 1964 coup against Khrushchev in Moscow and the abortive conspiracy of April 1965 at Sofia, the possibility of a successful attempt cannot be discounted completely.

DOMESTIC AND FOREIGN RELATIONS

The Economy.   Since the end of the Second World War, Bulgaria has imposed currency reforms on three different occasions, in 1947, 1952, and 1962. Each time, the revaluation was imposed to drain off excess purchasing power, curb existing inflation, and redistribute income. Since the currency reform of 1962, the low average wage has been the main reason for the depressed standard of living. To remedy this situation, wages and salaries (mainly for low-paid workers) were raised by from 4 to 12 percent in three phases during 1970. The minimum wage increased to eighty leva per month in 1973 and it will go up to ninety leva by 1980, at the end of the seventh five-year plan.[40]

Forced industrialization, almost complete socialization of the land, and heavy reinvestment have also caused the standard of living to suffer. The perspective plan for the period 1961–1980, which was adopted by the BCP's ninth congress, envisages an investment rate of 27 percent. This long-range plan is intended to raise the annual national income to approximately twenty billion leva, about five times the 1960 level.[41]

40. Todor Zhivkov's report to the eleventh BCP congress in *Rabotnichesko delo*, 30 March 1976.

41. Todor Zhivkov, *Otchetnyi doklad* (Moscow, 1963), pp. 95–96. See also Stanko Todorov's speech on the Bulgarian economy in the next twenty years in *Rabotnichesko delo*, 5 March 1970.

In an obvious attempt to correct some of the serious deficiencies within the economy, Bulgaria began a reorganization of both government and economy away from the previous centralized lines. The so-called New Economic System, which was unveiled in April 1966 at a plenary session of the Central Committee, apparently did not work.[42] It has been superseded by a New Economic Mechanism (NEM), which is being implemented during the 1976—1980 planning period.

According to Stanko Todorov, the main features of the NEM will include the management by objective principle in the national economy; the strengthening of centralized planning; and more authority for the national economic complexes, production units, and individual managers.[43] Only time will tell whether these vague and contradictory formulations can solve the many problems that beset the Bulgarian economy.

Bulgaria presents an outstanding example of the fallacy of communist doctrine, both in the economic sense and in the type of society it provides. Regime leaders have imitated the Soviet Union in nearly every respect, but this has produced little of a positive nature aside from a degree of industrialization.[44] The price the Bulgarian people have paid for this achievement is a high one. Supposedly, they "cannot conceive of building a developed socialist society and then communism" other than "in conditions of increasingly organic relations between the People's Republic of Bulgaria and the great Union of Soviet Socialist Republics."[45] Yet they have survived other "organic relationships" under Byzantine and Ottoman role, always reclaiming their role in the heart of the Balkans.

Collectivization. Agricultural collectives expanded at a more rapid pace in Bulgaria than in any of the other East European countries, even though collectivization policy moved through several distinct phases. The first of these phases involved persuasion, during the time when the communists were consolidating their power. This step was followed, commencing in 1948, by a most aggressive policy. Only two years later, some 43 percent of all the land had been collectivized; by 1960, it was claimed that 97.4 percent of the land belonged either in this category or in that of agricultural enterprises directly operated by the state.[46]

---

42. L. A. D. Dellin, "Economic Reforms: Bulgaria," in *Problems of Communism* (September—October 1970), pp. 44—52. NEM regulations appeared in *Darzhaven vestnik,* nos. 98, 99, and 100 (1970), with subsequent amendments.

43. *Rabotnichesko delo,* 5 December 1975.

44. Some 54.6 percent of the national income allegedly now comes from industry, according to Zhivkov, *op. cit.* (in note 39 above), p. 17.

45. *Ibid.,* p. 26. Economic targets for 1977 were announced by Sofia radio, 11 January 1977.

46. S. D. Sergeev and A. F. Dobrokhotov, *Narodnaya Respublika Bolgariya* (Moscow, 1962), p. 236.

The 1971 constitution of Bulgaria claims that "the land belongs to those who till it." As in the Soviet Union, the eventual desire of the Bulgarian communists probably is to bring all agricultural land into *sovkhozy* (state farms), although at present the greater part is in *kolkhozy* (collectives). Todor Zhivkov had ordered complete collectivization, despite the sometimes discouraging results already obtained. For example, in 1963 it became necessary to import some 100,000 tons of wheat from Canada, and a certain amount of food rationing had to be introduced. Although collectivization is pointed to with pride and declared to be irrevocable by officials, in practice measures are being taken to encourage production on private plots, a method that is more efficient. Bulgarian agriculture is not producing foodstuffs in sufficient quantities to supply the population adequately. (See table 13). Hence some compromise must be reached between production and collectivization if the country is ever to deliver more than the basic necessities. Although collectivized farmers have been eligible for old-age pensions, accident and health insurance, vacations, and child allowances since 1976, this may be inadequate to keep young people on the farm.[47]

TABLE 13

ACTUAL AND DESIRED ANNUAL CONSUMPTION LEVELS, 1970 AND 1980

		Consumption Levels		
Item	Measure	Actual 1970	Desired 1980	Scientific Norms*
Meat and meat products	Pounds per capita	91.3	165.4	176.4
Fish	do	12.1	22.0	22.0
Milk and milk products	do	335.4	551.3	573.3
Vegetable oils	do	27.6	30.9	28.7
Flour and flour products	do	376.1	330.7	221.0
Sugar	do	72.5	79.4	70.6
Vegetables	do	196.0	352.8	396.9
Fruits	do	326.8	442.0	442.0
Eggs	number per capita	122.0	250.0	265.0
Cotton fabrics	feet per capita	72.8	108.2	118.0
Wool fabrics	do	12.5	19.7	23.0
Shoes	pairs per capita	1.7	3.0	4.0
Radio sets	per 100 households	100.8	110.0	130.0
Television sets	do	42.0	80.0	105.0
Telephones	do	7.0	10.0	50.0
Washing machines	do	50.0	60.0	70.0
Refrigerators	do	29.0	90.0	100.0
Automobiles	do	6.0	30.0	40.0

SOURCE: Adapted from U.S. Department of Commerce, "Statistics on Rising Living Standard Given," in *Translations on Eastern Europe: Political, Sociological, and Military Affairs* (JPRS 58,480, No. 851, 1973); as cited by Keefe, *op. cit.* (in sources for table 12 above), p. 87.

NOTE: *As determined by research institutes at the Bulgarian Academy of Sciences.

47. Ivan Pramov interview with *Zemedelske noviny,* 17 March 1976; Prague.

Church-State Relations. The regime has been able to gain substantial control over religious life. This was accomplished in several distinct phases.[48] Minority faiths (Moslem, Jewish, Protestant, and Roman Catholic) were each handled separately, but with great effectiveness. The majority of the people belong to the Bulgarian Orthodox church, and the government has capitalized upon this fact:

> The Communists have patronized the church as the traditional national church of Bulgaria, not only to obtain support from the Church devotees, but also to unify national Orthodox Churches under the aegis of the Soviet-controlled Russian Orthodox Church. [Already] . . . Patriarch Kiril [had] clearly demonstrated his attitude . . when he thanked the regime for the reestablishment of the Bulgarian Patriarchate and called on all the faithful to support the Government in its policies.[49]

Control over the Bulgarian Orthodox church and other religions was greatly facilitated by a 1949 statute whereby all denominations were required to register with the Committee for Religious Affairs, which was attached to the Council of Ministers, and to obtain approval for their bylaws. This statute also specified that the leadership of all religious organizations "must be responsible to the state" and that members of each hierarchy could not "take office or be dismissed or transferred without the approval of the Committee."[50] Religious organizations are authorized to operate schools if state permission is obtained, but they are not allowed the right to engage in secular education. Such restrictions have curtailed virtually all religious freedom and converted religious leaders into spokesmen for the state.

Moslems of Turkish descent form the largest minority religious group and have fared less well than the Bulgarian Orthodox faithful. Approximately 150,000 of the Turkish Moslems were permitted to leave during 1950–1951, and the remaining 700,000 have been organized into communities numbering just over one thousand.[51] The Grand Mufti has repeatedly expressed his gratitude for the consideration shown to the Turkish minority; he undoubtedly retains his position under conditions that forbid any but favorable statements concerning the

---

48. On the techniques, see Z. Oshavkov *et al.* (eds.), *Izgrazhdane i razvitie na sotsialisticheskoto obshchestvo v Bulgariya* (Sofia, 1962), pp. 266–276.

49. Dellin, *Bulgaria,* p. 187. Sofia radio, 17 December 1974, broadcast a message from the new Bulgarian patriarch (Maxim) to the UN and the World Council of Churches, protesting Israeli imprisonment of a "clergyman-patriot."

50. Dellin, *Bulgaria,* p. 189. See also Ivan Sipkov, "Church and State in Bulgaria," in US Senate, Committee on the Judiciary, *The Church and State under Communism* (Washington, D.C., 1965), II, pp. 21–32.

51. Joseph B. Schectman, *Postwar Population Transfers in Europe, 1945–1955* (Philadelphia, 1962), pp. 345–354.

regime and the welfare of his group. Under a 1968 agreement with Turkey, Bulgarian Turks and families were allowed to emigrate. Repatriation commenced in 1969, but only 30,000 to 35,000 appeared to be eligible (those who had relatives in Turkey), and the number of those who had left apparently was smaller than this figure.[52]

The position of the Roman Catholic church is even worse. In September 1952 forty leading Catholics were tried at Sofia on trumped-up charges of spying. All of the defendants received death, imprisonment, or expulsion sentences. This action and the subsequent banishment of less important personnel sufficed to obliterate the church hierarchy in Bulgaria. The country still has about 56,000 persons of the Roman Catholic faith, but there are no church buildings or priests to conduct religious services for them.[53]

Protestants have suffered a somewhat similar fate, although their denominations are still active to a limited degree. Five separate groups were forcibly combined into one United Evangelical church. All denominational schools were closed, however, and many clergymen faced trial for espionage. In March 1949, fifteen pastors were sentenced to go to prison and to pay heavy fines for allegedly spying on behalf of the United States and Britain. Protestant churches in Bulgaria had exerted considerable influence on the educated class before the war, but now they remain under tight state control.

Another religious minority group comprises approximately 5,500 persons of the Jewish faith. The official leadership of this community has cooperated with the regime, since leaders of all recognized religious bodies have tenure that remains dependent upon the will of the communist government. After surviving the Second World War, the Jews in Bulgaria were allowed to emigrate to Israel. Some forty-five thousand did so, mostly during the 1949–1950 period. Fourteen synagogues still exist in Bulgaria for worship.[54]

What effect the control exercised by the regime over churches has had on the younger minds is impossible to judge. Religion still remains a stronghold of anticommunist feeling, however, and it is connected with a desire for genuine national independence. According to a Bulgarian expert on atheistic education, a recent survey[55] showed that more than one-third of the population was "religiously minded" to some degree.

---

52. RFE, *Situation Report*, 28 April 1976.

53. All priests, monks, and nuns were forced to leave the country in 1952, according to Sipkov, *op. cit.* (in note 50 above), pp. 29, 32. However, in June 1976 Todor Zhivkov called on Pope Paul VI, and Agostino Casaroli, secretary of the Vatican Council, reciprocated the visit later that same year. Sofia radio, 8 November 1976.

54. Dellin, *Bulgaria*, p. 192; Sipkov, *op. cit.* (in note 50 above), p. 32; Heinz Siegert, *Bulgarien Heute* (Vienna, 1964), p. 130. Some 3,500 Jews live in Sofia and another 650 at Plovdiv, according to the *San Francisco Sunday Examiner & Chronicle*, 8 November 1970.

55. Nikolay Mizov in *Politicheska prosvita*, no. 10 (1974); cited by RFE, *Situation Report*, 6 December 1974.

Foreign Trade.   Bulgaria became one of the original members of CMEA in 1949, when that organization was formed. Table 14 shows trade with the other East European states and the Soviet Union. By 1976 the bloc accounted for some 80 percent of Bulgaria's imports and exports.[56] East European states may now form temporary alliances or even subblocs within CMEA, and there is evidence that such arrangements had already occurred some time ago. On the other hand, the trade agreement for the period 1976–1980 involved transactions amounting to twenty-four billion rubles and increased Soviet-Bulgarian trade by four-fifths. The USSR has reportedly invested some two billion dollars in Bulgaria's economy.[57]

TABLE 14

BULGARIA-BLOC TRADE, 1963–1974

(in millions of leva)

Country	1963		1968		1974	
	Imports	*Exports*	*Imports*	*Exports*	*Imports*	*Exports*
Albania.	2.5	0.7	6.6	4.9	9.3	7.1
Czechoslovakia . .	95.2	82.0	96.8	103.6	169.8	149.8
East Germany . . .	113.7	94.5	176.1	141.5	380.2	284.3
Hungary	20.8	19.1	35.5	33.4	64.7	63.8
Poland	39.6	38.4	75.3	55.6	212.5	181.3
Romania	13.4	16.3	23.4	29.8	91.2	97.8
USSR.	585.5	521.5	1,107.0	1,045.8	1,830.7	1,871.9
Total.	870.7	772.5	1,520.7	1,414.6	2,758.4	2,656.0
All foreign trade. .	1,091.1	975.8	2,085.3	1,889.7	4,195.8	3,720.8

SOURCES: [Bulgaria], *Statistichesky godishnik 1964* (Sofia, 1965), p. 298; *Statistichesky yezhegodnik 1969* (Sofia, 1970), pp. 186–187; *Statistichesky godishnik 1975* (Sofia, 1976), pp. 312–313.

NOTE: One U.S. dollar equaled 1.17 leva and then 1.04 leva at official exchange rates prior to 1975, less than half the black market rate, but in 1976 it dropped to 0.96 leva.

Joint planning for 1971–1975 between Bulgaria and the Soviet Union resulted in cooperative efforts toward the construction of a gas pipeline and certain plants in the USSR that produce steel, cast iron, cellulose, and wood. Bulgarian workers in the tens of thousands were imported to work on these projects, and Bulgaria began to extend loans for the development of Soviet natural resources. By 1976 this cooperation involved fifty-four Soviet and twenty Bulgarian governmental agencies. Moscow is providing assistance for the construction of

---

56. Zhivkov interview (see note 21 above).

57. *Rabotnichesko delo,* 26 December 1975. Bulgarian investments in the USSR will total some 280 million exchange leva during 1976 alone, according to Stanko Todorov in *ibid.* 5 December 1975.

atomic and thermoelectric power plants, housing complexes, and a subway in Sofia.[58]

Relations with Border Countries. Bulgaria is touched on the north by Romania, on the west by Yugoslavia, and on the south by Greece and Turkey. The country has not had particularly good relations with its neighbors, including even communist-ruled ones. Its foreign affairs, however, are predicated upon satisfying the Soviet Union, and in this respect they have been conducted quite successfully. Foreign minister Petar Mladenov has stated that ''the basic goal of Bulgarian foreign policy is consolidation of the alliance with the USSR . . . . which is constantly moving forward and assuming ever-increasing new dimensions.''[59]

Bulgaria has a friendship and mutual-aid treaty with Romania which was renewed in 1970. Despite the maverick role played by Bucharest within the bloc, Sofia's relations with it have improved. During 1972 Nicolae Ceausescu and Todor Zhivkov exchanged visits, and plans for joint projects such as Danubian hydroelectric works were subsequently affirmed. In 1976 the two countries entered into a series of agreements involving joint enterprises and vastly expanded trade.[60] Bulgaria undoubtedly attempts to avoid a public airing of any intrabloc differences.

Relations between Greece and Bulgaria were initially hindered by Bulgaria's failure to pay reparations of forty-five million dollars, which were assigned by the 1947 peace treaty, and by the fact that communist Greek insurgents were given sanctuary in Bulgaria during the ensuing civil war. The spring of 1964, however, witnessed talks that were held to establish full diplomatic relations between the two countries. An agreement finally provided for payment of seven million dollars in reparations as well as communications by telephone and air. A railroad linking Koulata in Bulgaria with the port of Salonika in Greece was scheduled for completion as an alternative to the port of Rijeka in Yugoslavia. The two countries signed a new trade and payments agreement covering the years 1970–1974.

From that time on, relations have steadily improved. Following the overthrow of the Athens military government in 1974, Bulgarian-Greek relations have included the expansion of economic and cultural exchange, culminating in visits by Premier Konstantinos Karamanlis to Bulgaria (in July 1975) and by Todor Zhivkov to Greece (In April 1976). The reasons for this rapprochement appear to be the need for Bulgarian neutrality in the event of a Greco-Turkish War and

---

58. The departure of youths for construction work in Siberia was announced by Sofia radio, 5 February 1976; other data are found in *Rabotnichesko delo*, 19 March 1976, and the Fedor Kulakov address to the BCP congress over Sofia radio, 29 March 1976.

59. *Rabotnichesko delo*, 17 May 1975.

60. RFE, *Situation Report*, 29 July 1976.

the apparent Bulgarian wish to improve relations on a bilateral basis with its Balkan neighbors.[61] Relations with Turkey have never been especially good, stemming in part from the fact that the Ottomans represented the occupation power in Bulgaria for about five centuries. Bulgaria and Turkey have long had agreements for the mutual repatriation of nationals. During 1950–1951, as mentioned above, approximately 150,000 Bulgarian Turks were permitted to be repatriated to Turkey. Yet relations were strained at that time. In 1973, a joint communiqué noted that the repatriation process had become regularized. During the preceding five years, more than forty thousand Bulgarian Turks had been repatriated.[62] (For a breakdown by nationality group, see table 15.)

TABLE 15

NATIONALITIES IN BULGARIA, 1976 (ESTIMATED)

Nationality	Number of persons (in thousands)	Percent of total
Bulgarians	7,663,910	85.5
Turks	770,756	8.6
Gypsies	226,973	2.6
Macedonians	218,223	2.5
Armenians	26,189	0.3
Russians	8,730	0.1
Other	34,919	0.4
Totals	8,949,700	100.0

SOURCES: Sofia radio, 2 January 1976, for total population, and L. N. Tolkunov (ed.), *Sotsialisticheskii lager* (Moscow, 1962), p. 62, for percentages, which were used to compute absolute numbers. Approximately the same figures appear in Keefe, *op. cit.* (see table 12 above), p. 65.

NOTES: The Turks are called Moslems at times, that is, they are designated by religion, although they often feel themselves to be Turks. This is not true of the 160,000 Pomaks in the group, who are Bulgarians converted to Islam. About 190,000 repatriated Turks should be subtracted from the above table.

The 1956 census in Bulgaria gave the number of Macedonians as 187,789; in 1965 only 8,750 were recorded; the 1976 figures are not available. These changes reflect the political goals of the regime: first to please Tito but later reverting to the alleged Bulgarian "character" of Pirin Macedonia inhabitants.

With regard to the Greco-Turkish dispute over Cyprus and the Aegean, Bulgaria (although it holds a basically pro-Greek position on Cyprus), like the Soviet Union, has been attempting to exploit Turkey's alienation from the Western alliance. In order to pursue this objective in the dispute, Bulgaria

---

61. *The Times*, 3 July 1975; London.

62. *Statistichesky godishnik 1975*, p. 66.

received Turkish premier Süleyman Demirel late in 1975, and BCP leader Zhivkov visited Ankara the following year.[63]

Bulgaria's relations with Yugoslavia have been determined primarily by the degree of warmth or coolness between the USSR and that country. The status of Macedonia province in Yugoslavia has been of prime concern and might become increasingly important if Bulgaria should ever break out from under Soviet control. This border region is inhabited by 1.4 million persons who had been a bone of contention between the two states even before World War II. Yugoslavia claims that the Macedonians comprise a distinct nationality and it has organized them into a federal republic. Belgrade would like Sofia to accord its own Macedonians of the Pirin district minority rights akin to those they enjoy in Yugoslavia. Bulgaria, however, views this population as Bulgarian. Since there are more Macedonians in Yugoslavia, but relatively few Bulgarians are listed as inhabiting Vardar Macedonia, the controversy could escalate into tension over a possible Bulgarian irredenta.[64] Apart from this problem, relations with Yugoslavia have been correct in recent years.

In other politics of a regional nature, Bulgarians participated in the Balkan conference at Athens during early 1976 but played a restrained role. This hesitancy probably had its origins in the ambivalent Soviet attitude toward multilateral conferences following the 1975 Helsinki agreement and in Bulgaria's disappointment that Greece, rather than one of the communist-ruled states, had initiated the meeting.

63. RFE, *Situation Reports*, 11 November 1975 and 17 March 1976.

64. RFE report (by Robert R. King), "Macedonian Question and Bulgaria's Relations with Yugoslavia," 6 June 1975. For a historical background, see L. A. D. Dellin, "The Macedonian Problem in Communist Perspective," *Suedost-Forschungen* (1969), pp. 238–264; Munich.

Chapter 3

Czechoslovak Socialist Republic

Before the Second World War, Czechoslovakia was the most prosperous and most democratic country in Eastern Europe. Its government was based on a Western-style constitution, which was adopted in 1920. Two successive presidents, Tomas Masaryk and Eduard Benes, guarded and nurtured the democratic principles laid down in the constitution. Although much of the world did not appear to be apprehensive regarding Nazi Germany, the absorption of Austria by the Third Reich in early 1938 and claims by Hitler to border territory within Czechoslovakia gave the government in Prague considerable reason for alarm. In September the agreement at Munich countenanced the transfer of this area to Nazi rule and thus began the process that would lead to the end of freedom for Czechoslovakia. The peace that the British prime minister thought he had purchased at Munich lasted only six months, and the remainder of Czechoslovakia fell under Nazi domination, to remain so until World War II had almost ended.

From the moment that the Red Army crossed the Czechoslovak frontier in October 1944, indigenous communists began to move into key positions from which to assume control over the country. The Italian and French comrades were also making rapid gains, but Stalin may have been uncertain how the West would react to open seizure of power in Czechoslovakia. As a result, the communists used political means to fulfill one of their long-standing ambitions: gaining control over a country through a coalition government.[1] This process took time and provided a brief respite for Czechoslovak freedom, which lasted until February 1948; at that time the communists executed a bloodless coup and established a people's democracy.

---

1. The basic agreement for a National Front government and an "action program" was announced in April 1945 at Kosice. For details of the Marxist view, see Ivan Bystrzhina, *Narodnaya demokratiya v Chekhoslovakii* (Moscow, 1961), pp. 196–205; translated into Russian from the original Czech.

CONSTITUTIONAL FRAMEWORK

Superficially the new regime, which was based on a constitution adopted in May 1948, was similar to those in other Soviet satellites because it combined Marxism with several features of the old "bourgeois" system. There were many reasons for this decision. The constitution was designed to mask the true nature of communist rule by providing a facade of democratic respectability.[2] The existence of a form of coalition government was also an important factor, since many of the provisions in the constitution had been formulated before the communists seized power.

The Constitution of 1960. The draft of a new constitution received approval in July 1960 from the National Assembly, or legislature, only after it had been sanctioned by the Central Committee of the Czechoslovak Communist Party.[3] Any attempt to explain why the party chose this particular time to adopt a new basic law would be difficult, although the rationale behind the step is fairly clear. The first and probably the main reason was ideological in nature. By adopting a new "socialist" constitution the party hoped to strengthen its position. The document also seems to have been intended to show that Czechoslovakia had successfully laid the foundations of socialism and to justify the policies that the communists had followed since gaining control.[4] It thus represented an adaptation to the Soviet system.

Although the 1960 constitution has no more real meaning than its predecessor, it did have propaganda value among other communist regimes in Eastern Europe. The party could proclaim that Czechoslovakia was the second country in the world to have achieved socialism. The document summarizes various claimed achievements in legal form and outlines a program for the transition from socialism to communism. The preamble states that "people's democracy, as a way to socialism, has fully proved itself" and has brought Czechoslovakia "to the victory of socialism."[5] The country is allegedly "proceeding toward the construction of an advanced socialist society and gathering strength for the transition to communism."

The 1968 Constitutional Law. On 1 January 1969 a federal system with separate governments for the ten million Czechs and four million Slovaks went

---

2. H. Gordon Skilling, *Czechoslovakia's Interrupted Revolution* (Princeton, N.J., 1976), p. 924.

3. A useful chronology of events from 1943 to early 1960 appears in M. P. Epifanov (ed.), *15 let svobodnoi Chekhoslovakii* (Moscow, 1960), pp. 186–191.

4. Skilling, *op. cit.*

5. *Sbirka zakonu CSSR,* no. 100 (1960); English translation: [Czechoslovakia], *The Constitution of the Czechoslovak Socialist Republic* (Prague, 1964), 3rd ed. Further references apply to this edition.

into effect.[6] Federal authorities maintain exclusive jurisdiction over foreign policy, national defense, natural resources, and protection of the constitution. Joint control by the federation and the two republics is exercised over planning, currency, prices, industry, agriculture, transportation, communications and mass media, labor, wages and social policies, and the police.

These changes would logically necessitate a new constitution. In view of the de facto occupation of Czechoslovakia since August 1968 by Soviet troops, permission for this will have to be granted by Moscow. The ultimate success of the new arrangement will also depend on the USSR, which in general has been less than enthusiastic toward regionalism. Recent information seems to indicate that this negative attitude prevails here, probably because the Soviets desire as little change as possible. The years since the Warsaw Pact invasion have seen an increased tightening of control and greater centralization, culminating in the May 1975 election of Gustav Husak, party leader and National Front chairman, as President of the Republic.

The Government.   Czechoslovakia is typical among communist-dominated states in that it has a real government (the communist party) and a formal government. The latter is a facade that carries out administration for the party, which alone makes policy. The formal government performs three functions: executive, legislative, and judicial. This represents an artificial division for discussion purposes only, because no real separation of powers exists. Nor is there any genuine system of checks and balances that might prevent arbitrary abuse of governmental authority, which is subject only to party controls.

The executive branch of the formal government consists of the President of the Republic and the cabinet. The president is elected by and is accountable to the Federal Assembly as the representative of state power. Although East Germany followed other satellites in installing a collective head of state, Czechoslovakia did not do so. Its constitution provides for a president having real executive functions; this is also the situation in Romania.

The Czechoslovak communists apparently decided to retain the one-man presidency, rather than to adopt the standard presidium, for two reasons. First, the party was trying to capitalize on the prestige and stature that the office had acquired under Presidents Masaryk (1918–1935) and Benes (1935–1948). Second, the office represented a valuable political asset. Each of the five communist presidents (Klement Gottwald, 1948–1953); Antonin Zapotocky, 1953–1957; Antonin Novotny, 1957–1968; Ludvik Svoboda, 1968–1975; and Gustav Husak, 1975–date) was eager to occupy Hradcany Castle and cloak himself with the mantle of respectability. Attempts to abolish the presidency

---

6. The constitutional law on the Czechoslovak federation, published in *Sbirka zakonu CSSR*, no. 143 (1968), was ratified on 31 October 1968. It supersedes most of the 1960 constitution except for Articles 1 through 38, which deal with the social order as well as the rights and duties of citizens.

have also been complicated by the fact that until 1968 the office had been occupied by the leader of the communist party; this is again the case today.

The duties of the Czechoslovak president include most of those discharged by chiefs of states that have parliamentary systems of government. He must sign all laws enacted by the legislature, but may not veto legislation. He can declare a session of the Federal Assembly ended, although his authority to dissolve it is limited to cases in which the two chambers are in disagreement. The president represents the state in foreign relations, negotiates and ratifies treaties, and appoints and receives envoys. He has the right but not an obligation to submit a "state of the republic" message and recommend courses of action. He is supreme commander of the armed forces.

The president is "elected" by the Federal Assembly for a term of five years, and there is no provision for impeachment. In theory he is responsible to the Federal Assembly for the conduct of his office. There is no provision, however, for enforcing this accountability. In practice each communist president's power and prestige were derived not from the presidency but from his position in the ruling party. An exception to this rule was Ludvik Svoboda.[7]

The federal cabinet is composed of the premier, an unspecified number of deputy premiers, and the ministers. It is defined as "the supreme executive organ of state power" and is responsible only to the Federal Assembly. The president has the right to appoint and recall the cabinet. He must do the latter if the Federal Assembly votes the cabinet out of office (collectively or individually). The federal cabinet is organized into three distinct levels of authority: first, the premier; second, the government presidium, which is not mentioned in the constitution; and, third, the federal Council of Ministers.

The federal cabinet safeguards the fulfillment of state tasks, directs and controls the work of ministries and other central organs of administration, and issues ordinances that are based on and implement the laws. The federal ministers issue binding regulations also on the strength of government ordinances. Thus the constitution seemingly has assigned to the federal cabinet a decisive executive role. In practice, however, this organ is nothing more than a body of routine administrators. Issues of importance are decided in advance by the presidium of the communist party before they are even considered by the cabinet.[8]

If the federal cabinet really exercised the authority granted it by the constitution, the premier would hold more political power than the president. As

---

7. Svoboda commanded Czechoslovak troops in the USSR during the Second World War, and until March 1950 he served as Defense minister. Arrested and jailed during 1952, he worked the next three years as an accountant on a collective farm and then returned to public life. Heinrich Kuhn (comp.), *Biographisches Handbuch der Tschechoslowakei* (Munich, 1969). On 20 April 1970, Svoboda received the Order of Lenin at a ceremony in Moscow. He celebrated his eighty-first birthday, according to Prague radio, on 24 November 1976.

8. Edward Taborsky, *Communism in Czechoslovakia, 1948–1960* (Princeton, N. J., 1961), p. 200.

matters stand, the federal premiership is assigned to a second- or third-ranking communist, whose actual power is directly connected with his position in the party oligarchy.[9] It is apparent that the federal premier may never attain the same importance that other communist premiers enjoy, as long as the presidency is fillèd by a man of top rank. The government presidium, which is composed of the premier and (at present) seven deputy premiers, is empowered to control the activities of the various ministries and agencies and to direct and control the entire work of the cabinet.

The federal Council of Ministers patterns itself after the Soviet model. In 1976 it had twenty-seven members. The cabinet has never exercised the role of supreme policymaker that was assigned to it by the constitution. The federal ministers have so little real importance that the trend has been to appoint mediocrities to many of the cabinet posts. This has also provided a supply of scapegoats who can be sacrificed when difficulties develop.[10]

The Legislative Branch. According to the 1969 innovation, the Federal Assembly is the supreme organ of state power and the sole statewide legislative body. In theory, this gives it a lawmaking monopoly and, thus, considerable influence over all other central-government agencies within areas of exclusive jurisdiction. The powers of the Federal Assembly would seem to be almost unlimited, since only it has the power to amend the constitution, from which it draws its authority.

The Federal Assembly is headed by a chairman. If he is a Czech, the first deputy chairman is a Slovak, or vice versa. The chairman presides over the Assembly and its presidium, signs all laws and legislative measures, and reports to the Assembly on any action taken by the forty-member presidium (which includes deputies from each chamber, half Czechs and half Slovaks from the Chamber of Nations) while the full body is not in session. What looks like an "inner presidium" represents the second level of authority. The chairman of the Federal Assembly and the deputy chairmen are elected from the members of the regular presidium. This inner group handles all important matters and is the directing organ of the Assembly. It disposes of current business, drafts the Assembly's agenda, and controls the work of all committees. It is charged with the task of directing the work of the Federal Assembly and has the power to enact laws when the Assembly is not in session. It is explicitly accountable to, and can be recalled by, the Assembly.[11] This is the group that would act as the collective head of state in a typical communist government.

The Federal Assembly comprises 350 members, of whom 200 are in the

---

9. Since 1970, the federal premier has been Lubomir Strougal, who served during 1961–1965 as Interior minister. His biography appears in Kuhn, *op. cit.*

10. Taborsky, *op. cit.*, p. 201.

11. RFE report (by Henry Frank), "Czechoslovakia Becomes a Federation," 1 January 1969.

Chamber of the People. The Chamber of Nations consists of 150 deputies, of whom 75 are Czechs and 75 are Slovaks. The Assembly normally meets in the spring for one session and in the fall for another, although more than two sessions may convene annually. The near-perfect attendance record at these sessions before 1968 was surpassed only by the record of unanimity. Between 1948 and 1960 there was never so much as one dissenting vote and no amendment of any type was offered from the floor. Thanks to this harmony, the Assembly enacted legislation with amazing speed. The only incidents that slowed down the proceedings were the "spontaneous outbursts of enthusiasm" and "stormy applause"—carefully graduated according to the speaker's importance— that greeted even such dry reports as the one on the annual budget.[12] Since the Soviet occupation, there has been little or no evidence of parliamentary debates akin to those of the 1968 "Prague Spring." All parliamentary deputies who actively participated in that reform movement have been weeded out or silenced.

The Judiciary.   The prewar judicial system in Czechoslovakia was not unlike those of other Western parliamentary democracies. Judges were appointed to life tenure by the President of the Republic or the cabinet, and their independence was guaranteed. The law represented the foundation of the judicial system, and justice was its goal.

The present organization bears no resemblance to the former one. It is a copy of the Soviet model, specifically designed to serve the will of the party and allegedly intended to protect the socialist state, its social order, and the rights and true interests of its citizens and of the organizations of the working people.

Courts are also assigned the task of educating citizens so that they will be devoted and loyal to their country and to the cause of socialism and will observe the laws and the rules of socialist conduct. These principles include respecting socialist property, maintaining labor discipline, meeting production quotas, informing about hostile acts, and fulfilling obligations imposed by the state.

Constitutional courts were established for the country as a whole and for each republic separately in 1968. The judicial bodies now consist of three tiers: the supreme courts of the federation, the Czech Socialist Republic (which began its activities on 1 May, 1970), and the Slovak Socialist Republic; below the latter two are regional and district courts. Only one appeal is permitted from a lower instance. Professional and lay judges have equal status.

Qualifications for a judgeship include being at least twenty-four years of age and being known for devotion to "the purpose of socialism."[13] Professional judgeships have the added requirement of legal training. Judges are expected to

---

12. Taborsky, *op. cit.,* p. 256.

13. Source in note 6 above. See also the interview with Justice minister Jan Nemec in *Tvorba* (15 December 1976); translated in RFE, *Background Report,* 3 January 1977.

interpret the laws and regulations in accordance with the "socialist legal spirit." This means that civil and criminal cases are basically political in nature and must be decided accordingly. Judges are accountable for their actions and are subject to recall.[14]

The traditional roles of judge, public prosecutor, and attorney are not applicable to Czechoslovak courts. The defense lawyer must place the interests of society above those of his client, and lawyer-client communications are not often privileged. Many of the powers formerly held by judges have been transferred to the prosecutor, who is in effect a direct representative of the party.

The Office of the Procurator General exercises "supervision over the precise fulfillment and observance of laws and other legal regulations." Its primary duties include the enforcement and strengthening of socialist legality, the implementation of party policies, and the education of the people in socialism. The Procurator General of the Czechoslovak Socialist Republic (CSSR) is appointed by the president. He is responsible only to the Federal Assembly and probably has more power than any court in Czechoslovakia. The following provision eliminates any possible misunderstanding with regard to the role and responsibility of the procurator: "The organs of the Procurator's office form a coherent, centralized system, headed by the Procurator General of the CSSR, where lower procurators are subordinated to the higher ones. They discharge their functions independently of local organs."[15]

Local Government. The units of local goverment are organized on three levels: regional (eleven units), district (more than one hundred units), and local (about fourteen thousand units). The cities of Prague, Bratislava, and Brno form additional territorial units with regional status. The local administrative agencies, known as National Committees, are defined as "the organs of state power and administration in regions, districts, and localities," working "under the leadership of the Communist Party." Each committee has from 11 to 130 members, and even more for the districts, depending upon the level and the population of the area. Members normally serve terms of four years, after direct elections.[16] The organization on each tier is identical. The executive organ for any National Committee is a council composed of the chairman, his deputy or deputies, the secretary, and varying numbers of members.

These local councils, although nominally chosen by the committeemen and responsible to them, are indirectly subordinate to their respective republic-level

---

14. In this connection, see "Law on the Organization of Courts and Election of Judges," *Sbirka zakonu CSSR*, no. 19 (1970). On 27 May 1970, seven justices of the Supreme Court were dismissed.

15. "Law on the Procurator's Office," *ibid.*, no. 20 (1970). During that same year, a purge of public prosecutors took place.

16. "Constitutional Law on Extension of the Electoral Term for National Committees, National Councils, Federal Assembly, Supreme Court, Regional, District, and Military Courts," *ibid.*, no. 117 (1969), extended the deadline for elections (last held in 1964) to 31 December 1971.

governments. The councils perform some legislative functions by issuing decrees and ordinances. They "direct and control the activity of the National Committees." The local councils are assisted by commissions, elected or appointed by the National Committee, that are responsible for the operation of various administrative activities at the local level. Of the 147,409 National Committee members in the Czech Socialist Republic alone, some 12,721 (8.6 percent) either resigned or were recalled during the 1969–1970 purge.[17]

The National Committees have gradually been given more administrative authority, but they are not permitted to make policy. Their task is to organize and direct all economic, social, and cultural activity in the specific area. Regional and district administrations are organized into functional departments for planning, finance, agriculture, transportation, and so on. There is no mandatory departmentalization for the local levels; they are permitted to organize, with the approval of the next higher level, as the particular needs of the area dictate. Most of the effort expended by local government is devoted to the fulfillment of the state economic plan from indigenous resources and to the strengthening of the political system. As is generally true in East European countries, increasing agricultural production and protecting socialist property are two of the priorities.

Local administrations, despite the extensive theoretical power they exercise in areas ranging from national defense to recreation programs, do little more than carry out the directives of higher authority and have no self-government in the true sense. The principle of democratic centralism, with each level subject to the absolute authority of the next higher level, is strictly enforced. Members of the party dominate all levels of government and ensure that the party remains in fact "the leading force in the state and society."

The Slovak National Council, which was once a powerful organ of local government with its own executive Board of Commissioners, enjoyed unique autonomy under the 1948 constitution. (For a listing of national minorities see table 16.) The 1960 constitution abolished the Board of Commissioners and described the Council as "the national organ of state power and administration in Slovakia" (Article 73). Its legislative and executive actions may be repealed by the National Assembly. This loss of autonomy generated many problems and caused much resentment among Slovak communists and noncommunists alike. This dissatisfaction certainly contributed to the establishment of the federation on 1 January 1969 and of a separate Slovak Socialist Republic with its own government. However, centralized planning for the whole country has been maintained by the communist party. The Soviet Union has been cool toward any kind of regionalism, due to its possible effects on the Ukraine.

The Electoral System.   Voting in Czechoslovakia is direct and universal. Elections are normally held every four years to send representatives to all levels

---

17. Deputy Interior minister Antonin Balak in *Rude pravo,* 29 April 1970.

TABLE 16

NATIONALITY COMPOSITION OF CZECHOSLOVAKIA, 1975

Nationality	Population	Percent of Total
Czechs	9,509,000	64.3
Slovaks	4,443,000	30.0
Hungarians	585,000	4.0
Germans	77,000	0.5
Poles	71,000	0.5
Ukrainians and Russians	62,000	0.5
Others and unidentified	48,000	0.2
Total	14,795,000	100.0

SOURCE: V. Srb, "Thirty Years of Population Development in Socialist Czechoslovakia," *Demografie*, no. 2 (1975), pp. 97–105.

of the government. The "democratic" character of these elections is ensured by procedures that are typical throughout the communist bloc. At the latest election, in 1976, there was only one candidate per seat, and no write-in names were permitted. Even the ballot was merely a formality. The communist-dominated National Front, which includes three subordinate political parties and representatives of the mass organizations, has complete control over the conduct of elections and the tallying of the ballots. It nominates the members of the electoral commissions on all levels from among the party faithful. As a final measure of control, the National Front is given the right to recall any "unworthy members" who might be elected.

In past elections the National Front has held the exclusive right to nominate candidates for the electoral list. This reportedly is to be changed. Henceforth the right to nominate candidates will allegedly extend to political parties, meetings of workers, social organizations, and like groups. It is doubtful that the voters will be given a greater choice as to who "represents" them, since only one candidate acceptable to the National Front—and thus, in reality, to the communist party—can appear on the ballot for each office.[18]

The party in Czechoslovakia shares the passion for unanimity that prevails throughout the communist world. Although there is no legal obligation to vote, the force of the party and the governmental apparatus is brought to bear on the individual so that the "will of the people" shall be properly expressed in support of the regime. According to official statistics, which the communists have made public, almost perfect success has been achieved in getting out the vote. In the most recent general elections (October 1976) 99.7 percent of those who were eligible voted, and 99.97 percent of these participants cast their ballots for National Front candidates.

18. "Law on Elections to the National Assembly,' in *Sbirka zakonu CSSR*, no. 113 (1967).

Government Controls. Tight controls are the essence of most totalitarian states that seek to maintain the masses in submission, and Czechoslovakia represents no exception to this rule. The communist party, of course, is in control. It has followed the Soviet model in establishing a firm grip on the administrative apparatus.

Perhaps the decisive power in Czechoslovakia is still external. The Soviet Union can influence the communist leaders in Prague via official channels. This method might be likened to the surface current of a stream. The real power is in the invisible undercurrent that is represented by Moscow's network of native and Soviet agents. This network has proven to be an efficient device for keeping the native Czechoslovak rulers and party in line, although force had to be applied in August 1968. After that intervention, the presence in Czechoslovakia of Soviet advisors was openly admitted.

The police provide the most effective internal control device, and it is the secret, not the uniformed, police that generate fear in those who might be tempted to deviate. Secret agents have been infiltrated into every organization of the Czechoslovak Socialist Republic. The efforts of police functionaries are augmented by the extensive use of informers. The role of the Procurator General's office has already been discussed and requires little further amplification, except to note that it is in a position to accuse and is supported by its power of judicial prosecution. The Central Commission of People's Control[19] also represents a control device. This agency may investigate, recommend corrective action, and take disciplinary measures that include initiation of criminal prosecution against party members.

The state economic plan at one time represented yet another effective method of control. It worked as a yardstick by which all persons were measured. Fulfillment of a goal or a quota used to be of the utmost importance to the individual since, in the communist world, results were taken as an indication of his personal effort and intent. Failure, regardless of the cause, could and did have dire consequences for the person responsible for it. This led to falsified reports, among other things. During the Dubcek era a new system for economic management was gradually introduced that was based in part on the law of value, the relationship between supply and demand, and certain principles of a traditional market economy.[20] Since the August 1968 occupation by USSR troops, this development has been reversed.

Problems of Administration. Czechoslovakia has experienced the same administrative difficulties that plague most of the communist bloc: bureau-

---

19. "Law on the Commission of People's Control," *ibid.*, no. 70 (1967); promulgated 29 June 1967. Modifications appeared in *ibid.*, no. 85 (1968).

20. RFE report (by Harry Trend), "Return to Economic 'Normalcy' in Czechoslovakia," 20 June 1970.

cratism, disloyalty, incompetence, and dishonesty. The hard core of the communist party was small in 1945, but many opportunists were inducted during the rapid expansion which followed. The initial shortage of trustworthy communists was compounded by the rapid growth of governmental machinery, which was brought about by extensive nationalization.

Although the communists obtained the necessary manpower, the government continued to be filled with formerly middle-class people. After the purging of these "bourgeois" individuals, incompetent and frequently untrustworthy communists were put in to fill the vacancies. Further cycles of purge and reorganization have followed, but inefficiency and apathy still prevail. The average educational level of persons in high government positions is quite low. For example, among all of the leading officials in the state administration in 1965, some 61 percent had acquired only an elementary-school education, about 10 percent had attended lower special school, approximately 9 percent had completed their secondary education, and only about 9 percent were university graduates.[21]

A cumbersome administrative machinery has resulted in overlapping and poorly defined areas of responsibility. This situation is advantageous for any bureaucrat who prefers to remain anonymous and escape responsibility. An organization that accepts no excuse for failure makes experimentation dangerous. It is easy to understand, thus, why initiative has been stifled. A massive bureaucracy is also an ideal breeding place for corruption, and the spoils system has flourished. Stealing from the state seems to be an accepted practice in most communist-ruled countries.

In an effort to alleviate some of the discontent resulting from such difficulties and to respond to the popular demand for the correction of wrongdoings in the Stalinist era, President Novotny was forced to dismiss premier Viliam Siroky[22] in August 1963 and to agree to the removal of two other old Stalinists from high positions. There can be little doubt that one of the factors contributing to these changes was pressure by younger liberals who wanted to modernize the system and reverse the trend toward deterioration. However, the reorganization of the government did not seem to satisfy the liberal elements; instead it probably raised their hopes for more freedom and a higher standard of living. They maintained their pressure on the regime, and the Stalinist leadership repeatedly had to give way.

Novotny resigned on 5 January 1968 and was replaced as head of the party by Alexander Dubcek, the first time that a Slovak had become the political leader of the country. The so-called Prague spring did not last long, because the Soviets

---

21. *Kulturni tvorba*, 9 September 1965. The remaining 11 percent presumably had not even completed elementary school.

22. His biography in Vladimir Krechler (ed.), *Prirucni slovnik k dejinam KSC* (Prague, 1964), II, p. 891, explains the dismissal on the basis of insufficiencies, unspecified errors, and poor health.

apparently feared "contamination" in other parts of Eastern Europe and perhaps in their own country. Dubcek seemed to weather the invasion by Warsaw Pact troops in August 1968, but his days as party leader were obviously numbered. On 17 April 1969 he was succeeded by another Slovak, Gustav Husak, who is known as an opponent of Novotny and a victim of Stalinist justice but a much tougher man and one who does the bidding of Moscow. Dubcek reportedly had refused to engage in self-criticism. Recalled from political exile as ambassador to Turkey, he was subsequently expelled from the party and from all his posts.[23] (See table 18 for the 1976 leadership.)

THE COMMUNIST PARTY: ORIGIN AND ACTIVITIES

Although Czechoslovakia was formerly known for its political democracy, it has been since 1948 a communist one-party state. This reversal of political social, and economic orientation resulted from international developments and domestic conditions that culminated in the February 1948 coup. Because it took place while Soviet armed forces were not present in the country, a fundamental question arises. What were the contributing factors that enabled the Communist Party of Czechoslovakia (*Komunisticka Strana Ceskoslovenska*—KSC) to seize and maintain control?

The First World War and the resultant independence of Czechoslovakia had an important effect on the realignment of political parties in that territory. The outward appearance of communist party growth and legality provided a facade behind which doctrinal struggles took place. In the aftermath of severe criticism in 1928 of KSC leadership by Moscow at the sixth congress of the Comintern, Klement Gottwald became the general secretary of the Czechoslovak party.[24] Immediately upon taking office he instituted a large-scale purge.

From 1930 until 1938 Gottwald concentrated on the bolshevization of the party and the recruitment of young unskilled workers. This program, however, was not successful in producing a mass party. Official figures indicate that the KSC had 350,000 organized followers when it was founded, but continued to lose strength and had fewer than 50,000 card-carrying members in 1938. After the Munich crisis in September of that year, the party was banned from all political activity. By the time the Germans completed their occupation of Czechoslovakia, in March 1939, the majority of the KSC leadership had fled the country. By what "appeared to be a prearranged plan," they took refuge

---

23. Prague radio, 26 June 1970. See the explanations in *Rude pravo*, 16 July 1970 and 11 December 1974.

24. Josef Korbel, *The Communist Subversion of Czechoslovakia, 1938–1948* (Princeton, N.J., 1959), p. 28. Gottwald is eulogized in an article by Vasil Bilak, *Pravda*, 23 November 1976; Moscow.

abroad: in Moscow, London, or Paris.[25] Some communists were apprehended while trying to escape and were later sent to Nazi concentration camps.

Hitler's invasion of the USSR brought the communists into superficial cooperation with the Benes government-in-exile. A portent of the future was the signing of the Soviet-Czechoslovak agreement in December 1943 at Moscow. Benes regarded the treaty as "one of the links in the postwar system of security."[26] Article 5 precluded Czechoslovak participation in any alliances that were not acceptable to the USSR. For the KSC, this was the first step towards its ultimate goal: communist control of the country.

Penetration Tactics. Benes decided to negotiate with the representatives of various political parties about the establishment of a government in the liberated areas of the country. In March 1945 he arrived in Moscow from England. The talks began in an atmosphere of intimidation, with Gottwald pressing home "the tremendous psychological and political advantages accruing to them [the communists] from the Red Army's control over Czechoslovakia and the overt Soviet support of their cause."[27] Benes accepted a plan for a "government of the National Front of Czechs and Slovaks" in which communists were assigned eight of twenty-five cabinet seats. The communists demanded and obtained the important government ministries of Interior, Agriculture, and Information, among others.[28]

At the national, regional, and local levels, communist-dominated National Committees were acting as organs of government. Since these committees had not been regularly elected but had been established under Red Army occupation and hence under communist control, they were of a revolutionary nature. From these bases the KSC began an intense drive, during which the party made rapid strides toward the attainment of political and economic power. The communist program was facilitated rather than hampered by the withdrawal of the Red Army at the end of 1945 since that action could be interpreted by many Czechs and Slovaks as evidence of Soviet nonintervention.

A historian of the KSC has described how the political, social, and economic structure underwent a revolutionary assault. Actions included the confiscation of

---

25. For names see R. F. Staar, "Czechoslovakia," in Witold S. Sworakowski (ed.), *World Communism: A Handbook, 1918–1965* (Stanford, Ca., 1971), pp. 108–115.

26. Edward Benes, *Memoirs of Dr. Edward Benes* (London, 1954), p. 258.

27. Taborsky, *op. cit.* (in note 8 above), p. 13.

28. The separate communist parties of Czechoslovakia and Slovakia and four other political groups received three portfolios each. In addition, seven cabinet members qualified as "experts," including two communists and the left-leaning Defense minister General Ludvik Svoboda. The communists also had two deputy premiers and the fellow-traveling premier, Zdenek Fierlinger, who fulfilled Gottwald's directives. In this connection see Jozef Lettrich, "Czechoslovakia," in U.S. Senate, Committee on the Judiciary, *A Study of the Anatomy of Communist Takeovers* (Washington, D.C., 1966), pp. 17–25.

property; the prohibition of certain "bourgeois" political parties; and the transformation of parliament, "actuating the further development and consolidation of the revolution into a direct instrument for the socialist building of the country."[29] Meanwhile, since to achieve parliamentary control it was necessary for the KSC to increase its voting base, a communist recruitment campaign strove for mass enrollment.

Opportunists saw real advantages in joining the party. Significant inducements and the lack of any ideological tests resulted in great success for the recruiting effort. At the end of the war the party had 27,000 members. A year later, just before the general election, there were 1,159,164 registered communists.[30] (See table 17 for the party's subsequent growth.) The objective of the KSC was to gain an absolute majority in the May 1946 voting for a Constituent Assembly to establish the postwar government. The results were a disappointment to the communists because they polled only 38 percent during the balloting. Since the KSC had received more votes than any other party, however, communist leader Gottwald became premier in a cabinet of twenty-six members, only nine of whom officially belonged to his party. The communists, with 38 percent of the votes, and the Social Democrats, with 13 percent, together obtained 151 (114 plus 37) of the 300 seats in the Constituent Assembly. Clearly, Zdenek Fierlinger, a fellow traveler and the leader of the Social Democratic party, looked like the key to KSC strategy.

Cooperation was encouraged by Fierlinger, but this attempt failed in November 1947 when he was ousted and anticommunists took control of the Social Democratic party. Other political groups employed parliamentary maneuvers to impede the KSC programs. A plot to murder three noncommunists, the deputy premier, the Foreign minister, and the Justice minister (who had been sent packages with explosives), was discovered by the organs of security and the judiciary. An investigation suggested that the conspiracy had originated with a local KSC organization in Moravia. In addition, the Soviet demand that Czechoslovakia withdraw from announced participation in the Marshall Plan conference at Paris had served to undermine the KSC's prestige. The decline in communist strength also showed on a poll conducted by the Institute of Public Research, a branch of the KSC-controlled Information Ministry.[31]

Seizure of Control.   The coup of February 1948 followed the resignation of twelve noncommunist cabinet officers in protest over the refusal by the Interior

---

29. Jan Kozak, "How Parliament Can Play a Revolutionary Part in the Transition to Socialism," reprinted in U.S. House of Representatives, Committee on Un-American Activities, *The New Role of National Legislative Bodies in the Communist Conspiracy* (Washington, D.C., 1961), p. 17. See also his article on the years 1945–1948 in *Voprosy istorii KPSS* (July–August 1962), pp. 72–91; Moscow.

30. Paul E. Zinner, *Communist Strategy and Tactics in Czechoslovakia* (New York, 1963), p. 124. The author cites official party sources.

31. Taborsky, *op. cit.*, p. 19.

TABLE 17

CZECHOSLOVAK COMMUNIST PARTY MEMBERSHIP, 1949–1976

Date	Members	Candidates	Total
May 1949	1,788,383	522,683	2,311,066
February 1951	1,518,144	159,299	1,677,443
June 1954	1,385,610	103,624	1,489,234
June 1958	n.a.	n.a.	1,422,100
July 1960	1,379,441	179,641	1,559,082
October 1962	1,588,589	92,230	1,680,819
July 1963	1,624,197	55,286	1,679,483
January 1965	*ca.* 1,627,000	*ca.* 57,000	1,684,000
January 1968	–	–	1,699,677
December 1970	–	–	1,173,183
January 1974	*ca.* 1,200,000	*ca.* 124,000	*ca.* 1,324,000
April 1976	1,214,975	167,885	1,382,860

SOURCES: *Rude pravo*, issues of 2 July 1949; 23 February 1951; 12 June 1954; 22 June 1958; 8 July 1960; 5 December 1962; 26 January 1975. *Zivot strany* (October 1963 and May 1965). Prague radio, 14 December 1970 and 21 April 1976.

NOTES: The thirteenth KSC congress abolished candidate status and provided that by September 1966 all should be full members. In February 1973 candidate membership was reinstated.

The communist party, which was undergoing a thorough purge in 1970, reportedly had a healthy core, or *aktiv*, of 200,000 members. Prague radio, 1 June 1970. In the period 1968–1975 about 460,000 members (nearly one-third of the party) were purged. *Rude pravo*, 13 September 1975.

minister, a KSC member, to replace several ranking police captains who were guilty of violating the constitutional rights of citizens. Under normal conditions this action would have forced new elections. But the communists utilized key organizations, such as workers' councils, the Interior (police) and Information ministries, a workers' militia armed by the communists, and the "action committees," for the purpose of executing a coup d'etat. These last groups, which had been operating clandestinely, revealed themselves and took over the direction of all government and industrial activities.[32]

Communist pressure on Benes was severe. Demonstrations, the loss of government control to action committees, and the threat of civil war caused Benes, a sick man, to accede to the demands presented by Gottwald. A former Czechoslovak diplomat has described the situation as follows: "Once Benes had come to the conclusion that the only alternative to surrender was a bloody civil war, with strong likelihood of direct or indirect Soviet intervention, he was incapable of acting otherwise."[33]

In assuming control of the country, Gottwald enjoyed many advantages that had not accrued to Lenin after his seizure of power in Russia. Some of these

32. Pavel Tigrid, "The Prague Coup of 1948," in Thomas T. Hammond (ed.), *The Anatomy of Communist Takeovers* (New Haven, Conn., 1975), pp. 399–432.

33. Edward Taborsky, "The Triumph and Disaster of Edward Benes," *Foreign Affairs* (July 1958), p. 684.

centered on the experience that the communists had gained during their active participation in the government over a three-year period prior to the coup. Major industries had been nationalized, and no large segment of the population offered opposition to the regime.[34]

Transmission Belts. All political organizations, including the two communist parties (a separate one exists for Slovakia), comprise the National Front. It actually represents a coalition of KSC-dominated political groups and mass organizations. The retention of subordinate organizations has been useful in preserving the fiction that a multiparty system and political freedom exist in Czechoslovakia. These groups also act as transmission belts to population segments that reject doctrinaire communism. They are large enough for their support to be required in achieving communist objectives.

Even since the adoption of the 1960 constitution, which proclaimed the KSC as the leading force in society, the National Front facade has been retained. Communist control over the National Front at the highest level is exercised through the KSC presidium. The chairman or one of the deputy chairmen of the National Front has always been a member of that body. As of 31 March 1970, the presidium discontinued its activities to rehabilitate the victims of the Gottwald and Novotny regimes.[35]

Mass organizations are also necessary under the communist concept of population control. The communists will exploit the help of nonparty elements so long as they work for KSC purposes and are subordinate to its leadership. Mass organizations transmit the party line in their particular spheres of activity. These groups parallel in structure the organization of the ruling party, and communist control is maintained by the appointment of important KSC members to key positions at all levels.

From a political and an economic point of view the Revolutionary Trade-Union Movement (ROH), which has a membership of 5.5 million, is the most important of these organizations. The ROH is a symbol of the worker-KSC alliance. It is, however, more concerned with party goals than with traditional West European trade-union objectives. There are thirteen unions in the ROH. The organization is headed by Karel Hoffman,[36] a member of the KSC presidium.

The Czechoslovak Socialist Youth League (SSMC), like the Komsomol in the USSR, serves as an apprentice organization for the party, with membership

---

34. During this initial period the communists applied the Leninist principle of "kto kogo?" (meaning "who [will eliminate] whom?"), according to Bystrzhina, *op. cit.* (in note 1 above), pp. 263–264.

35. Prague radio, 7 April 1970. According to the same source, on 8 July 1970 the rehabilitation law was amended to prevent "acquittal of persons who had been justly sentenced under legislation valid at that [i.e., Stalinist] time."

36. *Ibid.*, 11 March 1971, announced his appointment.

beginning at the age of fifteen years. Its propaganda seeks to develop an early dedication to communism. Advancement in industry and higher education are practically impossible for those who fail to join. Yet, according to newspaper comments, apathy and indifference are the hallmarks of the SSMC. This organization was launched in 1970 to unify the eighteen youth organizations that, during 1968 and 1969, had proliferated over the country.

The Union for Cooperation with the Army (SVAZARM) claimed 690,000 members, organized into almost 10,000 units, in 1976.[37] It performs the same function as the Soviet DOSAAF in support of paramilitary-technical training and also serves as an umbrella organization for voluntary organizations, including all kinds of hobbies and sports. Another of these mass organizations is the USSR Friendship Society, which sponsors cultural and social ties with the Soviet Union. Much of its propaganda effort emphasizes Soviet scientific and cultural achievements, together with USSR support for Czechoslovakia; the objective, of course, is the strengthening of ties between the two countries. Communist control over mass organizations from the national down to the local level is facilitated by the parallel structure of all organizations, in which both vertical and horizontal controls are utilized.

The Communist Party. The KSC or Communist Party of Czechoslovakia, comprising approximately 9 percent of the total population, in 1976 had 1,382,860 members (among whom 167,885 are candidates for membership).[38] By comparison, the Communist Party of the Soviet Union (CPSU) has in its ranks only about 6 percent of the total population of the USSR. The organizational structure of the KSC is established by the party statute. Its pyramidal system, in which final authority is held by a small group at the top, closely parallels that of the CPSU. In reality, the operating procedures and the locus of power are entirely different from the formal structure.

The Presidium (formerly called the Politburo) of the Central Committee determines policies for the KSC. A self-perpetuating body that is formally elected by the Central Committee and is insulated from rank-and-file party members by several layers, the Presidium holds supreme authority. It currently numbers eleven full members and two candidates. (See table 18.) The rank and file underwent a purge by means of party-card exchange during 1970 that took place at the basic organization level.

The Secretariat is allegedly the administrative arm of the Presidium, but in fact it is the party organ of real authority. Its activity is officially restricted to the implementation of policy and it is nominally subject to review by the Presidium. The Secretariat transmits party orders from top to bottom and supervises the

---

37. *Rude pravo*, 4 November 1976.

38. Gustav Husak, "Confidently and Creatively along the Leninist Road," *World Marxist Review* (June 1976), p. 12.

TABLE 18

CZECHOSLOVAK COMMUNIST PARTY LEADERSHIP, 1976

Name	Born	Position and responsibility
Presidium full members (11)		
*Bilak, Vasil	1917	Secretary (interparty relations and ideology)
Colotka, Peter	1925	Premier of Slovak Socialist Republic
Hoffmann, Karel	1924	Chairman, Trade Union Central Committee
Hula, Vaclav	1925	Deputy premier (state plan)
*Husak, Gustav	1913	KSC Secretary-General; President; National Front chairman
Indra, Alois	1921	Federal Assembly chairman
Kapek, Antonin	1922	Leading secretary, Prague city
*Kempny, Josef	1920	Secretary (economy)
Korcak, Josef	1921	Premier of Czech Socialist Republic
Lenart, Jozef	1923	First secretary, Slovak Communist Party
Strougal, Lubomir	1924	Premier of Czechoslovakia
Presidium candidate members (2)		
*Baryl, Jan	1925	Secretary
Hruskovic, Miloslav	1925	Secretary, Slovak Communist Party
Secretariat (including four secretaries as indicated above by *):		
Fojtik, Jan	1928	Propaganda and mass media
Havlin, Josef	1924	Education, science, culture
Secretariat members		
Kabrhelova, Marie	1925	Czechoslovak Women's Union chairman
Lovetinsky, Cestmir	1924	Politico-Organization Department head
Polednik, Jindrich	1937	Czechoslovak Socialist Youth Union chairman
Svestka, Oldrich	1922	*Rude pravo* editor-in-chief

SOURCES: RFE, *Situation Report,* 21 April 1976; RFE, *Communist Party-Government Line-Up* (Munich, 7 December 1976), pp. 6–9; birth dates from Heinrich Kuhn, *Biographisches Handbuch der Tschechoslowakei* (Munich, 1969), no pagination; and various issues of *Dokumentacni prehled CTK.*

selection and activities of secretaries at lower party levels. Together with the secretaries of the region, district, and city committees and other full-time functionaries, its staff comprises the *apparatchiki* (backbone) of the party. Three of the six secretaries at the national level (Husak, Kempny, and Bilak) are also Presidium members and, thus, the most powerful persons in the country.

The current Central Committee, which was elected at the fifteenth party congress in April 1976, consists of 121 full members and 52 candidates.[39] Theoretically, it is the official ruling organ of the KSC when the party congress is not in session. In reality, its powers are in the hands of the Presidium and the Secretariat. The Central Control and Audit Commission, comprising thirty members, is responsible for making disciplinary investigations, screening KSC members, and hearing appeals against decisions of lower party organs. Another of its function is to audit the records of all KSC organizations in economic and

---

39. RFE, *Situation Report,* 21 April 1976.

financial matters. About one-half million members were purged from the party after the Soviet invasion (see table 17), and Husak announced to the most recent congress that about 390,000 technically are eligible for readmission.

The Communist Party of Slovakia (KSS) has a special position within the formal structure of the KSC. The 1968 plan to federalize the KSC and establish a separate party organization for the Czech provinces, a counterpart to the KSS, was abandoned three years later. In 1976 there were about 319,000 Slovak communists who made up 22.5 percent of the party membership in Czechoslovakia; in contrast, the population of Slovakia was about 30 percent of the total for the country.[40] The retention of the KSS as an "independent" organization is a concession to Slovak nationalist sentiment and tradition. The KSS presumably cherishes the fiction of its equality with the KSC, but it is definitely subordinate. Firm KSC control is maintained by an interlocking directorate in which three full members of the seven-member KSS Presidium are also members or candidates in the Presidium of the KSC. Statements by Slovak communist leaders emphasize their subordination. For instance, Jozef Lenart, the KSS first secretary, was premier of the Czechoslovak government from 1963 through 1968, during the Novotny and Dubcek eras.[41]

Connecting the top party organs with the broad base of primary units are the territorially graduated levels that correspond to the state administrative structure. Below the national level are the regional organizations, each of which in turn is broken down into districts. At the city, district, and regional levels the roles of committee, bureau, and secretary have ascending importance. Orders from above, conveyed through the secretaries at the regional and district committees, who are appointed by the next higher level, outweigh the influence of the grass roots.

The primary party units form the base of the organizational pyramid. Some 43,506 of these units exist (about 10,000 in Slovakia), mostly on an individual plant and office basis.[42] A minimum of three members is prescribed for a basic unit, and its establishment must be approved by the appropriate district or city committee. The essential functions of such units are to

> Improve training in the fundamentals of communism;
> Safeguard the security of the party dictatorship;
> Disseminate the party line on all domestic and foreign policy;
> Recruit and train new party members;

---

40. The KSS has been a separate organization theoretically since the 1939 Nazi occupation of Czechoslovakia, according to Krechler, *op. cit.* (in note 22 above), I, 329–330. See RFE, *Background Report,* 30 March 1976, for statistics.

41. His biography and those of other new KSC Presidium and Secretariat members were broadcast over Prague radio, 29 January 1970.

42. The thorough purge in 1970 reportedly reduced the KSC by 20 percent. *Rude pravo,* 23 September 1970.

Ensure that party economic goals are fullfilled and workers' morale is strengthened.[43]

Because of its structure the party is able to control the government's activities on all levels and to direct all its economic, social, and cultural undertakings. This very power, however, poses significant problems. It is apparent that the communists consider party discipline to be the most important factor in this process. The concept of democratic centralism is invoked to compel discipline.

The party has difficulty in recruiting young blood. This condition is reflected in the Czechoslovak Socialist Youth League, in which only 15 percent of those eligible are currently enrolled, although the Young Pioneers claim 1.2 million members.[44] The party is getting mostly young opportunists who are ready to buy personal advantage via the youth movement. It would appear that after more than three decades in power, the party holds little attraction for the young generation. Despite its efforts to recruit young persons, the average age of KSC members is high, with young party members and candidates for membership (twenty-five years old and younger) comprising only one-fourth of the total.[45] Apparently the majority of the present membership, on a national scale, joined the party between 1945 and 1949 (especially during 1948–1949), when it was expedient to do so.

Another effort of the party is to achieve a member ratio of approximately 60 percent industrial workers, 20 percent collective farmers, and the remainder in other categories. Its social composition for 1966 and 1973 is shown in table 19. The party is admittedly weakest among industrial workers, farmers, and young persons. Problems with recruitment in general have been encountered in Slovakia, for fundamental reasons. The Slovaks are a strongly religious (primarily Catholic) people who are more conservative than the Czechs. The depredations of the Red Army during the immediate postwar period are well remembered. In addition, despite the facade of unity, the Slovaks resent the traditional centralism emanating from Prague.[46] It appears ironic that the Czechs now speak of a "Slovak mafia," that is, too many Slovaks in the federal government.

---

43. Party rules were published by Heinrich Kuhn, *Der Kommunismus in der Tschechoslowakei* (Cologne, 1965), pp. 275–299.

44. Article in *Nova mysl,* as given by RFE, *Situation Report,* 13 November 1974; "The Pioneer Organization," *ibid.,* 28 April 1976.

45. Husak, *op. cit.* (in note 38 above), p. 12.

46. Communists in predominantly rural Slovakia also probably resent allegations in the official KSC history that the Slovak uprising against the Germans in August 1944 had been started "without sufficient political preparation," and that the Communist Party of Slovakia had been penetrated by right-wingers who "weakened the revolutionary nature of the movement." Pavel Reiman (ed.), *Dejiny Komunisticke Strany Ceskoslovenska* (Prague, 1961), p. 450. Reiman served as director of the KSC History Institute at that time.

TABLE 19

CZECHOSLOVAK COMMUNIST PARTY SOCIAL COMPOSITION,
1966 AND 1973

	January 1966		January 1973	
Occupational status	*Number of members*	*Percentage of total membership*	*Number of members*	*Percentage of total membership*
Industrial workers	511,917	30.2	544,194	44.1
Agricultural laborers	46,062	2.7		
Collective farmers	91,109	5.4	57,998	4.7
Government officials	113,350	6.7		
Public workers	27,246	1.6		
Scientific workers	3,796	0.2		
Engineering and technical workers	293,277	17.3	389,944	31.6
Workers in arts and culture	9,218	0.5		
Teachers and professors	64,787	3.8		
Students	6,372	0.4		
Housewives	68,659	4.0		
Pensioners	293,577	17.4	241,864	19.6
Other	168,641	9.8		
Total	1,698,011	100.0	1,234,000	100.0

SOURCES: *Zivot strany* (September 1966), as reported in *Czechoslovak Press Survey*, 13 October 1966; *Otazky miru a socializmu* (July 1973), pp. 91–92.

NOTE: Prague radio, 6 June 1970, revealed that industrial workers comprised 26.1 percent and collective farmers 5.2 percent of the party membership. Percentages in 1969 were 36 and 6.4 respectively, with 57.6 percent described as office workers, intelligentsia, and others by *World Marxist Review* (August 1970), Supplement, p. 6. Gustav Husak has stated that the percentage of workers had stopped decreasing for the first time in 23 years. *Ibid.* (June 1976), p. 12.

DOMESTIC AND FOREIGN AFFAIRS

The party's formerly solid grip on the populace has loosened, but there appears to be no alternative to the communist regime at present. The population has become less critical and outspoken, perhaps because of the "social engineering" that has altered the class composition (see table 20) and the traumatic experience of August 1968. Czech and Slovak domestic resistance movements against the Nazi occupation, the valor of Czechoslovak armed forces abroad in the Second World War, and the uprisings toward the end of that conflict all indicate that the people will also act against tyranny in the future. Withdrawal and apathy, which have been evident since the Warsaw Pact invasion, could be interpreted as pragmatism in the face of a situation that can not be changed for the time being. However 300 writers, journalists, scientists, politicians, and others active in the short-lived movement to liberalize communist rule had the courage to sign "Charter 77" in January 1977, petitioning the Prague regime to uphold constitutional rights and United Nations' covenants as well as the Helsinki declaration.[47] Many of those who signed were arrested.

TABLE 20

CLASS COMPOSITION OF CZECHOSLOVAKIA: 1945, 1961, 1975

	1945		1961		1975	
Class	Number	Percent	Number	Percent	Number	Percent
Factory workers	7,650,000	53.5	7,738,000	56.3	9,010,000	60.9
Office employees	1,810,000	12.7	3,834,000	27.9	4,139,000	28.0
Collectivized farmers	–	–	1,466,000	10.7	1,240,000	8.3
Cooperative workers	–	–	164,000	1.2	250,000	1.7
Private farmers	3,000,000	21.0	484,000	3.5	134,000	0.9
Craftsmen	960,000	6.7	51,000	0.3	12,000	0.1
Capitalists	880,000	6.1	–	–	–	–
Professionals	–	–	9,000	0.1	10,000	0.1
Total	14,300,000	100.0	13,746,000	100.0	14,795,000	100.0

SOURCE: V. Srb, "Thirty Years of Population Developments in Socialist Czechoslovakia," *Demografie*, no. 2 (1975), pp. 97–105.

Economic Planning.   The Czechoslovak communist regime has encountered difficulties and has found no effective means to facilitate the execution of its plans. Unforeseen circumstances forced the government to abandon its collapsing third five-year plan in 1962. An emergency one-year plan was subsequently introduced for 1963. Although its goals were eventually reported to have been attained, they were admittedly met only after various adjustments. Makeshift annual plans followed until 1966.

The fourth five-year plan in sequence was to guide the economy through 1970, and a different and more realistic approach could be seen in its details. Instead of setting rigid quotas or goals for the entire period, it planned for only twelve months at a time. Subsequent years had variable targets, with considerable latitude to allow for setbacks. Thus, the chances for a "successful plan" were increased and the attendant propaganda value was enhanced.

The Czechoslovak economy has shown significant growth beyond the goals of the fifth consecutive five-year plan (1971–1975), although shortcomings in several sectors have become evident. Power, fuel, labor productivity and

---

47. For documents on the "normalization" in Czechoslovakia, see Skilling, *op. cit.* (in note 2 above). The text of "Charter 77" appeared in the *New York Times,* 27 January 1977, reprinted from *The New Leader* (31 January 1977).

agricultural problems still represent weaknesses.[48] With the success of the fifth five-year plan, ambitious goals have been set for the sixth five-year plan. For example, industrial production is supposed to increase by 32−34 percent, industrial exports by nearly 50 percent, and marketed supplies by about 25 percent.[49] The prospects of attaining these goals are jeopardized by an adverse foreign-trade balance, due particularly to the increase in Soviet and world oil prices. Petroleum imports from the USSR totaled 15½ million tons during 1975, at a cost that had quadrupled since 1971.

With the exception of the years 1965−1968, Czechoslovak economic planning has been under the distinct influence of doctrinaire Marxist thinking. This adherence to the classics handicapped the communists in that they found themselves with an overabundance of heavy industrial products and a consequent shortage of consumers' goods. Nonetheless, the Czechoslovak economy has proven beneficial to the economic growth of the Soviet Union and other East European countries.

A low population-growth rate during the 1960s compelled the Czechs and Slovaks to take a closer look at their utilization of manpower.[50] By 1976 Czechoslovakia's birthrate was the highest in Europe, but it will take some time before this phenomenon affects the labor force. The economy has reached the limit of its labor potential and further expansion will be predicated upon greater efficiency in agriculture and industrial productivity. The latter has increased recently (see table 21), although private enterprise has been thwarted by a continued purge over the years. In 1955 approximately forty-eight thousand private entrepreneurs remained within the economic system, but by 1959 their number had dropped to nine thousand. A limited revival of private enterprise was allowed after 1964, and by 1974 some twelve thousand artisans were working. About 9 percent of the farmland is still in private hands.

Another weakness in the Czechoslovak economy is overspecialization; a disproportionate emphasis on certain areas of the economy and a concurrent neglect of others. A prime example is found in the transportation system, wherein railroads have received the benefit of technological advances and

48. For an official account of economic affairs, see "Czechoslovakia between the 14th and 15th Congresses of the Communist Party of Czechoslovakia," *Czechoslovak Economic Digest,* no. 1 (January 1976).

49. Lubomir Strougal, "Report on the Main Trends in Economic and Social Development in the Czechoslovak Socialist Republic in 1976−1980," *Rude pravo,* 14 April 1976; English translation in *Czechoslovak Economic Digest,* no. 4 (June 1976), p. 22.

50. Increases of employment totaled 450,000 during 1961−1965, some 330,000 in 1966−1970, but only 120,000 for 1971−1975. About 800,000 persons, or 28.3 percent of the labor force, changed industrial jobs in one year. Interview with official in federal labor and social welfare ministry, published by *Svet hospodarstvi,* 17 April 1970, pp. 1−2. Because of a labor shortage, Czechoslovakia has had to import foreign workers from Poland, Yugoslavia, Vietnam, and Cyprus. RFE, *Situation Report,* 10 March 1976.

TABLE 21

DEVELOPMENT OF THE CZECHOSLOVAK ECONOMY, 1969–1975
(Changes compared with the preceding year in percentages)

Index	1969	1970	1971	1972	1973	1974	1975
Industrial production	4.5	8.0	4.8	4.9	5.3	6.6	7.0
Building	–	5.1	10.4	13.3	4.4	5.3	8.1
National income (overall)	6.2	5.5	5.0	6.3	5.2	6.0	6.0
National income (without agriculture)	4.2	7.5	5.3	6.7	5.4	6.4	–
Labor productivity in industry	4.2	–	–	–	6.7	6.3	6.1

SOURCES: Federal Office of Statistics, *Statistical Survey of Czechoslovakia 1976* (Prague, 1976), tables 16 and 44, pp. 24 and 53; *Rude pravo*, 27 January 1976.

improvements while roads and highways have been neglected. The economic situation in Czechoslovakia, as in most communist countries, reflects the imbalance in planning that results from a narrow and specialized approach.

During the fifth five-year plan, one of the seven principles of financing and monetary policy dealt with that problem in the same frame of mind. One expert called upon the authorities[51]

> to start strict regulation of investments and at the same time to ensure that the necessary financial means are available for projects included in the plan investments. . . . In contrast to the years 1967–1969, when the prevailing principle was that investments are made by those who have money, without there being an order of precedence as to how the means are to be expended, now the priorities are determined strictly by the State plan of investments.

During 1970, on the eve of the fifth five-year plan, federal subsidies were running at 38.5 billion Czechoslovak crowns (an increase of 2.7 billion crowns from 1969).[52]

Industry. The extension of communist control over the country's vast industrial complex was facilitated through the nationalization policy started in October 1945 by the Czechoslovak coalition government. After this first wave of nationalization, about 40 percent of production (only in certain exempted industries) still remained in private hands. A second wave beginning in 1948 brought nearly every type of industry and business under state operation. The seizure of wholesale and retail businesses and of all foreign trade occurred during

---

51. Leopold Ler, "Financial Policy in the Fifth Five Year Plan," *Nova mysl* (May 1975); English translation in *Czechoslovak Economic Digest*, no. 5 (August 1975), pp. 6–7.

52. Article by Finance minister Rudolf Rohlicek, "About Financial Policy in Czechoslovakia," in *Pravda*, 3 March 1970; Bratislava. Guidelines for 1976–1980 stress expansion of the engineering industry, according to RFE, *Situation Report*, 8 December 1976.

this second period, after which only 5 percent of industrial production and 17 percent of the physical plant remained in private hands.[53]

Although Czechoslovakia's industrial output is a significant factor within the Soviet orbit, its products have failed to regain the prestige they once enjoyed on the world scene. The craftsmanship and skills of earlier days are not apparent today. The quantity of the output has remained significant, but its quality has deteriorated.[54] One reason for this may be that bloc requirements were initially, and are even now, less stringent than those imposed by prewar customers. Another, certainly, is that the USSR has been exploiting all East European countries by paying lower than world market prices, and that inferior products help to make up for this price reduction.

The importance of Czechoslovak industry to the bloc is most evident in its supplying of certain special requirements of the other countries. Eastern Europe, including the Soviet Union, has relied heavily on Czechoslovak machinery in building up its industrial sector. Entire plants are manufactured in Czechoslovakia for shipment and installation throughout the bloc. More than three-fourths of all types of machinery made in the world are available from Czechoslovakia. A considerable part of its industrial production involves armaments; as a result, Czechoslovakia has often been referred to as the aresenal of Eastern Europe. Also, arms captured from insurgent forces in many of the world's trouble spots have been found to have originated there.

Agriculture. Nationalization has not been quite so thorough in the agricultural sector of the economy as it has in industry. Nevertheless, through expropriation of large landholdings the communists were able to exert influence and control over agriculture relatively easily. Six months before the 1948 seizure of power, private farms had already been limited to fifty hectares each. From this base, a collectivization program was initiated. When Stalin died in 1953, it came to a temporary halt; two years later the program had regained momentum.

To centralize control over agriculture further, many of the weaker and less successful collective farms have been amalgamated into a state farm system. In addition to communist ideological considerations, the idea of more profitably applying the advantages of large-scale production and improved methods of management may have been behind this policy. However, during 1960 and 1965 agricultural output was actually below that of Czechoslovakia in 1936.

---

53. Bratislava radio, 28 October 1965.

54. During 1965 the value of rejects totaled one billion Czechoslovak crowns. Prague radio, 15 January 1966. The quality of products was to be stressed so as to increase exports. *Ibid.*, 15 July 1970. However, "dead billions [of crowns]" in unutilized stocks of materials "are lying in the warehouses of enterprises," according to *Nove slovo*, 18 November 1976; translation in RFE, *Background Report*, 7 December 1976.

Cooperative farming has suffered a net loss of 224,000 workers since 1961, leaving in 1975 a labor force of 1,240,000 for this sector.[55]

In general, the agricultural economy has been beset with numerous difficulties. Output has fallen far short of established quotas and expectations. Up to the Second World War, Czechoslovakia was almost self-sufficient in food. During 1974 the country had a trade deficit of 2.5 billion crowns in agricultural commodities, and food products made up more than 10 percent of its total import trade. These included over one million tons of grain. In 1976 the agricultural-production deficit totaled 16 percent.[56]

The total number of farm workers dropped from more than three million before the war to fewer than 1.4 million in 1975. Only about 9.5 percent of the population is engaged in agriculture.[57] Each farmer is permitted to cultivate a private plot of land that can be up to an acre in size, and he may have a cow to provide dairy products for his family. For the distribution of agricultural land in Czechoslovakia, which is almost 90 percent collectivized or nationalized, see table 22.

TABLE 22

AGRICULTURAL LAND DISTRIBUTION IN CZECHOSLOVAKIA, 1975

	Arable Land	
Type of unit	Area in hectares	Percent of total
Collective farms	4,163,000	59.1
State farms	2,122,000	30.2
Private farms and plots	690,000	9.8
Other (research institutes, schools, etc.)	67,000	0.9
Total	7,042,000	100.0

SOURCE: *Statistical Survey of Czechoslovakia 1976* (Prague, 1976), table 53, p. 58.

Agricultural progress in Czechoslovakia and in the other communist-dominated countries is predicated upon one of two developments. The first, and quickest, way to increase production is to return the land to individual farmers. The private entrepreneur who owns his land and livestock is concerned about erosion, weeds, waste, and the well-being and care of his animals and equipment. Pride in ownership, which is missing from the collective, stimulates the individual farmer into actions that rarely occur under the present system. It is to be understood that such a drastic measure is unlikely to be adopted under a

---

55. *Statistical Survey of Czechoslovakia 1976*, pp. 16 and 56.

56. *Ibid.*, pp. 78–79; Bratislava radio, 27 November 1976.

57. *Statistical Survey* (in note 55 above), p. 16.

firmly established communist regime, although this did happen in Poland after October 1956, as well as even earlier in Yugoslavia.

A second development appears to be in consonance with theoretical policies in several communist-ruled states to varying degrees, but it would take many years to complete. It consists essentially of achieving vertical integration by turning farms into factories, with agricultural workers being indoctrinated along the same line as their counterparts in the industrial plants. An essential prerequisite for this program is the passing from the scene of the current generation of farm workers. Most of these persons are becoming old (the average age is over fifty-eight) and have grown up on the land they are now forced to cultivate for the benefit of the state. The majority of them are women. Many are malcontents who long for the "good old days." The eradication of this group might lead to an atmosphere somewhat like that found in a factory. A wage system, patterned after that of the industrial program in theory, could provide incentives and bonuses. A scientific, technological, and impersonal approach to agriculture is envisioned, of course, under the current state farm system.[58]

Church-State Relations. Roman Catholicism had been the dominant force in Czechoslovak religious history until the Reformation, which established Protestantism throughout Bohemia and Moravia. Unlike some of the other East Europeans, the Czechs have been tolerant and even indifferent toward religion as a rule. In Slovakia, the Catholic church still plays a considerable role, especially in rural areas. But the Protestant minority there, which is larger than that in the Czech provinces, remains equally active. Throughout the Czechoslovak state, however, all religious schools, orders, and publications have been abolished. Suppression of the clergy has been intermittently relaxed as the tactics of party leaders have varied.

In 1952 relations with the Vatican were severed. Even before that date, the regime had imprisoned numerous high-ranking clergymen. In 1963, when the Soviet Union attempted to improve relations with the Vatican, the authorities in Prague released a number of those jailed. Yet there is no noticeable change in the basically hostile attitude toward any kind of religion, and an Institute of Scientific Atheism has been established in connection with Bratislava University. The church does not appear to have much potential for active resistance to the current regime because all of its activities are effectively controlled. Negotiations with the Vatican brought about the departure from Czechoslovakia of Archbishop (later Cardinal) Josef Beran, who died in Rome, and the appointment of Bishop Frantisek Tomasek as apostolic administrator. By 1970, however, new

---

58. For recent agricultural plans of this type, see the report by Jan Baryl, "Questions on Further Development of the Agriculture and Food Industry," *Rude pravo*, 8 October 1975; English translation in *Czechoslovak Economic Digest*, no. 8 (December 1975).

restrictions had been imposed on religious activities.[59] A regime-sponsored association of Catholic clergymen, "Pacem in Terris," appears to be circumventing the bishops and dealing directly with the state.

FOREIGN AFFAIRS

The Council for Mutual Economic Assistance (CMEA) and the Warsaw Pact provide the framework for the nature and extent of Czechoslovak activities within the Soviet sphere. Czechoslovakia was an original signatory to the statutes of both organizations and it currently supports them in a comparatively wholehearted manner. The Soviet attempt at manipulating the controls of CMEA so that the other members will become increasingly dependent economically on the USSR has succeeded to some extent in the case of Czechoslovakia.

Almost all of the petroleum (96 percent) used by the country comes from the Soviet Union, as do large proportions of the iron ore (68 percent) and cotton (41 percent) and a significant part of the nonferrous metals. During 1974 trade between the two countries totaled more than twenty-four billion crowns and represented more than 28 percent of Czechoslovakia's foreign trade.[60] Consequently the USSR is in a favorable position to exert economic pressure that should guarantee support by Czechoslovakia when and if required. Without petroleum and iron ore, Czechoslovakia would find it difficult to operate its industries and its transportation system. Strategically valuable uranium deposits also exist at Jachymov and Pribram;[61] these have been and may still be under Soviet control and supervision.

Intrabloc Relations. The sustantial output of complete industrial installations by Czechoslovakia has assisted the expansion of heavy industry in the Soviet Union and other communist-dominated countries. As mentioned already Czechoslovakia is the main supplier of machines and plants to the bloc. The specialization program of CMEA conflicts in many ways with the Czechoslovaks' new system of management. It is possible that this incompatibility will continue to grow rather than decrease.

Many of the East European communist leaders within the Soviet sphere are

---

59. *Christ und Welt*, 1 May 1970; statement by Catholic clergy in *Lidova demokracie*, 14 May 1970. On the Uniates, see *Pravda*, 1 September 1970; Bratislava.

60. *Statistical Survey* (in note 55 above), pp. 68, 72–73, 75, and 78. For an official view of Czechoslovakia's energy needs vis-a-vis other bloc states, see M. Virius and J. Balek, "Cooperation Among CMEA Countries in Securing Supplies of Fuels and Energy," *Planovane hospodarstvi* (January 1976); English translation in *Czechoslovak Economic Digest*, no. 3 (May, 1976), pp. 25–44.

61. Josef Krejci, chairman of the Federal Committee on Industry, reaffirmed contractual obligations during 1970–1975 for sale of the metal to the USSR, over Prague television, 1 December 1969. The Soviet Union will aid in construction of two nuclear power stations over the current decade, according to Moscow radio, 24 July 1970.

unhappy with CMEA because of certain features of the program and the resulting outside interference with what these men consider to be purely domestic matters. Czechoslovakia has also expressed dissatisfaction, but for an entirely different reason. The Prague regime complains of lax enforcement procedures for CMEA decisions. Because of the country's heavy industrial output and contributions to CMEA, official Czechoslovak opinions must carry some weight.[62] Still, the USSR holds the key to future economic success, and the leadership in Prague realizes this.

Czechoslovakia has been a member of the Warsaw Pact since 1955 and it apparently responds well to Soviet military directives. Like Hungary, Poland, and East Germany, Czechoslovakia has Soviet military personnel on its soil. Including security forces, the country is thought to have the equivalent of ten divisions available for deployment. These forces are well equipped with modern arms. The defensive capability of the Czechoslovak troops probably outweighs their offensive potential. The influence of the USSR is maintained throughout the armed forces by the placement of Soviet officers as advisors in the Prague high command.[63]

The production of arms and munitions makes Czechoslovakia a key member of the Warsaw Pact. With its industrial capacity and its relatively limited manpower, Czechoslovakia is an "ideal" associate of the Soviet Union. It is able to make a significant material contribution to the armed forces of the Pact. Article 5 of the new twenty-year treaty of 6 May 1970 even provides the basis for sending Czechoslovak troops to the Chinese border.[64]

Extrabloc Relations.   Foreign aid to countries outside the bloc has played an important part in Czechoslovakia's political and economic activities. Prague has spent more than all of the other East European states combined (except for the USSR) on foreign aid and technical assistance. The primary beneficiaries of its largesse have been Egypt, Syria, Ghana, Guinea, Ethiopia, Sudan, Mali, India, Morocco, Cuba, Brazil, and Argentina. The political implications of the foreign-aid and technical-assistance programs have been repeatedly explained to the people by the Czechoslovak press in order to lessen internal resentment and resistance toward the program.

The population has tended to blame the outflow of goods for the shortages experienced in certain commodities at home. Government officials have told the people that it has been necessary to conduct and continue the aid program for a

---

62. For official attitudes, see Frantisek Fojtik, "Some Theoretical Problems of Joint Planning in the CMEA Countries." *Zahranicni obchod* (October 1975); English translation in *Czechoslovak Economic Digest*, no. 3 (May 1976), pp. 12–24.

63. This has been simplified by a 1958 agreement on dual citizenship. The complete text appeared in J. Cerny and V. Cervenka (comps.), *Statni obcanstvi CSSR* (Prague, 1963), pp. 199–202.

64. Text in *Pravda*, 7 May 1970; Moscow.

number of reasons, the foremost being propagation of the socialist doctrine among neutralist or uncommitted countries by exhibiting the strength of the socialist order. Another reason given has been the allegation that the West allegedly blocked Czechoslovakia from its normal channels of trade, and that as a result new markets had to be found for the export of finished products and the import of needed raw materials. In recent years, however, economic aid to the developing areas has decreased considerably. This has especially been the case since August 1968.

During the 1960s Czechoslovakia also attempted gradually to reinstitute the trade ties with the West that had been so lucrative before the Second World War, and that were cut off almost entirely immediately after the war by communist policy. The regime made important commercial agreements with Britain, France, Spain, the Scandinavian countries, and others.[65] Even the United States was approached by Czechoslovak officials. More recently, Czechoslovakia again has shown considerable interest in trade with the West. This trade has already resulted in a manageable adverse balance of payments, and that situation, in turn, makes the regime cautious about incurring debts that must be repaid either in hard currency or in quality exports.[66]

This indebtedness will increase because of a disappointing harvest. Several billion crowns worth of agricultural products must be imported during 1977, "above all from the capitalist countries," according to Premier Strougal. Supplies of potatoes, vegetables, and fruit are insufficient, and it is anticipated that "over one billion crowns worth of meat" must be purchased abroad.[67] Whether the quality of Czechoslovakia's exports to the West can be improved remains to be seen.

65. Czechoslovak foreign trade and policy outside the socialist bloc is discussed in RFE, *Background Report,* 14 January 1976, and by Zdenek Orlicek, "Thirty Years of Czechoslovak Foreign Trade," *Zahranicni obchod* (May 1975); English translation in *Czechoslovak Economic Digest,* no. 6 (September 1975), pp. 48–49.

66. See the essay by Zdenek Suda, "Czechoslovakia," in R. F. Staar (ed.), *1977 Yearbook on International Communist Affairs* (Stanford, Ca., 1977).

67. Quoted by Thomas E. Heneghan, "Czechoslovakia," RFE, *Survey of East European Developments in 1976* (Munich, 23 November 1976), p. 34.

Chapter 4

German Democratic Republic

In both East and West Germany, the initial postwar policies of the occupation authorities were directed more toward reparations than toward rehabilitation. The USSR pursued this goal with an almost exaggerated zeal. During its brief tenure as the sole power in Berlin, for example, the Soviet Union removed 75 percent of all capital equipment. Also in the first several months, machinery from about nineteen hundred industrial enterprises in the Soviet occupation zone was either partly or completely dismantled and shipped to Moscow. This practice, coupled with a policy of extracting reparations from current production, violated the letter as well as the spirit of the Yalta and Potsdam agreements and seriously hampered economic recovery throughout East Germany for many years. It is estimated that reparations to the Soviet Union in the postwar period amounted to 66.4 billion marks.[1]

The industrial property of "war criminals, National Socialists [Nazis], and militarists" underwent expropriation. These categories received broad interpretation, with the result that private enterprise was eliminated from all large and most medium-sized industrial firms.[2] In addition, control over approximately two hundred large firms whose plants had not been dismantled was given to Soviet joint stock companies (SAG). By 1948 only 8 percent of all East German industry had been socialized, but 40 percent of the country's total industrial output originated from these enterprises; another 25 or 30 percent was produced by SAG units.

> A comparison of these two figures shows clearly that only small plants and a few medium-sized enterprises, especially in the manufacture of consumption goods, like textiles, had escaped socialization.[3]

1. Stephen D. Kertesz (ed.), *The Fate of East Central Europe* (Notre Dame, Ind., 1956), pp. 160–161; [Federal Republic of Germany], Bundesministerium fuer gesamtdeutsche Fragen, *A bis Z* (Bonn, 1969), p. 530.

2. Elmer Plischke, *Contemporary Government of Germany* (Boston, 1969), 2d ed., pp. 182–183, describes the overall economic organization of East Germany.

3. Kertesz, *op. cit.* (in note 1 above), p. 154.

In other directions the Soviets proceeded more cautiously. During 1944 and 1945 they still looked forward to the eventual reunification of Germany and the extension of "socialism" over the whole country. Thus the sovietization of their occupied zone was accomplished under a facade of democratizing and antifascist activity that was designed to mislead both the noncommunist East Germans and the Western powers. The following measures were undertaken by the Soviet Union during this initial period:

> The *Laender* or provinces were allowed legislatures, based on free elections.
> All private banks and insurance companies suspended operations.
> Widespread seizure of agricultural and industrial property was justified on antifascist rather than anticapitalist grounds.
> Political activity was encouraged, and "antifascist" parties were licensed much sooner than in the Western zones.[4]

From the early days of the occupation, the USSR encouraged the formation of political parties. The Communist Party of Germany (*Kommunistische Partei Deutschlands*—KPD), which was reestablished in June 1945 throughout East Germany, came first, of course. Within a month, the Christian democrats, liberals, and social democrats followed. Using the typical "people's front" tactics that had been adopted in other satellite countries, all four East German parties in July 1945 joined the Antifascist Democratic Bloc, which was subsequently renamed the "Democratic Bloc of Parties and Mass Organizations." In October 1949 this became the National Front.[5] The communists apparently believed that they could win control over East Germany through free elections, and they wanted to maintain at least the pretext of separate parties.

At first many politicians regarded the Soviet reforms as a positive step. The socialists, during the summer and fall of 1945, actually suggested a merger of their party with the KPD but were turned down by the communists.[6] By November 1945, however, the KPD had come to regard the Socialist party as a serious competitor since it had a large following in the industrial areas. Despite the fact that most socialists now opposed the move, a forced merger with the

---

4. For an official East German chronology of events from April 1945 to June 1964, see Stefan Dornberg, *Kurze Geschichte der DDR* (East Berlin, 1964), pp. 513–547.

5. Five political groupings operate in East Germany. For the names of key members in the four subordinate movements see [Federal Republic of Germany], Bundesanstalt fuer gesamtdeutsche Aufgaben, *Der Staats- und Parteiapparat der Deutschen Demokratischen Republik* (Bonn, 15 August 1976), pp. 36–38.

6. [Federal Republic of Germany], Bundesministerium fuer gesamtdeutsche Fragen, *SBZ von 1945 bis 1954* (Bonn, 1961), pp. 10, 21, 23–27.

KPD was effected in April 1946 to form the Socialist Unity Party of Germany (*Sozialistische Einheitspartei Deutschlands—SED*).

In the fall of 1946 the last relatively free elections were held in East Germany. An active SED campaign and interference with the activities of the other parties (such as forbidding rallies and banning candidates) still did not bring the absolute majority victory that the communists had wanted. However, SED candidates were given key positions in all five *Laender*.[7] This was also the last time that voters were given any choice of candidates. Subsequent national elections have presented only a single list on the ballot, and the voter has had no option but to approve it.

In late 1947 the SED formed from among its own membership a People's Congress. Despite the fact that it had no popular basis, this body assumed the task of establishing a government for East Germany. In March 1948 the Congress named a four-hundred-member People's Council. This group, in turn, appointed a committee to draft a new constitution; this assignment was completed by October.

To add an element of legality, national elections were held in May 1949 for representatives to the People's Congress. The ballot, however, consisted of a typical "unity list" that was packed with communists. The draft constitution received no mention during the campaign. After the election, a new People's Congress convened and promptly approved the constitution. The German Democratic Republic (*Deutsche Demokratische Republik*) was thus established. Its administrative agencies are located at Pankow, a borough of East Berlin, which represents a violation of agreements among the four occupation powers.

The Congress also appointed a new People's Council, which declared itself the provisional People's Chamber, or parliament, and promulgated the new constitution. Since the basic law envisaged the People's Chamber as a popularly elected representative body, the fact that this body actually appointed itself gave the German Democratic Republic (GDR) the unique distinction of starting with a government that had no legitimacy and was, in fact, unconstitutional.

CONSTITUTIONS OF 1949 AND 1968

It has been noted that "a good constitution may be the backbone of a state or it may be window-dressing."[8] The latter situation is nowhere more true than in the case of East Germany. Its first constitution provided for a strong central

---

7. They took four out of five *Laender* premierships, the same ratio in the Interior ministry, three out of five in Economics, and all five in the Education ministry. Kertesz, *op. cit.*, (in note 1 above), p. 158.

8. U.S. Office of the High Commissioner for Germany, *Soviet Zone Constitution and Electoral Law* (Washington, D.C., 1951), p. 1.

government based on a multiparty, parliamentary system. The power of government was concentrated in an elected representative body, the People's Chamber. The concept of separation of powers, which was common to the United States and most Western democracies, did not appear in the document. In many ways, however, the GDR's constitution[9] looked like a remarkably liberal document and it could have provided the basis for a stable and representative government.

> The East German constitution of 1949 was phrased so that, if properly implemented, a genuine democracy, in which basic rights were preserved, could have functioned under it. However, the wording of the Constitution also was framed so that, once the Communists were in control, they could interpret and apply it to maintain their system of centralistic statism. This was more patently recognized by the even less"democratic" constitutional system of 1968.[10]

It should be mentioned that the 1949 constitution had been written for all of Germany and purposely resembled the Weimar Constitution, on the assumption that the East and West zones eventually would be reunited. In regard to this prospect of reunification, it paralleled also the Basic Law in the Federal Republic of (West) Germany.[11] With its 17 sections and 144 articles, the 1949 constitution was also similar to the West German legislation in being long, thorough, and complex.

The 1968 Socialist Constitution.   In typical communist fashion, only two months elapsed between the establishment of a constitutional commission and the publication of a draft document. Eight weeks later, the People's Chamber incorporated several minor changes and gave its approval. A national referendum in April 1968 polled 94.5 percent in favor, and the new basic law for the GDR went into effect. In October 1974 certain amendments to this constitution were introduced; the following discussion reflects these changes.[12]

Article 1 proclaims the GDR to be "a socialist state of workers and farmers" (the 1968 terminology had been "German nation") and its capital to be Berlin.

---

9. For the text with amendments through 1960 see Siegfried Mampel (ed.), *Die volksdemokratische Ordnung in Mitteldeutschland* (Frankfurt/Main, 1963), pp. 56—79.

10. Plischke, *op. cit.* (in note 2 above), p. 210.

11. The Basic Law (*Grundgesetz*) for the Federal Republic of Germany specifically states that it is temporary, makes provision for ratification by other *Laender,* and proclaims that it will be superseded when a "constitution adopted by a free decision of the German people comes into force." See Article 146 in Amos J. Peaslee (ed.), *Constitutions of Nations* (The Hague, 1956), 2d ed., II, 59.

12. [German Democratic Republic], *The Constitution of the German Democratic Republic* (Leipzig, 1968), p. 37. The German text appears in *Deutschland Archiv,* I, no. 2 (May 1968), pp. 166—181. Amendments are discussed and the complete text given in Dietrich Mueller-Roemer (ed.), *Die neue Verfassung der DDR* (Cologne, 1974), p. 12.

The so-called National Front of political parties and mass organizations, however, rather than the (communist) Socialist Unity party, is identified as the "alliance of all forces of the people" in Article 3.

Since elections held in the GDR have been neither free nor secret, ultimate power over the government does not reside with the people, as the 1968 constitution proclaims. Other paradoxes and contradictions appear in the constitution's extensive listing of civil rights.

Every citizen allegedly may "express his opinion freely and publicly," and "freedom of the press, radio, and television is guaranteed" (Article 27). The right of peaceful assembly is also supposedly guaranteed: "The use of material prerequisites for the unhindered exercise of this right of assembly, such as buildings, streets, and places of demonstration, printing works, and means of communication, is guaranteed" (Article 28).

Nevertheless, about seven thousand political prisoners were being held in the GDR as of 1975. Many of them are incarcerated on charges of "slander against the state" because they had been exercising their constitutional rights of free speech and public assembly.[13]

Perhaps also of questionable validity is Article 103, which states that "every citizen may submit petitions (proposals, suggestions, applications, or grievances)" and that these petitioners "may be exposed to no disadvantage as a result of exercising this right." The demonstrations at Erfurt, Dresden, Frankfurt/Oder, and East Berlin toward the end of August 1968 represented a vocal grievance against the invasion of Czechoslovakia. The regime's answer included arrest and prison terms of from fifteen to twenty-seven months for each defendant.[14]

THE GOVERNMENT

The regimes of East and West Germany seem, at first sight, to have much in common. Both evolved from an occupation status in 1949, achieved formal sovereignty during 1954–1955, and now have military forces integrated with their respective alliance systems.[15] In the West, the Federal Republic of Germany has developed into a free democratic country whose political and economic growth has been the envy of neighboring states. The GDR, on the other hand, remains under the strongman rule of Erich Honecker, who continues to coordinate indigenous requirements with the interests of the Soviet Union, and in return can count on its support and protection. It should be noted that the East German standard of living is higher than that of other bloc countries, including even the USSR.

---

13. *Die Welt*, 13 August 1975; Hamburg.

14. *New York Times*, 30 October 1968.

15. Arnold J. Heidenheimer, *The Governments of Germany* (New York, 1966), 2d ed., pp. 182–183.

Abolition of the Laender. The provinces, or *Laender*, had traditionally been the basic units of German government. Evolving from the past, they had served as centers of political and social life. The 1949 GDR constitution recognized this fact and established the provinces as semi-autonomous entities that were represented in the central government through an upper chamber of parliament.

In July 1952 the governments of the *Laender* and their legislative bodies were abolished by law. This action was technically unconstitutional, since Article 110 provided that any change in territory required either an amendment to the constitution or a plebiscite in the *Land* concerned. The dissolved provinces were replaced by fourteen administrative areas, called districts, each of which had fifteen or more counties. A fifteenth district was established for East Berlin. This move completely eliminated local government as a source of even potential opposition and increased the power of the central government, thus assuring greater control by the ruling communist party.

With the elimination of the *Laender*, the political basis for the upper chamber of parliament disappeared. It continued in existence for several years to fulfill such constitutional requirements as the election of the president. In December 1958 it, too, was formally abolished. With this move, the legislative body of the GDR became unicameral, and the last vestige of federalism disappeared.

Elimination of the Presidency. In October 1949, two days after the adoption of the constitution and the day after the nominal transfer of administrative powers from the Soviet Military Administration to the East German regime, Wilhelm Pieck became the first and, as it has turned out, the only president of the GDR. In 1953 he won reelection, and in 1957 his tenure was extended for a third term. This last action should have been preceded by a change in the constitution, since Article 101 required that the president be elected by a joint session of the two parliamentary chambers. By this time, of course, the upper house had become a relatively meaningless body. Thus it is possible that the regime considered that the formality of an election was not worth arranging.

In September 1960 Pieck died in office. Instead of holding an election to determine his successor, the People's Chamber voted, without debate, to amend the constitution. A twenty-six-member Council of State, which was elected by the People's Chamber to a four-year term of office, superseded the presidency. This new body not only assumed the duties of chief of state, but also was empowered to issue orders and interpret the law.[16] This step established for East Germany a collective executive with fairly sweeping powers. Walter Ulbricht was elected the chairman of the new State Council by the People's Chamber. He thus became the head of the state, in which he already held the supreme authority

---

16. For a discussion of the Council of State, see I. P. Ilinskii and B. A. Strashun, *Germanskaya Demokratischeskaya Respublika* (Moscow, 1961), pp. 133–139.

as SED first secretary. This type of arrangement, which ensures the domination of a country by a single trusted communist, has prevailed from time to time both in the Soviet Union and in other East European countries. Ulbricht assumed the honorary position of SED chairman in 1971, and after his death in 1973, Willi Stoph succeeded him as chief of state. On 29 October 1976 party leader Erich Honecker assumed the chairmanship of the State Council. (See table 23.)

The National Defense Council.   Called into being by legislation in February 1960, the National Defense Council has a chairman and at least twelve members. It remains the only leading governmental organ whose personnel are appointed by the Council of State (although it was established chronologically before the Council).[17] A law in September 1961 empowered this body to direct the defense and security of the state. All government agencies were required to carry out regulations and orders issued by the Defense Council. The 1968 constitution, however, restricted the powers of the Defense Council by making it accountable to the People's Chamber and the State Council.

According to the January 1962 law on universal military training, the Defense Council is authorized to issue rules implementing this legislation. These appear as regulations in the official journal of laws. The defense minister also remains subordinate to the Defense Council, which is chaired by Erich Honecker. Since Honecker is also the SED secretary-general, perhaps the functions of the minister have been kept vague on purpose. It is possible that the Defense Council is intended to become fully operative only in time of hostilities, paralleling the Soviet organ that had a similar name during the Second World War.

Government Organization and Control.   According to the 1968 constitution of East Germany, final authority allegedly rests with the people. Control is supposed to proceed upward to various popularly elected assemblies and councils at each level of government. In practice, this flow is reversed. Ultimate authority rests with the SED control apparatus and is implemented by councils that appear at all levels of government. Much important legislation takes the form of executive orders issued by the State Council or the Council of Ministers.

The SED rules the state, and "the decisions of the communist party constitute the highest scientific generalizations derivable from political practice."[18] Control is applied indirectly. The Politburo makes decisions, and the Secretariat is responsible for carrying them out. SED members are detailed to governmental agencies and business enterprises, where they supervise and report. Periodic

---

17. Lech Janicki, *Ustroj polityczny Niemieckiej Republiki Demokratycznej* (Poznan, 1964), p. 156. Note also the new law on civil defense in *Gesetzblatt*, no. 20 (1 October 1970), pp. 289–290.
18. Speech by a Central Committee functionary, quoted in Heidenheimer, *op. cit.* (in note 15 above), p. 184.

TABLE 23

East German Communist Party (SED) Leadership, 1977

Politburo	Born	Secretariat	Other SED post	Government Position
FULL MEMBERS (19)				
Honecker, Erich	1912	Secretary-General		Chairman, National Defense Council and Chairman, State Council
Axen Hermann	1916	Secretary (international affairs)		
Ebert, Friedrich	1894			Deputy chairman, State Council
Felfe, Werner	1928	Secretary (agriculture)	First Secretary, Halle	
Grueneberg, Gerhard	1921	Secretary (culture, science and		
Hager, Kurt	1912	education)		Defense minister
Hoffmann, Karl-Heinz	1910			
Krolikowski, Werner	1928	Secretary (economy)		State security minister
Lamberz, Werner	1929	Secretary (agitation)		First Deputy premier
Mielke, Erich	1907			
Mittag, Guenter	1926		Chairman, Control Commission;	
Mueckenberger, Erich	1910		First Secretary, Frankfurt/Oder	
			First Secretary, East Berlin	
Naumann, Konrad	1928			First Deputy premier
Neumann, Alfred	1909			
Norden, Albert	1904	Secretary (propaganda)		President, People's
Sindermann, Horst	1915			Chamber
				Premier
Stoph, Willi	1914			

TABLE 23 (Cont.)

EAST GERMAN COMMUNIST PARTY (SED) LEADERSHIP, 1977

Politburo	Born	Secretariat	Other SED post	Government Position
Tisch, Harry	1928			Member, State Council
Verner, Paul	1911	Secretary (security)		
CANDIDATE MEMBERS (9)				
Dohlus, Horst	1925	Secretary (organization)		
Herrmann, Joachim	1928			Director, Ancient History and Archeology Institute
Jarowinsky, Werner	1927	Secretary (trade and supply)		
Kleiber, Guenther	1931			Deputy premier; Agricultural Machines and Vehicle Manufacturing minister
Krenz, Egon	1937		First Secretary, FDJ	
Lange, Ingeborg	1927	Secretary (women)		
Mueller, Margarete	1931			Member, State Council; Secretary, Trade Unions
Schuerer, Gerhard	1921			Deputy premier; Chairman, State Planning Commission
Walde, Werner	1926		First Secretary, Cottbus	

SOURCES: [Federal Republic of Germany], *Staats-und Parteiapparat der DDR* (Bonn, 15 August 1976), pp. 26–27; RFE, *Communist Party-Government Line-Up* (Munich, 7 January 1977), pp. 10–13.

review and criticism are also conducted by party organs. East German political, social, and economic life is thus dominated by a single organization whose membership constitutes almost 12 percent of the population.

The continued existence of the communist regime in East Germany is guaranteed by the presence of approximately twenty Soviet divisions with 370,000 troops. The late Walter Ulbricht, in an article published in Moscow, referred to the circumstances of the installation of his government in these terms:

> Protection and aid of the Soviet Union, which at that time had a military form, made it easier for the antifascist democratic forces of Germany to fulfill their historic task [and] deprived the class enemies of the possibility of resorting to measures of open violence.[19]

The facts of the situation can be discerned behind these phrases. Even today, if the threat of Soviet military power were removed, the communist East German government might be in serious danger of collapse.

The USSR has always had a particular interest in East Germany, not only as a buffer between the other East European states and the West, but also as a source of industrial power. When the failure of the Berlin blockade stymied Soviet expansionist aims in Europe, the USSR turned its attention to integrating East Germany with the bloc. This goal was thought to have been accomplished, but the workers' revolt in June 1953 demonstrated that the situation had not become stabilized. Communist authority almost disintegrated and could be restored only by Soviet armed forces.

Elections.   The formalities of nominating candidates and holding elections have been carried out regularly in East Germany despite the fact that these amount to meaningless exercises. Through mass organizations and subordinate political movements, the SED has been able to maintain control over most of the vote. Four subordinate parties are allowed to propose their candidates, but the choice of candidates is made in "consultation" with the SED. The communists have a veto power over any name that may be presented.[20] Until recently all ballots contained only a single "unity list," and voters were given no opportunity for a choice. In June 1965 the SED propaganda chief Albert Norden proposed that "more candidates be nominated than the number required for election" at regional levels; no similar proposal has been offered with regard to national voting.

Article 54 of the East German constitution, which was amended in 1974, stipulates that elections to the People's Chamber are to be held every five years. In 1962, however, merely through a vote by the Council of Elders in the

---

19. *Pravda,* 30 December 1961; Moscow.

20. The 1963 electoral law appears in Otto Gotsche, *Wahlen in der DDR* (East Berlin, 1963), pp. 17–21.

legislature, elections required by the constitution were delayed for a year. This postponement may have been due to preparations for the sixth SED congress, which was held in January 1963.

Meetings of "electors" take place at which candidates are approved for inclusion on the ballot. The ballot then offers no choice to the voters, who turn out and record approval almost unanimously (although some do not vote). Ballots are constructed to assure a predetermined composition of the five-hundred-member parliament. The current People's Chamber was elected in 1976, and the SED, with its affiliated organizations, holds the controlling number of seats. The general character of the ballot can be illustrated by returns from local elections held throughout the GDR on 17 October 1976, when 98.58 percent of those eligible went to the polls and 99.86 percent of them reportedly voted for the National Front's list of candidates.[21]

Loyalty. Although East Germany celebrated its twenty-seventh anniversary as a separate state in 1976, it remains under the strong influence of the USSR. This provides stability for the regime and has produced an outward appearance of popular support. This domination is also responsible for such acts of subservience as the passive acceptance by the GDR of the Oder-Neisse line as its eastern boundary. On 7 October 1975 East Germany signed an agreement[22] with the Soviet Union guaranteeing the inviolability of its own borders, while affirming its allegiance to the bloc. This special relationship is emphasized by the 1974 amendment to the GDR constitution; Article 6 of the amendment states that "the German Democratic Republic is forever an irrevocable ally of the USSR. The close and fraternal alliance with it guarantees the people of the German Democratic Republic further advance along the road to socialism and peace."

Agriculture. One of the earliest actions by the East German regime, based on Article 24 of the 1949 constitution, involved the confiscation of all privately owned farms that were more than a hundred hectares in size. Some of these became cooperative enterprises (LPGs) and others became state farms. Collectivization continued, and by 1959 about 52 percent of the country's arable land had come under cooperative or state control.

In 1960 a new drive started and, by the end of that year, agriculture was 98.7 percent socialized.[23] Over a three-month period, about 340,000 farmers had been forced to join LPGs or flee to the West. The German Democratic Republic's experience with collective farming, like that of most other East European states,

---

21. *Pravda*, 19 October 1976.

22. This treaty of friendship, mutual assistance, and cooperation appeared in *Pravda* the day after it was signed. Article 7 stipulates that West Berlin "is not a part of the Federal Republic of Germany and also in the future will not be governed by it."

23. L. N. Tolkunov (ed.), *Sotsialisticheskii lager* (Moscow, 1962), p. 163.

has been less than satisfactory. The agricultural plight reached crisis proportions in 1969 when the grain harvest dropped 12 percent below that of the preceding year and the potato and sugar beet crops lagged behind by 30 percent. As a result, additional imports of farm produce costing 350 million marks were required. Since 1964 the GDR has been purchasing more than one million tons of grain each year from the Soviet Union.

Substantial improvement has occurred since then, chiefly due to efforts to operate farms along industrial lines, investments in chemical fertilizers, and the employment of modern technology. Another reason for agricultural growth has been the introduction of efficiency and production incentives. Nevertheless, the GDR is still obliged to import food from abroad. Under a recent agreement,[24] the United States will supply between 1.5 million and two million tons of grain to East Germany annually through 1980.

Another serious problem involves the abandonment of the farms by the young East Germans to seek industrial employment in the cities. The average age on many collective farms is sixty. Reportedly, fewer than 5 percent of the farm workers are under twenty-five years of age. The situation has deteriorated to such an extent that local government agencies are permitted to declare harvest emergencies and draft factory workers to help with the crops. Attempts to recruit students for summer work in agricultural production have failed during recent years.[25]

Disaffection and Intellectual Ferment.   The most striking indicator of dissent among East Germans toward their communist regime was the constant stream of refugees until the last gap in the border was sealed by construction of the Berlin Wall. In the period 1950–1961 an estimated three million persons fled from East Germany, making it one of the few countries in the world to have a declining population. Since that time, about thirty East Germans per week, on the average, manage to elude border guards and escape to the West. From the time the Wall was built, in 1961, through 1969, some 254,187 persons are estimated to have left East Germay permanently.[26] Included were thousands of aged and invalids who were granted exit permits because they were a burden to the GDR. But approximately half that total consisted of refugees who were outside the country when the border was sealed and refused the option to go home and later escapees who managed to foil the tight security along the East German frontiers. During the first ten months of 1976 only 529 persons escaped directly across the border, but 4,379 others escaped through other countries, mainly Yugoslavia and Hungary.[27]

---

24. *New York Times*, 27 November 1976.

25. *Die Welt*, 20 August 1975.

26. *New York Times*, 16 August 1969. A total of 171 persons are known to have been killed while trying to cross the Wall or border fortifications. *Die Welt*, 10 August 1976.

27. *Die Welt*, 9 November 1976. About 500 doctors have fled since 1973, according to *Frankfurter Allgemeine Zeitung*, 29 October 1976.

The GDR has maintained generally close supervision over its intellectuals. One of the more vocal dissidents has been Robert Havemann, former professor of chemistry at Humboldt University in East Berlin. A lifelong communist, he maintained that the dogmatic SED leadership had replaced logic with authority and tradition. His thesis was that all mistakes and shortcomings should be discussed publicly, and he advocated "human socialism." Havemann was fired from his teaching position in 1966 and ousted from the SED because of "continued damage to the party and an outlook foreign to the party." Later he was openly attacked in an open letter by the Academy of Sciences; shortly thereafter his name was removed from the list of Academy members.[28]

Despite this punishment, the mere fact that Havemann was not executed or even imprisoned could have been perceived as a sign that intellectual regimentation might be relaxed. This hope disappeared in 1968 when all dissent over the occupation of Czechoslovakia was quickly suppressed. Havemann's two sons, in fact, were at the time tried and sentenced to prison for "antistate incitement." Stricter curbs were reimposed on intellectuals in the wake of these developments. A recent case involves the dissident poet-singer Wolf Biermann, who was deprived of GDR citizenship in late 1976, while performing at Cologne.[29]

Ulbricht's Successor.   With the death of Walter Ulbricht in 1973, leadership passed to Erich Honecker, who had already served for two years as SED first secretary, Willi Stoph, chairman of the State Council, and Horst Sinderman, premier. Honecker currently holds the most important post, that of party chief (secretary-general), since constitutional amendments in October 1974 made the post of State Council chairman a less significant position.[30] However, as mentioned above, on 29 October 1976 Honecker became chairman of the State Council, with Stoph resuming his former position as premier.

Born in the Saar in 1912 the son of a miner, Erich Honecker became a roofer by trade and joined the communist children's organization at the age of eight. A decade later he was a student at the Lenin Academy in Moscow, but he returned the following year to become secretary of the youth movement for the Saar. Arrested in 1935, he did not leave the penitentiary until the end of World War II. His early postwar activities centered on the youth movement, then he became a candidate Politburo member from 1950–1958 (with one year of training in Moscow), and since that time he has been a full Politburo member and a member of the Secretariat.[31]

---

28. See the interview with Havemann in *Der Spiegel* (12 October 1970), pp. 204–207, and an article about him in *ibid.* (22 November 1976), pp. 49–50.

29. Interview with Biermann published by *ibid.* (22 November 1976), pp. 36–46; East Berlin radio, 19 November 1976.

30. *Neues Deutschland*, 8 October 1974; *Die Welt*, 30 October 1976.

31. Guenther Buch (comp.), *Namen und Daten* (Berlin, 1973), p. 120.

THE RULING PARTY

Although the Socialist Unity Party of Germany (SED) is farther removed geographically from Moscow than any other such East European movement, it has been characterized by the greatest obedience to Soviet directives. During a decade of destalinization and superficial liberalization, both in the USSR and to varying degrees throughout the bloc, the SED has retained its essential and original harshness.[32] Functionally, it is something of a mirror image of the Soviet communist party, operating through similar organs of control. Yet the nature of the East German people, the character of the leadership, and the conduct of the party congresses all give the SED its own peculiar form and character.

Party Membership. Of the approximately 17 million people in East Germany, only 2,043,697 were in 1976 either full members or candidates for membership in the Socialist Unity party.[33] Like other ruling communist parties, the SED originally assumed a mass form; this lasted from 1946 until 1948, when the order came to reorient it into a cadre-type organization. Since that time the requirements for membership have become more stringent, and some of the opportunistic elements have probably been removed in the process. Membership now comes only after acceptance as a candidate and a probationary period under the careful scrutiny of party functionaries. These functionaries derive largely from the white-collar and intelligentsia classes.[34]

Candidacy in the SED requires recommendation by other party members or, if the candidate is enrolled in the Free German Youth, by the local youth organization's functionary. The social composition of the SED once again shows a large white-collar and intelligentsia component. (See table 24.) Although the collectivized peasants in the German Democratic Republic numbered 770,000 in 1975, just over 5 percent of the SED membership belonged to that class.[35]

Party Organization. The organization of the SED follows that of the Soviet communist party. The smallest unit is the primary party organization (74,306 of these existed in 1976), which permeates all activities on farms and in factories, government agencies, the armed forces, and so on. The next administrative level is the town, above this is the county, and then comes the district organization,

---

32. Note, for example, the article by Bozidar Dikic on the Nazi pasts of certain SED theoreticians that appeared in *Politika*, 21 February 1970; Belgrade.

33. *Neues Deutschland*, 21 May 1976.

34. Peter Christian Ludz, *DDR Handbuch* (Cologne, 1975), pp. 743–764. See also Hermann Weber, *Die Sozialistische Einheitspartei Deutschlands, 1946–1971* (Hannover, 1971).

35. [German Democratic Republic], *Statistical Pocket Book of the German Democratic Republic 1975* (East Berlin, 1975), p. 28.

TABLE 24

EAST GERMAN COMMUNIST PARTY (SED)
SOCIAL COMPOSITION, 1947–1976
(percentages)

Category	1947	1957	1961	1970	1976
Industrial workers	48.1	33.8	33.8	47.1	56.1
Officials and intelligentsia	22.0	42.3	41.3	28.1	20.0
Farm workers	9.4	5.0	6.2	5.8	5.2
Others	20.5	18.9	18.7	19.0	· 18.7
Total	100.0	100.0	100.0	100.0	100.0

SOURCE: Eduard R. Langer, "Zum Bildungsstand der SED Funktionare," *Die Orientierung*, no. 2 (1968), double issue, p. 7 (primary sources are given in a footnote by this source); *World Marxist Review* (August 1970), Supplement, p. 6; East Berlin radio, 18 May 1976.

which in turn reports to the Central Committee. This group is elected by the party congress once every five years and, in theory, evolves from its membership a Politburo and Secretariat. (The ninth congress met 19–24 May 1976).

In actual practice, the Politburo is a self-perpetuating body. Through the Secretariat it instructs lower levels on the accomplishment of goals; that is, the Secretariat oversees the implementation of policy decisions that are made by the Politburo. Instructors are assigned by the Central Committee apparatus to district headquarters; other instructors go from the district to the county, town, and primary organizations. These men and women are assigned either individually or, to assure the fulfillment of important plans, in teams.

The SED Central Committee in 1976 included 145 full members and 57 candidates.[36] The Politburo consisted of 19 members and 9 candidates in that year and the Secretariat had eleven persons who were designated as secretaries, in addition to secretary-general Erich Honecker. There are forty departments within the Central Committee's apparatus: cadres, agitation, foreign, women, youth, security, party organs, ideology, and so on.[37] Some of these are duplicated in the 15 district and 269 county organizations and remain under the supervision of district and county secretariats comprising five or six secretaries each.

Organs of Control. Certain among the organizations through which the SED maintains control over the East German population are unique, while others can be found in one form or another either in the USSR or in other bloc countries.

---

36. A report on the statute, that is, party rules, adopted by the ninth SED congress appeared in *Neues Deutschland*, 24 May 1976. See also K. W. Frickh, H. D. Schulz, and E. Nohara on this congress in *Deutschland Archiv* (June 1976), pp. 561–576.

37. *Staats–und Parteiapparat der DDR* (see note 5 above), pp. 32–33.

The ruling party itself is an organ of control, as are the four subordinate political movements already mentioned. During recent years, the National Front has been upgraded in importance. It represents a concept that the Soviets have implemented with varying degrees of success throughout their orbit. The 1968 East German constitution declares in Article 3 that the National Front serves to unite all forces of the people to act jointly in accordance with the principle that each is responsible for all.

The Free German Youth (FDJ) organization is probably the most effective agent of SED control. It has affiliations with its Soviet counterpart, the Komsomol, and with other bloc youth organizations, as well as with the World Federation of Democratic Youth. It has 2,157,734 members ranging in age from thirteen to twenty-five, many of whom also belong to the Socialist Unity party. The directorates of both organizations interlock. The FDJ secretary, Egon Krenz, is a candidate member of the SED Politburo.[38] The standard fare of Marxist-Leninist indoctrination is given to all FDJ members as preparation for membership in the ruling party. Admission to this youth organization takes place via a typical military ceremony.

Young children from the ages of six through twelve are urged to join the Pioneers. Membership in the Pioneers and in the older youth movement is promoted by monopolies over sports facilities[39] and education; these are controlled through FDJ cooperation with the trade unions. All vacations and entertainment, as well as entrance examinations for universities and educational scholarships, are administered by these regime organizations. Non-membership or even poor performance as a member may deprive the young East German of an opportunity for advancement.

A particularly useful function of the Free German Youth movement for the SED is its activity in observing and reporting. Every school class has at least one FDJ member who reports on the teacher and on other students. These young informers are also used to watch older officials in government agencies, factories, and businesses. Consequently, the FDJ attracts many opportunists and unprincipled youths to its ranks. It is not by any means a popular organization. Many young persons refuse to join despite its monopoly position.

The Free German Trade-Union Federation (FDGB), like labor organizations in all communist-ruled states, has no real bargaining power for the improvement of wages or working conditions. It is an instrument of control, supervision, observation, and reporting. About 96 percent (more than eight million members) of East German workers belong to one of the 250,848 trade-union groups.[40] Most are employed in state-owned industries, where organizational control by

---

38. For his biography, see Buch, *op. cit.* (in note 31 above).

39. An excellent series on GDR sports appeared in the *New York Times*, 20 through 22 December 1976.

40. *SK: Das Sozialistische Nachrichtenmagazin* (January 1975); Hamburg.

SED activists is tight and well disciplined. Workers in the diminishing private sector represent only a small percentage of the population; here the FDGB exercises somewhat less influence.

The primary usefulness of a trade union to the regime is its ability to organize the labor force to increase productive efforts and fulfill national goals. For these purposes the East Germans have copied the Stakhanovite system from the USSR. Throughout the GDR the example for other laborers is a miner named Adolf Hennecke. In 1948 he supposedly became dissatisfied with his normal output of 6.3 cubic meters of coal during an eight-hour shift and surpassed this quota by about 400 percent. This achievement and similar efforts in other industries are held before workers as examples of efficient production.

Such "records" are usually produced under optimum conditions. Teams of workers with party activists as leaders challenge one another in socialist competition. Often those who are not engaged in such contests attempt to hold down the norms by resisting the incentives given for overfulfillment. Activists, on the other hand, have the task of obtaining more work out of one or two select squads in order to provide a justification for raising the norms.

In a typical case the activist is given a project with a team of fresh laborers and the best equipment to show that a rate of production significantly higher than the norm is possible. Then a union meeting is held to honor the team and to vote "voluntarily" for increasing the norm by a certain percentage. At times this is done in honor of a forthcoming event or even a prominent individual. It is considered unwise for a member to speak against an increase, abstain from voting, or vote negatively when one of these proposals is brought up at a trade-union meeting. Other methods for increasing production include the payment of wages[41] on the basis of piecework and the encouragement of "volunteering" for extra shifts.

The Democratic League of Women has a membership of approximately 1.3 million. It allegedly works for the equal rights that are guaranteed by the constitution. These include the rights to perform all kinds of manual labor and to provide half of the support for a family. According to official statistics, almost four million women comprise about half the total East German trade-union membership. Nearly 85 percent of all women between the ages of eighteen and sixty hold jobs in the GDR.[42]

The Fighting Units of the Working Class are militia groups that are recruited by local SED organizations and are politically responsible to the ruling party. Militarily, they report directly to the Interior ministry's chief administration for the East German people's police. Politically reliable persons from twenty-five to sixty who work in industry, farming, or administration are sought out to become

41. The minimum wage has been increased by fifty marks to four hundred marks per month. East Berlin radio, 8 December 1976.

42. *Tribuene,* 4 June 1975; East Berlin.

members. Training is conducted by SED members who are officers in the people's police and by the East German armed forces. These fighting units receive four hours of training per week in light arms, are uniformed, and number about five hundred thousand men organized into battalions that comprise three or four companies; there are about a hundred members in each company. One battalion out of four is given the heavy equipment that would be allocated to an equivalent army unit of motorized infantry. A number of autonomous mobile companies also exist, all heavily equipped for action outside their own districts in cooperation with the regular armed forces. The purpose of the other units is to suppress local disturbances and, in accordance with the oath taken by members, to protect socialist achievements with their lives.[43]

The Society for Sports and Technology is steadily gaining in importance both as a premilitary and a paramilitary organization; it has about 1.5 million young participants. The avowed purpose is to instill socialist soldierly virtues in members and to prepare them for service in the National People's Army.[44] Youngsters are attracted by free courses in auto mechanics, parachute jumping, driving, marksmanship, etc.

Ideology.   The habit of ideological mimicry, which requires quick adjustment to keep in step with the Moscow line, has been followed in East Germany with few signs of the independent developments that have appeared in other parts of the bloc. The party line is coordinated with that of the USSR and embarrassment over mandatory reversals of position seems to have been minimal.

In GDR economic theory, which is closely coordinated with Marxist-Leninist principles, centralized control and ideological aims usually supersede purely economic considerations. Even so, the ideas of Soviet economist Yevsei Liberman, whose concept of "profitability" appeared rather un-Marxist, began to show up in East German writings after experimental application in the USSR. The SED sixth congress even reversed its positions by endorsing the concept of profit as well as the law of supply and demand. This led to the adoption of the "New Economic System," which advocated economic planning based more on expediency than on ideological imperatives. Since its introduction, the New Economic System has gone through several modifications, with the "leading role" of the SED reemphasized. In the 1968 constitution (Article 9), even after the 1974 amendments, the socialist planned economy is said to combine central state planning with individual responsibility by commodity producers and local state organs.

---

43. *Deutsches Monatsblatt* (June 1975); Ludz, *op. cit.* (in note 34 above), pp. 456–457; *Neues Deutschland*, 27–28 November 1976.

44. *Die Welt*, 5 June 1974.

DOMESTIC AND FOREIGN POLICIES

The already mentioned October 1975 treaty of friendship between the Soviet Union and the German Democratic Republic was signed because the GDR allegedly "has become a sovereign, independent socialist state, a full member of the United Nations."[45] It would be difficult, however, to find instances in which East Germany has exercised any such prerogatives, even at the UN, which it joined in 1973. Under the leadership of Walter Ulbricht and Erich Honecker, the GDR has echoed every major Soviet policy since it came into existence. Even the introduction of visa requirements on 1 January 1977 must have received USSR approval, especially since it violates four-power agreements regarding Berlin.

Paradoxically, only in its reluctance to follow the Soviet lead in destalinization has East Germany displayed some independence, or so it would appear. In response to Moscow's policy that was enunciated in early June 1953, Ulbricht promised an easing of some restrictions and a greater emphasis on the production of consumers' goods. He failed, however, to modify a decision to increase work norms that had, in effect, brought about a reduction in wages. The result was an uprising during which workers demanded economic reform, free elections, and the release of political prisoners. The disorder spread throughout East Germany, but was put down by Soviet troops. Ulbricht immediately fell back on the tried and trusted remedy of a purge in the SED hierarchy and reprisals against leaders of the rebellion.

In 1956 a period of liberalization again seemed to be in the offing after Khruschev's secret denigration of Stalin at the twentieth congress of the Soviet communist party. The response in some of the bloc states was a turn toward national communism and attempts to gain limited freedom from total domination by the USSR. Ulbricht's reaction to these attempts took the form of purges, although he paid lip service to destalinization and was, indeed, the first among East European leaders publicly to denounce Stalin. This did not prevent him from continuing to apply the old methods of repression.

As political tensions increased over the Berlin question in mid-1961, the number of refugees grew from more than thirty thousand during the month of July to more than forty thousand in the first ten days of August. On the night of 13 August the border was sealed on the orders of the German Democratic Republic, but some three million East Germans had already fled to the West. The Berlin Wall slowed the flow of refugees to a comparative trickle, but left the GDR condemned in the eyes of the world as a police state that retained control over its citizens primarily by physical means.[46]

---

45. Preamble, as given by *Pravda*, 8 October 1975.

46. Between 1961 and 1969 arrests for political reasons in the GDR involved 10,090 persons. *Sueddeutsche Zeitung*, 8 August 1969; Munich. More than 100,000 East Germans applied for exit permits during 1976, according to the *New York Times*, 20 January 1977.

Like the USSR, the East German regime limits the rights of free speech and assembly through its power of licensing. Nothing may be printed without a government permit. No meetings may be held unless official authorization is obtained. These devices are particularly important in the contest between church and state. In matters of religion, the regime is primarily concerned with Protestant churches rather than Roman Catholic ones, which remain in a minority. A religious census in 1965 showed that close to 80 percent of the population, or about 13.6 million East Germans, belonged to the Evangelical (Lutheran) church. A more recent estimate (1975) gives 12.5 million Protestants and 1.28 million Catholics.[47]

After the final separation between East and West Germany at the end of the 1940s, pressure on the churches in the GDR became increasingly evident. The regime made attempts to censor sermons of pastors and simultaneously to gain the political support of the Evangelical church. The basic position of the church was stated in a letter to the Soviet military governor, Marshal V. D. Sokolovskiy, by the presiding bishops.[48] According to this document, Christians were obligated to obey the orders of the state as long as these did not contravene moral law. The church claimed the right to support or criticize governmental measures, but only on moral and not on political grounds. Despite the government's attempts to isolate the East German churches, close ties have been secretly maintained with their Western counterparts.[49]

Church and state have come into conflict also on the issue of education. Although the church accepted the removal of religion as a subject from the public school system after the war, it has registered opposition to the use of schools for preaching atheism. The church has also taken a stand against the regime's electoral practices, particularly the wording of referendum questions. It has aroused the anger of state officials by its refusal to grant a blanket endorsement to regime policies by way of a loyalty oath.

Over the years attacks against the church by the government have assumed various forms. Travel and contact between East and West are severely restricted. The church press and its meetings have been controlled through the licensing power. State subsidies have been withdrawn, and the right of the church to conduct door-to-door solicitation drives has been restricted. Church relief agencies have been closed and their leaders arrested. On the other hand, about sixty "progressive" pastors established a formal organization at Leipzig that is subsidized by the regime.

Probably the most successful mechanism the state has employed against the church has been the usurpation of rites and ceremonies. Government rituals now exist for such occasions as baptism, marriage, and death. The best known is the

47. Ludz, *op. cit.* (in note 34 above), p. 713.

48. Richard W. Solberg, *God and Caesar in East Germany* (New York, 1961), p. 59.

49. *New York Times*, 4 April 1976.

youth consecration (*Jugendweihe*), which is akin to the ceremony of church confirmation; in it young people between the ages of twelve and sixteen dedicate themselves to socialism rather than to Christianity. Failure to participate in this ceremony often closes the door to further education or favorable employment opportunities. An East German pastor, Oskar Bruesewitz, immolated himself in front of his church at Zeitz (Anhalt) as a protest against the regime's infringement upon access to religious life by young people.[50]

The 1949 constitution still contained detailed regulations concerning the relationship between church and state. The 1968 document, as it was amended in 1974, severely limits the power of the church (Article 20), but does add that every citizen has the right to profess and practice a religion. For may years the Evangelical Church of Germany withstood numerous attempts to end its existence as the one remaining all-German organization and thus bridge between East and West. In 1968, however, announcement was made of the pending amalgamation of the churches in the German Democratic Republic into a newly established "Federation of Evangelical Churches in the GDR." The break was formalized in September 1969 when the first synod of this federation was held at Potsdam.[51]

Life is also difficult on the economic front. In proper communist fashion, the economy has been oriented toward heavy industry at the expense of consumers' goods. Farm policies in East Germany have been just as disastrous as they have elsewhere in the bloc. Official food rationing was abolished in 1958, but each consumer was required to purchase his basic food supplies from a particular store. This requirement in effect continued rationing, but his policy has been abandoned and reinstituted during the 1960s in accordance with the availability of supplies. Even in good times distribution remains a major problem. Two major reasons can be cited for the inability of the GDR to fill its agricultural requirements. The cession of the lands east of the Oder and Neisse rivers to Poland resulted in the loss of one-fourth of the arable land possessed by all of prewar Germany. Probably even more important is the fact that collectivization and communist mismanagement have stifled production.

Collectivization came rather slowly to East Germany. At the end of the war about one-third of the total agricultural land was seized from large landholders and redistributed to individual peasants and to collective farms. By the end of 1959 only half of all farms had been collectivized. Between February and April of 1960, however, the program was pushed through almost to completion in a manner similar to that employed during the early 1930s in the Soviet Union. The results were very much the same. An immediate decrease in grain production

---

50. *Der Spiegel* (30 August 1976), p. 36.

51. *Christ und Welt*, 6 March 1970. A report on "trustful talks" between Berlin-Brandenburg Evangelical Church representatives and GDR officials appeared in *Neues Deutschland*, 27–28 November 1976.

took place, and even today the annual deficit totals several million tons per year. Major shortages of meat and of livestock products followed. Farmers are not interested in collective work and they devote as much time as possible to their private garden plots. Remedial actions taken by the GDR have included the "industrialization" of agriculture, increasing political controls, and the pressing of communist youth groups into emergency service during crucial times during the year. However, this last device has failed, as mentioned earlier. (See table 25.)

Elsewhere the German Democratic Republic displays an economy that is seriously distorted by the demands of the Council for Mutual Economic Assistance (CMEA). East Germany, which became a member of that organization in 1950, today specializes in the production of machinery, chemicals, certain consumers' goods, railroad rolling stock, ships, optical goods, and scientific instruments for the bloc. Raw materials are imported mainly from the other East European countries and from the USSR, and their rising prices have adversely affected the East German economy. Seventy percent of the GDR's foreign trade remains with other communist-ruled countries, and the Soviet Union is its principal trading partner.[52].

Despite the fact that it was looted of some ten to twenty billion dollars worth of industrial capital goods and production in the years following the Second World War, by the late 1950s East Germany could show a fair measure of economic vitality. In 1959 it adopted a seven-year plan that included the goal of surpassing West Germany by 1961 in per capita production. During 1959 a growth rate of 12.4 percent was claimed. This declined to 8 percent in 1960, then to 6.2 percent during 1961, and subsequently averaged close to 6 percent through 1969. Obviously the goal of overtaking the Federal Republic of Germany could not be achieved, although it was subsequently claimed that this would occur by 1975; this, of course, did not happen.

In the past East Germany's economic performance has not always been up to its optimistic forecasts, although in many ways the country is credited with its own "economic miracle." The seven-year plan for 1959–1965, with its ambitious goals, had to be abandoned two years early; by the middle of 1962 it became clear that the plan had been based on faulty estimates of capacity and costs. It was replaced by the 1964–1970 "perspective plan," which was revealed at the sixth SED congress. Fundamental changes in the economy, based on the socialist system, and preparations for a new 1971–1975 plan were next announced by the Council of State. The changes envisaged a combination of

---

52. Half of all machine tools and instruments plus over one-third of the heavy engineering machinery exported by CMEA to the USSR during 1976–1980 will come from East Germany, which has undertaken most of the work on several large projects in the Soviet Union: a gas pipeline, a pulp plant, an asbestos combine, and an electric power grid. *Christian Science Monitor,* 5 November 1976. For details on the 1977 GDR-USSR trade agreement, totaling 6.4 billion rubles, see *Neues Deutschland,* 15 December 1976.

TABLE 25

EAST GERMAN GRAIN DEFICIT, 1964–1974
(in thousands of metric tons)

Production, imports and consumption	1964	1966	1968	1970	1972	1974
Apparent total grain available for consumption	8,143.6	7,688.5	9,468.1	—	—	—
Domestic production	6,184.6	5,917.5	7,829.1	6,456,465	8,563,239	9,703,236
Total imports	1,959.0	1,771.0	1,639.0	—	—	—
Imports which the Soviet Union provided	1,236.0	1,160.0	1,216.0	1,694,000	1,209,000	1,453,000

SOURCE: *Statistisches Jahrbuch der Deutschen Demokratischen Republik 1975* (East Berlin, 1975), pp. 194–195, 277, and 64 of appendix.

strong central planning for "structure-determining tasks" and the assignment of responsibility for production to individual enterprises and local state authorities. In fact this meant a curtailment of power at the factory level and the elimination of what previous reforms had hailed as "a certain self-regulation in the economic system." The most recent five-year plan (1976–1980) increases the integration of the GDR economy with the USSR and other CMEA member states.

There are several reasons for the economic difficulties East Germany has experienced. These include forced industrialization, which resulted in such errors as an expenditure of six hundred million dollars for construction of a huge steel combine at former Stalinstadt that has been unable to produce anything except crude pig iron. Normal development was also hindered by Soviet and CMEA requirements. Plans for the development of Rostock as a major shipbuilding center and seaport were suspended because of competition with the Polish port of Szczecin. The aircraft industry was abandoned altogether. Automobile and textile plants were held back. An industrial complex for uranium mining that employs 140,000 workers is being maintained at the Wismuth Aktiengesellschaft works simply to fulfill the needs of the USSR. There is no evidence that the East German regime has resisted CMEA policies as some of the other bloc countries have done rather successfully. Yet the GDR has attained the highest standard of living within the bloc, and despite all obstacles and demands it has achieved the rank of tenth most industrialized country in the world.[53]

In the area of foreign policy, the GDR is vitally concerned with its own relationship with the Federal Republic of Germany. For years after World War II the division of Germany remained an emotionally charged and utterly unacceptable condition for both German states. Yet by 1969 it had become clear that bringing the two parts of the country together might be impossible because of various conflicting interests, and that reunification was not a realistic goal. In the East the chances for reunification were limited by Soviet design and by the fears of GDR rulers for their socialist achievements; in the West they were circumscribed by Allied and NATO security requirements and concern over the status of West Berlin.

Moreover, the 1974 constitutional amendment defining the German Democratic Republic as a "socialist state of workers and farmers" implies that the maintenance of two separate German states is inevitable. This recognition had been underscored by long-standing verbal attacks that accused West Germany of revanchism, militarism, support for neo-Nazism, and the creation of obstacles to détente in Europe. Separateness had also been a clear factor in East German demands for full recognition of the GDR as a sovereign state under international law, the renunciation of the Federal Republic of Germany's (FRG) claims to sole representation abroad, and the acceptance of existing frontiers.

---

53. Part of this success has been due to almost five billion dollars in loans from the West, interest payments on which total about four hundred million dollars annually. *Christian Science Monitor*, 5 November 1976.

After years of diplomatic probes, an agreement between the two Germanys[54] on diplomatic recognition came into force in June 1973. The document, known as "The Treaty on the Basis for Relations between the GDR and the FRG" (Basic Treaty) included establishment of diplomatic relations and arrangements to facilitate transit by West German visitors. The new *Ostpolitik* of the FRG and this treaty have not effected an easing of tensions between East and West, however, but rather have delineated and intensified them. The East German government also reaped the benefits of wide international recognition, one of its basic objectives, through this treaty and the subsequent Helsinki agreement of 1 August 1975. The attainment of international status is being used by the GDR to affect the status of West Berlin vis-a-vis the FRG and to further enhance its position as the "other Germany."

The GDR regime has devised other obstacles to impair East-West contacts that had been guaranteed in the Basic Treaty. Vigilance has been intensified, including the intimidation of citizens and the placing of restrictions on their contacts with Western relatives and friends. Administraive devices such as increased fees and inspection times before entrance into East Berlin have also been imposed.[55] A further development in the GDR-FRG relationship has been a decline in the ransoming of East German political prisoners by the Federal Republic of Germany. From 1971 to 1973 an average of 3,451 such prisoners were purchased each year at a price of up to forty thousand dollars per individual, paid in consumers' goods. During the first nine months of 1976 only 950 releases could be arranged. Since the practice began, about $250 million has been paid as ransom in this manner.[56]

Trade between the two Germanys has grown over the past decade. The Federal Republic is now the GDR's main Western outlet, and the East German debt to the FRG is about one billion dollars.[57] This exchange, which has been considered internal German commerce since the 1956 treaty of Rome, has raised consternation among Common Market neighbors of West Germany. They are concerned about the free circulation within the European Economic Community of exports from East Germany, a country belonging to a different bloc. GDR firms have also been trying to capture West German markets by undercutting prices, a practice that has brought a reaction from FRG authorities.[58]

Another important aspect of foreign relations involves de jure recognition of the German Democratic Republic by states other than communist-ruled ones. With FRG agreement, East Germany has been able to obtain diplomatic

---

54. Ruediger von Wechmar (introd.), *Der Grundvertrag* (Hamburg, 1973), p. 224.

55. *New York Times*, 4 April 1976. Visas good until midnight of the day issued cost five East German marks and $2.85 must be exchanged into GDR currency. *Neues Deutschland*, 1−2 January 1977.

56. *Die Welt*, 20 October 1976; *New York Times*, 4 December 1976.

57. *Deutschland-Union Dienst*, no. 132 (13 July 1976); Bonn.

58. *Die Welt*, 26 September 1975.

recognition from all West European countries and the United States (4 September 1974) along with membership in the United Nations. It has since then entrenched itself in many international organizations and become involved in worldwide activities. An East German source reported that the GDR had established diplomatic relations with 121 foreign countries.[59] Other contacts include national liberation movements, vis-a-vis which East Germany may be playing the role of proxy for the Soviet Union. Thus, on 7 December 1976, East Berlin radio announced that two special Interflug aircraft had flown "important consignments" to the African National Congress and the South-West Africa People's Organization.

---

59. *Neues Deutschland,* 19 May 1976. See also Eric Waldmann, "Germany: German Democratic Republic," in R. F. Staar (ed.), *1977 Yearbook on International Communist Affairs* (Stanford, Ca., 1977).

Chapter 5

Hungarian People's Republic

During the so-called liberation of Hungary, and under Soviet tutelage, a provisional government was established in December 1944 at Budapest while that capital was still occupied by the Germans. A temporary legislature also came into being based on five political movements, including a small but highly disciplined communist one.[1] The leader of the coalition was the Smallholders' party, a popular and moderate group. The provisional assembly included a plurality of communists, however, and the police force came under their direction. Real power remained with Red Army occupation forces, specifically the (Soviet) chairman, Kliment Voroshilov, of the Allied Control Commission.

Despite universal suffrage and the fact that the November 1945 elections were unencumbered by direct pressure from the USSR, the Hungarian communists still felt that they could win a plurality. To their surprise, they received only 17 percent of the vote.[2] During the ensuing struggle over the allocation of ministries, Soviet influence successfully placed a communist, Imre Nagy (and shortly afterward Laszlo Rajk), in the position of Interior minister. This gave the Soviet advisors control over the police.

By early 1948 the communists had penetrated every department of the government and actually dominated the Hungarian state apparatus.[3] The approach used by Matyas Rakosi, the leader of the Hungarian communist party, during this period has been described as follows:

> With the famous "salami tactics" he first went into a coalition with the Smallholders, Peasant, and Social-Democratic parties to crush the Conservatives, then annihilated the Smallholders party with the help of the

1. The five political parties (communist, social-democratic, citizens-democratic, smallholders, and people's peasant) organized themselves into a National Independence Front. Sandor Balogh, *Parlamenti es Partharcok Magyarorszagon, 1945–1947* (Budapest, 1972), chapters 2 and 3.

2. During the next election in August 1947, the communists resorted to various kinds of fraud and intimidation but could increase this figure to only 22.3 percent. *Ibid.*, pp. 98 and 525.

3. Ernst C. Helmreich (ed.), *Hungary* (New York, 1957), p. 81.

remaining two parties. Then he suborned the Peasant party and absorbed the Social-Democrats, killing off or imprisoning their party leadership. Politicians were bribed, blackmailed, driven to exile, imprisoned, or sentenced to death.[4]

As a prerequisite for a complete takeover and the promulgation of a new constitution, the so-called Hungarian People's Front for Independence came forth with a single list of candidates before the elections of May 1949; after that full communist control was established.

CONSTITUTION OF 1949

The principal feature of the constitution that was adopted after the takeover in 1949 was provision for the inauguration of a people's democracy[5] on the Soviet pattern. Like all satellite constitutions adopted subsequent to the expulsion of Yugoslavia from the East European bloc in June 1948, this one also mentions the prominent role of the USSR in making possible Hungary's development toward socialism. The preamble declares that

> A new era of our history began when in the course of her victories won in the Second World War, the Soviet Union liberated our country from the oppression of Fascism and opened the road to democratic development for the Hungarian people. With the friendly support of the Soviet Union, the working people rebuilt the country . . . in national unity, the Hungarian profile is busy in the complete building of socialism.[6]

A comparison between the Soviet and Hungarian constitutions show that most of the latter was inspired by the former. Variations exist, but these all emanate from the theoretical assumption that the USSR has achieved socialism, while Hungary has not. This difference appears in a number of instances, as in the articles dealing with the status of workers, the ownership of the means of production, and citizenship.

The USSR is said to be a socialist state, whereas Hungary still unofficially admits the existence of classes other than those of industrial workers and working peasants. The Hungarian constitution uses the term small-commodity producers in Article 12, which recognizes their "socially useful economic activities." The new intelligentsia remains a distinct class; industrial workers and peasants may

---

4. George Paloczi-Horvath, *The Undefeated* (Boston, 1959), p. 246.

5. Zbigniew K. Brzezinski, *The Soviet Bloc* (New York, 1961), rev. ed., p. 78. Actually, the third congress of the Hungarian communist party, in September 1946, had already announced a "people's democracy."

6. [Hungary], *The Constitution of the Hungarian People's Republic* (Budapest, 1972), consolidated text with amendments through 19 April 1972; henceforth cited as *Constitution*.

become transformed into intelligentsia by means of appropriate education. In Hungary, also, a degree of private enterprise is still permitted.[7] The Soviet constitution allows private ownership by its citizens "based on their labor and precluding the exploitation of the labor of others," meaning that no one outside the family may be hired. Hungary is still working to "dislodge capitalist elements," whereas in the USSR the capitalist system has allegedly been liquidated already.

Since the Soviet Union claims to have achieved the level of socialism in 1936, it is assumed that all persons in that country are instilled with the collectivist spirit. In the USSR, either a citizen will work or he will not eat. Hungary, which is still at the lower stage of a people's democracy, has not worded its constitution so strongly in this respect. As Article 14 of the basic law clearly states, Hungary only strives to apply the socialist principle: "From each according to his ability, to each according to his work."

In Hungary, higher education was at first guaranteed only to every worker. The right to an education for all citizens, even for those with a "class alien" background (meaning persons whose parents are neither industrial workers nor peasants), was not established until 1963. Faith in the "socialist order"—in other words, the regime—continues to be a prerequisite for all university applicants.[8] In the USSR each citizen allegedly has the right to an education. Again, the difference can be ascribed to the level of socialist achievement. Hungary admits to the existence of classes other than workers. On the other hand, exploiters theoretically have been eliminated from the Soviet Union.

Parliament.   Hungary has a unicameral system, with the parliament designated the highest organ of state authority. The constitution charges parliament with responsibility for passing laws, determining the state budget, deciding on the national economic plan, electing the Presidential Council and the Council of Ministers, controlling ministries, declaring war and concluding peace, and exercising the prerogative of amnesty. Despite these official duties, this "highest organ" is actually a constitutional fiction whose work is carried out by the Presidential Council[9] between sessions of parliament.

"The members of parliament . . . are elected by the constituents by universal, equal, and direct suffrage, by secret ballot," says the Hungarian constitution; like the constitution of the USSR, it provides for direct election of representatives to all legislative levels. Needless to say, the slate of delegates is

---

7. For example, a total of 10,814 private-entrepreneur retail shops and catering units still exist. [Hungary], *Statisztikai evkonyv 1975* (Budapest, 1976), p. 296.

8. Professionals who graduate from universities now must compete for listed positions and must work at least three years in jobs for which they are qualified. Decree in *Magyar kozlony,* 15 July 1976.

9. Note, for example, the Presidential Council's decree on the expropriation of private agricultural land that came into force on 1 January 1977. Budapest radio, 27 August 1976.

nominated and controlled by the Hungarian Socialist [communist] Workers' party, although a few multiple candidacies have been allowed.[10]

Parliament meets in regular session three or four times a year. Its speaker, two deputies, and six recorders are chosen from the membership. All issues are decided by a simple majority, except for constitutional changes, which require a two-thirds vote. Laws are signed by the chairman and the secretary of the Presidential Council and then are published in the official gazette.

Presidential Council. At its first sitting the parliament elects from its membership a Presidential Council consisting of a chairman, two deputies, a secretary, and seventeen members. According to the constitution, the functions of the Presidential Council include calling general elections; convening parliament; initiating legislation; holding plebiscites; concluding treaties, appointing diplomatic representatives, and receiving foreign diplomats; appointing civil servants; and performing the duties of parliament when it is not in session.

The chairman of the Presidential Council is the nominal chief of state.[11] It is interesting to note that a member of the cabinet, that is, the Council of Ministers, is ineligible for election to the Presidential Council. Article 30 of the constitution provides the Presidential Council with the authority to dissolve local organs of government "whose activities infringe [upon] the constitution or gravely imperil the interests of the people."

Council of Ministers. The third part of the national government, the Council of Ministers, is referred to in the constitution as the highest organ of state administration. At the end of 1976 it comprised a chairman or premier, five deputy premiers, and the heads of seventeen ministries and one agency.[12] Article 24 of the constitution established twenty-six ministries, but changes since that time, effected primarily by combining ministries, have reduced this number. The sole agency whose head has cabinet rank is the National Planning Office. Eight other agencies are chaired by state secretaries. The Council of Ministers exercises administrative powers involving the enforcement of parliamentary laws and decrees issued by the Presidential Council; the fulfillment of economic plans; the promulgation of decrees that do not infringe on parliamentary legislation or that emanate from the Presidential Council; and the supervision of subordinate, local organs. Article 39 states that "the Council of Ministers is responsible to Parliament for its activities. It is bound to render regularly account of its work to Parliament."

---

10. Article 71, *Constitution*, p. 55. In the last three elections, more than one candidate ran in nine (1967), then forty-nine (1971), then thirty-four (1975) out of 352 constituencies.

11. He is Pal Losonczi, who had been Agriculture minister from 1960 to 1967. RFE, *Communist Party-Government Line-Up* (Munich, 7 December 1976), p. 15.

12. The incumbents are listed in *ibid.*

Local Organs of State Power.   For the purpose of administration Hungary is divided into counties, districts, towns, and communities, with some larger towns or cities subdivided into precincts. Local organs of state administration exist at the county, district, and precinct levels.[13] Members of these councils are elected to four-year terms by voters in the areas they represent.

Local councils are given authority to supervise all state organs (except the armed forces) that deal with maintenance of social, cultural, health, and labor regulations. Although civil police organs are directly under the national government, they are theoretically required to submit reports concerning public-security conditions to council meetings and to their executive committees.

The councils functioned in essentially the same manner at all levels, with each receiving instructions directly from Budapest until in 1971 local government underwent a reform that provided the councils with greater policy autonomy and financial independence. This system allegedly provides an efficient administrative structure by assuring the implementation of directives as they filter down from the top to the lowest levels of government.[14]

The most important part of any local council is its executive committee, which is elected at the first organizational session. It is presided over by a chairman, who is assisted by one or more deputies and a secretary. The executive committee exercises control over the local administrative apparatus. Its relation to the local council approximates that of the Council of Ministers to parliament: theoretically subordinate but actually dominant. On the county and district levels, the executive committee is supported in its work by a secretariat and a number of specialized administrative organs. One of the party devices for supervising the work of executive committees is the establishment of permanent committees. These units report via the communist-party chain of command to Budapest.

The Judiciary.   Justice in Hungary is administered by the Supreme Court and county and district courts. The highest tribunal supervises the judicial activities of all of the lower ones. Specifically, according to the constitution, the courts "protect and guarantee the political, economic and social order of the state, the rights and lawful interests of the citizens, and inflict punishment on the perpetration of criminal acts."[15]

Government in Practice.   Constitutionally, the Presidential Council has a list of functions that appears most impressive. In reality, it does not play any

---

13. These councils, which are equivalent to soviets in the USSR, are mentioned in an amendment to the constitution. See Law VIII, published in *Magyar kozlony* (1954), no. 73; Russian translation in Ya. V. Yakimovich, *Vengerskaya Narodnaya Respublika* (Moscow, 1960), p. 27.

14. See Article 43, *Constitution,* p. 34, for the specific responsibilities of the people's councils.

15. Article 50, *ibid.*, p. 40.

policy-making role in government. The fact that Istvan Dobi, who was the nominal chief of state between 1952 and 1967, had formerly been a leader in the Smallholders' party is indicative of his subservience to the communists.[16] Since the leading members of the ruling party are concentrated in the Council of Ministers, and the members of the Presidential Council may not be appointed to ministries, the Presidential Council is composed mostly of people who have limited influence.

It is likely that parliament has even less actual power and influence than the Presidential Council. In practice, all policies are formulated by the communist party hierarchy and sent to the Presidential Council for rubber-stamp approval while parliament is not in session. Since parliament is rarely in session, and since approval by the Presidential Council is binding, the requirement that all enactments by the Council be submitted to parliament is purely academic.

A list of individuals in government shows that the premier, one of his deputies, the National Assembly chairman, the head of trade unions, and several members of the Presidential Council also sit on the Politburo. (See table 26). According to the constitution, the Council of Ministers is subordinate to both the Presidential Council and parliament. However, in practice, it is subordinate to the Hungarian communist party, which controls all political, economic, social, and cultural activities.

Participation by nonparty members in responsible positions of the People's Patriotic Front once led some observers to conclude erroneously that this organization might become an opposition party. Janos Kadar, the communist party's first secretary, in a speech before the Front, clarified this point by presenting official government policy as follows:[17]

> In the service of determined political purposes the Western bourgeois papers publish quite often articles about the liberalization, the loosening of the Kadar regime. The writers of such articles and the politicians standing behind them are taking their wish-dreams for reality. . . . They would like to promote and bring about our weakening; this is why they write that the detente of international atmosphere makes possible such a People's Front movement which can lead to the revival of the coalition parties.

HUNGARIAN SOCIALIST WORKERS' PARTY

Bela Kun, the leader of the Hungarian communist party in the aftermath of World War I, in 1919 attempted to establish a communist republic.[18] After the collapse of his regime, the communist movement almost disappeared. Many of

16. Helmreich, *op. cit.* (in note 3 above), p. 85.

17. Kossuth radio, 19 March 1964. Proceedings of the Front's sixth congress were broadcast over Budapest radio, 17-19 September 1976.

18. Ivan Volgyes, *The Hungarian Soviet Republic, 1919* (Stanford, Ca., 1970), p. 90.

TABLE 26

COMMUNIST LEADERSHIP IN HUNGARY, 1976

Political Bureau (15)	Born	Other responsibility	Government post
Aczel, Gyorgy	1917		Deputy premier
Apro, Antal	1913		Chairman, National Assembly
Benke, Valeria	1920	Editor, *Tarsadalmi szemle*	
Biszku, Bela	1921	Secretary (cadres)	
Fock, Jeno	1916	–	–
Gaspar, Sandor	1917	Secretary General, Trade Unions	
Huszar, Istvan	1927	Planning Office Chairman	Deputy premier
Kadar, Janos	1912	First Secretary	
Lazar, Gyorgy	1924		Premier
Loszonczi, Pal	1919		Presidential Council Chairman
Marothy, Laszlo	1942	First Secretary, KISZ	
Nemes, Dezso	1908	Rector, Party Academy	
Nemeth, Karoly	1922	Secretary (economy)	
Ovari, Miklos	1925	Secretary (agitprop)	
Sarlos, Istvan	1921	Secretary General, Patriotic People's Front	

SOURCES: *A Magyar Szocialista Munkaspart XI. kongresszusa 1975. marcius 17 – 22* (Budapest, 1975), p. 244 (henceforth cited as *Eleventh Congress*); RFE, *Communist Party Line-Up* (Munich, 7 December 1976), pp. 14 – 16; and RFE, *Situation Report*, 25 March 1976.

its members fled to the USSR and continued to work there under Soviet direction. Others stayed behind to engage in revolutionary activities. Some of the emigrés formed the nucleus for a new communist party of Hungary as the Second World War was approaching its end. Matyas Rakosi, Erno Gero, Imre Nagy, and others returned to Hungary in 1944 to assume the leadership of the party at Debrecen, the temporary government capital on "liberated" soil. Another group of indigenous communists, headed by Laszlo Rajk, Janos Kadar, and Gyula Kallai, had been active during the war at Budapest. In February 1945 these two groups merged.

The party remained small at the end of the war. Under a policy of rapid expansion that was adopted at that time, the usual high degree of selectivity with regard to membership was disregarded in an effort to attract recruits. As a result, the number of members grew from two thousand in 1944 to more than 1.4 millon by 1949. Part of the increase was achieved through a merger with left-wing Social Democrats in 1948, and at that time a new name was adopted: the Hungarian Workers' party.[19] Discipline became tighter as the party gained more power.

Matyas Rakosi's wing of the communist movement, which was known as the "Muscovites," received support from the USSR and the Red Army. This man

19. For a study covering the early postwar period see Robert Gabor, *Organization and Strategy of the Hungarian Workers' [Communist] Party* (New York, 1952), especially pp. 1 – 15.

controlled the party and ruled Hungary from 1945 to July 1956, although his power was temporarily lessened when Imre Nagy held the premiership. Rakosi fell out of step with the destalinization program, however, and Khrushchev had him removed. He was succeeded by Erno Gero, but the Hungarians associated Gero with Rakosi's policies.

No discussion would be complete without some comment about the 1956 uprising and its effect on the people. This event not only left its mark on the participants but also colored subsequent internal and external policies. There is no doubt that one of the reasons why the revolt spread in Hungary was the brutal intervention by Soviet armed forces. The seeds of revolution, however, go back to the Stalinist hard line of Rakosi. Between 1953 and 1955 Hungarians enjoyed the more moderate policies of premier Imre Nagy.[20] This occurred because Moscow had dictated that Rakosi give up the premiership, although he retained the position of communist party leader.

In early 1955 the line shifted, Rakosi returned to full power, and Nagy was expelled from the party. As the government became more and more tyrannical, dissident elements (primarily students and the intelligentsia) began discussing open revolt. Although Rakosi was ousted by the Soviet Union in mid-1956, as mentioned above, by then the Hungarian communist party and the pro-Soviet government had lost control: they could neither effectively govern nor even rely on the armed forces. Great sympathy existed among the military for the revolutionary movement. The secret police (AVH) had become too weak to defend the regime alone.

The uprising in Hungary was to be short-lived; it became doomed to failure when its Freedom Fighters[21] were opposed by superior Soviet military power. The leaders of the USSR could not allow one of their satellites to defect from the bloc or even become neutral, let alone Western-oriented, because of the impact this might have on other East European states. It is against such a background that current Hungarian policies must be viewed. Details of the rebellion and its suppression are well known.[22] Janos Kadar, who was chosen by the Soviet

---

20. Subsequently, however, Nagy was accused by a Soviet writer of "left-wing errors" and "revisionism" during this period. M. A. Usievich, *Razvitie sotsialisticheskoi ekonomiki Vengrii* (Moscow, 1962), p. 132.

21. The name Freedom Fighters (*szabadsagharcosok*) originated during the 1848 insurrection led by Lajos Kossuth against Hapsburg rule. Russion troops aided the Austrians in putting down the insurrection. For the part played by the United States in allegedly "fomenting" the 1956 revolt see I. I. Orlik, *Vengerskaya Narodnaya Respublika* (Moscow, 1962), pp. 51−53.

22. See, for example, Ferenc A. Vali, *Rift and Revolt in Hungary* (Cambridge, Mass., 1961), p. 590. Some 32,000 refugees (including 1,800 students) came to the United States. *New York Times*, 31 December 1976. During the aftermath, about 63,000 Hungarians were deported to Siberia. Reportedly, 463 participants still remained in the central prison at Budapest; another 143, who were under eighteen in 1956, were executed as they came of age. Rev. Bela Fabian and Imre Kovacs, "Kadar's Hungary," *New York Times Magazine*, 24 January 1965, p. 6.

Union to be the new premier and party leader, took over both posts on 4 November 1956. The movement as it exists today has been shaped by Kadar. Its name, the Hungarian Socialist Workers' party (*Magyar Szocialista Munkaspart—MSZMP*), is the one he gave to the new organization.[23]

Membership and Support. The only relatively free elections held in Hungary since the Second World War took place in November 1945. The communists suffered a defeat, since 83 percent of the votes went to other parties, but they obtained representation in the government because of pressure by the Kremlin and the physical presence of Soviet troops in the country. In fact, the USSR gave permission for the elections only after receiving promises from the noncommunist parties that they would include communists in the future government.[24]

Following the 1956 revolt, the Kadar regime did not attempt to reconstruct the party along its former lines. The leaders became more selective and allegedly brought into membership only those who genuinely supported the communist movement; they hoped thus to develop a new hard core. During this period Kadar gradually purged the Rakosi and Gero elements. Starting with local and county organizations and ultimately moving to the top echelon, he eliminated dogmatic officials from responsible positions. In several cases die-hard Stalinists at the highest levels even found themselves expelled from the party.

By the fall of 1962 the strength of the Hungarian Socialist Workers' party had risen to more than half a million members.[25] This number amounted to about 5 percent of the population. With the passage of time, the composition of the party has also changed. For example, in 1966 the party claimed that more than 40 percent of its membership consisted of workers or former workers (at desk jobs, presumably) and 37.3 percent of the intelligentsia.[26] This would indicate that educated Hungarians were no longer boycotting the party. Because the leadership remained dissatisfied with the number of new members, ideological indoctrination had to be stepped up to increase the proportion of white-collar workers in the party (see table 27 for recent figures on social composition).

Local and factory organizations provide a lower-level course in communist policies and principles, townships offer intermediate instruction, and county and major city organs conduct advanced training. In addition to the Hungarian

---

23. A decision taken allegedly on his own initiative, according to a Soviet biography. Yu. Egorov (ed.), *Yanosh [Janos] Kadar* (Moscow, 1960), pp. 622—623.

24. Jozsef Koevago, "Establishment and Operation of a Communist State Order," in Robert F. Delaney (ed.), *This is Communist Hungary* (Chicago, 1958), p. 197.

25. Yanosh [Janos] Kadar, *Otchetnyi doklad Tsentralnogo Komiteta Vengerskoi Sotsialisticheskoi Rabochei Partii na VIII sezdu partii* (Moscow, 1964), p. 75. It was admitted that some 38 percent of these joined after May 1957, that is, following the revolt.

26. *Nepszabadsag*, 29 November 1966.

TABLE 27

HUNGARIAN SOCIALIST WORKERS' PARTY
SOCIAL COMPOSITION, 1970 AND 1975

Category	Tenth Congress (November 1970)		Eleventh Congress (March 1975)	
Industrial workers (including farm workers)	282,674	42.7	343,070	45.5
Intelligentsia (white-collar workers)	252,222	38.1	347,594	46.1
Others (armed forces, students, pensioners)	127,104	19.2	63,336	8.4
Total	662,000	100.0	754,000	100.0

SOURCES: *Nepszabadsag*, 29 November 1970; *Eleventh Congress*, pp. 6–7.

Socialist Workers' party, mass organizations such as the Communist Youth League (KISZ) and the Women's Association assist the communists in indoctrination work among the population. KISZ, for instance, has about 800,000 nominal members organized into 25,600 primary units.[27] They can be used by communist leaders to spread propaganda or to inform on nonmembers.

Party Organization.   The structure of the communist party is a familiar one that in general emulates the Soviet model. At the bottom of the pyramid are approximately 24,500 primary party organizations.[28] These include members in all types of work. The next level up consists of district party organizations in town and cities. Members of primary party organizations send representatives to district conferences. There is no democracy in this procedure, however, as the delegates are handpicked by district committees. Regional party organizations correspond to the nineteen major political subdivisions of the country and are run by regional committees elected at district conferences.

The national party congress meets every five years (the eleventh congress was held 17–22 March 1975) and elects a Central Committee to carry out policies. It now consists of 125 members[29] and no alternates. From the Central Committee in turn comes the Politburo, which has 15 members and no candidates; its chairman is the party leader. The Secretariat of the party, which is also part of the Central Committee, has 7 members and is responsible for supervising the implementation of Politburo decisions. Janos Kadar holds the office of First Secretary, that is, party leader.

27. *A Magyar Szocialista Munkaspart XI. kongresszusa 1975. marcius 17–22* (Budapest, 1975), p. 18.

28. *Ibid.*, p. 8.

29. *Ibid.*, pp. 236–244, lists all names.

Since the revolt in 1956, the Kadar regime has encouraged the development of a more relaxed political atmosphere. Probably because of this official attitude, party organization at the lower echelons is rather poor. The general level of schooling among rural party leaders remains inadequate. Up to 1960 national party leaders were interested above all in political reliability, and they cared little about formal education. Hence most villagers have gradually reached educational levels that are superior to those of the rural party chieftains. Kadar saw the danger in this development and began emphasizing the selection of nonparty experts for government work. Knowledge of particular fields is apparently held to be more important than blind adherence to communist ideology. There have been complaints about this trend, even though sensitive posts (such as in foreign affairs, police, and defense) cannot be held by nonparty members.

Party Leadership.   Most of the men who built up the party during 1944 and 1945 have by now died or gone into semiretirement because of disfavor. Of those who formally reestablished the movement toward the end of the war, other than Kadar, only a few (Apro, Biszku, Fock, Gaspar, Nemes) remain in good standing. (See table 26.) Today the highest posts in the party are held by a younger group than has been the case at any other time. During the years 1945−1956 these men had worked in lower-level party organizations, in the mass movements, or within government agencies. Kadar, as leader of the party, is assisted by a deputy, Bela Biszku, and five other national secretaries. Biszku is believed to be the heir apparent, although Karoly Nemeth may also be a competitor.

Policies.   At the eighth congress of the Hungarian communist movement in November 1962, Kadar placed emphasis on policies that suggested that the party had broken with its Stalinist past. One of these policies, involving amnesty for 1956 revolutionaries, has had international significance. It has removed a main obstacle to the acceptance of the Kadar regime by the West in general and by the United States in particular.[30]

Speaking about his type of communism, Kadar later stated: "If anybody stands today to the left of the socialist order of the state, the order of building socialism, then he actually stands for nothing but petty bourgeois radicalism and a great many confused ideas."[31] However, his chief ideologist warned against

---

30. The USA raised its diplomatic relations with Hungary to the ambassadorial level on 28 November 1966. Subsequently, agreement on the repayment of debts for American goods purchased after the Second World War and on U.S. pensions to certain Hungarians was reached, according to Press Release no. 242, U.S. Department of State, *Bulletin* (15 August 1969), p. 214. See also U.S. Congress, Subcommittee on Europe, Committee on Foreign Affairs, "Hungarian Claims Legislation," *Hearing* (Washington, D.C., 4 April 1974); and *New York Times,* 5 December 1976, about the crown of St. Stephen as well as other treasures held at Ft. Knox, Ky.

31. Quoted in *East Europe* (April 1964), p. 42.

the West as the enemy who plays the old tune "according to which the personality cult [Stalinist-type terror] is the logical product of the socialist system." This man added that for many persons, even in Hungary, this conclusion had been "confirmed by the way in which Comrade Khrushchev was relieved of his duties."[32]

Although the party has liberalized some of its policies, provided the population with more freedom of action, and even restricted secret-police activities, it still rules Hungary. If the regime considers it necessary, it can and will institute tighter and harsher controls. Although Kadar stated that "he who is not against us is with us," this does not mean that persons who express themselves openly against the regime will go unpunished. The security police are powerful and ready. Even for a Kadar, there is no possibility of bridging the ultimate ideological gap and allowing an opposition party to function.

DOMESTIC AND INTRA-ORBITAL AFFAIRS

In Hungary, as in much of Eastern Europe, agriculture had fallen into a state of crisis during the years just before the Second World War. A catastrophic slump in farm prices, coupled with an uneconomic division of the land, had created a chaotic farming situation.[33] In 1945, with the approval of Soviet authorities, the communist Agriculture minister Imre Nagy ordered the expropriation of large landholdings and their distribution as small allotments to the peasantry. Some collectivization was introduced immediately because the communist party wanted to assist the "inevitable development" of *kolkhozy*, but the major drive was launched only after 1948.

Agricultural Policies.   The five-year plan covering 1950–1954 set extremely ambitious goals for the population. Statistics reveal that no governmental approach can so mismanage agricultural production as one based on a communist philosophy. The production of bread grain for this period totaled less than it had during 1911–1915, when the population had been nearly 25 percent smaller.[34] One of the former breadbaskets of Eastern Europe became an importer of grain.

The headlong rush by communists to collectivize after their 1948 takeover caused widespread dissatisfaction and antagonism. Agricultural production showed a decline because of poor organization and the use of coercion by regime leaders. Abortive means used to stimulate production included compulsory deliveries, high taxes, fines for alleged violation of administrative regulations,

---

32. Istvan Szirmai in *Tarsadalmi szemle* (April 1965); translated by *Hungarian Press Survey*, 20 April 1965.
33. Hubert Ripka, *Eastern Europe in the Post-War World* (New York, 1961), p. 9.
34. Vali, *op. cit.* (in note 22 above), p. 87.

and penalties ranging from admonition to death.[35] It is significant to note in table 28 the rapid increase in collective farms throughout Hungary during a period of less than four years (1959–1962); this expansion was due to the new policy under Kadar that, after initial excesses, avoided terror and stressed methods of persuasion as well as indirect pressure. It is apparent that one criterion for judging the effectiveness of any communist leadership is its ability to promote collectivization, which frequently occurs in direct proportion to the amount of pressure applied. By the end of 1975 some 94.7 percent of all arable land had been organized into collective or state farms. (See table 29.)

During 1975 the privately cultivated half-hectare household plots and ancillary farms, which occupied 18 percent of all cultivated land, accounted for a much larger percentage (50.5) of agricultural production than their total area would seem to justify.[36] One inference that can be drawn is that despite massive government efforts to promote collectivization, the profit motive still remains an important aspect of peasant psychology. Recent communist pronouncements seem to encourage intensive cultivation of existing household garden plots. The party also appears to recognize the importance of incentives in agriculture. One reason for this recognition is the fact that total employment in farming, especially of young people, has declined over the years, and that by 1980 another one hundred thousand persons, or 20 to 25 percent of those now working on collective farms, will have retired.[37]

As in other communist-ruled countries, the government in Hungary faced the problem of putting into effect impossible agricultural policies. A Budapest newspaper reported in 1969 that 2,840 collective farms had been studied for purposes of classification. These farms covered 28.5 percent of the country's arable land and employed about one-fourth of all collectivized farmers, yet they contributed only 20 percent of gross agricultural production.[38] A shortage of meat during the past several years was caused by a lack of incentives for fattening cattle. Comparative figures released by the regime indicate that in 1935 Hungary had 1,911,000 cattle; by 1975 this number had increased only to 2,017,000, and about 437,000 of these were on household plots.[39]

The country is again self-sufficient in food, as it was before the war. Hungary suffers, however, from a shortage of fertilizer, a situation that is prevalent

---

35. Even in 1957 there were no more than three thousand kulaks or wealthy peasants who "exploited" the labor of others. G. V. Barabashev, *Gosudarstvennyi stroi Vengerskoi Narodnoi Respubliki* (Moscow, 1961), p. 21, n. 2.

36. *Mezogazdasagi statisztikai zsebkonyv 1976*; cited in RFE, *Situation Report,* 14 December 1976. Kadar has stated that Hungary ranks first in per capita meat and second in egg production, compared with all CMEA and Common Market countries. *Nepszabadsag,* 15 December 1976.

37. Budapest radio, 19 and 23 November 1976; cited by RFE, *Situation Report,* 7 December 1976.

38. *Nepszabadsag,* 2 August 1969.

39. *Statistical Pocket Book of Hungary 1975*, p. 167. However, a record wheat yield of more than five million tons reportedly was achieved the following year. Budapest radio, 20 September 1976.

TABLE 28

AGRICULTURAL PRODUCTION COOPERATIVES, 1958–1976

Year	Number	Active members	Family workers (as of December 31)	Employees	Arable land (as percentage of total) (as of May 31)
1958	2,755	—	—	—	11.1
1959	4,158	—	—	—	28.1
1960	4,507	653,000	—	—	59.9
1961	4,204	815,000	—	—	75.1
1962	3,721	811,000	—	—	75.5
1965	3,278	684,000	171,526	62,612	76.5
1970	2,441	637,951	127,993	120,687	76.6
1972	2,314	578,233	112,890	121,911	76.7
1974	1,917	529,473	—	124,469	77.1
1975	1,598	514,884	—	120,599	77.6
1976	1,462+	—	—	—	—

SOURCES: *Statisztikai evkonyv, 1958*, p. 157; *ibid., 1959*, p. 139 and 165; *ibid., 1960*, p. 151; *ibid., 1961*, p. 134; *ibid., 1962*, pp. 164 and 182; *ibid., 1965*, pp. 54 and 142; *Magyar statisztikai zsebkonyv, 1968*, p. 235; *Statisztikai evkonyv, 1970*, p. 232; *ibid., 1972*, pp. 243 and 273; *ibid., 1974*, p. 250; *ibid., 1975*, pp. 205, 207, and 221; and *Magyar mezogazdasag: informaciok* (1 September 1976).

NOTES: Retired members of agricultural production cooperatives are not included.

+Situation at the end of August

TABLE 29

HUNGARY'S FARM AREA BY SECTOR, 1975

	Arable land	
Category	*Percent*	*1,000 hectares*
Cooperative sector*	80.7	4,015
State sector	14.0	697
Private sector	5.3	264
Total	100.0	4,976

SOURCE: [Hungary], *Statisztikai evkonyv 1975* (Budapest, 1976), pp. 11 and 205.
NOTE: *Private garden plots comprise 444,900 hectares within this category. This subcategory does not include ancillary farms.

throughout the bloc. Although production has recently received great emphasis, Budapest is still dependent on Moscow for many of its agricultural chemicals. Moreover, production alone will not solve the problem. Fertilizers that are already available have been inefficiently used because of inadequate storage facilities, transportation bottlenecks, and peasant indifference.

In general, the doctrinaire approach of communism fails to recognize that among East European peasants there exists a traditional attachment to the land. The soil is viewed by those who work it with a sense of affinity that is difficult to erase by regime decree. These psychological attitudes have brought about a paradoxical situation: some peasants have been willing to join the party in Hungary but not to work on collective farms. Notwithstanding such problems, the regime encourages mechanization (partly through the purchase of Western agricultural machinery) and has improved the standard of living for agricultural workers. All of this has had a favorable impact on productivity.[40]

Industrial Development. By March 1948 all large industrial enterprises (those having a hundred or more employees) had been nationalized in Hungary. The development of heavy industry was fostered with even more fanatical zeal than the transformation of agriculture. The initial five-year plan, covering the years from 1950 through 1954, was actually intended to transform Hungary first from an agricultural to a balanced agricultural-industrial economy, and then to change it into an "iron and steel" country.[41] This attempt took place at the expense of farm production and the manufacture of consumers' goods. Progress toward developing heavy industry could be achieved only at considerable sacrifice by the population, whose standard of living would be lowered.

40. In an effort to encourage production, higher procurement prices have been set for certain agricultural commodities. *Nepszabadsag,* 19 August 1976. However, frozen foods and canned goods were raised in price from 16 to 35 percent according to Budapest radio, 8 January 1977.
41. Vali, *op. cit.* (in note 22 above), p. 82.

Even before Stalin's death in 1953, a slowdown occurred in the rate of industrialization throughout the East European bloc. The slackened pace could be attributed to an unrealistic basis for the forced drive to achieve industrialization and to pressure by the people for a decent standard of living. The declining rate of industrial output in the bloc countries during this period is reflected in the following comparisons, where production of the previous year is given as 100 percent: 130 percent (1951) and 108 percent (1955).[42]

As was the case in agriculture, there appeared to be a direct relationship between industrial output and the amount of pressure exerted on the workers. After an unsuccessful five-year plan ended in 1954, a one-year plan was adopted. It stressed an increase of consumers' goods. With the removal of Imre Nagy from the premiership in April 1955, however, heavy industry again became emphasized. Such vacillations in the economy took their toll in both human motivation and resources.

The effects of the 1956 rebellion and the Soviet reoccupation exerted an incalculable influence on Hungary. Large credits had to be granted by the USSR[43] and by other East European states to aid in the recovery from the damage to physical assets, the reduced productivity of workers, and the loss of skilled technicians who had been killed or had taken refuge abroad. Since the country is relatively deficient in raw materials but experienced in the manufacture of certain commodities, the CMEA "division of labor" had great appeal to Hungarian communist leaders. The adoption of this concept gave every indication of completely reorienting Hungary's industrial development, which was to become compatible with and complementary to that of other member economies. During the period 1957–1965, however, Hungarian trade with the bloc resulted in a foreign-exchange deficit of almost 3.5 billion forints. In a single recent year (1975), Hungary's adverse balance of payments in all foreign trade totaled almost 9.4 billion exchange-rate forints.[44]

Industrial development in Hungary suffers from the same problems that beset the Soviet Union and the other East European states. There is widespread popular dissatisfaction with a living standard that remains low in comparison to that of Western Europe. Communist leaders have made it clear, however, that increased investment in Hungarian industry, the need to repay credits granted by the USSR, and high expenditures for the armed forces militate against any substantial or rapid increase in consumers' goods. In Hungary, as in the other Soviet

---

42. Edward Taborsky, "The 'Old' and the 'New' Course in Satellite Economy," *Journal of Central European Affairs* (January 1958), p. 383.

43. Reportedly credits totaled $320 million during 1956–1958. Lucjan Ciamaga, *Od wspolpracy do integracji* (Warsaw, 1965), pp. 39–40.

44. *Statisztikai evkonyv 1975*, p. 258. During 1975 the deficit in trade with the USSR alone totaled over 1.2 billion foreign-exchange forint. *Ibid.*, pp. 259–260. The trade imbalance with the United States in 1976 was about $70 million because of sizeable feed grain imports. *New York Times*, 28 December 1976.

dependencies, politically expedient economic measures (such as the purchase of Cuban sugar at artificially high prices, submission to Moscow's import requirements,[45] and compulsory aid to underdeveloped countries) limit economic development.

New Economic Mechanism. An enlarged Central Committee plenum met in May 1966 to adopt a new economic reform that became part of the five-year plan. Six months later, the ninth congress of the ruling party approved two basic decisions: a change in economic management and the introduction of a new economic mechanism (NEM). The reform went into effect on 1 January 1968. It maintained central direction over long-range tasks, yet provided for implementation by individual enterprises based on market demand. Each factory prepared its own plan. The state established credit, price, and interest policies to influence effectiveness indirectly. Even wages were established by individual factories, within certain limits that depended upon profits. The government provided financial assistance to plants that incurred additional costs because of technological improvements. On the other hand, tax penalties were levied against industries that turned out goods of inferior quality. Enterprises that reduced costs by 1.2 percent were authorized to give their workers twelve to thirteen days' pay as a bonus, with an extra day's wages added for each reduction of 0.1 percent below this target. A new quota bonus was fixed at 70 percent of the bonus paid the previous year. It could be increased to 100 percent or even 130 percent depending on the extent of profit-plan overfulfillment.[46]

The decisive feature of NEM was a new price system that attempted to reflect the true value of each article. By mid-1970, the number of prices fixed by central planners had dropped from approximately one million to about one thousand. Production could be planned better, and the ratio of consumers' goods could be increased. Official data, however, indicate that productivity improved only slightly, labor efficiency remained unsatisfactory, and the economic situation in general was uneven. To eliminate these difficulties, the government's Economic Committee has issued new guidelines on the further development of economic regulators. The aim is to achieve greater differentiation on the basis of quality work, managerial responsibility, and improved manpower utilization.

NEM radically changes the economic picture and also inevitably affects various parts of society. The coordinating role of central organs, however, assures firm party control. For this reason, the Soviet Union probably considers that the NEM represents economic reorganization rather than a basic

---

45. Some 370,000 tons of wheat during 1977 and up to 460,000 tons by 1980, more than 108 tons of meat, plus about 25 percent of all Hungarian agricultural and food products are being exported annually to the USSR. Budapest radio, 9 September 1976. The Soviet Union will supply Hungary with one billion cubic meters of natural gas during 1977. *Ibid.*, 10 December 1976.

46. Article by Jozsef Balint in *Pravda*, 27 March 1970; Moscow. Note also the experiment with "direct democracy," being conducted at fifty enterprises. Budapest radio, 22 September 1976.

reform that might bring major social change or even undermine communist rule in Hungary.[47]

Church-State Relations. In the mid-1960s there were indications that government restrictions on clerical activity were being relaxed. Five bishops and one apostolic administrator traveled to Rome and were received by the pope. The leader of the Hungarian delegation, Bishop Endre Hamvas, told the Vatican Council that there were signs of a "growing understanding" between Roman Catholics and other Christians who were faced with "the common danger of atheism."[48] On 15 September 1964 the Vatican signed an agreement with the regime in Budapest that was the first of its kind to be negotiated with a communist-ruled state.

Of all the forces at work in a society, probably none is more annoying to communists than a well-organized religion. This is particularly true of a church that owes its loyalty to a center outside the Soviet bloc. Religion works on the mind, and it is the mind that must be made subservient to the state or neutralized as a center of resistance to communist ideology. In addition, religious influence on the young must be eliminated just as ties with foreign countries must be severed.

Taking exception to any tolerance vis-a-vis the Roman Catholic Church, the initial Hungarian postwar regime under Rakosi recognized that religion posed a serious threat to communism. In early 1949 Jozsef Cardinal Mindszenty was arrested and, after "confessing," was sentenced to life imprisonment. Rakosi miscalculated the effect of this move, and the cardinal-primate became a martyr. The churches became filled with both the "religiously" religious and the "politically" religious.[49]

During the 1956 rebellion churches were among the first to shed the restrictions placed upon them by the regime's control apparatus. By attending religious services, people manifested their deep-seated love of liberty. After the revolt had been crushed, state control over the churches was reinstituted. Several new policies were developed and, while the government refused to grant complete freedom to the churches, it did recognize the influence of religion on the population.

Late in 1957 the government resumed the payment of subsidies to the Catholic Church,[50] and the communist-sponsored "peace movement" of priests dis-

47. Only 3.4 percent of the employed population work as artisans or small shopkeepers, what is left of private enterprise. Budapest radio, 17 September 1976.

48. "Hungarian Bishops Abroad," *East Europe* (January 1964), p. 42.

49. Vali, *op. cit.* (in note 22 above), p. 65.

50. Resumption marked a step in an attempt by the state to regain financial control over the church. U.S. Senate, Committee on the Judiciary, *The Church and State Under Communism* (Washington, D.C., 1965), VI, pp. 10–11.

banded. While these steps indicated a temporary desire to "coexist," the state continued to exercise considerable control over the church and its leaders. This situation continued until after the 1958 elections; the results of the election then apparently made the regime feel strong enough to drive what it considered to be a lasting wedge between the people and their religion. Catholic as well as Protestant bishops were required to take oaths of allegiance to the state, and the Office for Religious Questions was reestablished.

Ten years after the Vatican-Budapest agreement mentioned earlier, Pope Paul VI retired Cardinal Mindszenty, who had already left Hungary after more than two decades in prison and a period of self-imposed exile at the United States Legation. He died in Vienna. Appointment by the pope of Laszlo Lekai[51] as the new primate and later as cardinal finally filled all three positions of archbishop and eight of bishop in Hungary. Whether this "normalization" will last may depend on Kadar's successor.[52]

---

51. *Nepszabadsag,* 28 April 1976. Lekai had served as Cardinal Mindszenty's secretary in 1945 at Veszprem. An important article on church-state relations by deputy premier Gyorgy Aczel appeared in *Vilagossag* (October 1976); translated in RFE, *Background Report,* 14 December 1976.

52. See also Bennet Kovrig, "Hungary," in R. F. Staar (ed.), *1977 Yearbook on International Communist Affairs* (Stanford, Ca., 1977). Note that Kadar made his first official visit to a Western country when he spent 6−8 December 1976 in Austria. His next trip will take him to the Federal Republic of Germany. Hungary's foreign debt has almost reached two billion dollars.

Chapter 6

Polish People's Republic

The USSR accomplished a classic operation when it installed a puppet communist regime at Warsaw. All odds were against such a transformation.[1] The countries of Eastern Europe seemed more receptive to democracy after the Second World War than they had been after the First. The populations had become completely disenchanted with semidictatorships and disgusted by ruthless Nazi and Soviet occupation forces. The Poles, in particular, with their homogeneity and intense nationalism, craved such basic democratic attributes as self-government, freedom of speech, and private ownership. They also sought freedom to practice their Roman Catholic religion, an ideology that was diametrically opposed to the atheistic communist system soon to be imposed upon them from the outside.

Given the foregoing factors, and assuming that it had freedom of choice, Poland would have been the East European country least likely to fall under Soviet domination. Yet it did, and even today it remains under the control of a communist regime. The governmental structure is patterned, in all important aspects, after that of the USSR. Although two subordinate political organizations exist, there is no doubt as to who rules in Warsaw: the Polish United Workers' party (*Polska Zjednoczona Partia Robotnicza—PZPR*).

Historically, Soviet leaders have maintained a belief that whoever controls the East European countries will ultimately dominate all of Europe. A corollary is that the power that holds Poland will be in a key position in Eastern Europe. At the Yalta conference, Stalin agreed in February 1945 to a formula for establishing a Polish government through "free and unfettered elections as soon as possible on the basis of universal suffrage and secret ballot."[2] But the Soviets interpreted the words "free" and "unfettered" in a totalitarian manner. Their

---

1. Susanne S. Lotarski, "The Communist Takeover in Poland," in Thomas T. Hammond (ed.), *The Anatomy of Communist Takeovers* (New Haven, Conn., 1975), pp. 339–367.

2. U.S. Senate, Committee on Foreign Relations, *A Decade of American Foreign Policy* (Washington, D.C., 1950), p. 30.

understanding of a government friendly to the USSR, which the formula also proposed, meant only a regime that would act in blind obedience to the Kremlin. Therefore, they quickly exploited the early postwar situation and pushed ahead with typical Trojan-horse tactics. These consisted of infiltration, subversion, purges, and terrorism, all directed toward obtaining control over communications, elections, and sensitive government positions—particularly the Interior ministry and its security police.

ELECTORAL PROCEDURES

In the years since the Second World War there have been eight occasions on which the communist leadership asked the people of Poland to decide on the composition of goverment by means of parliamentary elections. The first, in 1947, came during an intermediate stage in the subjugation of Eastern Europe by the USSR. The goal was clear: to eliminate all opposition by any means necessary (including violence, deception, and falsified results). The campaign was directed primarily against the Polish Peasant party[3] and the Roman Catholic church. Despite widespread dissatisfaction and disillusionment on the part of the population, a ruthlessly conducted campaign rewarded the communists with success.

By 1952 there was little need to fire bullets or falsify ballots. The communists were in full control. Statutes had been promulgated that made it impossible for an opposition candidate to be considered for election. All of the unopposed 425 United Front candidates for parliament (including the communists, candidates from two bogus political parties, and a few independents) received overwhelming majorities. As might have been predicted, it was announced that more than fifteen million persons, or 95 percent of the electorate, had voted.

The characteristics that distinguished the elections that took place between 1957 and 1976 will probably continue to prevail during the predictable future. They include (1) an apparent but superficial relaxation of the dictatorial stranglehold on the population, (2) a real yet subtle and sophisticated communist totalitarianism, and (3) public awareness of the true conditions, resulting in widespread apathy.

In 1957 the elections were somewhat modified when the communists allowed more candidates to run than there were seats available in parliament (a total of 750 candidates for 459 seats). In view of the fact that all genuine opposition parties had been liquidated in 1947 and none had been allowed to come into

---

3. Other prewar political parties had already been banned. For an account of this election by an eyewitness, the leader of the Polish Peasant party, see Stanislaw Mikolajczyk, *The Rape of Poland: Pattern of Soviet Aggression* (New York, 1948), pp. 180–202.

For subsequent political developments, see R. F. Staar, *Poland, 1944–1962* (Westport, Conn., 1975), 300 pp., which also discusses the so-called United Front.

existence in the ten years since then, the ruling party presumably considered this a safe concession. Even so, the communist leadership had misgivings about the turnout at the polls and about the possibility of widespread crossing-out of communist-proposed names from the ballot by voters.

To eliminate these doubts, the communist first secretary Wladyslaw Gomulka delivered a major speech to the nation shortly before the election. "Deletion of our party's candidates," he warned, "is synonymous with obliterating Poland from the map of Europe."[4] The implication was that unless support appeared to be overwhelming, Poland might suffer the fate of Hungary. The voters heeded the warning.

However, in 1961 support was noticeably less overwhelming. For example, in Warsaw only 55 percent of the eligible voters bothered to register. The emotion of the electorate could best be described as apathetic. There was no hope for outside help other than the aid that had been provided by Western radio broadcasts. The tragedy in Hungary had offered proof that an uprising would be crushed by Soviet armed forces.

In the 1965 elections there were 617 candidates for the 460 seats in parliament. The formality of voting took place on 30 May with the results shown in table 30. In only one way could the population manifest its discontent—by crossing out the names of persons belonging to the communist elite. Among districts with large populations and thus several seats, a candidate whose name had been crossed off by numerous voters could still be elected if he received more than half the ballots. However, his ranking within the district would drop below those of other successful candidates who received larger numbers of votes. This kind of ranking can serve as a basis for judging the public image or popularity of each candidate.

The 1972 electoral campaign involved 625 National Unity Front candidates running for 460 seats. Two-thirds of those elected were newcomers. Although the voters could not influence the outcome, they rearranged the order of preference in all eighty constituencies; in only seven of these constituencies did the top-listed candidate keep that position.[5] Four years later the electorate returned only 15 of the 71 candidates at the top of the list with a majority, and 6 of the 9 Central Committee secretaries dropped in the final ranking. Voter turnout in 1976 was lowest in Gdansk, Gdynia, central Lodz, and Szczecin, the cities in which most of the December 1970 rioting had occurred.[6]

THE 1952 CONSTITUTION

The farce of the Polish people's democratic governmental structure extends to its very foundation, namely the constitution. On the surface this basic law

---

4. Wladyslaw Gomulka, *Przemowienia 1956–1957* (Warsaw, 1957), p. 193.

5. RFE, *Situation Report*, 24 March 1972.

6. *Ibid.*, 26 March 1976.

TABLE 30

POLISH PARLIAMENTARY ELECTIONS: 1965-1976

Party or other group	Seats won				Percentage of seats - 1976
	1965	1969	1972	1976	
Polish United Workers' party	255	255	255	261	56.8
United Peasant party	117	117	117	113	24.5
Democratic party	39	39	39	37	8.1
Nonparty	36	35	36	36	7.8
Catholic activists	13	14	13	13	2.8
Totals	460	460	460	460	100.0

SOURCES: *Trybuna ludu,* 3 June 1965, 5 June 1969, 21 March 1972; RFE, *Situation Report,* 26 March 1976; *Polityka* (3 April 1976), p. 4.

NOTE: For the background of the above political groups, see R. F. Staar, *Poland 1944-1962* (Westport, Conn., 1975), pp. 227-240.

possesses all the elements of a progressive instrument written by the people to serve the people. In actual fact, it was prepared by a hard core of Soviet-trained communist party leaders. In most respects it derives from the 1936 "Stalin" constitution, which still remained applicable to the USSR at the end of 1976.

The preamble to Poland's basic law provides an opening clue to the unreality of the democratic facade. Unlike its 1921 and 1935 predecessors, this document expresses no religious dependence. References to God have been replaced by verbiage about allegiance and gratitude to the Soviet Union. A second clue can be found in the obvious alignment with the governmental structure of the USSR, which at that time claimed to be centered on the proletariat. The Polish constitution of 1952 avowedly relates itself to "the historical experience of the victorious socialist constitution in the USSR, the first state of workers and peasants."[7]

Following the preamble, the document consists of three principal segments divided into ten chapters and ninety-one articles. The opening and closing chapters describe in general terms the political, social, and economic structure of the people's democracy. Aesopian language comes into full play throughout Chapters I and II, in the descriptions of free elections, social and economic equality, and a government operated by and for the peasants and workers. The middle section, Chapters III through VI, deals with principal state organs: the legislature, the executive, and the judiciary.

The 1952 constitution was amended in February 1976, but in a modified form because of a wave of protest that had begun the previous December in response to a draft. As a result, statements about the leading role of the PZPR, Poland's unbreakable ties with the Soviet Union, and the need to make civil rights

---

7. *Dziennik ustaw,* 23 July 1952. See also Kazimierz Gosciniak, *Czym jest, a czym nie jest Konstytucja PRL* (Warsaw, 1969), p. 155.

dependent upon the performance of duties were removed from the phraseology. The amendments[8] proclaim Poland to be a socialist state, name the PZPR as the leading force in the construction of socialism, urge friendship with the Soviet Union and other socialist states, and finally exhort citizens to fulfill their obligations.

Legislature.   The parliament, or *Sejm,* is described as the supreme organ of state authority. Its 460 members are elected to four-year terms. Full sessions are held once every six months. Theoretically, the *Sejm* makes laws, controls other state agencies, and appoints and recalls the government. It formally elects the Council of State. In actual practice, this body merely gives official approval to drafts of laws proposed by the executive organs of government and also rubber-stamps Council of State decrees. In recent years, however, there has been considerable debate in the *Sejm.* Although regime proposals always pass, some of the deputies have recorded negative votes on legislation.

Council of State.   This body, which is elected from and by parliament to four-year terms in office, consists of a chairman who acts as chief of state, four deputy chairmen, a secretary, and eleven other members.[9] The Council of State possesses the authority to call elections, summon parliament, interpret laws, appoint and recall diplomatic representatives, supervise local people's councils, and issue decrees during the intervals between *Sejm* sessions.

In general, the Council of State performs most of the functions formerly assigned to the presidency. It is not a vitally important policy-making body but it remains useful to the ruling party as a vehicle for issuing decrees. The elimination of the presidency and the transfer of its functions to the Council of State aligned the governmental structure more closely with those of the Soviet Union and other East European countries.

Up to 1952 the post of president was filled by Boleslaw Bierut, who also headed the Polish communist party. During the next fourteen years, Aleksander Zawadzki served as chairman of the State Council. After his death in 1964, Edward Ochab became chief of state. (It was Ochab who had stepped down from the party leadership in October 1956 in favor of Wladyslaw Gomulka.) He resigned from the Council of State because of poor health in 1968. Former defense minister Marian Spychalski and former premier Jozef Cyrankiewicz each served two years in succession. Since March 1972, the titular chief of state has been former education minister Henryk Jablonski.[10]

---

8. Council of State chairman, Henryk Jablonski, discussed the changes that were approved the same day by the *Sejm.* Warsaw radio, 10 February 1976.

9. For the new Council of State see RFE, *Communist Party-Government Line-Up* (Munich, 5 April 1976), p. 18; henceforth cited as *Line-Up.*

10. Photograph and biographic data in *Trybuna ludu,* 13–14 December 1975.

Council of Ministers. This body is defined as the highest executive and administrative organ of state authority. Its duties include the coordination of ministries, the preparation of the budget and economic plans, supervision over public law and order, and the control of foreign and defense policies. In 1976 the Council of Ministers consisted of forty-one members headed by a chairman or premier.[11]

This instrument of the government is supposedly the key policy-making agency. Just as in the USSR, however, it is interesting that all but four of the ministers are also important members of the ruling Polish United Workers' party. These four belong to either the United Peasant or the Democratic party, both of which are communist-controlled subordinate organizations. The Council of Ministers has been headed since December 1970 by Piotr Jaroszewicz, who is thus premier.[12]

The People's Councils. These organs are similar in all respects to the soviets in the USSR. They comprise local administrative units existing in each of the 2,365 communes, 836 towns, 392 counties, 33 city districts, and 49 provinces. The term of office for all 3,675 councils is four years.[13] Their main functions include the adoption of local economic plans and budgets, supervision over local law enforcement, the maintenance of public services and, in general, the linking of local needs to state tasks. Executive organs called presidia are responsible to the next higher echelon, with the province-level presidia subordinated in turn to the Council of State.

The activities of the people's councils are defined in a law of 25 January 1958. They have jurisdiction over the protection of public order; agriculture; local industry and handicrafts; local building and the development of towns and villages; communal housing arrangement and policy; domestic trade; government purchases; public transportation and the construction and maintenance of roads; the management of waterways; education and culture; health, and tourism; unemployment; social welfare; and finances. In all 6,740 councilors were elected in 1976 from 9,618 candidates in the forty-nine province-level people's councils.[14]

The Judicial System. This area of government is administered by the Supreme Court for the country as a whole. Province, county, and special courts

---

11. *Line-Up*, pp. 18–19.

12. His biography appears in *Trybuna ludu*, 13–14 December 1975.

13. Extended from three years by legislation in December 1963. Figures from [Poland], *Concise Statistical Yearbook of Poland 1975* (Warsaw, 1975), p. 8.

14. Warsaw radio, 23 March 1976. At all levels, there are 135,169 councilors, according to *Contemporary Poland* (February 1976), p. 10.

operate at successively lower levels. Justices on the Supreme Court are elected to five-year terms by the Council of State. Lower-ranking judges receive their appointments from the Justice minister.[15] The makeup of the judicial system shows the absence of any separation of powers. No provision exists for judicial review, and the interpretation of laws belongs to the Council of State, which is a a body theoretically created by parliament. A prosecutor general investigates offenses that are deemed harmful to the safety and independence of the Polish People's Republic. He is assisted by a militia (regular uniformed police) and a secret police.

Constitutional Practice.   In any discussion of the governmental structure, it would be a serious error to overlook a concept adopted by the communist hierarchy and known as "constitutional practice." Under this practice, directives are issued that supposedly interpret the real meaning of provisions in the constitution. Changes are made in the content of some provisions, while other provisions are rejected. New regulations or institutions that were not envisioned by the constitution are introduced.

There were several examples of "constitutional practice" between the adoption in 1952 of the fundamental law and its 1976 amendments. By passing an ordinary resolution, for instance, it is always possible for the *Sejm* to expel members. This concept has also enabled members of parliament to ignore constitutional provisions forbidding them to hold government posts and preventing government officials from holding more than one post simultaneously. In effect, there is no binding consitutional law. The constitution can be manipulated and reinterpreted in any manner that the ruling party sees fit and that will best serve its needs.

Democratic Centralism.   A key principle in communist governmental systems is designated by the term "democratic centralism," which refers to an organizational theory developed by Lenin and also to a technique that he first put into practice. The principle, in both aspects, arose from Lenin's demand for tight, centralized control that would at the same time allow for flexibility of execution and mass participation in administrative activities. The principle is thus used vertically, in centralized control, and horizontally, in mass participation. This system has also been called "dual subordination."

All policy decisions and directives emanate from the top and filter down vertically to the lowest echelons of the governmental structure. There is little room for interpretation and none for interference or disagreement. At the same time, a horizontal line of activity is carried on by the various territorial units. Each of these performs specific administrative tasks within its own limited

---

15. An evaluation of the new penal code was provided by the Justice minister, Stanislaw Walczak, over Warsaw radio, 27 December 1969.

sphere. It is apparent that once again the Aesopian language needs interpretation. What the propaganda statements allude to as "local democratic autonomy" is not in fact local, democratic, or autonomous. Such statements merely signify that the implementation of centralized directives is locally administered.

THE COMMUNIST PARTY

The population of Poland is just over thirty-four million. Of this number, approximately 2.5 million belong to the ruling political movement. (See table 31.) Like the Communist Party of the Soviet Union, the Polish United Workers' party—the PZPR— mantains a dictatorship in the name of the working class,[16] which itself has only minority representation in the party. How is it possible that a few men in control of an organization that has only a minority of the people as members can maintain such regimentation over a nation? The answer lies in the structure of the party and in the principle of democratic centralism.

TABLE 31

GROWTH OF THE POLISH COMMUNIST PARTY, 1942–1976

Date	Number of Members	Date	Number of Members
1942 (July)	4,000	1959 (March)	1,067,000
1943 (January)	8,000	1961 (July)	1,270,000
1944 (July)[a]	20,000	1963 (January)	1,397,000
1945 (January)	30,000	1965 (January)	1,640,000
1946 (July)	364,000	1966 (June)	1,848,000
1947 (July)	848,000	1967 (May)	2,000,000
1948 (December)[b]	1,500,000	1970 (October)[c]	2,296,000
1950 (December)	1,360,000	1971 (December)	2,270,000
1952 (June)	1,129,000	1975 (November)	2,453,000
1954 (March)	1,297,000	1976 (December)	2,500,000
1956 (January)	1,344,000		

SOURCES: R. F. Staar, *Poland, 1944–1962* (Westport, Conn., 1975), p. 167 (citing various Polish sources for the years 1942–1961); Tadeusz Galinski (ed.), *Rocznik polityczny i gospodarczy 1963* (Warsaw, 1963), p. 98; *Trybuna ludu,* 31 October 1965, 14 August 1966, and 17 May 1967; Warsaw radio, 3 November 1970; *VI zjazd* (Warsaw, 1972), p. 67; *Polish Perspectives* (November 1975), p. 5; Warsaw radio, 1 December 1976.

NOTES: [a]Some eight thousand of these returned from the USSR with the advancing Red Army. *Nowe drogi* (January–February 1951), p. 235.

[b]After the fusion congress with the socialists.

[c]Includes 206,640 candidates for membership or 9 percent of the total.

General Organization. The Polish communist party is organized along five distinct levels: the primary party organization (PPO) at the bottom, then the

---

16. *Contemporary Poland* (February 1976), p. 8.

commune, county, province, and national levels. With the exception of the PPO, each of the lower levels includes a body of delegates to the next higher echelon. At the intermediate levels these bodies are called conferences; when delegates are assembled on a national scale, they form the party congress. Conferences and congresses are too large for handling routine party business. Therefore they form committees for day-to-day activities. The committees then elect bureaus and even smaller organs, secretariats, to handle party affairs. In effect this system represents a duplication of the government's administrative structure, but it costs more than the state bureaucracy because of the higher salaries paid to party officials.

These units and the individual secretaries theoretically are responsible to the parent group on the same level, reporting to it on the implementation of tasks.[17] All meetings, committees, organs, and individual secretaries also remain sensitive to direction coming from higher levels and report to them. In this horizontal and vertical network of responsibility the principle of democratic centralism, or dual subordination, manifests itself. The tripartite division of authority at each level (meeting, committee, organ) is in reality a device used to create the feeling among rank-and-file party members that they are involved in decision making. The real authority rests with the occupant of the key post at each level, the secretary or first secretary who heads the executive organ.

Relationships among the five-party levels are governed by a statute issued at the third PZPR congress in 1959 and amended by subsequent congresses through the seventh at the end of 1975. This document defines the principle of democratic centralism. Relations among the various levels are guided by the following rules, which appear under Chapter II, paragraph 17, of the statute:

> All directing authorities from the lowest to the highest are elected in a
> democratic manner.
> All party resolutions are passed by a majority vote.
> All party authorities are required to report to the party organizations
> [which elect them].
> Maintenance of party discipline [is required], and the minority
> is subordinate to the resolutions of the majority.
> Resolutions and directives from higher party authorities must be carried
> out by lower ones.[18]

These rules comprise a system of checks and controls that allows only one man freedom of action. That man is the first secretary of the party, Edward

---

17. Names of incumbents at province levels appear in CIA, *Directory of the People's Republic of Poland Officials* (Washington, D.C., 1977); hereafter cited as *Directory*.

18. Polish United Workers' party, *III zjazd PZPR* (Warsaw, 1959), pp. 1213–1237. The amendments did not change these principles. See *IV zjazd PZPR* (Warsaw, 1964), pp. 783–802; *V zjazd PZPR* (Warsaw, 1968), pp. 863–874; *VI zjazd PZPR* (Warsaw, 1972), pp. 207–224; and *VII s'ezd PORP* (Moscow, 1976), pp. 176–188 (translation into Russian).

Gierek (since 20 December 1970). An important aspect of this situation for Gierek is the unknown degree of control that Moscow maintains over him. It is no longer a matter of dictation; this has been replaced by more sophisticated techniques.

Theoretically, ultimate control in the party rests with the meetings of members—at the highest level, the congress; at intermediate levels, the conferences; at the bottom level, the primary party organization meeting. In actual practice, these bodies are little more than rubber-stamp organs whose consent serves to legalize, in the eyes of the rank and file, the actions taken by the party leaders. Some 75,200 primary party organizations[19] represent the base of this vast facade for the few who actually make decisions in Poland today. There are three types of primary party organizations:

> *Institutional,* for those working in factories, mines, railroad yards, government agencies, hospitals, or universities.
> *Village,* in rural areas for peasants, artisans, teachers, and doctors.
> *Territorial,* in urban areas for those employed by small shops that do not have a primary party organization and the unemployed (e.g., housewives).

Of the three types, the institutional is normally the largest. If the organization has more than a hundred members it can be subdivided into brigades, aggregate units, work areas, or shifts, according to the specific production links of the industry involved. General meetings of the primary party organizations are being replaced by institutional, village, and territorial conferences of delegates from the smaller units. Since these conferences avoid convening the lowest party level, they provide much tighter control over the participation of individual members. Whether it occurs at the level of the primary party organization, the commune, the county, or the province,[20] all activity and work is theoretically handled in accordance with the principle of democratic centralism. The concentration of power in the hands of a small elite is perpetuated through this procedure.

All meetings, conferences, commission sessions, and the like, supposedly expressing the attitudes of Polish United Workers' party's rank-and-file members, remain open to influence from above. Itinerant groups from higher authority attend meetings to see whether all is proceeding in accordance with the first secretary's wishes. A good example of this principle on an international scale occurred during the eighth plenary session of the party's Central Committee. The meeting had just begun when the chairman announced the arrival of

---

19. *VII s'ezd Polskoi ob'edinennoi rabochei partii* (Moscow, 1976), p. 57.

20. The number of provinces was increased from twenty-two to forty-nine, allegedly to streamline administration. *Trybuna ludu,* 13 May 1975. In actual fact, this caused the fragmentation of the regional PZPR power structure.

Nikita Khrushchev, Vyacheslav Molotov, Lazar Kaganovich, and Anastas Mikoyan, among others. The top hierarchy in Moscow, having learned that standard operating procedures were not being observed in Poland, had come to investigate. This took place in October 1956 and was accompanied by simultaneous Soviet troop movements in the direction of Warsaw. After an all-night discussion, the Soviet leaders agreed to the election of Wladyslaw Gomulka as first secretary.

The National Congress. The ruling party's first postwar congress[21] convened at the end of 1945. There have been seven congresses since that time. The "fusion congress" of 1948 involved a forced merger of left-wing socialists with communists; for that reason it is known as the first. Party congresses have been convened as follows:

First postwar (PPR) congress .... 6−12 December 1945
First PZPR (unification) congress ....15−21 December 1948
Second PZPR congress .... 10−17 March 1954
Third PZPR congress .... 10−19 March 1959
Fourth PZPR congress .... 15−20 June 1964
Fifth PZPR congress...........................11−16 November 1968
Sixth PZPR congress .... 6−11 December 1971
Seventh PZPR congress .... 8−12 December 1975

At first the party congresses were scheduled to meet at least once every three years, but this interval was changed to four years in the new statute adopted by the third congress, and it was extended at the seventh congress to five years.[22] The meeting held in June 1964 was fifteen months overdue. This postponement probably resulted from uncertainty regarding the control exercised by Gomulka. Extraordinary national party conferences may be called by the Central Committee or by application of a majority of the province committees. So far only one extraordinary conference has been held, in October 1973, to discuss a socioeconomic development program for the country.

A total of 1,811 delegates attended the seventh congress in December 1975. Present were representatives from sixty-five other communist parties, including a Soviet delegation headed by Leonid I. Brezhnev. It was here that the CPSU secretary-general gave strong endorsement to the policies of Edward Gierek. Nothing ever happens at any of these congresses that has not been arranged in advance down to the smallest detail. Elections are rigged with one candidate for each post, and a rubber-stamp balloting or acclamation registers approval to the actions of the party leadership.

---

21. Wladyslaw Gomulka-Wieslaw, *Ku nowej Polsce* (Katowice, 1945), 108 pp., gives Gomulka's four speeches and the final resolution of the congress.

22. Chapter IV, Article 28 in *III zjazd PZPR*, p. 753; and *VII s'ezd*, p. 182.

The Central Committee. This organ is chosen by the party congress. Again, only enough names are placed in nomination to fill the total number of seats (140 full members and 111 candidates were elected in December 1975). The Central Committee is supposed to meet at least once every four months in plenary session. It has the following functions: to represent the party externally with other communist parties, to establish party institutions and direct their activities, to nominate the editorial boards of party newspapers, and to control party cadres that are sent into the field. [23]

Almost 75 percent of the full members and nearly 93 percent of the candidates for membership on the Central Committee in 1976 had been elected at either the sixth or the seventh PZPR congresses. [24] The total of 251 members includes full-time PZPR apparatus employees (100), government officials (51), industrial workers (49), intellectuals (21), generals (12), farmers (8), technocrats (3), and others (7). As this list indicates, this elite is hardly representative of the rank-and-file working class.

The Political Bureau. According to the party statute, a Politburo is elected by the Central Committee from among its own membership and is entrusted with directing the work of that body between plenary sessions. This agency parallels in importance the position of the Soviet communist party's Political Bureau. It is the most powerful among all the organs and represents the summit of the party hierarchy. All of its members can be found on a January 1977 list of the power elite. (See table 32.)

It is in the Politburo that one sees the principle of interlocking directorates at work. As members of the Politburo, the hierarchs make policy; as Secretariat members, certain of them see to it that policy is carried out by the party apparatus; as government officials, they legalize policy in the form of laws and decrees that become effective throughout the country. The internal operations of the Politburo are cloaked in secrecy. The chief of this organ is Edward Gierek, who also serves as first secretary of the Central Committee.

Gierek was born on 6 January 1913 at Porabka near Bedzin in Silesia. After the death of his father in a coal-mine accident, the family migrated in 1923 to France. According to an official biography, Gierek began work as a miner at age thirteen and five years later he joined the French communist party in the Pas-de-Calais area. Deported to Poland in 1934 because of strike activities, he served in the Polish armed forces as a draftee. [25] He emigrated again in 1937, this time to Belgium.

After transferring his membership to the Belgian communist party, Gierek

---

23. *Ibid.,* p. 754 (Chapter IV, Article 32, of the statute).

24. RFE Report (by Ewa Celt), 15 January 1976, gives the breakdown.

25. Not mentioned by Warsaw radio, 20 December 1970. However, see R. F. Staar, *Poland, 1944–1962* (Westport, Conn., 1975), pp. 183–184.

TABLE 32
POWER ELITE IN POLAND, 1977

Politburo and Secretariat	Date of birth	Government office	Joined party	Party office and/or area of responsibility
POLITBURO MEMBERS (14)				
*Babiuch, Edward	1927	State Council member	1948	Secretary (cadres)
*Gierek, Edward	1913	State Council member	1931	First secretary (Party leader)
Grudzień, Zdzisław	1924	–	1946	First secretary, Katowice province
Jabloński, Henryk	1909	State Council chairman	1948	Higher education
Jagielski, Mieczysław	1924	Deputy premier; CMEA representative	1945	–
Jaroszewicz, Piotr	1909	Premier	1944	–
Jaruzelski, Wojciech	1923	Defense minister	1947	–
*Kania, Stanisław	1927	–	1945	Secretary (military and security)
Kepa, Józef	1928	Deputy premier	1948	–
Kowalczyk, Stanisław	1924	Interior minister	1948	–
Kruczek, Władysław	1910	State Council deputy chairman	1932	Trade Union Council chairman
*Olszowski, Stefan	1931	–	1952	Secretary (economy)
Szydlak, Jan	1925	Deputy premier	1945	–
Tejchma, Józef	1927	Deputy premier; Culture minister	1952	–
POLITBURO CANDIDATES (3)				
Barcikowski, Kazimierz	1927	Agriculture minister	ca. 1948	–
*Lukaszewicz, Jerzy	1931	–	ca. 1949	Secretary (propaganda)
Wrzaszczyk, Tadeusz	1932	Deputy premier; Planning Commission chairman	ca. 1954	–

TABLE 32 (Cont.)

POWER ELITE IN POLAND, 1977

Politburo and Secretariat	Date of birth	Government office	Joined party	Party office and/or area of responsibility
SECRETARIES (11)				
Frelek, Ryszard	1929	—	1953	Director, Foreign department
Karkoszka, Alojzy	1929	—	1951	First Secretary, Warsaw City
Pinkowski, Józef	1929	—	ca. 1952	Agriculture
Werblan, Andrzej	1924	Sejm deputy speaker	1948	Director, Marx-Lenin Institute
Zandarowski, Zdzislaw	1929	—	1948	Director, Organization department
SECRETARIAT MEMBER (1)				
Kurowski, Zdzislaw	1937	—	1957	Federation of Socialist Unions of Polish Youth chairman

SOURCES: Warsaw radio, 12 December 1975; *ibid.*, 2 and 7 December 1976; *ibid.*, 21 January 1977.
NOTES: *Secretary of the PZPR Central Committee
Italics signify promotion at the December 1975 congress or December 1976 Central Committee plenum.

reportedly belonged to the anti-German resistance movement during the Second World War. He also participated in the communist-sponsored Union of Polish Patriots and served two years after the war as chairman of the Polish National Council in Belgium. He did not return to Poland until 1948, having lived abroad for more than two decades.

Gierek began to work full-time in the party as an instructor for the central apparatus in Warsaw, then as deputy director of the organization department on the Katowice province staff (1949). He became second secretary for economic affairs of the same department (1951), then director of the heavy industry department in the central apparatus at Warsaw (1954), and finally a secretary of the Central Committee two years later. Since 1957 he had served as first secretary of Katowice province and has also been on the Political Bureau that long. He succeeded to the highest party office on 20 December 1970 because of an economic crisis that resulted in riots, especially along the sea coast. Replacement of five party leaders (including Wladyslaw Gomulka) on that day resulted from these disturbances, which were triggered by a government announcement only nine days before Christmas that food prices had been raised by an average of 30 percent without any increase in wages.[26] Dock-yard workers along the Baltic coast struck, and during the ensuing disorders communist-party headquarters were burned at Gdansk and Szczecin.

The Secretariat, which is considered the hub of party activity, is nominally elected by the Central Committee in plenary session, just as the Politburo is. There are currently eleven national secretaries, including Gierek. Under the direction of these men, about a dozen departments, three bureaus, and four commissions operate at this top level.[27] The Secretariat maintains a constant check on local party officials throughout the country. It also remains in permanent contact with the Politburo, since six of the eleven secretaries are Politburo members or candidates for membership on that policy-making body. (See table 32.)

Composition of the Party.   The social composition of the party is shown in table 33. What does not appear is the quality of membership. The proportion of intellectuals (including white-collar employees) has risen from less than 10 percent to almost 43 percent within three decades, and many of these persons are probably opportunists. On the other hand, the hard core of the party consists mainly of those members who were activists and functionaries during the 1940s.

---

26. *Trybuna ludu*, 16 December 1970, listed the new ones compared with 1965 prices. In terms of average wages, it would have taken four hours' work to purchase one kilogram of frozen beef (3.3 hours in 1965); five hours' work for pork (four in 1965); 8.4 hours for ham (6.4 in 1965); and 2.2 hours for fish (1.1 in 1965). Computed from official figures in the source above.

27. *Directory* (in note 17 above), lists the directors and other officials.

Few of these are left on the current leadership list, although some twenty-two thousand current PZPR members belonged to the pre-1938 Polish communist movement and its youth affiliate or to the socialist party's left wing.

Since 1942, when the party was reconstituted,[28] its membership has grown almost steadily (see table 31). This growth, however, has been accompanied by the purging of considerable numbers. The main reasons have been theft, bribery, embezzlement, misuse of official positions, and drunkenness. Table 34 shows the party's losses since 1955.

There has been condemnation by the party's leadership of the trend toward an increasing percentage of intelligentsia in the party. This shift toward control by the better educated is more than just a trend; it is in reality a current problem. Only about 40 percent of the PZPR membership belongs to the proletariat or industrial labor force in Poland. The goal set by Gomulka reportedly was 90 percent industrial workers and 10 percent "mental" workers. The proportions have developed in the reverse direction, with each of the two groups providing roughly 40 percent of the membership in 1975 (see table 33).

Despite these problems, temporary stability has been achieved within the party leadership. Acceptance of many younger province secretaries and workers from large factories into the Central Committee after the sixth and seventh PZPR congresses possibly could have become a threat to Gierek. These individuals, who have grass-roots contacts, probably desire an increased living standard for the workers. Among them may be a dark-horse candidate for party leadership, one who will combine support from the intellectuals and the young people. This represents a long-range proposition, although developments during the latter half of 1976 may have brought it closer.

A possibility that should not be excluded is intervention by the Soviet Union; the USSR may decide that Gierek must be sacrificed to avoid even more serious disturbances among a population that has never been noted for its procommunist and especially its pro-Russian sympathies. The two precedents, in October 1956 and December 1970, which saw the rise and fall of Gomulka, are probably on the minds of those who make decisions both in Warsaw and in Moscow.

Regardless of any differences among party factions, the winner will always be a communist. The PZPR can be expected to continue to be patterned after its counterpart in the Soviet Union. The goal of the party still remains that of a "socialist" state, and the maintenance of control over the nation by a self-perpetuating elite is considered a prerequisite for the attainment of this

---

28. The prewar Polish communist party was dissolved by the Comintern in 1938, and most of its leaders (who had taken refuge in Moscow) were executed or sent to Soviet forced-labor camps. Their posthumous rehabilitation by the USSR Supreme Court came after October 1956. *Polityka*, 21 August 1965.

See also M. K. Dziewanowski, *The Communist Party of Poland* (Cambridge, 1976), 2nd ed., which covers the period up to 1973.

TABLE 33

POLISH COMMUNIST PARTY, SOCIAL COMPOSITION, 1945–1975

Category	December 1945		September 1957		October 1970		November 1975	
	Number	Percent	Number	Percent	Number	Percent	Number	Percent
Industrial workers	130,620	62.2	511,917	39.9	939,064	40.9	995,918	40.6
Peasants	59,220	28.2	164,224	38.8	266,236	11.6	242,847	9.9
Intellectuals	20,160	9.6	497,804	38.8	975,890	42.5	1,052,337	42.9
Other (artisans, retired, housewives)	–	–	109,055	8.5	114,810	5.0	161,898	6.6
Total	210,000	100.0	1,283,000	100.0	2,296,000	100.0	2,453,000	100.0

SOURCES: *Nowe drogi* (January–February 1947), p. 29, and (May–June 1948), p. 30; *Zycie Warszawy*, 25 October 1957; *Trybuna ludu*, 18 November 1957; Warsaw radio, 3 November 1970; *Polish Perspectives* (November 1975), p. 5. Absolute figures computed.

NOTE: Only 15 percent of the members have complete or incomplete university educations and another 26 percent have high school diplomas. *VII s'ezd Porp*, p. 56.

TABLE 34

PURGES IN THE POLISH COMMUNIST PARTY, 1955–1975

Year	Number of members purged	Year	Number of members purged
1955	55,000	1968	40,100
1956-1964	400,000	1969	52,300
1965	41,900	1970	53,600
1966	44,100	1971	163,900
1967	117,100	1972-1975	206,000

SOURCES: *Nowe drogi* (December 1958), p. 87; *Trybuna ludu,* 16 January and 16 June 1960, and 16 March 1961; Warsaw radio, 15 April 1964; *Trybuna ludu,* 26 February and 14 August 1966; *Zycie Warszawy,* 18 April 1968; *Zycie partii* (March 1970), p. 2; *VI zjazd PZPR* (Warsaw, 1972), p. 68; *Nowe drogi* (February 1971), pp. 79–94; *Trybuna ludu,* 26 June 1974; *Zycie partii* (May 1975), p. 25. Glos robotniczy (Lodz), 5 December 1975.

NOTES: Between 1959 and June 1970, a total of 525,700 members had been purged from the party according to *Nowe drogi* (February 1971), p. 90.

Proceedings of the 7th Congress in December 1975 revealed only that the number of party members and candidates increased by 105,000 over the preceding four years. *VII zjazd PZPR* (Warsaw, 1975), p. 49.

Figures for 1972–1975 include 32,000 party candidates.

objective. Even the so-called destalinization and "liberalization" have not changed this fact of life.[29]

DOMESTIC AND INTRA-ORBIT RELATIONS

Poland remains unique among the East European countries within the Soviet power bloc. This is not only due to the remarkable success of the communists in fettering the people and establishing a regime despite seemingly insurmountable socioreligious and political barriers. There are other reasons for its uniqueness, among which perhaps the most interesting remains the "deviationist" manner in which Poland's agriculture has been permitted to develop. The unusual modus vivendi between church and state would be another, but it has deteriorated. In the past, however, this arrangement permitted such incompatible ideologies as those of the Roman Catholic church and of communism to coexist within the country.

The Agricultural Program.   Even before the cessation of hostilities in the Second World War, radical land reform was introduced by the communist-dominated provisional government. It consisted principally of expropriating

29. R. F. Staar, "Destalinization in Eastern Europe: The Polish Model," in Andrew Gyorgy (ed.), *Issues of World Communism* (Princeton, N.J., 1966), pp. 66–85.

large landholdings and redistributing them among the peasantry and the new Polish settlers in the so-called Recovered Territories to the east of the 1939 Polish-German boundary. Little was done toward the collectivization of agriculture, as the communists were concentrating on the consolidation of their control over the government during the early years. This postponement of collectivization represented in Poland, as in some of the other "people's democracies," merely a tactical divergence from the traditional Soviet path toward the so-called socialist state. Deferment was permitted by Moscow during the formative years of the bloc as a temporary means toward the desirable end of solidifying communist control.

By 1947, however, Stalin had decided that the time was ripe for establishing more uniformity within the diverse East European satrapies. The organization of the Cominform[30] was the signal for the beginning of his conformity drive. Gomulka, nominally the leading communist in Poland at that time, reportedly indicated his coolness toward establishment of this international organization and, by implication, objected to forced agricultural collectivization, which had not given brilliant results elsewhere. He was removed as party leader by a September 1948 plenary session of the Central Committee. By the following year, collectivization patterned after the Soviet model had been launched in Poland.

This forced process was conducted by such coercive devices as compulsory state deliveries, heavy land taxes, and punitive visits by party activists and police to farm areas where opposition to the program had been encountered. Between late 1949 and the fall of 1956 some 10,600 collective farms came into being. The resentment of the peasants against the abrogation of their property rights mounted. The farmer in Poland not only considers his land to be a source of income but he also attributes to it sentimental and traditional values.

This growing discontent finally came to be recognized by communist authorities. It was probably this fact more than any other that tempered the degree of force and violence subsequently used in Poland to achieve the aims of the program. A much more severe campaign of terror and coercion was applied in the other East European satellites. As a result, collectivization of farms in Poland showed only a 3 percent growth between 1950 and 1958, in contrast with increases of 48 percent in Bulgaria and 52 percent in Czechoslovakia.[31]

Production figures that have subsequently been released indicate that Polish farms remaining in private hands outproduced those in the socialist sector (both collective and state operated) by a considerable margin. This led Gomulka, after his return to power in 1956, to suggest the dissolution of the collective units that

30. Eugenio Reale, *Nascita del Cominform* (Rome, 1958), 175 pp., gives an eyewitness account of the establishment of the Cominform.

31. Zbigniew K. Brzezinski, *The Soviet Bloc* (Cambridge, Mass., 1960), p. 98.

were operating at a deficit.[32] He also announced more liberal regulations pertaining to organizing production cooperatives, as collective farms are euphemistically called. The reaction probably represented a barometer of peasant attitudes toward collectivization. Taking the speech of Gomulka literally, the peasants began to dissolve the cooperatives. By the summer of 1957 more than 8,500 of the 10,600 previously existing collectives had been disbanded.[33] Further liberalization of control over agriculture resulted in the reduction of compulsory deliveries to the state, increases in the prices paid for agricultural commodities, and more autonomy within rural areas. (See table 35.).

What is the current farm picture in Poland? A review of the results achieved indicates a substantial decline in the production of pork, animal fat, poultry, dairy products and sugar; a drop in total agricultural trade; and an increase in retail food prices. Furthermore, sizable annual grain imports (eight million tons in 1976) from the USSR and the West have been found necessary and are continuing.[34] A certain amount of mismanagement and three poor harvests in succession have led to a decrease in the number of cows, which also adversely affected milk supplies.

Although Poland is the only country within the Soviet bloc in which collectivization has not been actively pursued since 1956, the communist regime there did not ignore the idea entirely. It instituted "agricultural circles" to inculcate collectivist attitudes among the peasantry. These state-controlled organizations are designed to favor members over strictly private-entrepreneur farmers in the procurement of agricultural supplies and in arrangements for distribution and sale of produce. Apart from the introduction of these circles, heavy taxes were reimposed on individual nonaffiliated farms. With a membership of 2.8 million, agricultural circles cultivate about three hundred thousand hectares of their own land.[35]

Poland's stumbling agricultural economy presents a serious problem to the government, as party leader Gierek admitted at the seventh PZPR congress when he stated that the demand for some agricultural products, especially meat, considerably exceeds the supply. Stable prices "for most food products," in Gierek's words, obviously will not cover an item that is relatively scarce. To justify the necessity for future price increases, Gierek blamed inflation which had affected the cost of imported oil, grain, feed, steel, leather, edible fats, machinery, and equipment.

---

32. *Nowe drogi* (October 1956), pp. 24−25 (complete issue on the eighth plenum of the PZPR Central Committee).

33. *Trybuna ludu*, 28 August 1957.

34. *The Economist*, 11 December 1976; London.

35. Warsaw radio, 3 November 1950, and *Kultura*, 26 October 1975; both cited by Stefanowski (see table 35).

TABLE 35

CHANGES IN THE OWNERSHIP OF ARABLE LAND, 1970–1980 (PROJECTED)
(in hectares)

	1970		1975		1980 Percent
Type	Area	Percent	Area	Percent	(Projected)
Individual farmers	12,636,500	83.7	12,000,300	81.3	70
State farms	2,198,600	14.6	2,373,700	16.1	20
Collective farms	193,500	1.3	225,400	1.5	10
Other state land (including State Land Fund)	61,300	0.4	164,700	1.1	–
Total	15,089,900	100.0	14,764,100	100.0	100

SOURCES: *Maly rocznik statystyczny 1970*, pp. 163–165; *Rocznik statystyczny 1975*, p. 245; Warsaw radio, 5 December 1976; RFE report (by Roman Stefanowski), "Agricultural Perspectives," 20 January 1976.

NOTE: According to Warsaw radio, 20 December 1976, the state took over about 700,000 hectares from private-entrepreneur farmers in return for pensions during the past five years. It anticipates that this figure will total 1½ to 2 million hectares between 1976 and 1980.

Within six months the government had announced that meat would go up 70 percent, sugar 100 percent, and grains 40 percent in price. The following day (25 June 1976), strikes, public protests, and riots occurred in several cities throughout the country. Communist-party headquarters in Radom were burned. Within twenty-four hours, the proposed price increases were withdrawn. However, thousands of those who were involved in the disturbances are in prison or have been dismissed from their factory jobs.

The problem facing the regime is that 12 percent of the annual budget or about four billion dollars will have to be expended in food subsidies during 1977. For example, a loaf of bread can be purchased for twenty cents or the equivalent of the grain itself, without adding processing or sales costs, not to mention a profit. Gierek announced on 1 December 1976 that Poland will import grain and meat in 1977 worth $1.5 billion, and this amount will have to be added to a debt of more than eight billion dollars already owed the West.[36]

Church-State Relations.   The prewar Roman Catholic population of Poland numbered about twenty-three million out of a total of almost thirty-four million inhabitants. In addition to more than three million Jews (of Hebrew religion), the

---

36. R. F. Staar, "Poland: The Price of Stability," *Current History* (March 1976), pp. 101–106 and 133–134; *Christian Science Monitor*, 20 December 1976; *New York Times*, 21 January 1977.

remainder included Ukrainian (Uniate), German (Lutheran), and Belorussian (Eastern Orthodox) minorities. Now, after the Nazi holocaust and the annexation of Polish territory in the east by the USSR,[37] the minority groups comprise fewer than seven hundred thousand persons, or two percent in a total population of more than thirty-four million of whom the overwhelming majority adheres at least nominally to the Roman Catholic faith. (See table 36.)

TABLE 36

MINORITY RELIGIONS IN POLAND, 1970

Name	Approximate number	Percentage of minority total
Eastern Orthodox	440,000	70.8
Lutheran	100,000	16.1
Polish National Catholic	30,000	4.8
Old Catholic Mariawit	22,000	3.5
Seventh-day Adventist	6,500	1.1
Jewish	6,000	1.0
Reform Lutheran	5,000	0.8
Catholic Mariawit	4,000	0.6
Free Association for Bible Study	3,400	0.5
Epiphany Lay Movement	2,000	0.3
Moslem	1,700	0.3
Bible Study Association	800	0.1
Karaimi (Tartars)	250	less than 0.1
Total	621,650	100.0

SOURCE: *Zycie Warszawy,* 18 May 1970. Percentages computed.

In 1945 the new, communist-dominated Council of Ministers declared null and void the twenty-year-old concordat between Warsaw and the Vatican. This agreement had regulated church activities in Poland. In abrogating the concordat, the regime charged that the church had allegedly violated its provisions by favoring Germany during the war. From that time on, a slowly intensifying campaign against the church was waged, beginning with press campaigns against the hierarchy and the teaching of the catechism in public schools. It gradually expanded to include the arrest and trials of clergy and the suppression of the Catholic news media.

---

37. Twelve years ago, there were about 1.4 million Poles in the USSR, scattered as follows: Belorussia (539,000), Ukraine (363,000), Lithuania (230,000), the Russian Soviet Federated Socialist Republic (118,000), Latvia (60,000), Kazakhstan (53,000), and other republics (17,000). *Polityka,* 30 October 1965, p. 10. The latest Soviet census gave the total as 1,167,000, which represents a substantial decline. [USSR] *Narodnoe khoziaistvo SSSR v 1970g.* (Moscow, 1971), p. 15.

In January 1949 Archbishop Stefan Wyszynski was appointed primate of Poland. He immediately opened negotiations with regime authorities to clarify the position of the church in relation to the state. These talks became seriously hampered by a Vatican decree ordering the excommunication of all Catholics who actively supported communism. The regime in Warsaw, claiming that this constituted interference in the internal affairs of the country, retaliated by announcing that priests who attempted to enforce the excommunication order would be punished under Polish law.

Despite these difficulties, a modus vivendi was signed in April 1950 between the church and the regime.[38] In essence, the church agreed to abstain from all political activities and to restrain its clergy from opposition to the government. The state, in turn, guaranteed freedom of worship, permission to conduct religious education in public schools, and noninterference with the Catholic press. The wording of the agreement, however, appeared flagrantly one-sided and provided the basis for subsequent government interference. In almost every case where specific guarantees of freedom were given, the regime carefully qualified them with restrictive phrases.

The communists took advantage of this terminology and reverted to their campaign against the church almost immediately. In the following years, persecution by the government mounted in intensity. The new Polish constitution (1952) omitted any mention of safeguards for religion. In the fall of the next year Cardinal Wyszynski was secretly arrested and forbidden to carry out the functions of his office. Arrests of other clergy followed. The state even went so far as to require, and insist on obtaining, its own approval whenever changes in clerical assignments or new appointments were contemplated.

In 1956, immediately after Gomulka's return to power, Cardinal Wyszynski and the other arrested clergymen were released. Persecution of the church halted temporarily. A new, more liberal church-state agreement[39] was announced whereby religious instruction could once again be provided on a voluntary basis in the schools, government control over certain clerical appointments was relaxed, and other concessions were made. At this time communist control had weakened throughout the country because of the October upheaval, and there was fear of a revolt.

Subsequent events showed that the new church-state agreement represented more a political expedient to gain temporary church support than a sincere intention to liberalize former restrictions on religious activities. Once the communists had gained sufficient strength, persecution in one form or another followed and, indeed, persists to this day. It is apparent that the communists want not only to separate church and state but also to eliminate religion totally from the lives of the people.

---

38. The text of the agreement appears in Henryk Swiatkowski (ed.), *Stosunek panstwa do kosciola w roznych krajach* (Warsaw, 1952), pp. 132–137.

39. Published in *Trybuna ludu,* 8 December 1956.

The future of the church in Poland does not look bright. Nevertheless, the large Catholic population is still a powerful factor in domestic politics. The church hierarchy remains well aware of communist desires to rid the country of religion. It continues to fight for religious freedom despite nearly continuous oppression during the postwar years. In the fall of 1965 Cardinal Wyszynski and Archbishop Antoni Baraniak of Poznan were attacked by the regime media for making speeches at the Ecumenical Council meeting in Rome without mentioning "the avoidance of war, disarmament, and world-wide cooperation by states and peoples on behalf of peace."[40]

Shortly afterward the Cardinal and thirty-five Polish bishops, who had participated in the sessions in Rome, sent a letter inviting the Catholic bishops in all of Germany to attend the forthcoming celebration of the millennium at Czestochowa. The letter reviewed relations between the two countries, made a plea for a "dialogue," and offered forgiveness and asked for it in return. The regime in Warsaw reacted vehemently by accusing the church hierarchy of meddling with foreign affairs. On 15 December 1969 Cardinal Wyszynski gave Pope Paul VI a memorandum from the Episcopate requesting the appointment of regular bishops in the Oder-Neisse territories. The Vatican finally recognized the former German territories as de jure part of Poland on 28 June 1972, when it confirmed the appointment of six Polish bishops who had been officiating there as apostolic administrators.[41]

More recently, church-state relations have deteriorated to the extent that an episcopal letter was read on 28 November 1976 in all churches throughout the country. It mentioned that the government continued to wage a "hate-filled and brutal campaign against religion" and that "one can constantly feel a secret conspiracy against God." Then came a detailed indictment listing discrimination against believers, limits placed on new church buildings, atheism in schools, and even use of the legal system against religious persons.[42] During the first half of December, Cardinal Wyszynski in two different sermons criticized the government for having used force against demonstrators during the June 1976 food riots.

INTRABLOC AFFAIRS

Poland belongs to those treaty organizations that are sponsored by the Soviet Union. Among them, the Council for Mutual Economic Assistance (CMEA) is perhaps the most consequential, owing to the effects of its program of economic integration within the bloc. Involvement in this group has proven rather

---

40. An article whose title can be translated as "Pig-Headed and Intolerant" apeared in *Zycie Warszawy*, 16 October 1965; excerpts were repeated in the PZPR daily, *Trybuna ludu*.

41. See R. F. Staar, "Poland: Old Wine in New Bottles?," *Current History* (May 1973), p. 227.

42. Vatican radio, 28 November 1976, broadcast the letter. Note also the pastoral letter on education, cited in the *Washington Post*, 4 January 1977.

expensive to Poland, as it has to several other bloc countries. Large capital investments have been diverted to long-range CMEA economic-improvement projects. This capital has been badly needed for shorter-range domestic programs that have been delayed or remained abortive. Heavy expenditures for construction of the Polish section of the Danube-Oder canal and exploitation of brown-coal deposits in the Turoszow area are two examples of such large investments. The best illustration, perhaps, is the "friendship" oil pipeline, the northern spur of which crosses Poland from the USSR and ends at Schwedt in East Germany. An expensive refinery has been constructed at Plock, Poland, to process this Soviet crude petroleum. Part of the cost of the construction of the pipeline itself has also been borne by the government in Warsaw.

Polish economists, however, seem to recognize the problems that the long-range investments required by CMEA are generating in their domestic economy. They apparently no longer follow blindly the dictates of Moscow. For example, on the fifteenth anniversary of the CMEA, then deputy premier Piotr Jaroszewicz admitted that economic differences existed within the organization:

> Even a husband and wife who love each other are not always of the same opinion about investments. It is hard to imagine that eight countries are also of the same opinion. In Comecon [CMEA] the only method is to use persuasion through economic arguments.[43]

It seems likely that Poland's membership in the CMEA has been one of the factors contributing to a faltering economic development. It may be, however, that when the large investments in CMEA projects begin to provide a return, the government will be able to invest more funds in the domestic economy. This might conceivably remove some of the current economic weaknesses that beset the country. One attempt to improve the system has involved a cautious change that has led to some decentralization by transferring planning and responsibility down to the intermediate level of industrial unions for similar plants, though not to the level of the individual factory.[44]

Aside from the purely organizational aspects of intrabloc relations, a geographical issue loomed large among the postwar problems involving Poland and other countries. This issue involved the ratification of the country's new western boundary along the Oder and Western Neisse rivers.

The Oder-Neisse Line.   The origin of the problem concerning the boundary between Poland and Germany dates back to the latter part of the First World War.

---

43. Warsaw radio, as cited in *New York Times* 28 April 1964.
44. The Central Committee resolution on the "New System of Incentives" for the Polish economy, published in *Trybuna ludu*, 25 May 1970. This established during 1971 premiums for technological progress, lowering the rate of idleness of machinery and reducing shoddy production.

Roman Dmowski, the chairman of the Polish National Council that was then recognized by the West as the government of Poland, defended Poland's right to the Oder-Neisse river line as a frontier. Wladyslaw Sikorski, who was premier of the Polish exile government at London early in the Second World War, suggested the Oder River as the future boundary between the two countries after the war. In 1943 the Polish communists living in Moscow echoed the same proposal and further indicated that this extension of the boundary to the Oder River in the west should be considered compensation to Poland for the territories annexed by the USSR in the east (as a result of the 1939 Nazi-Soviet nonaggression pact).

The Big Three discussed Germany's future boundaries in the course of three conferences during and immediately after the war. At Teheran, in November 1943, Stalin proposed the boundary along the Oder River. The other two participants, Churchill and Roosevelt, agreed in principle, but no firm agreement was reached. Later, at the Yalta meeting during early February 1945, the border question again came up. The final communiqué after this conference specified that Poland would receive accessions of territory in the north and west, that the Poles themselves were to be consulted prior to a final settlement, and that the ultimate demarcation of borders would be determined at the peace conference after the war.

During the Potsdam meeting, in August 1945, the three heads of government agreed that "pending the final determination of Poland's western frontier, the former German territories east of a line running from the Baltic Sea and thence along the Oder River to the confluence of the Western Neisse River and along the Western Neisse to the Czechoslovakian frontier [should] be under the administration of the Polish State."[45] A procedure was also agreed upon for the removal of German citizens from these "Recovered Territories," as they have come to be known. This implied that Poland was to repopulate the vacated area.

Despite the provisional nature of the Potsdam agreement, the USSR in that same month signed a treaty of friendship with Poland that included an agreement for the demarcation of the Polish-Soviet frontier.[46] In June 1950 a Warsaw communiqué issued at the close of negotiations between East Germany and Poland announced agreement over their existing frontier and established cultural cooperation between the two countries. Finally, the new Brezhnev leadership in the Soviet Union traveled to Warsaw in April 1965 and reaffirmed the 1945 pact, signing a twenty-year extension[47] that specifically guarantees the inviolability of the Oder-Neisse border.

---

45. U.S. Senate, Committee on Foreign Relations, "The Berlin (Potsdam) Conference, July 17– August 2, 1945," in *A Decade of American Foreign Policy: Basic Documents, 1941–49* (Washington, D.C., 1950), pp. 43–44.

46. Text in S. M. Maiorov (ed.), *Vneshnyaya politika Sovetskogo Soyuza v period Otechestvennoi Voiny* (Moscow, 1947), III, pp. 386–387.

47. Text published in *Trybuna ludu*, 9 April 1965.

The regime has consolidated its hold over the Recovered Territories. Besides asserting legal and historical rights to these lands, the Warsaw goverment has repopulated them with more than eight million citizens of Polish nationality. Reconstruction efforts have been so successful that more than a third of the country's annual gross national product is attributed to production from these former German lands.[48] Many countries had apparently come to regard Poland's hegemony over the territories as a fait accompli, and most states in the West gave it tacit recognition.

Regardless of the earlier Western stand that Warsaw only administered the territories, it would seem that Poland's sovereignty over the area indeed represented a fait accompli. Only a major conflict or a significant shift in the world balance of power could result in a revision of the present boundary between Germany and Poland. During 1970 it appeared that the government of Chancellor Willy Brandt would recognize the border de jure, the Soviet-West German treaty in August of that year removing the main obstacle to recognition.[49] A visit by foreign minister Walter Scheel to Poland during early November solved certain problems and Chancellor Willy Brandt was invited to initial a treaty, which he signed on 7 December 1970 at Warsaw.[50]

Despite this agreement, it was not until after the foreign ministers of the two countries met again at Helsinki on 31 July 1975 (during the conference on security and cooperation in Europe) that a comprehensive settlement of the issues could be agreed upon. A new nineteen-article treaty[51] specifies that Poland will receive 1.3 billion marks ($543 million) in pension claims as indemnity to Polish victims of Nazi concentration camps and one billion marks ($416 million) in low-interest credits.

In return, Poland obligated itself to issue between 120,000 and 125,000 exit visas over the next four years to individuals of German extraction who wish to join their families in the Federal Republic. More than one-half million people had been resettled in this manner during the preceding two decades. Whether the Polish government will meet its obligation regarding ethnic Germans is impossible to predict, although the promise made by former foreign minister Stefan Olszowski that fifty thousand people would be allowed to leave during 1974 apparently was not kept.[52]

---

48. See R. F. Staar, "Poland: Myth versus Reality," in *Current History* (April 1969), pp. 218–223.

49. This treaty recognizes the inviolability of borders, "including the Oder-Neisse line." Article 3, as given in *Krasnaya zvezda*, 13 August 1970; Moscow.

50. Text broadcast over Warsaw radio, 20 November 1970; i.e., in advance.

51. Published in *Trybuna ludu*, 10 October 1975.

52. Cited by RFE, *Situation Report*, 3 December 1976. However, a later report from the Federal Republic of Germany indicates that about 2,600 ethnic Germans are coming out of Poland each month. *Christian Science Monitor*, 11 January 1977.

Chapter 7

Socialist Republic of Romania

The history of Romania has indelibly affected the makeup of its population. While the communists seek to create a new world in Eastern Europe, the path of their type of "socialism" is no longer the same for all countries. The roots of the past not only affect the attitudes of the great masses of people whom totalitarian regimes hold captive; this very same past is also locked into the attitudes of the current leaders.

These men lay claim to an infallible interpretation of Marxism-Leninism, but what they practice is far removed from ideological purity. The contemporary Romanian dictatorship may have as firm a hold on the nation as any previous regime had. Impeding the road to a national variety of socialism and a new world, however, are historical influences that express themselves in a variety of ways.

From the background of this land emanates the strong influence of a Latin heritage. Romanians point to it with pride today, claiming that they are Latins and not Slavs. As proof they cite the fact that more than 60 percent of the words in their language have Latin roots, while only 20 percent are of Slavic derivation. Because of this heritage, among other reasons, the views of the people have generally been pro-Western. Perhaps this is why much of the leadership of the Romanian communist party in the past came from ethnic minorities that felt no compunction about aligning their goals with those of Russia and other Slavic groups.[1]

Because of Romania's alliance with the Axis powers until August 1944, the USSR took steps early to press for a government that would be essentially pro-Soviet. Even so, provisions regarding the organization and functioning of central and local agencies contained in the communist-inspired constitutions of 1948, 1952, and 1965 (amended in May 1974) have been applied only when it has been convenient for the rulers. The postwar regime in Romania has generally

---

1. D. A. Tomasic, "The Rumanian Communist Leadership," *Slavic Review* (October 1961), p. 478.

shown a discrepancy between its professed theory of constitutional government and its actual practice.

In February 1945 the USSR's political representative, Andrei Vyshinskiy, peremptorily ordered King Michael to appoint Petru Groza, a communist-selected front man, as premier. The cabinet proposed by Groza included representatives from a number of different political parties. Communists were placed in the key Interior, Justice, and Public Works ministries. They soon expanded their power from these important positions. The monarchy lasted two more years, acting as a passive restraint, but it remained powerless to prevent this consolidation.[2]

The war-crimes trial of Romanian leaders who were held responsible for supporting the Axis assisted in immobilizing all opposition and prevented the establishment of a liberal and peasant coalition. In addition, the USSR seemed to favor Romanian claims to that part of Transylvania taken away by the Axis Powers in 1940, and this generated some support for the communist program. Opposition groups were intimidated by the use, or even threat, of violence. From a base of fewer than 1,000 members in 1944, through a rapid recruitment up to 217,000 by September 1945, the Romanian Workers' (communist) party soon attained the numbers to staff its regime.

During the consolidation period, the essential features of the prewar government were retained. The Grand National Assembly was reinstated in 1946, though as a unicameral parliament. Suffrage was extended to women, and the voting age was lowered to eighteen. Parliament experienced a purge of noncommunist deputies and underwent transformation into a rubber-stamp type of legislative body. In December 1947 King Michael was forced to abdicate. Soon thereafter parliament passed Law 393, illegally abolishing the existing constitution of 1923 and calling for a constituent assembly to decide upon a new basic law. A draft constitution actually appeared before the constituent assembly could be elected; it was published by the People's Democratic Front (the front, as in other bloc countries, represented an elector organization for the communist party and its ancillary groups). The new constitution, which introduced the designation "Romanian People's Republic," was adopted in April 1948. Communist rule now superficially appeared to have a legitimate basis.[3]

NEW CONSTITUTIONS

The basic law of 1952 represented a modification of the one introduced four years previously. Like the 1936 Stalin constitution, after which it was closely

---

2. Zbigniew K. Brzezinski, *The Soviet Bloc* (New York, 1962), rev. ed., p. 16. See also Ghita Ionescu, *Communism in Rumania, 1944–1962* (London, 1964), for a complete account of this process.

3. A. V. Mitskevich, *Gosudarstvennyi stroi Rumynskoi Narodnoi Respubliki* (Moscow, 1957), p. 15, discusses the new people's democracy.

patterned, the Romanian document appeared to grant all fundamental rights to the people. These rights, however, were subordinated to the interests of achieving socialism. The interpretation of "interests" rested with the ruling party. The Romanian Workers' party gained its official mandate in Article 86, which proclaimed it to be the "vanguard of the working people" and the "leading force of organizations of the working people as well as of the State organs and institutions."[4]

Therefore, as in the USSR, the ruling party interpreted the constitution, made laws, and maintained complete dictatorial power. Judicial prerogatives also transcended constitutional rights. From the standpoint of the individual citizen, since no judicial review over the constitutionality of government acts existed, the articles of the constitution pertaining to basic rights remained unenforceable. The constitution prescribed the various organs of government, including the ministries, but even these frequently did not correspond to the written outline and were in a constant state of change.

The subsequent constitution, which was adopted on 21 August 1965, did not substantially change the system.[5] It merely proclaims in Article 1 that Romania is now a socialist republic, meaning that the country has reached the level of development previously attained by the USSR (1936), Yugoslavia (1958), and Czechoslovakia (1960). In keeping with Article 1, the name of the country no longer included the reference to a people's republic; it became the Socialist Republic of Romania.

Governmental Structure. The present governmental system is similar, both structurally and functionally, to the one established by the 1952 basic law. The fundamental difference is that Article 3 of the 1965 constitution proclaims the entire regime to be led by the "Romanian Communist party."[6] This control is most direct at the administrative level because party members hold key positions in executive and legislative organs as well as in the judicial arm of government. Although the organizational provisions of the constitution are generally upheld, the composition and action of the various agencies follow the directives of the party.

The central government consists of the Grand National Assembly or parliament, the Council of State, the Council of Ministers, and the court system. Functions are not clearly defined because the communists reject the concepts of separation of powers and checks and balances. The Grand National Assembly is theoretically supreme. It remains essentially a legislative branch, although its function is to provide approval rather than to act in a deliberative capacity. The

---

4. "Constitution of the Rumanian People's Republic," in Amos J. Peaslee (ed.), *Constitutions of Nations* (The Hague, 1956), 2d ed., III, p. 251.

5. [Romania], *Constitution of the Socialist Republic of Rumania* (Bucharest, 1965), p. 34.

6. The party's ninth congress, 19–24 July 1965, adopted this name, *Partidul Communist Roman*. See the article on these changes in *Polityka*, 24 July 1965; Warsaw.

Council of State, which was formerly called the presidium of parliament, plays the role of a collective presidency for the country. The Council of Ministers is the supreme administrative and executive organ.[7] The courts are in charge of administering justice.

Grand National Assembly.   According to Article 43 of the 1965 constitution, the Grand National Assembly has twenty-three specific powers that range from adopting and amending the constitution to appointing and recalling the supreme armed-forces commander. This legislature is elected every four years and has one representative for each sixty thousand citizens. The balloting on 9 March 1975, for example, elected 349 deputies, all of whom were Front of Socialist Unity (formerly People's Democratic Front) candidates.[8] Laws are adopted by a simple majority and are signed by the president and the secretary to the Council of State. The Assembly convenes twice a year for ordinary sessions. Extraordinary meetings may be called when one-third of all Assembly members or the Council of State considers it necessary.

The Assembly elects a chairman and four deputies to preside over sessions and guide the flow of business. All members are entitled to address enquiries to the government and to individual members of the Council of Ministers. They are immune from arrest or prosecution and can not be held legally responsible without the consent of the Grand National Assembly or, between its sessions, the Council of State. Such privileges, however, do not alter the fact that the Assembly is merely a facade that helps to perpetuate the appearance of democracy. It is unlikely that the new rules will change this situation, although they do call for more activity on the part of the members.

State Council and the Presidency.   The Council of State presently consists of twenty-six members elected by the Grand National Assembly who, from among themselves, elect a chairman and his three deputies. Theoretically accountable to the Assembly under the constitution, the State Council functions more like a legislature than does the Assembly. It exercises power through decrees that are subsequently approved by the Assembly. This fact is evident from the small number of laws passed by the legislature itself and from the large number that are officially enacted only after having originated with the Council of State. Lawmaking, however, is a secondary matter. The primary

---

7. The 1965 constitution created a permanent Standing Bureau, attached to the Council of Ministers, that comprised an inner cabinet for "collectively settling problems which require an urgent solution." It probably included the premier and perhaps all or several of the ten deputy premiers. RFE, *Communist Bloc Party-Government Line-Up* (17 December 1976), p. 22; henceforth cited as *Line-Up.*

8. It was claimed that 99.9 percent of all registered voters had gone to the polls. Bucharest radio, 10 March 1975.

function of both bodies, like that of the USSR Supreme Soviet and its presidium, is their joint role in the ratification of decrees issued by the government's executive branch.

At the end of a legislative term the Council of State orders elections to be held within three months, but it remains in power until the new Assembly has had an opportunity to elect another Council. In an emergency the Grand National Assembly may extend the mandate of the Council for the duration.

Until 1974 the chairman of the State Council was ex officio the titular head of state, that is, the president. In 1948 and again in 1952 a noncommunist was elected chairman for tactical reasons. In 1961 the party leader Gheorghiu Gheorghiu-Dej was elected to this post, and upon his death in 1965, Chivu Stoica became chairman. He was replaced on 13 March 1969 by Nicolae Ceausescu.[9] Five years later the constitution was amended to provide for the position of President of the Socialist Republic of Romania. Although the State Council continues to exist, the President is now ex officio also its chairman. He has additional prerogatives by virtue of the office of the presidency, being entitled to issue decrees and to take other measures on his own initiative without State Council approval.

The Executive.   The administration of the government is centered where the ruling communist party can best exert its influence and control, in the Council of Ministers. It is significant that more members of the party's Executive Committee serve there than on the Council of State. All key positions are filled by trusted communists.

The Council of Ministers is elected by the Grand National Assembly; theoretically it is responsible to that body and, between its sessions, to the Council of State. Decisions by the Council of Ministers are formulated as orders that are binding throughout the country. A good example is the decree authorizing public meetings to decide on contributions in money and labor to works of "public interest," such as schools, maternity homes, roads, and bridges. A summary of the Council's eleven official prerogatives appears in Article 70 of the new constitution.[10] This document also fully describes the functions of the ministries.

The large number of ministers and agencies under them reflects the specialization as well as the centralized nature of the economy and the extensive administrative apparatus of the government. The exact number of ministries and agencies is in constant flux, with fusion or separation reflecting current needs. In 1976 there were thirty-eight units.[11]

---

9. This man also heads the Romanian communist party.

10. See also the new law adopted on the organization of the Council of Ministers. *Scinteia,* 18 December 1969, gives the full text.

11. RFE, *Line-Up,* pp. 22–23.

Local Government.   The administrative subdivisions of Romania include thirty-nine counties and the municipality of Bucharest. Within these units there are 236 towns and 2,706 communes. According to official estimates, the total population of 21.5 million is about 57 percent rural and 43 percent urban.[12]

The local instruments of state power are called people's councils; they correspond to soviets in the USSR. These operate under the principle of democratic centralism, with a downward flow of guidance that limits the initiative of subordinate units. People's councils operate at county, municipal, district, town, and commune levels. More important administrative organs within the councils are called executive committees. It is noteworthy that while the constitution proclaims the supremacy of the councils themselves, the executive committees are packed with trusted party members who exercise the real power.

Elections in counties and municipal districts are held every four years, in towns and communes every other year. Upon the expiration of its term, the executive committee retains power pending the election of a new council, in direct parallel with the State Council and the Grand National Assembly at the top of the organizational pyramid. The latest elections at the local levels coincided with those held nationally in March 1975, and approximately 165,000 deputies were chosen.[13]

Under the electoral provisions in the constitution, suffrage is universal for all persons eighteen years of age and older. Candidates for the people's councils must be at least twenty-three. The right to nominate candidates is reserved to the Front of Socialist Unity. Article 25 of the constitution denies suffrage to citizens who are considered unworthy and unreliable, including "mentally alienated and deficient people."

Judicial System.   The fundamental tasks of the judiciary, as they are defined in the constitution and subsequent laws, include, since 1965, defending the regime of socialism, the rights of the working people, and the interests of state agencies and institutions. Theoretically the judiciary must ensure the observance of justice and, furthermore, it must educate the people in the spirit of devotion to the fatherland and to the construction of socialism. Here, as is usual under communist regimes, politics becomes the basis for law. Legal rules must be interpreted in the light of the class struggle, and justice is deemed to be the will of the working class.

The task of administering justice is carried out by the *procuratura* or the office of the prosecutor general,[14] and by regular and special courts. Regular courts, which are known as people's tribunals, hear civil, penal, and any other cases

---

12. *Anuarul Statistic al Republicei Socialiste Romania, 1975,* pp. 5 and 9.

13. RFE, *Situation Report,* 14 March 1975.

14. The criminal code is discussed in RFE report (by Michael Cismarescu), "The New Rumanian Code on Criminal Procedure or the Limits of Socialist Legality," 24 January 1969.

within their competence. The jurisdiction of each court is graduated in accordance with the level of government at which it functions. Military courts hear cases and announce the penalties provided by law to punish such enemies of the people as traitors, spies, those sabotaging the construction of socialism or committing "crimes against peace and humanity," warmongers, embezzlers, and those who destroy socialist property. Courts in the city of Bucharest and at the county level hear cases that are on appeal from the people's tribunals. The supreme court, theoretically, is entrusted with control over the judicial activities of the other courts; it meets for this purpose at least once every three months. Soviet practices are copied here also, since the supreme court has no power to review the constitutionality of statutes. Judges of all courts are nominated exclusively by the Romanian communist party. People's tribunal judges play a larger role than is specified in the constitution. For example, the Justice minister can move them from court to court to meet exigencies.

The prosecutor general possesses the highest supervisory authority over the observance of the law by all central and local government organs. Naturally he must be a trusted member of the party. He is "elected" by the Grand National Assembly for a term of five years. He then designates his deputies and prosecutors to serve at lower levels for periods of four years. All prosecutors are independent of local government organs since they are formally responsible to the Assembly or, between its sessions, to the State Council. However, the *procuratura* is really an organization that is directed exclusively by the party.[15] It is modeled closely after the corresponding agency in the USSR. The prosecutor general enjoys a "consultative" vote in the Council of State and in the Council of Ministers.

Education. The structure of Romanian education is founded on three basic enactments. These are the August 1948 educational reform law; the July 1956 joint decree of the party's Central Committee and the Council of Ministers that implemented the resolutions of the party's second congress; and the October 1961 decree transforming into law the resolutions of the third party congress.

Since October 1961 compulsory education has encompassed the first eight grades, a change that was made to parallel the system extant in the USSR. This period comprises elementary school grades one to five, and intermediate grades six through eight. Four additional grades, from nine through twelve, provide a complete secondary education. These upper grades are oriented toward either the humanities or the physical and mathematical sciences. If they are complemented

---

15. RFE report (by Michael Cismarescu), "The Reform of the Rumanian Judiciary and the Procuratura," 21 February 1969. *Procuratura* prerogatives have been restricted, according to new legislation. See also the Ceausescu speech to interior ministry leadership cadres dealing with this in *Scinteia,* 24 December 1976.

by two years of employment and practical experience, they can lead to a higher education.

Admission to the six universities and to some thirty-six other institutions of higher learning in Romania is based upon both successful completion of an entrance examination and political reliability, with the latter requirement generally certified by the communist party or the youth organization unit at the applicant's place of residence.[16] The aims of the educational system, thus, include political conformity. Vocational training is provided at special schools. Technicians who teach at these schools have both specialized training and practical experience. The November 1976 "Action Program for Ideological, Political, and Cultural-Educational Work" stipulates that all textbooks must be revised and improved within a period of two years.

ROMANIAN COMMUNIST PARTY

A communist movement was established in 1921, only to be outlawed three years later. The party continued its agitation underground, but effective government police harassment prevented the maintenance of a viable political organization. Determined action in 1936, which led to the arrest and conviction of nearly all the communist leaders, virtually eliminated the party as a political force. The movement had little or no war record of partisan activity to give it prestige, and in 1944 its reduced leadership included a large number of Jews, Ukrainians, and Hungarians.[17]

In August, King Michael forced a change of government and took Romania out of the war it had been fighting as a German ally. Hitler responded by bombing Bucharest, following which the king formally declared war on Germany and brought in his fifteen divisions on the side of the Red Army.

> Romania's change of front, together with the Teheran decision not to open a front in the Balkans, decided the fate of Central Europe, decided that the Soviet Union should dominate the whole region, that its new order should be a communist new order. Generalissimo Stalin therefore had good reason later to award to King Michael the highest Soviet decoration, the Order of Victory.[18]

In most of the other countries within the USSR orbit, communist-dominated "front" governments assumed power immediately after Red Army occupation. In Romania, however, a so-called bourgeois government (although it included

---

16. Randolph L. Braham, *Education in the Rumanian People's Republic* (Washington, D.C., 1963), p. 115. The universities are at Bucharest, Iasi, Cluj, Timisoara, Tirgu Mures and Craiova. According to *Scinteia*, 26 November 1976, none of them have textbooks for all subjects that are taught.
17. Biographic data on this point are in Tomasic, *op. cit.* (in note 1 above), pp. 480–489.
18. Hugh Seton-Watson, *The East European Revolution* (New York, 1956), p. 90.

communist-party representation) was tolerated for a short time. In March 1945 the USSR ordered the king to install a People's Democratic Front regime. This was done, and the communists received the three ministries they had demanded: Interior, Justice, and National Economy. They sought mass support by redistributing confiscated land to peasant smallholders and promising improved working conditions to factory workers. National and local government administrations were controlled by placing trusted personnel in key positions.

In February 1948 the communists and the left-wing social democrats merged to form the Romanian Workers' party. A new Central Committee and Politburo drew a majority of their members from the previous communist organization, and the new party, from its inception, clearly came under the leadership of the old communists. Thus, in the period between 1944 and 1952, an initially insignificant communist movement, working with assistance of Soviet advisors and supported by the presence of Soviet troops, ousted and destroyed all political opposition to make itself the sole ruler of Romania.

Central Organization. The supreme organ of the Romanian communist party is the congress, to which delegates are elected by regional conferences. Congresses are to be called at least every five years; at these times delegates hear and approve reports by central organs, adopt programs, and establish basic policy. They elect a Central Committee and a Central Audit Commission, which controls party finances. After performing these functions, the congresses then delegate their authority to the Central Committee until the next session.[19]

As the seat of power between congresses, the Central Committee provides a rostrum for publicizing the party program, directs and controls party as well as government organs, and also administers party finances. It has the responsibility for electing the Political Executive Committee and the Central Committee Secretariat. These bodies are not elective but actually consist of leading party personalities who are chosen by an inner group and then rubber-stamped by the Central Committee.

As the foremost consultative body of the party, the Central Committee tends to include the top stratum of government after the familiar model of interlocking directorates. (See table 37.) Of the thirty-eight persons listed as members of the Council of Ministers in 1976, the majority hold membership or candidate status on the Central Committee of the party. According to an excellent but dated analysis,[20] in 1961 half the Central Committee was made up of hard-core party professionals, with 80 percent of this half being drawn from the inner circles of

---

19. At the most recent (the eleventh) congress, the 2,450 delegates reelected Nicolae Ceausescu secretary-general and also elected 203 members and 153 candidates for membership on the Central Committee. Names are listed in CIA, *Directory of Officials of the Socialist Republic of Romania* (Washington, D.C., July, 1976), pp. 72–78; henceforth cited as *Directory*.

20. Tomasic, *op. cit.* (in note 1 above), p. 492.

government or industry and the remaining 20 percent from lesser positions of power.

As has been mentioned previously, the locus of party power rests with the Political Executive Committee. It functions as the primary policy-making body and also reviews work of the Secretariat and the Central Collegium (formerly known as the Party Control Commission), which maintains party discipline.[21] (The Collegium has been downgraded in recent years; it now performs only control and investigative functions.) The Political Executive Committee selects a Permanent Bureau, which is at present composed of nine members. Although this small group is concerned with day-to-day matters of high-level significance, it is not equivalent to a Politburo in the other East European ruling parties or to the former Standing Presidium, which had existed until spring 1974 in the Romanian party. The Political Executive Committee now appears to be the policy-making body. Those who decide policy are, as often as not, the ones who implement it. The ten-member Secretariat sees to it that policies are executed. Although the Secretariat is nominally elected by the Central Committee, it is really appointed by the party leadership and represents one of the main power centers.

Decisions and policies established by the leaders and checked by the Secretariat and the Central Collegium are supposed to be reviewed critically and then approved by plenary sessions of the Central Committee at least four times a year.[22] This procedure, however, merely provides a forum through which the party leadership can submit to the Central Committee for its rubber-stamp approval the party line as established by the Political Executive Committee.

Regional Organization. The county is the intermediate organizational echelon within the party.[23] Committees at this level are near duplicates of the Central Committee at the top, both organizationally and functionally, although they are smaller in size.

The supreme organ of the country is the conference, which is called to meet by its respective committee every two years. It reviews and approves reports, debates problems connected with party activities, and elects a new party committee as well as delegates to the conference of the next higher party organization or to the national party congress. Conferences are basically sounding boards, and the policies and directives issued by the Central Committee are implemented by lower committees and secretariats that are subordinate to them.

---

21. RFE report, "The New Statutes of the Rumanian Communist Party," 9 October 1969, includes a translation of the statutes as published in *Scinteia,* 7 August 1969. They describe the functions of these organs.

22. RFE report, "The New Rumanian Central Committee," 25 August 1969, contains an excellent analysis.

23. For incumbents in these local organizations, see *Directory* (in note 19 above), pp. 87–113.

TABLE 37

Romania's Interlocking Directorate, 1977
Political Executive Committee

Members (23)	Government position	Other party post
Ceausescu, Nicolae	President; Chairman, State Council	Secretary-general; member, PermBuro
Bobu, Emil	Deputy Chairman, State Council	Secretary (military and security)
Burtica, Cornel	*Deputy premier*	*Member, PermBuro*; Secretary (press and propaganda)
Ceausescu, Elena	Head, Chemical Research Institute	*Member, PermBuro*
Cioara, Gheorghe	Deputy premier	–
Ciobanu, Lina	Light Industries minister; Chairman, Council on Women	–
Dinca, Ion	Head, Bucharest People's Council	First Secretary, Bucharest
Draganescu, Emil	Deputy premier	–
Fazekas, Janos	Deputy premier	–
Ionita, Ion	Deputy premier	–
Lupu, Petre	–	*Chairman, Central Collegium*
Manescu, Manea	Premier	Member, Permburo
Niculescu, Paul	Deputy premier	–
Oprea, Gheorghe	Deputy premier	Member, PermBuro
Pana, Gheorghe	*Labor minister*; Chairman, trade unions	–
Patan, Ion	Deputy premier	Member, PermBuro
Popescu, Dumitru	Chairman, Radio and TV Council	Secretary (mass communications)
Radulescu, Gheorghe	Deputy premier	*Member, PermBuro*
Rautu, Leonte	–	Rector, Stefan Gheorghiu Academy
Trofin, Virgil	–	First Secretary, Brasov
Uglar, Iosif	Chairman, Committee on People's Councils	Secretary (nationalities and complaints)
Verdet, Ilie	–	*Member, PermBuro*; Secretary (state party organizations and cadres)
Voitec, Stefan	Deputy Chairman, State Council	–
Candidates (15)		
Andrei, Stefan	–	Secretary (foreign relations); Member, PermBuro
Banc, Iosif	Chairman, Workers' Control	Secretary
Coman, Ion	Defense minister	–
Coman, Teodor	Interior minister	–
Dalea, Mihai	Director, Chem Import Export; Chairman, Soviet Friendship Society	–
Dobrescu, Miu	Chairman, Culture and Education Council	First Secretary, Suceava
Fazekas, Ludovic	Head, Harghita County People's Council	First Secretary, Harghita

TABLE 37 (Cont.)

Romania's Interlocking Directorate, 1977
Political Executive Committee

Candidates (15)	Government position	Other party post
Gere, Mihai	Deputy to National Assembly	−
Giosan, Nicolae	Chairman, National Assembly	−
Iliescu, Ion	Head, Iasi County People's Council	First Secretary, Iasi
Mocuta, Stefan	Head, Cluj County People's Council	First Secretary, Cluj
Patilinet, Vasile	Forestry and Construction Materials minister	−
Telescu, Mihai	Head, Timis County People's Council	First Secretary, Timis
Ursu, Ion	Chairman, Scientific and Technical Council; Director Atomic Physics Institute	−
Winter, Richard	Deputy Chairman, German Nationality Working People's Council	First Secretary, Sibiu

Secretariat (3 plus 7 above = 10)		
Dascalescu, Constantin	—	Agriculture
Duma, Aurel	—	Chief of Chancery
Stanescu, Ion	Deputy premier	—

Source: CIA, *Directory of Officials of the Socialist Republic of Romania* (Washington, D.C., July 1976), pp. 226 passim; Bucharest radio, 3 November 1976 and 25 January 1977; *Scinteia*, 27 January 1977.
Note: Italics indicate new appointment in January 1977.

The county committee is supposed to meet every three months. It always remains in contact with the party apparatus at the center through the county first secretary, who is usually a member of the Central Committee. The town or commune committee meets every two months and represents the immediate superior to the basic party organizations that comprise the base of the pyramid.

Basic Party Organization.   By statute, these units constitute the party's foundation, since they are the ultimate executors of the policies and directives issued by the Central Committee. They exist in government, industry, agriculture, schools, and military units. Their size can vary from a minimum of three to a maximum of three hundred members. The larger ones are headed by bureaus. If they contain fewer than ten members, the leadership comprises a secretary and one deputy. These lowest-ranking organizations (of which there are about seventy thousand)[24] play a dual role; they are the executors of party and government policies and directives and supervisors over the activities of local administration and other nonparty organs. This arrangement is indicative of the manner in which party and government functions overlap and of the fact that the party and its organs are placed above the government and its institutions.

Party Membership. Probably the most astonishing aspect of the communist movement has been its growth during the postwar years, due to different kinds of pressure. Its size is estimated to have increased from about one thousand members[25] in 1944 to almost one million only four years later. Over the next several years it fluctuated between six hundred thousand and nine hundred thousand members. In 1964, when the party had 1.2 million members and candidates, about 16 percent or two hundred thousand of these were classified as activists. In 1976, total membership was reported to be almost 2.5 million, or a little more than 10 percent of the Romanian population.[26]

Like the communist parties in the other East European countries, the party in Romania has had difficulty in maintaining a proper representation of factory workers in its ranks. Even with mass recruitment during 1947 the proletarian component comprised less than 40 percent, with the majority of the members coming from white-collar employees and the intelligentsia. This emphasis on derivation from the industrial workers follows from the glorification of the proletariat in communist doctrine and from a conviction that the leaders within this class—the competitive "Stakhanovite" types who have a zeal for surpassing production goals—are generally more reliable, more susceptible to indoctrination, and easier to control. Recruitment procedures were relaxed for this group, and by 1960 the party could claim an increase in the percentage of factory workers. By 1975 the total in this category had not quite reached the 1960 level. (See table 38.) Lack of verification for these figures and the uncertain definition of a worker make such regime statistics questionable. A 1976 report on cadre policy states that the party now has more members with a higher education than it had two years before.[27] Of course, those with a working-class background are given preference in promotion.

Mass Organizations. The Union of Communist Youth (UTC), which was originally founded in 1922 and reorganized in 1948 as a junior branch of the party, comprises a mass organization of some 2.3 million members.[28] It is

24. *Scinteia,* 25 July 1975.

25. U.S. Department of State, *Moscow's European Satellites* (Washington, D.C., 1955), p. 12.

26. V. N. Vinogradov (ed.), *Istoriya Rumynii novogo i noveishego vremeni* (Moscow, 1964), p. 382; *Scinteia,* 20 March 1970; RFE, *Situation Report,* 7 May 1976.

27. RFE, *Situation Report,* 7 May 1976.

28. *World Marxist Review* (August 1970), supplement, p. 9.

TABLE 38

ROMANIAN COMMUNIST PARTY SOCIAL COMPOSITION, 1960, 1970, AND 1975

Category	June 1960 Number	Percent	March 1970 Number	Percent	December 1975 Number	Percent
Workers	426,000	51.0	867,290	43.4	1,288,717	ca. 50.0
Peasants	186,000	22.0	531,447	26.6	515,487	ca. 20.0
Intelligentsia	83,000	11.0	481,083	24.0	511,642	ca. 22.0
Others	131,000	16.0	119,900	6.0	103,088	ca. 8.0
Total	826,000	100.0	1,999,720	100.0	2,418,934	100.0

SOURCES: *Scinteia*, 21 July 1960, 20 March 1970, and 24 April 1976.

NOTE: About 108,000 persons joined the party in 1975. Their composition according to category was 66.9 percent workers; 12.5 percent peasants; and 20.6 percent intellectuals and white-collar employees.

patterned after the Komsomol in the Soviet Union. The UTC is organized similarly to the party, and party rules indicate that those in the age group of eighteen to twenty must belong to the UTC to be eligible for party membership. Apart from providing the core of future party members and cadres, the UTC has the responsibility for carrying out and supervising the execution of party policies as they affect the whole of Romanian youth within and above its age range.

Until April 1966, the UTC supervised the introductory Pioneers for children, whose membership of 1.3 million encompassed about 70 percent of the nine-to fourteen age group. The inspiration provided by a similar organization in the Soviet Union can be noted in the Pioneers' former motto: "In the fight for the cause of Lenin and Stalin, forward." They are under the direct control of the party. A cultural-ideological program approved on 2 November 1976 established a new organization called "Fatherland's Falcons" for children in the four-to-seven age group. Political indoctrination, henceforth, will include the entire population.

The General Confederation of Trade Unions is one of Romania's largest mass organizations. With a membership of 6,066,544, it covers the complete spectrum of workers and professional people.[29] Like the party, it is organized according to the principle of democratic centralism. The sixteen component trade unions maintain county councils that are superimposed upon some 11,600 basic units. Instead of representing workers, factory committees, and professional groups, the trade-union apparatus has the primary purpose of insuring the successful fulfillment of the government's economic plans. It exercises the additional responsibility of raising the cultural level, and especially the political con-sciousness, of its members. Indoctrination is generally carried out at the lowest level by party or UTC members who belong to the local trade-union council.

---

29. RFE report, "The Romanian Trade Union Organization Congress," 18 May 1976.

The Front of Socialist Unity, which in 1968 replaced the People's Democratic Front, is open to those who are eligible for membership in other mass organizations. In order to maintain the fiction of representative government, the party has chosen to consider all candidates in parliamentary and local elections as representing the Front of Socialist Unity. The Front accepts these nominees as its own, promotes the election, and presents a political program that is identical with the program of the ruling party. The activities of the Front are limited to election periods occurring every two and four years, that is, at both local and national levels.

DOMESTIC AND FOREIGN POLICY

The history of the people dates back to the second century, when Roman legions were stationed in what is today Romania. The language, a Romance tongue of Latin origin, can also be traced to this period. Somewhat modified by Slavic, Albanian, Hungarian, Greek, and Turkish influences in the centuries that followed, it still has today a majority of word elements that are derived from the Latin once spoken in the Eastern Roman Empire. This fact (noted earlier) continues to be important in the current situation, perhaps as important as the demographic and geographic features of the country.

Losses of territory occurring in the early part of World War II included parts of Transylvania, Bessarabia, Northern Bukovina, and Southern Dobruja. Transylvania was eventually recovered from Hungary; Bessarabia[30] and Northern Bukovina, however, were annexed in 1940 to the Soviet Union, recaptured by the Romanians in 1941, but lost again in 1944; Southern Dobruja has been kept by Bulgaria. The various modifications in borders have contributed to animosity between Romania and her neighbors, including the USSR.

National Minorities. Although the population is principally of ethnic Romanian origin, some 13 to 15 percent comprise minorities. The largest minority groups are the Hungarians (in 1966 they numbered 1.6 million or 8.5 percent of the population) and the Germans (almost four hundred thousand or 2 percent of the population), but there are also smaller groups of Jews, Ukrainians, Russians, Bulgarians, Gypsies, Turks, Tartars, and others.

The treatment of the Hungarian minority after 1948 represented an important issue, and one with which the goverment in Budapest was concerned. In 1952 a Hungarian Autonomous Region was established under the provisions of the Romanian constitution adopted that year. After unrest arose among the people in this autonomous region during the 1956 Hungarian revolution just across the border, however, the Romanian government began to restrict the rights of this

---

30. According to a Soviet source, ". . . in June 1940 the troops of the Red Army came to the aid of the toilers of Bessarabia." *Kommunist Moldavii* (May 1970), p. 78.

minority. In 1959 the Hungarian-language university of Cluj was merged with the Romanian-language university in the same city. During the following year the boundaries of the Hungarian Autonomous Region were redrawn to exclude a large homogeneous Hungarian population and thus to provide a mixed population that included a larger number of Romanians.

Since the advent of Nicolae Ceausescu to the party leadership in 1965, a more conciliatory policy toward minorities has been followed. However, limitations still restrict minority activity and links with Romania are emphasized. Although schooling in their mother tongues is permitted, minority youths are expected to learn Romanian. In the territorial reorganization of 1968, the Hungarian Autonomous Region was abolished, as were all fifteen other regions. Among the thirty-nine new counties that were created then, however, two had Hungarian majorities and several others had large Hungarian minorities.[31] Table 39 shows the ethnic composition of the country, together with the extent of change over the 1930—1966 period, the latest period for which census data are available.

TABLE 39

ETHNIC GROUPS IN ROMANIA, 1930, 1956, AND 1966

| | 1930[a] | | 1956 | | 1966[b] | |
Nationality	Number	Percent	Number	Percent	Number	Percent
Romanians	12,981,324	71.9	14,996,114	85.7	16,746,510	87.7
Hungarians	1,425,507	7.9	1,587,675	9.1	1,619,592	8.5
Germans	745,421	4.1	384,708	2.2	382.595	2.0
Jews	728,115	4.0	146,264	0.8	42,888	0.2
Ukrainians	582,115	3.2	60,479	0.4	54,705	0.3
Russians	409,150	2.3	38,731	0.2	39,483	0.2
Bulgarians	366,384	2.0	12,040	0.1	11,193	0.1
Gypsies	262,501	1.5	104,216	0.6	64,197	0.3
Turks	154,772	0.9	14,329	0.1	18,040	0.1
Găugăuzi (Tartar)	105,750	0.6	20,469	0.2	22,151	0.1
Others	295,989	1.6	124,425	0.6	101,809	0.5
Totals	18,057,028	100.0	17,489,450	100.0	19,103,163	100.0

SOURCES: *Anuarul Statistic al Rominiei 1939* (Bucharest, 1939); *Recensamintul populatiei din 21 Februarie 1956* (Bucharest, 1956); and Bucharest radio, 18 September 1966. Cited by Robert R. King, *Minorities Under Communism* (Cambridge, Mass., 1973), p. 267, from which the above table was taken.

NOTES: [a]The territory of Romania at this time included Bessarabia, Northern Bukovina, and Southern Dobruja.

[b]A new census has been announced for 5—12 January 1977 by *Scinteia,* 5 December 1976.

31. Robert R. King, *Minorities Under Communism* (Cambridge, Mass., 1973), pp. 35—44, 82—85, 146—169. An agreement between Bucharest and Budapest should improve the status of the 1.6 million Hungarians in Transylvania. *Christian Science Monitor,* 5 January 1977.

The 1965 constitution also makes special provision for minority groups. Article 22 states the following:

> In the Socialist Republic of Rumania, the coinhabiting national minorities are ensured the free utilization of their native language as well as books, papers, magazines, theatres and education at all levels in their own language. In districts also inhabited by a population of non-Rumanian nationality, all the bodies and institutions use the language of the respective nationality in speech and in writing and appoint officials from its ranks or from the ranks of other citizens who know the language and way of life of the local population.

At one time, two thousand Hungarian elementary schools and one thousand Hungarian high schools existed in the former autonomous province.[32] By December 1960, however, the southern part had been transferred to the ethnically Romanian province of Brasov. Hungarian archives and libraries were destroyed and buildings were torn down to provide stone for new construction. In education, a system of "parallel sections" added a Romanian curriculum, and after a period of time, the Hungarian curriculum was eliminated. However, in 1969 some 240,000 students were being taught Hungarian, German, and other minority languages.[33]

The Economy.   In the past Romania has been primarily an agricultural country. More than half the population is still classified as rural. Some 62 percent of the total labor force is employed in industry and nonagricultural work, but a manpower shortage persists. Although the rate of population increase declined from 10 per thousand in 1959 to 5.2 per thousand in 1966, it rose again to 9.7 per thousand during the 1970–1975 period. Romania is expected by 1990 to have twenty-four million inhabitants.[34]

In the years just preceding World War II, agriculture and forestry contributed more than half the national income. This proportion dropped to one-third in 1961, which was a good harvest year. During the period 1971–1975, Romania's industrial production reportedly expanded at an annual rate of more than 13 percent, and the total national income grew at the rate of 10 percent a year. The production growth rate planned for 1976–1980 is 30 percent for agriculture and only 11 percent for industry. Agriculture remains a problem, in part because of the low motivation of the farmers.

---

32. Mitskevich, *op. cit.* (in note 3 above), p. 43.

33. Ceausescu speech at the tenth party congress. Bucharest radio, 6 August 1969. He subsequently made it clear that Germans would not be permitted to leave the country in large numbers. *Christian Science Monitor,* 5 January 1977.

34. U.S. Bureau of the Census, *Projections of the Population of the Communist Countries of Eastern Europe: 1975–2000* (Washington, D.C., July, 1976), table 16, p. 27.

It should also be emphasized that in the new five-year plan much more concern has been shown than in the past for increasing the amount of consumers' goods. Three new bodies have been established to coordinate the production and sale of these commodities. It should also be mentioned that per capita income in Romania is only about one thousand dollars a year, compared to an average that is four times higher in developed countries. As a corollary, foreign-trade targets have been drastically raised, from 72 to 80 percent in the new 1976–1980 planning period.[35] Hence, the government will have to place considerable emphasis on controls and work discipline.

Investment has been concentrated in industry since the communists gained control. The Soviet party program emphasizes heavy industry in "creating the material and technical basis for communism" and, similarly, the leaders in Romania have sought to develop and expand this sector of the economy.

> The consistent Leninist policy of industrializing the country by concentrating on the development of heavy industry, and its main branch, the machine-building industry, has brought about deep changes in the structure of RPR [Romanian People's Republic] exports. Machines and equipment are gaining greater importance in export trade. . . .[36]

As a result of this concentration on heavy industry, the composition of Romanian foreign trade has changed. Before 1939, exports of cereals, oil, timber, livestock, and animal derivatives comprised 90 percent of the total. By 1961, machinery and equipment already accounted for 16 percent. In general, an increase in the export of finished products has taken place. Between 1948 and 1958 the proportion of food exports dropped from almost 50 percent to only 15 percent. The current principal imports—industrial machinery, vehicles, machine tools, iron ore, and coal—also reflects the continuing emphasis on industry.

The economic difficulties resulting from World War II and the subsequent exploitation by the Soviet Union took many years to overcome. Although the country changed sides in August 1944 and fought with the Allies, it was occupied thereafter by the Red Army. Under an armistice agreement with the USSR, Romania paid reparations of three hundred million dollars in goods at 1938 prices. Over a period of six years, the Soviet Union took petroleum in considerable amounts for about half of what it would have brought the Romanians on the world market. The total value of reparations actually extracted by the USSR between September 1944 and June 1948 has been estimated at more than $1.7 billion.[37] In order to continue these forced deliveries, several oil companies had to be subsidized by the government at Bucharest.

---

35. Ceausescu interview with *Frankfurter Rundschau,* 23 July 1976.

36. *Probleme economice* (September 1963); translated in *Romanian Press Survey* (15 October 1963). See also *East Europe* (January 1970), pp. 2–8, for reaffirmation of the foregoing.

37. Willard Thorp, U.S. delegate to the 1947 Paris peace conference, as cited by Alexandre Cretzianu (ed.), *Captive Rumania* (New York, 1956), p. 51.

Soviet occupation forces confiscated all property that had formerly been owned by Germans and Italians, including French, Dutch, and Belgian assets previously expropriated by the Germans. This was in addition to the reparations. By 1946 the USSR owned more than one-third of Romania's industrial and financial enterprises. Some of the seized property formed the basis for Soviet-Romanian joint-stock companies, which were called "Sovroms."

During the period 1946–1947, about 37.5 percent of the national budget had to be committed for the payment of reparations. In the next fiscal year, the amount rose to 46.6 percent.[38] Subsequently, the reparations were reduced but not abolished completely. Only in 1954 did Soviet premier Georgi Malenkov, in an effort to ease the economic situation and increase voluntary political cooperation by Romania, announce transfer of Soviet shares in the joint-stock companies to Bucharest. Control, except for that of uranium mining through "Sovromquartz," was handed over to the Romanian communists.

On the whole, the economy of Romania has had a growth rate higher than that of any other East European country. It is claimed that between 1950 and 1959 national income grew by 10.3 percent each year. The officially reported increase averaged 8.5 percent from 1960 through 1964, and the five-year plan for 1966–1970 envisaged an 8 percent annual growth; during 1971–1975 this rate increased to 10 percent. One of the reasons for such an accelerated growth rate, of course, is the low level from which it began. An admitted disparity still exists between the agricultural and the industrial sectors of the economy. By 1970 industrial production had reportedly risen fourteen times over the past thirty years, compared with only 1.6 times for agriculture. The index for industry during the 1971–1975 period expanded by 74 percent.[39]

Agriculture. Although more than half the population still lives in rural areas, as mentioned, less than one-third of the national income is produced by agriculture. The reasons for this include the long-standing opposition of the peasants to collectivization, the regime's emphasis on industrial investment and neglect of agriculture, high taxation, insufficient mechanization, the continuation of certain backward methods, mismanagement and inefficiency, and droughts. Over the past several years, however, farming has received increased attention.

The primary crops are corn and wheat. Romania is the only country in the bloc that is self-sufficient in cereals at the present time; in 1963 it even exported four hundred thousand tons of wheat to the USSR. The complete socialization of agriculture had been announced the year before, two years ahead of schedule, making Romania the first East European country to achieve this status.[40] The

---

38. Brzezinski, *op. cit.* (in note 2 above), p. 125.

39. Michael Cismarescu in *East Europe* (January 1970), p. 5; CIA, *Handbook of Economic Statistics 1976* (Washington, D.C., September, 1976), p. 39.

40. A. Lukovets (ed.), *Narodnaya Rumyniya segodnya 1944–1964* (Moscow, 1964), p. 18.

average annual production of cereals was only 14.8 million tons during 1971–1975, despite a record 16.9 million tons in 1972.

Land Reform and Collectivization.   An initial land-reform act was passed in March 1945. On the basis of this legislation, holdings in excess of fifty hectares and all real property belonging to certain categories of individuals (e.g., war criminals and Germans) were expropriated. Land reform had been designed in part to gain the support of the peasants by giving them small private plots. The major long-term objective, however, was the collectivization of agriculture. Gradual pressure on the peasants took the form of compulsory delivery quotas at artificially low prices; state ownership of expropriated agricultural machinery; socialization of credit institutions, mills, and oil presses; and the 1947 monetary reform, which practically eliminated peasant savings.

Because of resistance, socialization could be carried out only gradually and at different levels. The highest form is the state farm, which is patterned after the *sovkhoz* in the USSR. In this type of enterprise agricultural workers do not share in the profits but are paid wages.

Upon joining a collective farm, however, a peasant family turns over to the *kolkhoz* its land, farm implements, draft animals, vehicles, and other equipment. The house and a few head of livestock can be retained. A family is given a private garden plot of land ranging from two-thirds of an acre to one acre in size, depending upon the quality of soil. After the payment of various expenses, the delivery of compulsory quotas, and the setting aside of funds for investment, the earnings are distributed to the collective farm members by the management. This division is made on the basis of days worked during the year rather than the original contribution of land, animals, and equipment. The number of standard units credited to a member depends upon the type of job performed and can total more or fewer than the actual days worked. Many administrators give themselves several times the appropriate number.

In the district of Dobrudja, for instance, the average number of work days per *kolkhoz* member annually was 195, while the chairmen of the *kolkhozes* in this district credited themselves with an average of 711 work days annually.[41]

Because of strong resistance to collectivization, in 1951 the government introduced so-called agricultural partnerships. These involve a less rigid form of association. The peasant has a choice of how much he will contribute, and his share of the profits depends upon his contribution and the amount of work he performs. When agricultural partnerships tend to become permanent, higher-

---

41. Wolfgang Oberleitner, "Realities of Agriculture in Rumania," *International Peasant Union Monthly Bulletin* (July–August 1963), p. 19.

level agricultural associations and collective herds are established. In these organizations, cooperation is limited mainly to pooling land for plowing, with the rest of the work done by each individual member. In areas where grazing predominates, collective sheep herds and livestock farms have been established.

The collectivization of agriculture at first proceeded slowly. In late 1957 Bucharest radio announced that 13,065 collective farms had been established.[42] They covered less than one-fourth of the arable land. In June 1960 the third congress of the Romanian Workers' party adopted a new six-year economic plan. At that time 81 percent of all agriculture was said to be socialized. The largest part consisted of the lowest-level collectives. Only about one-third of the total consisted of *kolkhozes*. In early 1962 it was announced that the goal of 96 percent socialization of agriculture had been reached. In attaining this target, of course, production had been affected adversely. Because of strict controls (some 875,478 communist-party members worked in rural areas during 1970) and a low rate of investment, agricultural growth remained lower than capability. Hence, a new law on remuneration for agricultural products went into effect.[43] Small private plots are now also being allocated to state farm workers, as material incentive, within a framework of intensive agricultural development. (See table 40.)

TABLE 40

TYPES OF FARMS IN ROMANIA, 1975

Type	Areas in use (millions of hectares)	Percent of total cultivated area
State agricultural	4,492,130	30.1
Agricultural production cooperatives	9,047,241	60.5
(of which private plots)	(973,016)	(6.5)
Individual farms	1,407,064	9.4
Total	14,946,435	100.0

SOURCE: [Romania], *Anuarul Statistic al Republicii Socialiste Romania 1976* (Bucharest, 1976), p. 150.

Industry. As was the case in agriculture, the nationalization of industry lagged at first. By June 1948, however, most privately owned factories had been taken over by the government. In the following year, the state sector

---

42. Cited in *East Europe* (December 1957), p. 51.

43. *Romania Libera,* 7 January 1976. See also RFE, *Situation Report,* 10 December 1976, for official statistics comparing the output of state and collective farms. The latter occupy 79 percent of all agricultural land but produce only 63 percent of the output, according to *Era Socialista,* no. 2 (1976).

accounted for 85 percent of all industrial production; by 1960, it encompassed 98.8 percent.[44]

As mentioned previously, Romania has been concentrating upon the development of heavy industry. Between 1970 and 1975, approximately 58 percent of the total national investment was allocated by plan to this sector of the economy. Both imports and exports are oriented toward industry. In order to increase steel production, it has been necessary to bring large quantities of iron ore, coke, and rolled metals into the country. The trend of imports in machinery and equipment has been toward complete processing plants.

Beginning in 1962, Romania contracted with West European suppliers to build the largest steel-plate mill in the world. A tire factory and two cellulose plants for making paper and related products were obtained from Britain and set up during the following summer. An American company was granted a permit in 1965 to construct an oil cracking plant, and the British helped to set up an ore-processing factory at Galati.[45] Romania's largest trading partner outside the Soviet bloc, the Federal Republic of Germany, has built an iron and steel mill at Hunedoara in the central part of the country. The French installed a winery and a processing plant for sugar beets. Although economic agreements covering the period 1976−1980 have been signed with the USSR increasing the reciprocal exchange of goods by about one-third compared with the previous five-year period, it is likely that the Soviet share in Romania's foreign trade will continue to decline. To pay for advanced Western technology and the necessary raw materials, Bucharest depends upon exports and credits.

Foreign Trade.   Through direct seizure of certain industries, joint-stock companies, and the CMEA, the Soviet Union openly exploited the Romanian economy for more than a decade. Since 1954, however, Soviet control has lessened progressively. The agreement to sell its interests in industries that were expropriated during the occupation represented a first step in the process of returning the property stolen by Moscow to Bucharest.

The economies of the Soviet Union and Romania parallel each other in certain respects. Both countries are engaged in the process of industrialization, although, of course, at different levels, and both produce substantial agricultural commodities. Consequently they have similar needs, and these requirements are not complementary. The USSR is naturally reluctant to send Romania materials that are in short supply at home.

For many years Bucharest was deprived of an opportunity to obtain foreign exchange because of reparations, expropriation and arbitrary, as well as discriminatory, prices established by the Soviet Union. It is little wonder that the

---

44. N. Tolkunov (ed.), *Sotsialisticheskii lager* (Moscow, 1962), pp. 293−294.

45. Trade with capitalist states grew from 22.3 percent in 1960 to 35.7 percent of the total in 1968. Cismarescu, *op. cit.* (in note 39 above), p. 7.

Romanian communists were anxious to trade on a more equitable basis with capitalist countries. Romania's trade with France almost quadrupled between 1965 and 1974 and its trade with Britain will double by 1980. Its exchange of goods with the United States for 1976 was expected to surpass four hundred million dollars, and on 21 November of that year, a ten-year trade agreement was signed by the two countries.[46] Moscow, moreover, does not protest when Bucharest obtains the latest technology from the West.

Imports of coal and iron ore from the Soviet Union have been necessary for the continuing production of steel.[47] Other sources of iron ore have been explored by Romanian trade missions in Algeria, Brazil, India, and the United States, among others. Much emphasis has been placed on the chemical industry because oil, methane gas, coal, salt, and other raw materials are available locally. In the past, Romania has imported oil only from the Arab states and Iran.

One serious controversy has arisen between the Soviet Union and Romania, in connection with the CMEA and economic cooperation. (See table 41.) Moscow had originally wanted Bucharest to concentrate on producing raw materials for the industries of the more developed East European countries. The shortage of cereals and particularly wheat in the Soviet Union and throughout the bloc in general was probably one factor that prompted the USSR to press Romania to emphasize agriculture also.

Attempts to make Bucharest accept this role in the CMEA were made by high-ranking Soviet officials who visited Bucharest in person during 1963. Nikolai Podgorny, who is now president of the USSR, arrived first. Next came former premier Nikita Khrushchev, followed by first deputy foreign minister Vasilii Kuznetsov. A policy statement issued by the Romanian communists almost a year later said that Bucharest favored bringing all communist-ruled states into the CMEA (i.e., also Albania, China, and Cuba), but that each bloc country should remain sovereign over its own economic affairs and should not be forced by any supranational body to adopt measures against its will.[48] Since then Romania seems to have been successful in retaining the direction of its own economy by always emphasizing equality and noninterference in the affairs of other states.

Church-State Relations. As in other communist-ruled lands, the churches in Romania are allowed to exist as a temporary evil. Efforts have been made to

---

46. RFE, *Situation Report,* 2 December 1976. Romania owes the West about three billion dollars and suffers from a chronic adverse balance of payments. *Christian Science Monitor,* 13 December 1976, quoting from *The Times*; London.

47. About 80 percent of Romania's imported iron ore and ferroalloys, half of its coal, approximately 70 percent of its nickel, more than 40 percent of its cotton, and so forth, come from the USSR. *New York Times,* 19 April 1970, stressed Romania's almost complete dependence on the Soviet Union for coking coal which, of course, limits Romanian independence.

48. Agerpres (official Romanian news agency) communiqué, *Statement on the Stand of the Rumanian Workers' Party* (Bucharest, 1964), pp. 27–29.

TABLE 41

ROMANIAN TRADE WITH OTHER COMMUNIST-RULED STATES, 1965 AND 1975
(In millions of *lei* and percent of total)

Country	1965		1975	
Albania	33.6	0.2	81.2	0.15
Bulgaria	133.7	1.0	1,023.1	1.90
Czechoslovakia	989.0	7.6	2,446.7	4.60
China	291.0	2.2	2,164.4	4.10
North Korea	51.4	0.4	185.1	0.35
Cuba	14.6	0.1	127.3	0.24
East Germany	805.4	6.2	2,909.0	5.50
Yugoslavia	173.1	1.3	1,209.8	2.30
Mongolia	9.7	0.1	33.8	0.60
Poland	492.1	3.8	2,072.6	3.90
Hungary	399.3	3.0	1,603.5	3.00
Soviet Union	5,067.5	38.8	9,857.5	18.60
North Vietnam	32.6	0.2	57.8	0.01
	8,493.0	64.9	23,771.8	44.74
Other states	4,577.9	35.1	29,323.6	55.26
Totals	13,070.9	100.0	53,095.4	100.00

SOURCE: *Anuarul Statistic al Republicei Socialiste Romania 1976* (Bucharest, 1976), pp. 376–381.

NOTES: Romania's present trade within CMEA is double the 1970 level and, according to plan, will double again by 1980. Moscow radio, 19 November 1976.

The exchange rate is estimated to be 4.97 lei for one U.S. dollar.

use them for propaganda and cultural purposes, though they have met with limited success. The mere existence of church organizations is also meant to project an image of religious freedom.

Up to the time when the party gained control of the country, religion played an important part in the life of the people. The Romanian Orthodox Church had been the leading and the most powerful religious force prior to World War I. It continued afterward to be active in both local and state government, but its power gradually declined. In 1921 practically all church lands were expropriated. This measure did not affect the Roman Catholic Church as much as others because it had always been a minority organization.

The communist regime assumed control of all the churches in 1947 and 1948. This was achieved by arrogating to the government all authority over finances, property, and high-level administration; placing in key positions clergy who were subservient to the ruling party; and severing ties with church organizations in foreign countries. As an example, in July 1948 Bucharest abrogated its prewar concordat with the Vatican.

During 1962 the Holy See announced that of the fourteen Catholic archbishops and bishops in Romania, all but one were under arrest. Three years later it was reported that four of the five Catholic bishops remaining in the country had died in prison.[49] Legislation since 4 August 1948 had required that all denominations provide the regime's Department of Religious Affairs with inventories of their assets and revenues and that all clergy take an oath of allegiance to the government, pledging to obey and help enforce laws and to defend the state against all enemies.[50] Besides controlling the purse strings and the appointment of personnel in all churches, the Department of Religious Affairs designates the extent and type of catechism that may be taught under church sponsorship.

Apart from such direct techniques, the regime also applies indirect methods to reduce the influence of the churches. Attendance at religious services is not forbidden by law, but mass organizations such as the Union of Communist Youth and the Pioneers schedule activities on Sundays and religious holidays (Easter and Christmas are regular working days in Romania) to make church attendance difficult. The general atmosphere created by the communists discourages participation in religious activities by members of the armed forces and by those holding government positions. The communists have been successful in reducing the influence of the churches, and religious groups no longer pose any significant threat to the regime. Although the constitution, in Article 30, guarantees freedom of religion, in practice it is systematically repressed.

The largest religious denomination has always been Romanian Orthodox, which may now have about fourteen million nominal members. Before their forced union with this majority church in 1948, the Eastern-rite Catholics or Uniates represented the next largest group. Roman Catholics are next in size, with about 1.75 million members. There are approximately one million Calvinists, and about two hundred thousand communicants of the Lutheran and perhaps fifty thousand of the Jewish faiths.[51] The remaining denominations total fewer than one hundred thousand members. In general, atheistic propaganda among the youth has achieved poor results. Hence, long-term programs were organized in 1976 through so-called "educational brigades" that will attempt to shape a "new man."

Foreign Policy. Romanian foreign policy from 1945 until the early 1960s had been responsive for the most part to the lead of the Soviet Union. Until the

49. Cited by Constantin Visoianu in U.S. Congress, House of Representatives, Committee on Foreign Affairs, 87th Congress, 2nd session, *Captive European Nations: Hearings* (Washington, D.C., 1962), p. 180. For the names and fates of individual bishops see RFE, *Situation Report,* 10 December 1965.

50. See Virgiliu Stoicoiu (comp. & trans.), "Church and State in Rumania," in U.S. Senate, Committee on the Judiciary, *The Church and State under Communism* (Washington, D.C., 1965), II, pp. 4–5 for the oath. *Buletinul Oficial,* no. 103 (15 August 1970), published Decree no. 334, on the duties of the Religious Affairs Department.

51. According to Chief Rabbi Moses Rosen, there is only one other rabbi left in the country. More than 2,300 Jews were permitted to leave for Israel in 1975 and the same number in 1976. *Los Angeles Times,* 11 November 1976.

end of 1963, Bucharest always voted with the communist bloc on all questions at the United Nations, but in 1963 Romania did not support the USSR on two minor issues. At the same time the Romanians also began to exercise some independence in their relations with the Soviet Union in other areas. While most of the instances have been in the economic sphere, some also involved cultural areas. Already during 1960 and 1961 Bucharest had settled claims by the United States and West European countries. Although the full amounts due were not paid, these agreements probably helped to pave the way for several trade pacts that were signed later.

Romania also became the first bloc country to resume diplomatic relations with Albania after they were severed in 1961. A summary of Peking's polemical letters to Moscow, published in the newspaper *Scinteia*, may have been designed to assist the Romanians in the CMEA dispute that was developing at that time. Bucharest has been sending numerous delegations to Peking, resulting in regular trade agreements between the two governments. The Chinese granted Romania a $250 million loan in 1971, and both countries have signed a long-term goods-and-payments agreement covering the period 1976–1980.

Over the past several years Romania has been working closely with the nonaligned developing countries, seeking active support for admission to their conferences as an observer. Nicolae Ceausescu himself has visited more than thirty such foreign countries, speaking about "a new international economic order." As a result, Romania's trade with these states has multiplied five times since 1950. Some four thousand young Africans were studying in Romania during 1976 and twelve thousand Romanian specialists have been sent to African countries.[52]

In the field of culture, an Institute of Russian Language and Literature was absorbed by the foreign-languages faculty at Bucharest University. In elementary schools Russian has been eliminated as a compulsory language below the eighth grade. A survey made several years ago at all Romanian universities showed 55 percent of the students choosing French, 33 percent English, and only 10 percent Russian as a foreign language.[53] The regime has also stopped publishing *Timpuri Noi* (*New Times*), a Soviet periodical printed in the Romanian language. Its replacement is *Lumea*, a foreign-affairs magazine that frequently includes translations from Western works.

Balancing between East and West. Bucharest insists upon exercising sovereignty in economic planning and increasing its trade with the West (which has grown by 230 percent since 1970), but this does not represent a turning away

---

52. *Lumea*, 20 May 1976. *Scinteia*, 15 September 1975, announced that Romania had been admitted to membership in the "Group of 77," which was formed by the developing countries. African trade unionists are being trained in Bucharest, according to an Agerpres communiqué of 11 November 1976.

53. *New York Times*, 9 March 1969.

from communism.[54] The regime in Romania maintains strict internal controls that are tighter than those in many other East European countries. The fact that Bucharest desires and exercises a certain degree of independence from Moscow can not be interpreted as indicating a change from a communist to a democratic ideology. A new twenty-year treaty of friendship, cooperation, and mutual assistance between the two countries was signed in July 1970 at Bucharest.[55]

This was followed by a two-week visit that Ceausescu made to the United States. His meetings with businessmen resulted in a ten-million-dollar contract for an aluminum sheet-rolling plant, to be built by American Metal Climax, Inc. Agerpres announced that an agreement had been signed in New York to exchange researchers and university teaching staff. During Ceausescu's next visit to the United States in 1973, he signed a joint declaration concerning economic, industrial, and technological cooperation. When President Gerald R. Ford stopped off at Bucharest in mid-1975, he signed another trade agreement granting most-favored-nation status to Romania, as well as credits from the Import-Export Bank. The International Bank for Reconstruction and Development (World Bank) had already extended loans totaling $460 million to Romania.

It is interesting to note that Bucharest again during 1975 and early in 1976 raised the Bessarabian question. But in August 1976 Ceausescu officially visited this former Romanian province and subsequently met with Brezhnev in the Crimea; he reportedly told Brezhnev on that occasion that the Bucharest government accepts the postwar border with the Soviet Union. Brezhnev also paid an official visit to Romania during 22−24 November 1976 that apparently resulted in the reestablishment of a basis for closer relations between the two countries.[56] Ceausescu probably will attempt to maintain the autonomy which he has been able to develop within the USSR's sphere of influence.

Although the reasons for them are unknown, as of this writing, changes in senior Romanian communist party and government positions affected 35 persons at the end of January 1977. The ruling party's Permanent Bureau was increased from five to nine members, and the official news agency Agerpres explained that the shake-up had been made for the purpose of "consolidating the sphere of party and state bureaucracy."

---

54. Since a new foreign-trade law was adopted, Romania has been cooperating with Western firms that are allowed up to 40 percent participation in joint companies. RFE report (by Henry Schaefer), "Economic Reform and the Party in Romania," 22 March 1971. Note the agreement to establish Oltcit for production and marketing of small cars with Citroen, announced over Bucharest radio on 30 December 1976.

55. The text of the treaty appeared in *Krasnaya zvezda*, 8 July 1970; Moscow.

56. A statement on the visit, Brezhnev's first in ten years, appeared in *Pravda* for 25 November 1976. See also Robert R. King, "Romania," in R. F. Staar (ed.), *1977 Yearbook on International Communist Affairs* (Stanford, Ca., 1977). Note also the visit to Bucharest by Italian communist leader Enrico Berlinguer and the communiqué in *Scinteia*, 8 January 1977.

Chapter 8

Socialist Federated Republic of Yugoslavia

Yugoslavia is the only federal state in Eastern Europe and the most heterogeneous country on the continent, except for the USSR. It has received the following apocryphal description: one political party, two alphabets, three religions, four languages, five nationalities, six republics, and seven bordering states.[1] Even the name Yugoslavia connotes diversity and multiplicity. It means "land of the southern Slavs" and represents a collective designation for all peoples of Slavic origin who migrated southward across the Danube river during the sixth and seventh centuries A.D.

GENERAL SURVEY

The establishment of a single country in 1918 resulted from Yugoslavia's geographic location. The territory had served in the past as a passageway or land bridge between Western Europe and Asia. This corridor position influenced the development of the state both positively and negatively. For the most part mountainous, with hills covering about 70 percent of its total area, Yugoslavia comprises six federal republics that fall roughly into line with the geographic features. They are Serbia, Croatia, Slovenia, Bosnia-Herzegovina, Macedonia, and Montenegro. The autonomous regions of Voivodina and Kosovo-Metohija are located within Serbia.

Corresponding with this geographic division, ethnic groups can be differentiated within the total population of Yugoslavia, which was estimated in 1976 to be about 21.5 million.[2] Table 42 shows the sixteen identifiable ethnic groups

---

1. U.S. Congress, Senate Committee on the Judiciary, 87th Cong., 1st sess., *Yugoslav Communism: A Critical Study* (Washington, D.C., 1961), p. 3; prepared by Charles Zalar.

2. CIA, *National Basic Intelligence Factbook* (Washington, D.C., July 1976), p. 225.

that can each be found in one or more of the federal republics and autonomous areas. None of the divisions of the country is completely homogeneous.

The four basic languages—Serbian, Croatian, Slovenian, and Macedonian—are often treated as only three by joining Serbian and Croatian to form the Serbo-Croat language. These basic tongues arose from the slow evolution of dialects from a single language, the Old (Church) Slavonic that was spoken at the time when southern Slavs migrated to the Balkan peninsula.

TABLE 42

ETHNIC GROUPS IN YUGOSLAVIA
(1971 census)

Nationality	Number	Percent of Total
Serbs	8,143,246	39.8
Croats	4,526,782	22.2
Slovenes	1,678,032	8.2
Macedonians	1,194,784	5.9
Montenegrins	508,843	2.6
Moslems	1,729,932	8.4
Yugoslavs	273,077	1.4
Albanians	1,309,523	6.4
Hungarians	477,374	2.3
Turks	127,920	0.6
Slovaks	83,656	0.3
Romanians	58,570	0.1
Ruthenes	24,640	0.1
Bulgars	58,627	0.1
Italians	21,791	0.1
Czechs	24,620	0.1
Others and unidentified	281,555	1.4
Total	20,522,972	100.0

SOURCE: [Yugoslavia], *Statisticki godisnjak Jugoslavije 1975* (Belgrade, 1975), p. 100.

Religion is an important aspect of the diversity that is characteristic of Yugoslavia. More than 41 percent of the people are Serbian (Eastern) Orthodox, almost 32 percent are Roman Catholic, and more than 12 percent are Moslem, with the remainder belonging to other churches or to no religion. It is a significant fact that the Orthodox Church has strongly identified itself with the Serbian nationality, and the Catholic Church with the Croatians and Slovenes. These alignments have influenced nationalistic tendencies and differences that date back to the Middle Ages, when the latter two groups were under the direct spiritual jurisdiction of Rome. (During mid-August 1970, the Vatican and Yugoslavia resumed diplomatic relations after an eighteen-year break.)

For this reason, the two alphabets are Latin and Cyrillic, corresponding to the East-West religious division. Cyrillic is essentially based on Greek letters, augmented by additional symbols. It is generally used by the Serbs and the Bulgarians (as well as the Russians), who comprise in essence the Eastern Orthodox Slavs. The Latin alphabet, on the other hand, supplemented with diacritical marks, is utilized by the Croatians and the Slovenes (as well as the Poles and the Czechs), who comprise the Roman Catholic Slavs. Slovenian can be written only with Latin characters, and Macedonian only with Cyrillic letters.

The Second World War.   Yugoslavia fell early in 1941 to a German invasion. The first guerrilla operations, of the London-supported Chetniks, were headed by Colonel (later General) Draza Mihajlovic. In June of that year Germany's attack on the Soviet Union provided a signal for all communists to support Moscow. Shortly thereafter, a second resistance movement became active in Yugoslavia; Partisans, under the leadership of a mysterious figure known as Tito (Josip Broz, secretary-general of the Yugoslav communist party), began activities against the German occupant. Harsh reprisals became the order of the day. In one case, an entire community of about seven thousand inhabitants was massacred by the Germans.[3] Under Hitler's *Nacht und Nebel* ("night and fog") decree, between fifty and a hundred Yugoslavs were executed for every German wounded or killed. After initial cooperation in the struggle against the Germans, the forces led by Mihajlovic and Tito engaged in a merciless civil war against each other.

Tito proclaimed the establishment of a de facto government in the fall of 1943, contrary to the wishes of Stalin, who thought the time inopportune. The second session of the Anti-Fascist Council for National Liberation of Yugoslavia proclaimed itself (at a small town called Jajce in Bosnia during November) the supreme representative of the peoples and of the state of Yugoslavia as a whole, divested the royal Yugoslav government-in-exile of its legal rights, forbade King Peter II to return, and decided that the future state should be built on the federalist system.[4]

These moves, combined with British and American favoritism toward the Partisans, led to the abandonment by the West of the Chetnik leader and of the royal government-in-exile. Western military support and the entry of the Red Army into Yugoslavia during the fall of 1944 allowed the Partisans to seize power.[5] In a typical instance of communist tactics, they established a provisional coalition government.

The coalition provided Tito with twenty-three Partisan ministers out of twenty-eight, and he himself became premier as well as Defense minister. In November

3. Dragoljub Durovic (ed.), *Narodna vlast i socijalisticka demokratija, 1943–1963* (Belgrade, 1964), pp. 22–23.

4. *Ibid.*, p. 56, reproduces the beginning of the proclamation.

5. For a recent interpretation of Western policy toward the two rival resistance movements, see Walter R. Roberts, *Tito, Mihailovic and the Allies, 1941–1945* (New Brunswick, N.J., 1973).

1945 the monarchy was abolished. The establishment of the "Federal People's Republic of Yugoslavia" followed the promulgation in 1946 of a USSR-type constitution.[6] The last remnant of the former royalist regime faded from the picture when General Mihajlovic was captured and, after a mock trial, executed.

Postwar Developments. The end of the war saw Tito's resistance movement transformed into a constitutional regime. A significant factor has shaped the country, namely, the Yugoslav communists' seizure of power with Soviet military assistance combined with their own armed forces and political cadres. This situation, for all practical purposes, had no parallel in any of the other East European states that were overrun by the Red Army toward the latter part of World War II. It accounts for the early consolidation of the Yugoslav communist regime and its subsequent conflict with Moscow.

During the period 1945–1949, however, the Federal People's Republic of Yugoslavia was modeled after the USSR in both structure and operation. Its monolithic totalitarianism featured the complete nationalization of industry, centralized economic planning, a single communist-front organization, and the elimination of all opponents.

In the first two postwar years widespread starvation probably would have resulted had it not been for aid from the United Nations Relief and Rehabilitation Administration. Almost simultaneously, reconstruction and nationalization were set into motion, along with a vigorous campaign to collectivize all peasant holdings into producers' work cooperatives that "ran into passive resistance from the peasantry."[7] The first industrialization drive soon followed.

The planned goals, which were prepared by men with little experience, were too high. The "big leap" involved the hope that rapid conversion could take place from a basically agrarian economy to an industrialized one within the relatively short span of five years (1947–1951). The plan anticipated Soviet and other East European support in the form of long-term credits for industrial machinery and equipment. After this economic plan had been set into motion, two developments occurred.

First came unilateral moves by Moscow to extend both its economic and its political domination over Belgrade.[8] These were blocked by Tito. Next the Communist Information Bureau or Cominform—paradoxically suggested by the Yugoslav communists themselves—was established in September 1947 by Stalin to keep the satellites under control. Less than a year later, this body passed a

---

6. V. N. Durdenevskii (ed.), *Konstitutsii zarubezhnykh sotsialisticheskikh gosudarstv* (Moscow, 1956), pp. 389–408, gives the text in Russian.

7. Albert Waterston, *Planning in Yugoslavia* (Baltimore, Md., 1962), p. 7.

8. Alex N. Dragnich, *Tito's Promised Land, Yugoslavia* (New Brunswick, N.J., 1954), pp. 290–293. See also Vladimir Dedijer, *The Battle Stalin Lost: Memoirs of Yugoslavia, 1948–1953* (New York, 1971), especially chapter 3.

resolution condemning and expelling the Yugoslav communist party, anathematizing it as a "traitor" to the Moscow-directed world communist movement. The real reason for the dispute was Stalin's distrust of the leadership in Belgrade.

Tito probably had no desire to challenge Stalin, but the traumatic Cominform experience produced a degree of unity within the Yugoslav party in spite of, and perhaps because of, Soviet pressure. The deteriorating condition of the economy and the faltering of the five-year plan, combined with international isolation, forced Tito reluctantly to turn to the West for aid. The rapprochement with the West, and its resulting economic benefits, surpassed all that Yugoslavia could have anticipated. The net result was "Titoism," which has been defined in various ways depending upon the point of view and the time.[9]

Economic Planning. Yugoslavia has a complicated and confusing economy, but it insists on calling itself a socialist state. Industry and commerce engage relatively little private enterprise, yet technically there is no state ownership. A varied type of agriculture, which includes both private and cooperative efforts, is carried on by the peasants. The authoritative journal of the world communist movement adhering to Moscow reported the basic principle of the Yugoslav socialist economy to be "planned guidance."[10] The economy is, indeed, planned. The state, however, does not administer the various economic enterprises. Its purposes are accomplished by having them operate allegedly under the management of the workers themselves.

Yugoslav economic planning is unlike that of any other communist-ruled country, primarily because the plan is called "indicative" and, therefore, is not binding. Still, a federal planning bureau is responsible for drawing up the national economic plan. Economic planning takes place simultaneously on all levels, with an attempt at the continuous coordination of efforts among republics, districts, communes, individual enterprises, and economic chambers representing groups of enterprises.

Worker-Management. With the change of policy in the direction of a more decentralized economic system in the early 1950s, the concept of worker-management, and specifically the workers' council, surfaced. According to the latest constitution,[11] which was adopted in February 1974, the system is based on freely associated labor using socially owned means of production, self-

---

9. For example, Nikita Khrushchev, when still in power, stated that based "on objective laws, on the teachings of Marxism-Leninism, it is impossible to deny that Yugoslavia appears to be a socialist [i.e., communist] country." Quoted in P. D. Mineev and V. A. Tokarev, *Yugoslaviya* (Moscow, 1963), p. 29.

10. V. Zagladin et al., "Yugoslavia Today," *World Marxist Review* (March 1964), p. 66.

11. [Yugoslavia], *The Constitution of the Socialist Federal Republic of Yugoslavia* (Belgrade, 1974), p. 311; henceforth cited as *Constitution*.

management by the working people, and distribution of the social product. In theory the constitution provides every member of a working organization with the guaranteed "right to a personal income and other rights stemming from labor to an amount and volume that ensure his economic and social security." The personal income depends "on the general level of productivity of total social labor and on the general condition prevailing in the environment in which the worker lives."[12]

The working organizations, which are in theory independent and autonomous, may include professionally active individuals who form units that have the same status as those of industrial workers. Any such organization includes the following: a workers' council, which is the basic element, consisting of from fifteen to two hundred members, depending on the size of the enterprise; a management board, usually numbering from three to seventeen persons; and the director or manager of the enterprise, who supervises the business and executes the decisions of the workers' council and other management organs.[13]

All officials are elected from among the employees, with terms of two years for the workers' council and one year for the management board. Although nobody may be elected twice consecutively to the council or more than twice consecutively to the management board, the manager or director may be eligible for additional terms of office. This individual is nominated by the workers' council, after being proposed by an "appointments commission." It is through this commission that state and party control is exercised. In theory, however, the new constitution of 1974 states that self-government in working organizations includes the right of the workers to manage their respective enterprises, either directly or through elected bodies, organize production, and decide about expansion of the enterprise; to distribute income; to regulate working conditions; and to decide to associate with other enterprises.[14] Workers' councils represent one of the features of the Yugoslav system that distinguish it from other communist regimes.

Economic Reform.   Since the mid-1960s, the general economic policy of the ruling party and the government in Yugoslavia has involved a decentralization in decision-making. Market forces determine the distribution of investment funds through a price system, including realistic exchange rates. Only plants that are profitable can survive because state subsidies have been eliminated. Voluntary mergers may take place, however. Specific measures aimed at implementing these policies have included a new banking system and the devaluation of the dinar.

---

12. *Ibid.*, pp. 87–90.

13. Mirko Boskovic, *Drustveno-politicki sistem Jugoslavije* (Zagreb, 1963), pp. 121–126.

14. *Constitution*, pp. 84–87, 89.

Despite economic problems such as spiraling inflation and low labor productivity in recent years, decentralization has continued. In 1976, a law on associated labor was in preparation. It not only reaffirms self-management but also encourages limited private enterprise on a self-management basis.[15] The anomaly of less economic control and more political control appears to represent a "living Marxist contradiction" in Yugoslavia.

Agriculture. Yugoslavia has traditionally been a country of farmers, and agriculture represented the most significant branch of the prewar economy. In 1940 about 75 percent of the population lived on the land, but this proportion has been decreasing rapidly; during the most recent census it had dropped to 38.2 percent.[16] Yugoslavia's main goal in agriculture has been to increase production. To achieve this goal, government policy after the war involved a drive to collectivize the peasantry. The Yugoslav rulers were intelligent enough eventually to confess the failure of forced collectivization and to abandon this approach. A new program in 1953 disbanded most collective farms, with the land being returned to private ownership by the peasants. Compulsory delivery quotas were abolished, a free market for agricultural products was introduced, and the private sale and purchase of land was allowed. Farmers could own up to a maximum of ten hectares (24.7 acres) of land for each household.[17] Despite these concessions, agricultural production has not increased substantially, as table 43 shows.

TABLE 43

YUGOSLAV AGRICULTURAL PRODUCTION, 1961–1975
(In thousands of metric tons)

Commodity	1961	1964	1969	1974	1975
Wheat.	3,400	3,900	4,880	6,282	4,396
Corn (maize).	4,550	6,960	7,821	8,031	9,392
Sugar beets.	1,730	2,830	3,636	4,300	4,222
Sunflower seed	117	260	390	298	272
Potatoes	2,690	2,820	3,144	3,127	2,366
Plums.	1,130	760	1,292	682	951
Meat	670	679	806	1,012	–
Milk (millions of liters)	2,415	2,334	2,723	3,531	–

SOURCES: P. D. Mineev and V. A. Tokarev, *Yugoslaviya* (Moscow, 1963), p. 32; [Yugoslavia], *Statisticki godisnjak Jugoslavije 1970* (Belgrade, 1970), pp. 129–131 and 135–136; *ibid. 1975*, pp. 157–159 and 163–164; *Statistical Pocketbook of Yugoslavia 1976*, p. 52; Belgrade radio, 18 December 1976.

---

15. RFE report (by Slobodan Stankovic), "New Law Encourages Private Enterprise," 12 March 1976.

16. [Yugoslavia], *Statistical Pocket Book of Yugoslavia 1976*, pp. 22 and 26.

17. RFE report (by Zdenko Antic), "Private Farms Prosper in Yugoslavia," 30 July 1969.

The new policy is oriented toward a gradual socialization of agricultural activities, with increased cooperation between the socialist and private sectors encouraged so that the same goal can be achieved without the use of force. Four basic farm sectors exist today. The private sector predominates, as the peasants themselves in 1975 owned about 85 percent of all agricultural land, on almost 2.6 million private farms.[18] The three nonprivate sectors include peasant work cooperatives, which are collective farms similar to the Soviet *kolkhozy*; state farms, which are the Yugoslav equivalents of the *sovkhozy*; and general agricultural cooperatives, which are the least regimented. (See table 44.)

TABLE 44

AGRICULTURAL LAND DISTRIBUTION IN YUGOSLAVIA, 1974

Category	Units	Area (hectares)	Percent of Total
State farms	306	1,515,727	10.5
General agricultural cooperatives	832	454,547	3.1
Private farms	*ca.* 2,600,000	12,344,690	85.1
Experimental farms, schools, institutes, and other holdings	607	187,036	1.3
Total	2,601,745	14,502,000	100.0

SOURCE: *Statisticki godisnjak Jugoslavije 1975* (Belgrade, 1975), pp. 156 and 167.

Peasant work cooperatives are organized, like nonagricultural enterprises, under the worker-management system. They are voluntary, with the land being community owned and farmed. Only 40 of these existed in 1969 throughout the country—a drop from 6,625 in 1948 and 229 in 1959—and their role in production remains small. In 1959 there were 4,803 general agricultural cooperatives, by 1964 the number had decreased to some 2,400, and in 1974 there were only 832 (see table 44). The long-range plan to draw the individual peasant into dependence on the state can be seen from the fact that all government agricultural investments and subsidies are reserved for state farms and general agricultural cooperatives.

By and large, however, the Yugoslav regime has failed in its effort to persuade private-entrepreneur farmers to abandon their individual plots and join collectives. The peasants have followed plans of their own. By means of one-year contracts, variations in their annual plowing practices, and adequate fertilization of their land, the peasants are able to circumvent the state.

There are many forms of cooperation between the private sector and the

---

18. *Statistical Pocket Book of Yugoslavia 1976*, p. 50.

general agricultural cooperatives, but they fall into three basic categories: "rendering services," usually paid in cash by the private individual for the use of machinery, seed, and chemical fertilizers; "joint production," called a higher form of cooperation, in which socialist and private forces join to share proportionately in productive services and goods; and other forms, such as contracts by a cooperative with a private farmer for his expertise, labor, and products.

One method of comparing results in the private and the other two sectors is to examine their yields per hectare. It would appear from government statistics that the greatest yields come from the state farms (or the socialist sector) and the lowest from the private farms. Careful analysis, however, shows major discrimination by the government against the private farms. Government investments in the greatest yields come from the state farms (or the socialist sector) and the neurs can afford. Even so, yields are only 2.5 times higher in the socialist sector. Private entrepreneurs must pay twice as much for fertilizers as do the others. The socialist and cooperative sectors work the best land and work under the most favorable conditions.

The main objectives in agriculture are, for the private sector, to increase production (in order to remain outside the collectives) and, for the socialist sector, to show a profit. The latter, not infrequently, shows a deficit. This should raise doubts among communist leaders, since state farms were created especially to serve as focal points that would attract private farmers, who still cultivate 12.3 million of the 14.5 million hectares in agricultural land (table 44).

It is evident that the policy of persuasion has not induced the peasants to join collective farms. Only under the relative freedom of the individual farmer have there been any broadly positive results. This is significant, because nothing goes to the private entrepreneur. Little is provided even for general agricultural cooperatives. As far back as 1969, this situation was described by Executive Bureau member Mika Tripalo as follows:

> Our party recognized that uncritical imitation of foreign experiences has hampered not only our economic development but also deteriorated the political alliance with the peasantry which was the strongest army of our revolution.[19]

Industrial Growth and Resource Base.   Yugoslavia has followed Marxist dogma in giving priority to industrialization. Fortunately, the country has been in a comparatively advantageous position to achieve this goal. In contrast to agriculture, the means of industrial production were completely nationalized by the state after the war and have remained so. Primary emphasis has been placed on

---

19. *Vjesnik*, 28 July 1969; quoted by Antic, *op. cit.* (in note 17 above). For the latest data, see RFE report (by Slobodan Stankovic), "Yugoslav Satisfied with Wheat Harvest; Collectivization Rejected," 28 September 1976.

/

heavy industry, mining, electric power, and raw materials in the course of successive national economic plans. Shifts in policy, however, have prevented industry from developing evenly. For example, factory production during the spring of 1976 was up 8.6 percent compared with the previous year, but it was down from the 11 percent annual growth rate achieved during 1974, which represented a record.[20]

A measure of industrial growth is iron and steel production, which has increased to become the largest in the Balkans. Transportation, which has lagged in the past, is being improved. The new Belgrade-to-Bari railroad was completed in 1976 and construction was begun on a four-lane superhighway linking Yugoslavia and Greece to Western Europe with loans from the European Investment Bank.[21] The problems of surplus unskilled labor in areas too far removed from industrial enterprises and shortages of skilled manpower represent problems. Both may be solved by locating new factories in areas that have plentiful labor and by training local workers in areas where these plants are being constructed.

Yugoslavia is also fortunate in having substantial raw-material reserves to cope with ambitious plans for economic growth. Its mineral resources are abundant, with the exception of coking coal and petroleum. Despite intensive surveying and drilling over a seven-year period, only half of Yugoslavia's oil needs can be supplied from inside the country. In 1975 Yugoslavia produced 36 million tons of coal, about 3.5 million tons of petroleum, some 1.5 billion cubic meters of gas, and 40 billion KWH of electricity.[22] The first nuclear plant has been put into operation at Kalva, near the Bulgarian border, utilizing rich deposits of uranium from an active mine.

Nationalism. Without any doubt, nationalism represents the most important domestic phenomenon in Yugoslavia. Closely related is the problem of living standards. On the one hand, antagonism still exists among the various nationalities within the country; on the other, there is the desire for a better life throughout Yugoslavia. This desire certainly exists in the underdeveloped regions of Macedonia and Montenegro, as well as in the mountainous parts of Bosnia and Herzegovina, where living conditions have been relatively primitive. One cause for nationalist prejudice appears to be the regime's policy of bringing into better balance the economic development of all regions.

This policy has not been popular, despite the fact that the benefited areas have a more rapidly increasing population, a larger manpower base, and most of the natural resources. One-third of all investments in recent years has gone into these regions (see table 45); this is twice the amount allocated to the more developed

20. *Quarterly Economic Review,* no. 3 (1976), p. 8; London.

21. *Christian Science Monitor,* 28 May 1976; RFE report (by Zdenko Antic), "Yugoslavia to Build Highways," 12 March 1976.

22. *Politika,* 30 December 1975; Belgrade.

republic of Slovenia. Moreover, production in Slovenia and Croatia has increased more than twice as much as it has in the regions favored by generous regime investments.

TABLE 45

AID TO UNDERDEVELOPED REGIONS, 1974

Province	New Dinars (millions)	Population (millions)
Bosnia and Herzegovina	107,232	3.7
Kosovo (Serbia)	20,609	1.2
Macedonia	41,016	1.6
Montenegro	22.007	0.5
Total	190,864	7.0
Total for Yugoslavia	644,283	20.5

SOURCE: *Statisticki godisnjak Jugoslavije 1975,* pp. 367 and 499.
NOTE: During the first ten years of the regime (1945−1955), Slovenia and Croatia had been favored by generous investments.

This nationalist tendency boiling beneath the surface is connected with measures aimed at achieving centralization, which is euphemistically called integration. Liberal intellectuals object to pressures by party-apparatus workers. Their resistance in Slovenia and Croatia is directed against all centralizing measures, which they consider to be violations of nationality rights. The old Croat-Serb dispute also remains an issue, with the Croatians blaming the party (which they have incorrectly identified mainly with Serbia) for the creeping increase in prices that has adversely affected their ability to raise the living standard.

Nationality problems have become exacerbated in recent years and have led to crackdowns and the tightening of controls by party and government, as happened in Croatia during 1971−1972. Tension among national groups has been evident in almost every republic. In Kossovo the Shiptars have become a bone of contention between Yugoslavia and Albania, while the Macedonians are still a problem vis-a-vis Bulgaria. Furthermore, extremist emigré groups abroad have added to the differences by propaganda and terrorist acts. There has also been some indication that the Soviet Union is exploiting these problems for its own future advantage.

Standard of Living.   Tourism brought in about $850 million during 1975, and contact with the West is relatively free. With the common desire to be better off, a trend toward rising expectations has developed throughout the country. This and the difficulty of finding employment and housing drove some nine hundred thousand Yugoslav workers abroad in the late 1960s and 1970s, primarily to the Federal Republic of Germany, France, Austria, and Sweden.

As a result of the economic slowdown in Western Europe, Yugoslavia faces the problem of accommodating many of these returning *Gastarbeiter*. The government is attempting to cushion the impact of the returnees by expanding the economy and creating new jobs. Furthermore, it is promoting small business and private enterprise to achieve these goals.[23]

Another problem seriously affecting Yugoslavia's standard of living is the rate of inflation within the country, although during 1976 it did slow down considerably. Nevertheless, wages have not kept up with rising prices. To alleviate this problem and to spur economic expansion, the government has announced a tax reduction on building materials and consumer durables that reduces prices on these commodities by up to 10.5 percent.[24] Whether this and other measures can offset inflation on the one hand, and increase production on the other, remains to be seen.

Yugoslavia's standard of living is, of course, affected by the extent and availability of education. All children between the ages of seven and fifteen are required to attend eight years of school. The previously high illiteracy rate by 1964 had declined to about 21 percent, although it is still "widespread among elderly people and in the villages" and it is on the average "three times as high among women as among the men." According to one estimate, among the adults who took postwar reading and writing courses, some 70 percent, or 1.5 million persons, reverted to illiteracy. About four-fifths of the population above the age of ten allegedly remained illiterate or had completed at most only four grades of elementary school only a decade ago.[25]

The working class in Yugoslavia is probably dissatisfied with the limited access to educational opportunities for its children. Owing to the almost prohibitive cost of housing, food, and school supplies (which has been estimated at ten thousand old dinars per month per student) just one workers' family in four can send its children to a general secondary school. In 1974–1975, there existed only 450 such high schools, with about 203,000 students.[26]

---

23. RFE report (by Zdenko Antic), "Yugoslavia Confronted with Return of Gastarbeiter," 15 April 1976; *New York Times*, 24 October 1976, indicates that unemployment would almost reach 1.5 million if all of these workers returned to Yugoslavia.

24. *Vecernje novosti*, 20 May 1976; *Politika*, 17 May 1976.

25. The quotations and estimate of relapse are from Zagladin, *op. cit.* (in note 10 above), p. 70; Zagreb radio, 12 February 1966. However, the 1971 census reported that only 15.1 percent of the total population above the age of ten was illiterate and about one-fourth had completed three years of primary school or less. *Statistical Pocket Book of Yugoslavia 1976*, p. 24.

26. *Statisticki godisnjak Jugoslavije 1975*, p. 326.

STRUCTURE OF GOVERNMENT

The Constitution. The first postwar constitution was proclaimed in January 1946. Its main feature was the establishment of six constituent republics. This was not a genuine federal arrangement because the republics were subordinated in most important matters to the central government. The federal principle remained to a great extent theoretical, except that both houses of parliament had equal powers. There were twenty-four areas of jurisdiction in which the federation possessed exclusive competence, so that residual powers had almost no practical meaning for the republics.

The constitution underwent drastic modifications in January 1953 through a constitutional law, so that it became in effect a new one. Eight of the original fifteen sections were abrogated. It did not cover many important later developments in the political and social system. Hence, at the end of 1960, the Federal Assembly or parliament appointed a constitutional commission to prepare a completely new basic law. A preliminary draft was not ready until almost two years later. This third constitution, which had 259 articles, was adopted in April 1963. It received no fewer than forty-two amendments in three fundamental changes between 1967 and 1971. Due to these many additions, it was decided to adopt a fourth constitution, which was promulgated on 21 February 1974.

The current 1974 constitution[27] has 406 articles and is divided into six fundamental parts, except for the introductory "basic principles." It describes the Socialist Federated Republic of Yugoslavia, its social system, relations within it as well as the rights and duties of the federation, the organization of the federation, the procedure for amending the constitution, and transitional and concluding provisions. In its exhaustive definition of the social system and government, Yugoslavia's 1974 basic law is the longest and most detailed of all East European constitutions.

Legislature. Corresponding to a legislature or parliament is the Federal Assembly, which is divided into two chambers and has a total of 308 members. The Federal Chamber consists of 220 delegates from "self-managing organizations and communities and sociopolitical organizations in the republics and autonomous provinces," while the smaller Chamber of Republics and Autonomous Provinces is composed of delegations from "assemblies of the republics and assemblies of the autonomous provinces."[28]

The primary task of parliament is to discuss and approve legislation, acting in conjunction with any one of the four specialized units: sociopolitical; economic; education and culture; social welfare and health. Candidates for each of these units are selected by and from the appropriate working organizations. Danilo

---

27. *Constitution.*
28. *Ibid.*, p. 236.

Kekic is president of the Federal Chamber, while Zoran Polic currently heads the Chamber of Republics and Autonomous Provinces. Kiro Gligorov is president of the Federal Assembly as a whole.[29]

The Federal Assembly, or parliament, is the only body that is theoretically competent to amend the constitution, pass national laws, adopt federal plans and budgets, call a referendum, ratify international agreements, decide upon questions of war and peace, alter the boundaries of Yugoslavia, lay the foundation for internal and foreign policy, and supervise the work of the federal executive and administrative bodies. It elects the president and vice-president of the republic, the president of the Federal Executive Council, and members of the federal courts.

The Federal Assembly has a regular question period during which members may ask for information from government officials. However, legislative proposals by the Federal Executive Council are rarely amended, except in minor ways. The establishment of a joint parliamentary committee with broad powers to investigate expenditures and general policies at all levels, of Assembly standing committees with some authority over administration, and of the Constitutional Court may have been conceived to permit the Federal Assembly to act "safely" with more independence. In general, however, the 1974 constitution strengthens the control of the ruling party, as well as the new collective presidency.

The Executive. This branch of the government is led by Josip Broz-Tito, the president of the Socialist Federated Republic of Yugoslavia. He is also head of the presidency, which is a collective body of nine representing the six republics, two autonomous regions, and the communist party. Its main functions involve providing executive leadership, appointing civilian and military officials, and carrying out ceremonial duties. It was established to provide a smooth succession following Tito's death.

The president (who is also commander in chief of the armed forces) promulgates federal laws by decree, proposes judges for the Constitutional Court, appoints ambassadors, grants pardons, and, if the Federal Assembly and the collective presidency are unable to meet, declares war.[30] During hostilities or an immediate threat of war, the president may issue decrees on matters within Assembly jurisdiction. These must be submitted to the Assembly for approval as soon as it can meet. The president supposedly exercises his authority within the restrictions of the constitution and federal law.

The vice-presidency is the second most important position in the country since, in the event of a vacancy in the office of President of the Republic (whose

29. CIA, *Directory of Officials of the Socialist Federal Republic of Yugoslavia* (Washington, D.C., February 1976), pp. 37–43; henceforth cited as *Directory*.

30. *Constitution*, pp. 266–267.

incumbent concurrently heads the collective presidency), the vice-president becomes the interim successor. The vice-president serves a one-year term, according to a rotating schedule. The man appointed to this position on 7 May 1976 was Vidoje Zarkovic of Montenegro.

The Federal Executive Council, which is the source of legislative proposals, represents the most important governmental body in terms of day-to-day government operations. Its thirty-three members constitute a cabinet.[31] The collective presidency proposes a member of the Federal Assembly to be president of the Federal Executive Council; this candidate is then voted upon by the Assembly. The incumbent, until his death in an airplane crash on 18 January 1977, was Dzemal Bijedic who served as premier. The other Council members are elected by the Assembly on the recommendation of the premier, with one consideration being that the Council reflect the nationality composition of the country.

Local Government.   The decentralization of both political and economic power, which allegedly represents the basis for Yugoslavia's different approach to communism, is nowhere better illustrated than in local government. Broad administrative authority, a degree of autonomy, and extensive citizen participation are major factors in Yugoslavia's claim to have blended democracy with socialism. The basic local unit, which is called a commune, allegedly represents a genuinely new form of government.

By 1947 the people's committees had already been established as prime movers in both political and economic affairs. Seven years later, all authority other than that specifically delegated to the federal and constituent republics or autonomous region governments was given to these lowest units of administration. They exist at the level of commune, subdivision of a district, district, and city. At district and city levels, these committees are bicameral. Actually there are only two major levels of local government, commune and district, with the district consisting of a number of communes. Larger cities have district status, and smaller ones are governed by special town councils that operate under district or commune authority.

At present the districts hold jurisdiction over broad political matters, such as law enforcement and elections. They are responsible for coordinating activity within their general jurisdiction. But the communes have become key local units that have several primary concerns. One of these is economic, including planning, investments, internal trade, and supervision over economic enterprises. Another concern is municipal services, such as water supply, sewers, streets, and public utilities. A third comprises the area of "social management," that is, citizen control over public activities.

Judicial System.   The courts are divided into regular, self-management, and military categories. The federal Supreme Court (a regular tribunal) is the final

---

31. *Directory*, p. 10, lists the names.

appeal for all others, including military tribunals. Self-management courts, which do not consider criminal cases, mostly arbitrate disputes involving economic enterprises. That the judiciary can be used for political purposes is evident from the case of the dissident author Mihajlo Mihajlov, who was tried and sentenced for political crimes in 1965, 1966, and 1974. Currently serving a seven-year term for disseminating "hostile propaganda," he has been reported to be gravely ill as a result of a hunger strike.[32]

There is no jury trial in Yugoslavia. Economic and regular courts of the first instance and at district levels include both professional and "lay judges"; the latter are citizens legally untrained in law who are elected by people's committees for limited periods. Regular courts at the federal and republic levels consist of professional judges only. In judicial matters as in others, the autonomous regions are served just as the republics are.

The new Constitutional Court, which began functioning in 1964, decides on the conformity of laws and other regulations with the constitution, and of the laws of the republics with federal law; resolves disputes between sociopolitical committees on the territory of two or more republics; and decides whether any act of a federal agency violates the rights laid down by the constitution.[33] The president and the thirteen judges of this highest tribunal are elected for eight-year terms and may not hold office for more than two consecutive terms.

Elections. Ordinary voters submit names of candidates for commune, district, autonomous province, republic, and federal assemblies. This procedure takes place every two years by means of "preelection consultations." The votes of 10 percent of the registered voters in any electoral unit are sufficient to proclaim a candidate. Hence, communist-party members attempt to influence the choice and keep down the number of candidates.[34] Once communal assemblies have been constituted in this manner, they subsequently choose from among the candidates those who will become deputies to the district, province, republic, and federal legislatures.

All candidates are now elected indirectly by representatives chosen through sociopolitical organizations, economic enterprises, institutions, and government agencies. Deputies to both chambers of the Federal Assembly are elected by commune assemblies (to the Federal Chamber) or by province and republic assemblies (to the Chamber of Republics and Autonomous Provinces).

During the most recent elections, in 1974, three distinct phases were observed: (1) during March and April, more than one million delegates were chosen by

---

32. *New York Times,* 30 November 1976.

33. *Constitution,* pp. 286–287.

34. See the discussion of elections by Slobodan Stankovic in "Yugoslavia," R. F. Staar (ed.), *1975 Yearbook on International Communist Affairs* (Stanford, Ca., 1975), pp. 116–117.

voters; (2) early in May, these delegates elected about one hundred thousand individuals from their ranks to serve in commune, autonomous province, republic, and federal assemblies; (3) between 15 and 17 May the two chambers of the Federal Assembly elected their respective presidents and vice-presidents, the President of the Republic, and the premier.[35]

THE RULING PARTY

The movement that controls Yugoslavia today developed from a merger between left-wing social democratic and communist groups. Known initially as the Socialist Workers' Party of Yugoslavia (communists), it was founded at a 1919 unification congress.[36] The name was changed to the Communist Party of Yugoslavia the following year. The new party joined the Comintern and accepted the principles of revolution, the dictatorship of the proletariat, and a Soviet republic as the future form of government.

During elections in November 1920, the communists had the third strongest party in the country and succeeded in winning 58 out of 417 parliamentary seats. The party was outlawed after an attempt on the life of King Alexander and the assassination in 1921 of the Interior minister, Milorad Draskovic; after these events, it lost its unity and became wracked by factional strife. Eventually the Comintern had to intervene actively to solve the conflict between left and right elements.

In 1932 the party's Central Committee was dissolved by the Comintern and Milan Gorkic was appointed leader. Five years later, Stalin began his purge of ranking foreign ''comrades'' within the Comintern. He was on the verge of dissolving the party in Yugoslavia, as had already been done in Poland, but refrained from doing so, allegedly at the insistence of the Comintern secretary, the Bulgarian Georgi Dimitrov, who offered Josip Broz-Tito[37] an opportunity to reorganize the discredited movement. Gorkic was liquidated, and Tito became head of the party.

The Takeover.   An agreement signed in 1944 between Tito and premier Ivan Subasic of the exiled royal Yugoslav government stated that both sides would respect the will of the people with regard to the internal system, that the king would not return until a plebiscite had been held, and that a new legislative

---

35. *Politika,* 10 May 1975.

36. See Rodoljub Colakovic (ed.), *Pregled istorije Saveza Komunista Jugoslavije* (Belgrade, 1963), pp. 38–46, on this congress.

37. For a biography of Tito, see U.S. Department of State, Division of Biographic Information, *The Central Leadership of the Union of Communists of Yugoslavia* (Washington, D.C., 1958), p. 19; hereafter cited as *Central Leadership*.

assembly shall be established by combining Tito's followers in Yugoslavia and some numbers of pre-war Parliament.[38]

The first postwar election for a constituent assembly took place in November 1945. The communist-dominated People's Front provided the only candidates, while the registration of voters was managed by so-called people's committees. As a result, the single list of candidates won 90.48 percent of the vote and all of the seats. This constituent assembly abolished the monarchy and proclaimed a federal people's republic, and the country actually came under communist control.

The ruling party in Yugoslavia at first patterned itself after its Soviet counterpart and wholeheartedly accepted the hegemony of Moscow. No other communist movement adhered more closely to directives from the center than did the Yugoslav.[39] Tito believed that his party, like the Bolsheviks, had come to power after a true revolution. The dispute between Moscow and Belgrade, which finally led to the expulsion of the Yugoslav movement from the Cominform in June 1948, had many causes. The main ones were of a personal and psychological nature, including an underestimation by Stalin of the Yugoslav leadership and particularly of Josip Broz-Tito.

The statutes adopted at the party's fifth congress in July 1948 still followed the rules of the Communist Party of the Soviet Union (CPSU). By the time the sixth congress convened in 1952, the Yugoslav communists had withstood Stalin's challenge and were stronger than ever before. Party membership had almost doubled, despite the purge of its pro-Cominform elements. The leaders were convinced that they could advance toward communism in their own way, and this meant deviation from the Soviet model.

Everything possible was done to differentiate the Yugoslav party from the CPSU. At the sixth congress, the party name was changed to the League of Communists of Yugoslavia (*Savez Komunista Jugoslavije*—SKJ). Aside from distinguishing the Yugoslav party this action proclaimed the country's advancement to a higher level in its development toward the goal of a communist state. The leadership made it clear, however, that the one-party system would be retained in Yugoslavia. By 1970 specific plans appeared for transformation of the SKJ.[40]

Present Organization.   Despite a new name and new statutes, the SKJ still shows considerable similarity to all other communist organizations. It is operated

---

38. Robert Lee Wolff, *The Balkans in Our Time* (Cambridge, Mass.), p. 267.

39. Milovan Djilas, *Conversations with Stalin* (New York, 1962), pp. 11–12.

40. The need for transformation from a political party into a political-ideological force, internal SKJ democratization, and broader participation by members in forming and implementing policy were conclusions adopted by the SKJ Presidium and published in *Borba*, 24 April 1970.

to ensure that a small number of well-disciplined members make the major policy decisions and control all aspects of national life. There can be no fundamental criticism of Marxist-Leninist dogma as it is interpreted by the party, which adheres to the principles of democratic centralism.[41]

The highest SKJ organ, in theory, is the congress, which convenes every five years to pass resolutions, hear reports of the statutory control commission, adopt the party program, and determine the political line. The tenth congress, which was held in May 1974, was the most recent. The Executive Committee of the Presidium wields the real power, however. It consists of twelve members in addition to Tito: four Serbs, two Croats, two Macedonians, one Slovene, one Albanian, one Montenegrin, and one Moslem.

The 166-member Central Committee is composed of 46 Serbs, 25 Croats, 22 Slovenes, 22 Montenegrins, 18 Macedonians, 13 Albanians, 11 Moslems, and 9 of other nationalities. The Montenegrins are heavily represented in the party hierarchy, out of proportion to their percentage of the population and of party membership. In 1974 there were 41,150 Montenegrin party members and 27 in high SKJ positions. They hold as many posts as the Slovenes, who have 67,069 party members and more than three times the population.[42]

Tito became president of the party in December 1964; in this capacity he also heads the policy-making Executive Committee (see table 46). The social makeup of this body in 1958 was nine workers and six intellectuals. Five possessed university degrees, one was a graduate of a teachers' school, and six could claim only to have attended an elementary school; the rest presumably did not have even that much education.[43]

The Executive Committee supervises the work of the party organizations. It oversees the implementation of decisions that originate within the Presidium. In addition, five members of the Executive Committee head the following specific secretariats: ideology, organizational development, sociopolitical system, socioeconomic relations, and international relations. Six commissions under the Executive Committee deal with related interests.

The financial records of the party are checked by its Control Commission. The structure of the SKJ in the six republics and two autonomous provinces is similar to that at the federal level. The republics and autonomous regions and the army send representatives to a newly established 280-member Party Conference, which has replaced the Central Committee. The first such conference met during 29—31 October 1970.

---

41. See the party statute adopted at the ninth congress, 11—15 March 1969, and published in *Komunist,* 16 March 1969; Belgrade.

42. *Borba,* 4—5 April 1974. See also *1975 Yearbook* (cited in note 34 above), p. 114. This may change after the eleventh SKJ congress which will meet the end of May or early June 1978. Belgrade radio, 10 January 1977.

43. *Central Leadership,* p. 3. This refers to the group elected at the seventh congress, held 22—26 April 1958.

TABLE 46

EXECUTIVE COMMITTEE
LEAGUE OF COMMUNISTS OF YUGOSLAVIA, 1976

Name	Date of birth	Ethnic group	Joined party	Other position
Tito, Josip Broz (ex-officio member)	1892	Croat	1920	President of Yugoslavia; SKJ President
Dolanc, Stane	1925	Slovene	1944	SKJ Secretary
Bilic, Jure	1922	Croat	1941	SKJ Secretary (organizational development)
Grlickov, Aleksandar	1923	Macedonian	1943	Editor, *Socijalizam*; SKJ Secretary (international relations)
Kurtovic, Todo	1919	Serb	1941	SKJ Secretary (ideology)
Popovic, Mirko	1923	Serb	1941	SKJ Secretary (socio-political system)
Srzentic, Vojo	1934	Montenegrin	1952	SKJ Secretary (socio-economic relations)
Kukoc, Ivan	1918	Croat	1933	Colonel general; President, SKJ Commission for All-People's Defense
Mesihovic, Munir	1928	Moslem	after 1941	President, SKJ Commission for Economic Policy
Popovic, Dusan	1921	Serb	1944	President, SKJ Commission for Propaganda and Information
Stavrev, Dragoljub	1932	Macedonian	1950	President, SKJ Commission to Implement the Constitution
Sukrija, Ali	1919	Albanian	1939	President, SKJ Commission for Development and Personnel
Vidic, Dobrivoje	1918	Serb	1939	President, SKJ Commission for International Relations

SOURCES: Central Intelligence Agency, *Directory of Officials of the Socialist Federal Republic of Yugoslavia* (Washington, D.C., February 1976), pp. 107–165; Radosin Rajovic (chief ed.), *Jugoslovenski Savremenici: Ko je ko u Jugoslaviji* (Belgrade, 1970), passim, for dates of birth and first year of party membership.

Membership.   Until 1952 the criteria for membership in the communist party of Yugoslavia were the same as those of its Soviet counterpart. A prospective member was required to be eighteen years of age, to have recommendations in writing from two party members (who had been acquainted with him for two years and had themselves been members for at least two years), and to submit a written biographic statement.

Applications are still reviewed by one of the thirty-four thousand basic party organizations and forwarded to the next higher level. If the prospective member proves acceptable, he is placed on probationary status for eighteen months. At the eighth congress these requirements were modified to eliminate written recommendations and probationary status.[44] It appears that membership can be attained now on nomination by workers who are not necessarily party members themselves. The growth of the party's membership is shown in table 47.

TABLE 47

YUGOSLAV COMMUNIST PARTY, MEMBERSHIP, 1937−1976

Year	Number of members	Year	Number of members
1937	1,500	1956	635,984
1939	3,000	1960	898,300
1940	6,000	1964	1,030,041
1941	12,000	1967	1,046,018
1945	140,000	1970	1,111,682
1948	448,175	1974	ca. 1,100,000
1952	779,382	1976	ca. 1,400,000

SOURCES: Komunist, 15 October 1964 and 6 April 1967; Borba, 24 October 1970, 26 February 1975, and 18 October 1976.

Only one-fourth of the twelve thousand members in 1941 survived the war.[45] Thus, more than 90 percent of the 1976 membership joined the party during the preceding thirty-five years. The significant increase in membership between 1948 and 1952 is indicative of how much Stalin underestimated Tito's strength. The drop that occurred between 1952 and 1956 can be attributed to the confusion created by the new doctrine announced at the sixth congress and by the Milovan Djilas affair. (See the section below on "reconciliation with the Kremlin.") Both situations resulted in purges and disillusionment on the part of many members. From the beginning of 1958 through the end of 1964, some 108,236 persons were expelled from the party.[46] (See table 48.)

During the early 1970s purges intensified as a result of nationality problems within certain geographic parts of the country (e.g., Croatia) and infiltration by pro-Soviet elements. Although purges have decreased, up to six thousand members were expelled from the SKJ in 1974, with perhaps 37 percent of these dropped from party roles for political reasons. In November 1976 the SKJ

44. Komunist, 15 July 1965; paragraph 1 of statute, in Osmi Kongres SKJ (Belgrade, 1964), pp. 236−238.

45. Josef Korbel, Tito's Communism (Denver, Colo., 1951), p. 57.

46. Osmi Kongres SKJ (Belgrade, 1964), p. 139; Komunist, 15 July 1965.

TABLE 48

PURGES IN LEAGUE OF COMMUNISTS OF YUGOSLAVIA, 1959—1976

Year	New admissions	Expulsions	Voluntary resignations	Total number of members
1959	103,093	14,416	(see note)	935,856
1960	96,176	13,425	(see note)	1,006,285
1961	67,548	14,975	(see note)	1,035,003
1962	26,725	22,655	(see note)	1,018,331
1963	39,362	15,320	(see note)	1,019,013
1964	41,403	10,626	2,273	1,031,634
1965	51,398	12,878	5,762	1,046,202
1966	39,928	13,488	7,640	1,046,018
1967	33,986	11,195	11,182	1,013,500
1968	175,293	14,235	13,363	1,146,084
1969	152,000	11,176	9,447	1,111,628
1970	32,500	←——— 92,601 ———→		1,049,184
1971	47,606	n.a.	8,993	1,025,476
1972	58,262	12,941	14,449	1,009,953
1973	109,150	9,443	5,694	1,076,711
1974	152,673	n.a.	19,134	1,192,461
1975	110,377	n.a.	n.a.	1,302,843
1976 (Jan-June)	105,724	n.a.	n.a.	ca. 1,400,000

SOURCES: Belgrade radio, 24 January 1970; *Borba*, 19 March 1970. *Druga Konferencija SKJ* (Belgrade, 1972); *Cetvrta Konferencija SKJ* (Belgrade, 1973); *Deseti Kongress SKJ: Dokumenti* (Belgrade, 1974); *Statisticki godisnjak Jugoslavije 1975; Komunist*, 3 June 1971, 28 September 1972, 3 March and 16 June 1975, 25 October 1976.

NOTES: Until 1964, members who resigned of their own free will were listed together with those expelled.

The 1970 figure includes both expulsions and voluntary resignations.

numbered 1.4 million, after having admitted 216,101 new members during the eighteen months prior to the middle of that year.[47]

The social composition of the party is shown in table 49. Recent years have seen a constant decline in peasant membership, both in the percentage of the total and in absolute numbers. This can be attributed to the regime's approach toward agriculture and its emphasis on industry. The peasants have become disenchanted with the party because of past attempts to collectivize the farms. On the other hand, the intelligentsia component has increased markedly. This is probably a result of the system, which obliges a person to join the SKJ if he or she hopes to acquire a good post after completing his or her higher education. The number of pensioners has been increasing as well; this is characteristic of an "ageing" party.

47. *Borba*, 8 January 1976 and 3 November 1976; Belgrade radio, 9 November 1976.

TABLE 49

LEAGUE OF COMMUNISTS OF YUGOSLAVIA, SOCIAL COMPOSITION,
1959–1976

| | January 1959 | | January 1967 | | June 1976 | |
Category	Number	Percent	Number	Percent	Number	Percent
Workers (including peasants in collectives)	271,100	31.6	355,022	33.9	366,272	28.1
Peasants (uncollectivized)[a]	121,684	14.2	77,134	7.4	65,910	5.1
Intelligentsia	264,629	30.9	408,378	38.8	542,248	41.8
Other[b]	200,124	23.3	96,217	9.5 }	232,274	17.7
Pensioners	–	–	74,610	7.1 }		
Students	–	–	34,657	3.3	96,132	7.3
Total	857,537	100.0	1,046,018	100.0	1,302,836	100.0

SOURCES: *Jugoslovenski pregled* (July–August 1964), pp. 33–35; *Komunist,* 6 April, 1967; *Vjesnik,* 13 June 1976.

NOTES: [a]This category of peasant in 1946 comprised 49 percent of the party membership. *Komunist,* 25 May 1967.

[b]Includes members of the armed forces in 1976.

In Yugoslavia, just as in all other communist-dominated states, control over youth is both a matter of prime importance and a major problem. To supplement the basic education received at school, the Pioneers provide militant political indoctrination. During holidays or free time, participation in volunteer working brigades is encouraged. Yet the young people themselves have prevented the party from exercising tight control and have become disenchanted. This does not necessarily produce direct opposition to communism, but it does involve resistance to rigid conformity.

Of the 3,500,000 members of the Yugoslav Youth Union, more than a third of those who are eligible are neither in the SKJ nor in the Socialist Alliance front organization. Although this is the sole youth movement that is allowed, official figures indicate that only about 60 percent of the young people who were between fourteen and twenty-five in 1975 were members.[48] There is persistent discontent among students and other young people all over Yugoslavia.

Mass Organizations.   The most important mass movement in Yugoslavia is the Socialist Alliance of Working People (SSRN), formerly known as the People's Front, which has 8,582,000 members. It is composed of both organizations and individuals. To become an SSRN member, an individual must enroll in one of its basic organizations. The purpose is to involve as many people as possible in some type of activity over which the party has control.

---

48. *Borba,* 14 May 1975.

The SSRN platform has been designed so that it will be acceptable to practically everyone. A person with a distaste for the principles of the ruling party may find those of SSRN more to his liking. The movement has two fundamental purposes, one political and the other economic.[49] Politically, it helps to influence the masses along the general SKJ line, conducts elections, and on special occasions holds political rallies. The economic purpose consists of assisting in the fulfillment of national economic plans and explaining the need for social change.

The SSRN has an organizational structure similar to that of the ruling party. It extends from the national level down to the commune and is controlled by the SKJ at all levels. Party members are supposed to influence the SSRN by their own efforts and not only through their positions in the communist hierarchy. The president of the SSRN is Dusan Petrovic-Sane, an SKJ Presidium member, who succeeded to this position in 1974.

The Confederation of Trade-Unions in Yugoslavia is another communist-dominated mass organization. It operates as a means for implementing the party's economic policy. Until 1958 labor unions had control over the list of candidates for workers' councils. At that time, there were among 220,656 council members only 60,012 communists, or 27.2 percent of the total. In individual councils, party membership ranged from 10 percent to 85 percent. Although trade unions no longer control the candidate list, they retain influence within various industrial enterprises helping the party and the government control factories with their assistance. In 1975 the trade unions had 4,108,000 members.[50] The confederation is headed by Mika Spiljak, who belongs to the SKJ Presidium.

It is interesting to note that between January 1958 and September 1976 about two thousand strikes took place in Yugoslavia. Most of these occurred in Slovenia, followed by Serbia, and than Croatia. An official listing indicates a concentration in metallurgy, with textiles, wood products, and the construction industry following in number of strikes.[51] Both the communist party and the trade unions probably look upon the strikes as safety valves rather than real threats to the system.

Succession. There has been at least an attempt by the League of Communists to provide for an orderly succession after Tito: the new constitution states that the vice-president of the collective presidency (at the end of 1976, Vidoje Zarkovic) will head the government pending the election of a new president. Some danger lies in the lack of a fixed date for elections and in the lack of experience in electing any presidents thus far except Tito, who was elected for

49. Boskovic, *op. cit.* (in note 13 above), pp. 339–347.

50. *Yugoslav Survey* (May 1975), p. 17.

51. *Vecernje novosti,* 15 May 1976; RFE report (by Slobodan Stankovic), "Strikes in Yugoslavia: Neither Permitted nor Forbidden," 20 May 1976.

life. The strongest personalities to have emerged thus far, both Slovenes, are Edvard Kardelj and Stane Dolanc, Bakaric, who is a Croatian, also remains a contender. However, the chief organ of succession is the collective presidency, which may not prove viable. Tito's departure could revive the old ethnic conflicts and create additional tensions in the party.

As early as 21 September 1970, Tito had announced that "a sort of collective presidency of Yugoslavia" would succeed him as the head of state. He stressed the need to preserve unity by drawing into the collective leadership "the best people from individual republics."[52] Edvard Kardelj reiterated Tito's proposal, stating that every republic would elect "two to three or more representatives, depending on the total members of the body." The new organ was confirmed in the 1974 constitution, and representatives of individual nationalities will annually rotate as President of the Republic.

It is doubtful that the party will destroy itself through a struggle for power, even though it might become seriously weakened. There is no nonparty individual or organization in Yugoslavia capable of displacing the present regime. The communists long ago liquidated all opposition leaders and organizations they did not control. The only remaining power center that might affect the succession struggle is the armed forces.

The specter of intervention by Moscow in the Belgrade succession was revealed over the years 1974–1976, with the arrests and trials of "Cominformists" within the country who were forming a pro-Soviet party so that they could seize power after Tito's death. The possibility of USSR military action in Yugoslavia has not been ruled out, and there have been indications that the Soviet Union is exploiting the nationality problem to its advantage.[53] However, a personal visit by Leonid Brezhnev during 15–17 November 1976 allegedly resulted in assurances of USSR peaceful intentions vis-à-vis Yugoslavia.

FOREIGN RELATIONS

The foreign policy of Yugoslavia had reflected and had been mainly determined by the status of that country's relations with the Soviet Union. Tito, in taking certain exceptions to USSR policy, was at one time forced to orient himself toward the noncommunist world in order to survive. However, there can be no question about Yugoslavia's strong preference for alliance with the Soviet bloc. Despite this preference, it has steadfastly refused to become a satellite. While there has been no compromise of this independence, neither has there been

---

52. *Borba,* 23 September 1970.

53. RFE reports (by Zdenko Antic), "Yugoslav Leader Accuses Cominformist of Foreign Ties," 9 January 1976; and (by Slobodan Stankovic), "Cominform Trials in Yugoslavia," 15 January and 12 February 1976. See also the criticism of Soviet proletarian internationalism in *Politika,* 20 December 1976.

any lessening of the Yugoslav government's devotion to communist principles. The importance of this relatively small country has been magnified many times over by its ability, demonstrated in 1948, 1953, and 1968, to defy the Soviet bloc and to obtain Western economic and military assistance.

Aggressive Postwar Policies. Although provided with extensive wartime military aid by the United States and Britain, and disappointed by the failure of the Soviet Union to contribute substantially until the fall of 1944, the new postwar government of Tito openly oriented its foreign policies toward the USSR and considered the capitalist states enemies. Backed by an army that had received decisive aid from Soviet divisions toward the end of the war,[54] communist Yugoslavia attempted to expand its borders. It seems clear that Tito at this time had visions of a Balkan federation led by himself.

An initial argument with Italy concerned the border province of Venezia Giulia, including the port city of Trieste. Populated by a majority of Slavs, but ceded to Italy after World War I, the province had been occupied by Partisans in 1945 after the German retreat. The Western Allies subsequently entered the city, but it took nine years to reach a settlement. The Yugoslavs were disappointed by the Soviet failure (1948–1953) to support their claims, and the 1954 agreement was concluded in London without the participation of the USSR. It gave the city of Trieste to Italy and the hinterland to Yugoslavia.

In neighboring Albania, Tito's representatives had advised the newly founded communist party in 1941 and supported the successful guerrilla struggle against Italians and Germans in that country. By establishing joint-stock companies and stationing a few army units in Albania, Yugoslav communists exercised supervision both economically and militarily over their satellite. Imbued with somewhat the same independent spirit as their neighbors, Albanian communists resisted this domination. Annexation by Yugoslavia never took place (although it had previously been suggested by Stalin) because of the Tito regime's 1948 dispute with the Cominform.

Another plan for expansion included Bulgarian and Greek parts of Macedonia adjoining the similarly named republic in Yugoslavia. In August 1947 the Bulgarian communist party agreed to federation at some future date.[55] Tito also influenced the civil war in Greece by reestablishing a Macedonian partisan movement in that country. His plan for consolidating Macedonia was stopped (as in the case of Albania) after the Cominform's expulsion of the Yugoslav

---

54. Soviet divisions only passed through the northeastern part of the country, but they did assist the Partisans to capture Belgrade. Djilas, *op. cit.* (in note 39 above), pp. 88–89, reports that he discussed with Stalin the 121 reported cases of rape (111 of these also involved murder) and 1,204 registered incidents of looting by Red Army personnel in Yugoslavia.

55. Early in 1948 Stalin turned from his previous opposition and ordered an immediate federation between Bulgaria and Yugoslavia. *Ibid.*, p. 177. It never took place.

communist party in June 1948, together with the termination of the Greek civil war in the following year.

The Tito-Stalin Dispute. Yugoslav communists were completely dedicated to Stalin personally and to the Soviet Union in the early postwar years. This devotion persisted, despite several disappointments and differences during the war years and thereafter.[56] Proposals for joint-stock companies, which would have given the USSR control of the Yugoslav economy, were opposed. This was precisely the same procedure that Belgrade had adopted in seeking domination over Albania. Soviet military advisers insisted that the Yugoslav army be remodeled after the Soviet example, and brazen intelligence activities were conducted by Soviet representatives in Yugoslavia. Agents were recruited in the army, the government, and even the Central Committee of the Yugoslav communist party.

Relations had already become strained when Tito failed to obey Stalin's summons to Moscow in February 1948. In a series of letters the Yugoslavs were accused by Soviet leaders not only of deviation, arrogance, and ingratitude, but even of Trotskyism. (These charges also reopened the matter of the "insult" to the Red Army by Milovan Djilas in 1945 when he complained that Yugoslav women had been raped and murdered by Soviet soldiers.) Yugoslavia's replies, which were always conciliatory, contained pledges of loyalty and suggestions that the Central Committee in the CPSU might be the victim of misinformation. Belgrade offered time and again to prove its loyalty to Moscow. Tito and his colleagues hoped for reconciliation, almost irrationally and to the very end. The Soviets, however, remained adamant and demanded unconditional capitulation.

Failing in his attempt to eliminate Tito with denunciation and expulsion from the Cominform, Stalin turned to more direct methods of economic, political, and military pressure. Newspapers were smuggled into the country, and radio broadcasts viciously denounced Tito. Agents from neighboring states infiltrated Yugoslavia to incite national minorities, and an economic boycott was applied by the entire Soviet bloc. In August 1949, the USSR formally declared that it considered the Yugoslav government an enemy. Armed clashes with Soviet satellite troops along the Yugoslav borders became constant occurrences.

Tito Turns West. Reluctantly, but without a choice, Tito looked to the West for help. His economy had depended upon trade with East European countries and now was in danger of collapse. The Western response was gradual but positive. American-held Yugoslav assets were released, and a trade agreement was signed in December 1948 with Britain. During the following year, negotia-

---

56. Milorad M. Drachkovitch, "The Comintern and Insurrectional Activity of the Communist Party of Yugoslavia in 1941–1942," in Drachkovitch and Branko Lazitch (eds.), *The Comintern: Historical Highlights* (New York, 1966), pp. 184–213.

tions involving trade and a loan from the U.S. Export-Import Bank were completed. In 1950 surplus American grain was sent to alleviate hunger resulting from a serious drought in Yugoslavia.

During the next decade an estimated 3.5 billion dollars' worth of assistance came from the West. Nearly half of this was contributed by the United States. As of mid-1962 American economic aid to Yugoslavia had amounted to more than $1.5 billion and military assistance to about $719 million. UNRRA's help had totaled nearly one-half billion dollars.[57] An equal amount came from nongovernment charitable institutions such as CARE or in the form of loans from international banks. This provided an annual average of nearly $250 million, which materially assisted in alleviating the foreign-trade deficit. (See table 50 for figures on the continued adverse balance-of-payments problem.)

TABLE 50

YUGOSLAVIA'S FOREIGN TRADE, 1961 – 1975
(in millions of dinars)

Category	1961	1966	1970	1975
Imports	15,474	26,782	48,857	128,805
Exports	9,672	20,741	28,544	88,468
Total	25,146	47,523	77,401	217,273
Balance	- 5,802	- 6,041	- 20,313	- 60,337

SOURCE: [Yugoslavia], *Statistical Pocket Book of Yugoslavia 1976* (Belgrade, 1976), p. 80, which gives figures for each year between 1961 and 1975.

One of the hopes of the West had been to bring Yugoslavia indirectly into the North Atlantic Treaty Organization. A step toward this goal was the treaty of friendship and cooperation signed at Ankara in February 1953 by Yugoslavia, Greece, and Turkey. Several months later, a military pact was concluded between the same three countries. Late the following year and early in 1955, however, Tito toured India and Burma to expound the principles of "active coexistence," equality of nations, and noninterference in the internal affairs of other countries.[58]

Reconciliation with the Kremlin. After Stalin's death, the new Soviet communist-party leader, Nikita Khrushchev, realized that anti-Yugoslav policy represented a liability. The earliest sign of a thaw was the establishment of a

---

57. Milorad M. Drachkovitch, *United States Aid to Yugoslavia and Poland: An Analysis of a Controversy* (Washington, D.C., 1963), p. 121; *U.S. News & World Report* (8 November 1976), p. 36.

58. Note the speech at Rangoon in Josip Broz-Tito, *Selected Speeches and Articles, 1941–1961* (Zagreb, 1963), pp. 172–173.

Romanian-Yugoslav joint administration over their common part of the Danube River, obviously with Soviet approval. Moscow omitted the usual May Day criticism of Tito in 1953 and proposed that the two countries exchange ambassadors. The offer was accepted. The other satellite countries, one by one, adopted an identical course. Border clashes and subversion virtually ceased, and anti-Tito newspapers and radio stations in neighboring countries were shut down.

Two years later, during May 1955, in full realization of the need to heal the breach, Khrushchev and premier Nikolai Bulganin journeyed to Yugoslavia. Officially accepting Soviet responsibility for the break between the two countries, Khrushchev in a speech at Belgrade airport blamed the executed secret-police chief Lavrenty Beria for what had happened and asked Yugoslavia's forgiveness. He also proposed the renewal of friendly relations between the two governments and communist parties. In a joint declaration Tito and Khrushchev agreed to respect the sovereignty, independence, integrity, and equality of states; accepted the principle of noninterference, based on the premise that differing forms of social development are solely the concern of each individual country; and condemned aggression as well as political and economic domination.

For his part, Tito supported the USSR in its suppression of the 1956 Hungarian revolt. He had opposed the initial interference, while the local communists were still in control of the situation. After the rebellion got out of hand, however, he considered Soviet intervention to save the country for communism to be the lesser of two evils. In 1957 Tito extended diplomatic recognition to East Germany and, in an essay[59] published abroad, called for the dissolution of NATO and criticized the West for its negative attitude toward Moscow.

At the same time, no criticism of communism inside Yugoslavia or in the Soviet Union could be expressed. A good illustration is the case involving Milovan Djilas. Although earlier he had been considered the heir apparent to Tito, this man resigned from the communist party in 1954 and subsequently wrote a book entitled *The New Class*. It represents the most devastating and best-known indictment of the communist system. Another book, *Conversations with Stalin*, resulted in his imprisonment for allegedly disclosing "official secrets." After serving part of his sentence, Djilas was released on 31 December 1966. Several years later, regime officials withdrew his passport two days before he had planned to leave for a visit to the United States.[60]

The Second Soviet-Yugoslav Dispute.   Concerned with unrest throughout Eastern Europe and beset by differences of opinion within his own party leadership, Khrushchev decided it was time to reorganize the Soviet bloc. He had pre-

---

59. Josip Broz-Tito, "On Certain International Questions," *Foreign Affairs* (October 1957), 70–72.

60. Belgrade radio, 11 March 1970. See his interview with a reporter from the *Washington Post*, 25 November 1976, in which Djilas urges better relations with the United States.

pared and circulated a resolution on communist unity to be presented and signed at Moscow on the fortieth anniversary of the 1917 revolution. The document portrayed the world in terms of two uncompromising blocs, with the United States as the "center of world reaction." It equated the Soviet bloc with the Warsaw Pact and, in an allusion to the Yugoslavs, declared revisionism to be the greatest danger. Tito was shocked and dismayed. Refusing to attend the anniversary meeting himself, he sent Edvard Kardelj and Aleksandar Rankovic to Moscow with instructions not to sign the resolution.

The seventh congress of his communist party in April 1958 gave Tito an opportunity to present his version of communism to the world. He circulated drafts of the new party program and, in some instances, modified it in acquiescence to Soviet objections. The final document[61] represented a formal declaration of Yugoslavia's political and ideological independence. Tito's insistence on retaining the main substance of the draft program resulted in a boycott of the congress by the Soviet communist party as well as its East European allies. Although ambassadors from these countries attended as observers, all except the Polish representative ostentatiously walked out of the congress.

Moscow's attack on Yugoslav revisionism set the tone and the levels of criticism for its supporters to follow. The rift remained moderate in the beginning. Unexpectedly, however, the Chinese communists launched a vitriolic attack, declaring that the Cominform had been correct in its 1948 expulsion of the Yugoslav party.[62] Moscow announced a five-year postponement of its $285-million credit commitment to Belgrade, but no economic blockade or disruption of diplomatic relations followed.

Tito Again Turns West.   Shortly after the seventh party congress, friendship for the United States again became official Yugoslav policy. This was claimed not to be based on any requirement for assistance, yet at the same time a real need admittedly existed. Tito asked for $100 million in aid during October 1958, and the United States responded with a program encompassing even more.

There were limitations to Yugoslavia's leanings toward the West, as is evidenced by its active support of Fidel Castro, even to the point of jeopardizing American assistance. Renewed friendship with the West did not become as intimate as before, nor was the break with the Soviets as serious as the first one. Belgrade could not be convinced that the schism would continue, and Tito privately pictured Khrushchev as the leader of an anti-Stalinist faction that sincerely sought peace with the West. In the same vein, he criticized the

---

61. Translated in full in Stoyan Pribichevich (ed. and trans.), *Yugoslavia's Way: The Program of the League of the Communists of Yugoslavia* (New York, 1958).

62. *Jen-min jih-pao*, 5 May 1958; Peking. Just twelve years later, a Yugoslav ambassador arrived in Peking and the Chinese communists appointed an envoy to Belgrade. *New York Times*, 12 August 1970.

administration in Washington for failing to reach an accommodation with the USSR.

Tito next attempted to organize the nonaligned nations with "third force" proposals by organizing and addressing a conference of these states that met at Belgrade.[63] This effort brought him dangerously close to a rift with the West. While the neutralists condemned the existence of all "blocs," their policies approximated those of the USSR in outspoken support for the recognition of East Germany and the seating of Mainland China in the United Nations. There was resentment in Washington when Tito supported the Soviet Union during the Berlin crisis and failed to denounce the USSR's resumption of nuclear testing.

The Cycle Repeats Itself.   After the Sino-Soviet dispute had come into the open at the twenty-second congress of the Soviet communist party, Tito saw a chance to move closer to Moscow. Despite an amnesty for political prisoners, Milovan Djilas was rearrested in April 1962 because of the imminent publication in English of his book *Conversations with Stalin*, which was critical of the Soviet leadership during and immediately after the war. Since the USSR had split with both Albania and Mainland China, the Yugoslavs showed by this arrest that they desired closer relations.

Beginning with the late 1960s, however, the growing possibility of Soviet interference in the future of Yugoslavia has led the ruling party and regime to take a more sober attitude toward the USSR. This could be seen in Belgrade's condemnation of the Warsaw Pact invasion of Czechoslovakia (August 1968) and its vigorous prosecution of pro-Soviet elements within Yugoslavia during the mid-1970s.

On the other hand, commercial agreements provide for the equivalent of some fourteen billion dollars in trade with the USSR during the 1976–1980 period (compared with only six billion dollars in the previous five-year period).[64] By contrast, Yugoslavia's trade with the (West) European Economic Community amounted to about 40 percent of its total foreign turnover in 1975, causing it to incur a deficit with the Common Market countries. Trade with the United States is also of importance since American investments have grown over the last several years. The U.S. now occupies first place as a joint-investment partner with Yugoslavia, an example being the huge $750 million petrochemical complex built by Dow Chemical Company.[65]

Tito has stated that he has no intention of joining any of the existing military blocs. He proclaims neutralism, but his actions contradict this stand. In a speech at a party conference shortly after the 1959 dispute with the USSR and well before the Sino-Soviet split, and during a visit to Sverdlovsk in 1965, Tito said

---

63. His address is in *Selected Speeches and Articles* (in note 58 above), pp. 388–408.

64. Moscow radio, 10 and 15 December 1976.

65. *Ekonomska politika*, 24 March 1975; Belgrade.

flatly that he sided with the Soviet Union on all main problems of foreign policy. During an interview with a correspondent for the Soviet Army's daily newspaper *Krasnaya zvezda*, he said: "What must at present bring us together and link us more than anything else is the struggle for the common aims of socialist and communist construction, for implementation of the great ideas of Marx, Engels, and Lenin, and the struggle for peace, international cooperation, and democratic relations in the world."[66] The participation of the SKJ in the European Conference of Communist Parties in June 1976 reaffirmed its basic solidarity with the other movements, even though criticism of certain Soviet postulates remains. Nevertheless, uncertainty about the future of Yugoslavia after Tito leaves the scene has led to a dilemma in Yugoslav policy regarding East-West relations.

Typical of this problem vis-a-vis the western world is the present relationship between Yugoslavia and the Federal Republic of Germany. Belgrade has demanded indemnification for Yugoslav war victims and assailed the West Germans for their failure to accept reparation claims. Still, the Federal Republic of Germany remains Yugoslavia's current third-ranking economic trading partner, after Italy and the United States. Despite the obvious benefits from this relationship in the past, about seven billion dollars in debts to Western countries[67] had accumulated by the end of 1976. Whether these are met may provide some clue to the future.

The great complexity of Yugoslavia's domestic and international problems and the dominant role one man has played since the communists seized power at the end of World War II make any prediction about that country hazardous. In the past Tito's leadership and authority have been essential in holding the ruling party together, but there is a legitimate question whether Titoism without Tito will prove to be an enduring formula for political cohesion in a diversified country. Yugoslav-Soviet relations have oscillated in the past between extremes of friendship and hostility, and the current rapprochement between Tito and Brezhnev will be put to another test after one or the other leaves the political scene.[68] Recent disunity among regional communist parties (Serbian, Croatian, etc.), which Tito temporarily overcame, reflects deeper ethnic strivings in that multinational country. As yet inconclusive results from experimentation with the decentralized system of workers' self-management, which has from the beginning been incompatible with the one-party rule, represent another unsettling factor. Last but not least, the role the armed forces may play in case of internal disorders after Tito makes the picture even more uncertain.

One should add that more than any other East European country, Yugoslavia

---

66. *Borba*, 10 October 1974.

67. *New York Times*, 30 December 1976.

68. Note, for example, a letter reportedly sent by the SKJ leadership to all basic party organizations. It allegedly confirms that Brezhnev had asked Tito for military facilities in Yugoslav ports and air fields as well as rapprochement with Warsaw Pact policies. Tito "indignantly" rejected these Soviet demands. Rome radio, 7 January 1977; based on an ANSA dispatch from Belgrade.

has been open to the influence of the West. But this means that popular disposition toward a free political system, beyond the stranglehold of a single party, might also become an element to consider. Therefore, instead of an attempt to predict what will happen, the foregoing enumeration of several basic factors that may shape the future should suffice. The interplay among them should determine the course of events in Yugoslavia.

Chapter 9

Military Integration: Warsaw Pact

The establishment of a multilateral military alliance system in Eastern Europe that was announced by Moscow came ostensibly as a response to West German membership in NATO. The true reason for the Warsaw Treaty Organization was probably the USSR's desire to obtain legal justification for stationing its troops in East-Central Europe. The pact[1] was initialed in the capital of Poland on 14 May 1955, only one day before the signing of the state treaty in Vienna that restored sovereignty to Austria and obligated Moscow to evacuate its forces from Hungary and Romania within forty days after the Austrian State treaty had gone into effect. The Warsaw Treaty Organization (WTO) also provided an additional legal basis for the continued presence of Soviet troops in Poland and the German Democratic Republic. However, in the case of the GDR, such provision appeared to be superfluous, due to the absence of a peace treaty.

A Soviet declaration[2] at the height of the Hungarian revolution reaffirmed the right of this presence and added that Soviet forces in Poland had the additional justification of the Potsdam agreement. This official statement claimed that no military units existed in any other East European people's democracy—the German Democratic Republic, which had been proclaimed sovereign in October 1949, apparently did not fall into such a category—and that the Soviet government stood ready to discuss the question of its troops abroad with other signatories to the Warsaw Pact.

The subsequently negotiated status-of-forces treaties with Poland (December 1956), East Germany (March 1957), Romania (April 1957), Hungary (May 1957), and Czechoslovakia (October 1968) all remain in effect today except for

---

1. Boris Meissner (ed.), *Der Warschauer Pakt: Dokumentensammlung* (Cologne, 1962), p. 12. A translation of the Warsaw treaty into English appears in *United Nations Treaty Series*, CCXIX, Part I, p. 24. N. N. Rodionov et al. (eds.), *Organizatsiya Varshavskogo dogovora: 1955–1975* (Moscow, 1975); published documents and materials on the WTO, including the treaty.

2. *Pravda*, 31 October 1956.

the third, which lapsed in June 1958 upon the withdrawal of Soviet troops from Romania.[3] These agreements represented the first such arrangements to be made public, although secret accords may have existed in the past. The treaty with East Germany is unique in that it includes a safety clause allowing the USSR to intervene if it finds its own security endangered. Article 18 reads as follows:

> In case of a threat to the security of the Soviet forces which are stationed on the territory of the German Deomcratic Republic [GDR], the High Command of the Soviet forces in the GDR, in appropriate consultation with the GDR Government, and taking into account the actual situation and the measures adopted by GDR state organs, may apply measures for the elimination of such a threat.[4]

This situation has not changed as a result of the two bilateral friendship, collaboration, and mutual-assistance pacts signed in June 1964 and October 1975 between the two countries. (For other treaties, see table 51.)

Apart from the East German treaty, all of the status-of-forces treaties follow a uniform pattern. They deal with

1. the movement of Soviet forces in the host country;
2. jurisdiction over Soviet forces and individual soldiers, members of Soviet military families, and civilian Soviet employees while on the territory of the host country;
3. Soviet control and use of military installations on the territory of the host country;
4. the jurisdiction of local authorities in civil and criminal matters arising out of, or in conjunction with, the presence of Soviet troops;
5. matters subject to the exclusive jurisdiction of Soviet authorities; and
6. the settlement of mutual claims.

The inferior status of the German Democratic Republic can also be seen in certain differences in details. For example, the treaties with Poland and Hungary omit the article on the basis of which the GDR guarantees to the Soviet Union the use of military and nonmilitary facilities, including transport and communications, that were being used on the date the agreement was signed. Further divergencies exist regarding the movement of Soviet troops.[5] Such movement

---

3. On the withdrawal of Soviet troops from Romania see Guenther Wagenlehner, "Die politische Bedeutung des Warschauer Paktes," *Soldat und Technik* (March 1965), p. 115.

4. Meissner, *op. cit.* (in note 1 above), p. 128. For an English translation of the status-of-forces treaties see the RFE report, "Agreements on Soviet Forces Stationed in Czechoslovakia, the GDR, Hungary, and Poland," 24 October 1968.

5. Kazimierz Grzybowski, *The Socialist Commonwealth of Nations* (New Haven, Conn., 1964), p. 205. The most recent Soviet-GDR treaty appears in *Neues Deutschland*, 8 October 1975; the Russian text can be found in *Izvestiya* of the same date.

TABLE 51

EAST EUROPEAN BILATERAL TREATY SYSTEM, 1976
(Treaties of Friendship, Cooperation, and Mutual Assistance)

	USSR	GDR	Czecho-slovakia	Poland	Romania	Bulgaria	Hungary
USSR	—	7 October 1975	6 May 1970	8 April 1965	7 July 1970	14 May 1967	7 September 1967
GDR	7 October 1975	—	17 March 1967	15 March 1967	1 October 1970	7 September 1967	18 May 1967
Czechoslovakia	6 May 1970	17 March 1967	—	1 March 1967	16 August 1970	26 April 1968	14 June 1968
Poland	8 April 1965	15 March 1967	1 March 1967	—	12 November 1970	6 April 1967	16 May 1968
Romania	7 July 1970	1 October 1970	16 August 1970	12 November 1970	—	19 November 1970	24 February 1971
Bulgaria	14 May 1967	7 September 1967	26 April 1967	6 April 1967	19 November 1970	—	10 July 1969
Hungary	7 September 1967	18 May 1967	14 June 1968	16 May 1968	24 February 1971	10 July 1969	—

SOURCES: Malcolm Mackintosh, *The Evolution of the Warsaw Pact* (Adelphi Papers, no. 58; London: Institute for Strategic Studies, June 1969), p. 25; *Pravda*, 7 May 1970; *Krasnaya zvezda*, 8 July 1970; East Berlin radio, 1 October 1970; Bucharest radio, 12 November 1970; Sofia radio, 19 November 1970; Bucharest radio, 24 February 1971; Jean-Pierre Brule, "Le Pacte Varsovie a 20 ans," *Est & Ouest* (16–30 April 1975), pp. 2–16; East Berlin radio, 7 October 1975.

can occur allegedly in Hungary and Poland only with consent of the host government and with plans made in advance. The GDR agreement provides a general understanding on maneuver areas, but says nothing about troop movements. Again, the treaties with Poland and Hungary require the consent of the host governments to changes in the strength of Soviet military formations and to relocation of garrisons, whereas in the treaty with the GDR, only consultation is needed.

The treaty with Hungary is essentially the same as the one with Poland, except that the latter is much more elaborate. For example, its Article 5 reads:

> The regulations on entry and exits of Soviet troop units and members of the Soviet armed forces and their families into Poland or from Poland as well as questions concerning types of required documents in connection with their stay on the territory of the People's Republic of Poland will be governed by a special agreement between the contracting parties.[6]

In contrast, the Hungarian treaty simply refers to an agreement on the strength of Soviet troops and the places where they will be stationed.

Finally, the treaty with Poland differs from the other two by introducing a reference (in Article 15) to a special agreement defining "lines of communication, dates, orders, and compensation conditions for transit of Soviet troops and war materiel across the territory of the People's Republic of Poland."

The most recent such agreement[7] differs from all others since it is based on the consent of the governments in Bulgaria, Hungary, East Germany, Poland, and Czechoslovakia for some of the Soviet forces already in the country, as a result of the (August 1968) Warsaw Pact invasion, temporarily to remain there. It states that all other military units of WTO allies will be withdrawn over a period of two months and that the temporary presence of Soviet forces "does not violate the sovereignty" of Czechoslovakia (Article 2). However, Soviet troops, families, and other civilians are "exempted from passport or visa control when entering, remaining in, or leaving the Czechoslovak Socialist Republic" (Article 4).

A different problem is posed by Albania, which has been outside the bloc since Khrushchev attacked its leadership in October 1961 at the twenty-second CPSU congress. Although it was not expelled from the Warsaw Pact, Albania refused to attend sessions of its Political Consultative Committee. Since the ouster of Khrushchev, two attempts had been made to bring Albania back into active participation, but without success. In January 1965 Tirana rejected an

---

6. Meissner, *op. cit.* (in note 1 above), p. 118. See also Jens Hacker, "Zwanzig Jahre Warschauer Pakt," *Osteuropa* (May 1975), pp. 299–318.

7. *Krasnaya zvezda*, 19 October 1968; English translation in RFE report, *op. cit.* (in note 4 above), pp. 1–8.

invitation, extended by the Polish regime, to attend the seventh meeting of the Committee held in Warsaw. Exactly one year later, an invitation from the same source proposed that Albania send a delegation to a meeting of communist parties from Eastern Europe and "socialist" countries from Asia to discuss the coordination of military aid for North Vietnam. The following month, the official Albanian news agency published the texts[8] of both the brief invitation and the lengthy refusal. On 13 September 1968, Tirana radio announced Albania's official withdrawal from the Warsaw Treaty Organization because troops of the WTO's member states had invaded Czechoslovakia. A week later, Albania protested an alleged concentration of Soviet troops in Bulgaria.

Soviet leader Brezhnev informed his party's Central Committee in September 1965 that changes in the military alliance of the pact countries were under consideration. He stated:

> With a view to improving the activity of the Warsaw Treaty Organization, it is necessary to establish within the framework of this pact a permanent and operational mechanism for the evaluation of current problems. The complex international situation forces us to pay special attention to problems of military collaboration with the [other] countries of socialism. A great effort is taking place according to the following plan: standardization of equipment is being implemented, exchange of combat training experience [has been developed], and joint maneuvers are being conducted.[9]

It was not until 17 March 1969, at the Budapest meeting of the WTO's Political Consultative Committee, that certain agreements appeared to implement the "permanent operational mechanism" suggested by Brezhnev. This 110-minute conference agreed to establish a new WTO Defense Council and a Committee of Defense Ministers. (See chart 1.) Since that time few details have been released on the functioning of these two organs.

The Committee of Defense Ministers reportedly "exchanges experience obtained by the armed forces of member states, coordinates tasks concerning members, and works out proposals serving the effectiveness of joint defenses." It convened at Moscow on 22—23 December 1969, and may have designated certain flag-rank officers for assignment to the Unified Command. (see note 23 below.) A second meeting took place on 21—22 May 1970 at Sofia, with all of the defense ministers attending except the Romanian, who was represented by his chief of staff. The committee "looked at current problems of military preparedness." The most recent such meeting took place during 10—11 December 1976 at Sofia.[10]

---

8. Tirana radio, 12 February 1966.

9. *Krasnaya zvezda*, 30 September 1965.

10. Communiqués in *ibid.*, 23 May 1970; Sofia radio, 11 December 1976.

CHART 1

Warsaw Pact Structure, 1976

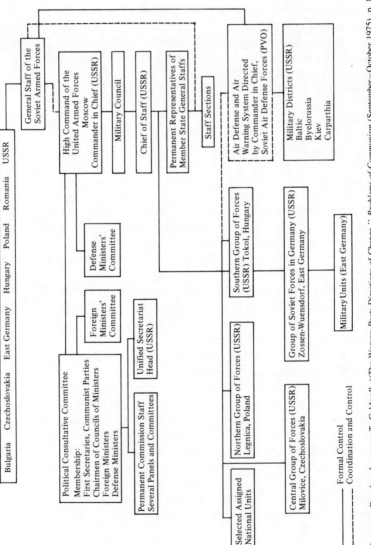

Bulgaria Czechoslovakia East Germany Hungary Poland Romania USSR

General Staff of the Soviet Armed Forces

Political Consultative Committee
Membership:
First Secretaries, Communist Parties
Chairmen of Councils of Ministers
Foreign Ministers
Defense Ministers

Permanent Commission Staff
Several Panels and Committees

Foreign Ministers' Committee

Unified Secretariat
Head (USSR)

Defense Ministers' Committee

High Command of the United Armed Forces
Moscow
Commander in Chief (USSR)

Military Council

Chief of Staff (USSR)

Permanent Representatives of Member State General Staffs

Staff Sections

Air Defense and Air Warning System Directed by Commander in Chief, Soviet Air Defense Forces (PVO)

Military Districts (USSR)
Baltic
Byelorussia
Kiev
Carpathia

Northern Group of Forces (USSR) Legnica, Poland

Central Group of Forces (USSR) Milovice, Czechoslovakia

Southern Group of Forces (USSR) Tokol, Hungary

Group of Soviet Forces in Germany (USSR) Zossen-Wuensdorf, East Germany

Military Units (East Germany)

Selected Assigned National Units

——— Formal Control

– – – Coordination and Control

Sources: Based on Lawrence T. Caldwell, "The Warsaw Pact: Directions of Change," *Problems of Communism* (September–October 1975), p. 8; CIA, *Directory of USSR Ministry of Defense and Armed Forces Officials* (Washington, D.C., September 1976), pp. 27–31; [German Democratic Republic], *Session of the Political Consultative Committee of the Warsaw Treaty States held in Bucharest, 25–26 November 1976* (East Berlin, 1976). pp. 28.

CHANGES WITHIN THE WTO

Established from the outset as a highly centralized system, the Warsaw Pact has had only four commanding officers to date. Marshal of the Soviet Union Ivan S. Konev was succeeded in July 1960 by Andrei A. Grechko, who also held that highest military rank in the Soviet armed forces and later became the Defense minister. Grechko's successor as WTO commander, Ivan I. Yakubovskiy, who was also a Marshal of the Soviet Union, died on 30 November 1976. He was replaced on 8 January 1977 by the fifty-five-year-old Soviet chief of Staff Viktor G. Kulikov, who was promoted to Marshal six days later. There have been five chiefs of staff for the WTO Unified Armed Forces Command, all of them career Soviet officers: Generals of the Army Aleksei I. Antonov, who died in office; Pavel I. Batov, who succeeded him in October 1962; from late 1965 to August 1968, Mikhail I. Kazakov; until his death in April 1976, Sergei M. Shtemenko; and, since October 1976, Anatoly I. Gribkov.[11]

Batov was a Khrushchev man who reportedly strove for rapid integration of pact's armed forces along supranational lines. Kazakov commanded Soviet troops in Hungary for four years after the 1956 revolution. He had been in charge of several military districts, most recently the one at Leningrad. His task may have included bringing Eastern Europe into line with Soviet military reorganization. Shtemenko's appointment came only two weeks before the invasion of Czechoslovakia. At one time he had served as Stalin's head of military intelligence, and later he was chief of the general staff in Moscow. Gribkov, at age fifty-seven, was transferred from the command of the Leningrad military district.

East European Defense ministers are ex officio WTO deputy commanding officers. (See table 52.) As can be noted from their appointment dates, relatively little change has occurred in the top-echelon military personnel during recent years, with the exception of Romania. One reason may be that many of these Defense ministers either received their training in the USSR or have had careers as political commissars rather than as professional military officers. This probably makes them seem more reliable in the eyes of the Soviet leadership and, indeed, more dependent upon advisors sent from Moscow.

On the other hand, a definite rotation system can be seen in the Russian military commands in pact countries where Soviet forces are stationed. The commanders in East Germany, Army General Y. F. Ivanovskiy; in Poland, Lieutenant General O. F. Kulishev; in Hungary, Colonel General F. F. Krivda; and in Czechoslovakia, Lieutenant General D. S. Sukhorukov, were in these positions during late 1976.[12] These men are not permitted to stay abroad for

---

11. Gribkov's appointment was broadcast over Moscow radio on 12 October 1976; the announcement also included a short biographic sketch.

12. CIA, *Directory of USSR Ministry of Defense and Armed Forces Officials* (Washington, D.C., September 1976), pp. 27−31 (henceforth cited as *Directory*); *Krasnaya zvezda*, 8 and 14 November 1976.

TABLE 52

WARSAW PACT, DEPUTY COMMANDING OFFICERS, 1977

Name	Rank	Country	Appointed Defense Minister
Jaruzelski, Wojciech	General of the Army	Poland	April 1968
Dzur, Martin	General of the Army	Czechoslovakia	April 1968
Hoffman, Karl Heinz	General of the Army	East Germany	July 1960
Coman, Ion	Colonel General	Romania	June 1976
Dzhurov, Dobri Marinov	General of the Army	Bulgaria	March 1962
Czinege, Lajos	Colonel General	Hungary	May 1960

SOURCES: Sofia radio, 11 December 1976; RFE, *Party-Government Line-Up* (Munich, 7 January 1977), p. 32.

extended tours of duty, perhaps lest they develop an attachment to the local milieu.

Not all of the functions of Soviet military commanders are known. They do represent a symbol of Soviet power in the four countries involved and they no longer seem averse to publicity. Their photographs appear from time to time in Soviet military newspapers, as do articles by them, and their positions are not concealed. The main contacts between the Soviet commanding officers and the regimes in Poland, Hungary, East Germany, and Czechoslovakia are probably the local Defense ministers. Representatives of the member countries are stationed at WTO headquarters in Moscow, and routine communications go through them.

Strategic Planning.   WTO was at first devised and regarded by the USSR as a defensive alliance, the forward area of which would provide a buffer and absorb an anticipated NATO attack. This attitude, however, has undergone a drastic transformation, resulting in a qualitative buildup of the East European armed forces. The change can be seen from a scenario implemented during quadripartite maneuvers in the German Democratic Republic. Former pact commander Marshal Grechko, in an interview with *Tass*, stated:

> . . . One must above all note the uniform military doctrine of the socialist countries united in the Warsaw Pact. . . . In case of aggression, our armies are ready not to conduct a passive defense but to engage in active military operations, which could be immediately transferred to the territory of the enemy. The armies of the Warsaw Pact countries also adhere to a uniform tactic of battleground action. As to armament, it has been standardized to a considerable degree. . . . Consistently, the methods of army training have been almost identical.[13]

13. Moscow radio, 21 February 1966.

Maneuvers in the 1965 code named October Storm included Soviet, East German, Czechoslovak, and Polish military units among the ten thousand troops involved, and provided substance for Grechko's remarks. Blue aggressors crossed the GDR border in the southwest and attacked Red defending forces. Concrete plans for such a NATO blitzkrieg supposedly envisage a general direction of attack toward

> Eisenach—Erfurt—Karl Marx Stadt [Chemnitz], as far as the upper reaches of the Neisse [River], then swinging north, in order to wrench the GDR out of the socialist camp within 36 to 48 hours. It was argued [by NATO] that if accomplished facts were created so quickly, a world war could be avoided by, as it were, a police action.[14]

In the course of October Storm, however, the Blue offensive was stopped, and the aggressor, "like a cornered beast," decided to risk all by using tactical atomic warheads. Responding "in greater numbers and with more powerful calibers of nuclear weapons," the Red side struck at the firing potential and troops of the aggressor. Nearly one thousand Polish paratroopers were transported by Antonov-designed AN−22 transports to the drop zone.[15] Their mission included the capture of an airfield near Erfurt and a subsequent attack on the enemy force from the rear.

The Red defenders advanced toward a strategically important bridge that had been identified by reconnaissance as being intact. "In the very last moment, when Blue forces were retreating already, West German workers disarmed a demolition crew and saved the bridge." Marshal Grechko and all of the pact Defense ministers attended as observers. The same high-ranking officers witnessed Operation Vltava, which was held in Czechoslovakia during the fall of 1966 with Soviet, East German, Hungarian, and Czechoslovak troops. Some three hundred nuclear warheads of a tactical nature were exploded under simulated conditions by both sides.[16]

Subsequent maneuvers included Rodopi (1967) in Bulgaria, Oder-Neisse 69 in Poland, Brotherhood in Arms (1970) in the GDR,[17] and Shield-76 in Poland, all of which employed large-scale landings from the air that preceded, or occurred simultaneously with, attacks by armored and motorized rifle formations in division strength. These massed forces, moving at speeds of between seventy and seventy-five kilometers per day, attempted to exploit the element of surprise

---

14. Deutschlandsender (East Berlin), 31 October 1965.

15. Warsaw radio, 21 October 1965.

16. "Pr." (Colonel Erich Pruck), "Erkentnisse aus dem Manoever Moldau," *Wehrkunde* (December 1966), p. 662.

17. These war games included some one hundred thousand troops from all seven WTO member states and represented the largest maneuvers held to date in Eastern Europe. Communiqué in *Krasnaya zvezda*, 20 October 1970.

with the objective of annihilating NATO troops that had survived the initial nuclear strikes.

That this doctrine is of an offensive nature is shown clearly in an article by the GDR's first deputy Defense minister, which repeats the remarks of the late Marshal Grechko quoted earlier. Writing in Russian for Soviet military readers, the East German said:

> The national mission of the NVA [GDR National People's Army] is to be prepared and able to. . . destroy the aggressor on his own territory by decisive, offensive action together with [other] brotherly socialist armies and to assist progressive forces in West Germany to liquidate the imperialist system [in that country].[18]

The fact that the Soviet military doctrine is being implemented, and the subordinate role of its East European "allies" in this strategy, can be seen from the provision of advanced surface-to-surface missiles (SSMS) capable of carrying nuclear warheads as standard equipment for all WTO armies at present, and from Russia's continued insistence on control over these weapons. The new T-72 main battle tank has recently made an appearance in the forward areas facing NATO.[19]

Decision Making.   Only fifteen meetings of the WTO Political Consultative Committee took place from 1956 through the end of 1976, although forty meetings should have been convened during this period on the basis of two per year, as the pact statute set forth. Table 53 gives data on the subjects considered at these sessions. The published communiqués deal mainly with issues of propaganda significance, but important questions are no doubt dealt with as well. As an example, the committee meeting held during 25−26 November 1976 at Bucharest issued a draft treaty[20] prohibiting the first use of any nuclear weapons, and proposed a freeze on membership in opposing military blocs. It also established a new committee of foreign ministers and broadened the scope of the "unified secretariat."

Even less is known about the operations of the Military Council, which was established in March 1969. It has held meetings about twice a year, with official announcements mentioning only discussions related to "further strengthening

18. Admiral Waldemar Verner, "Ten Years of the GDR National People's Army," *Kommunist vooruzhennykh sil* (February 1966), p. 78. See also GDR Defense minister Heinz Hoffman, "Streitkraefte in unserer Zeit," *Einheit* (March 1976), pp. 354−363.

19. "Frog-7: Das FK-Einsatzmittel des Warschau-Paktes auf Divisionebene," *Soldat und Technik* (March 1975), pp. 124−127. See also Phillip A. Karber, "The Soviet Antitank Debate," *Military Review* (November 1976), pp. 67−76. The 20,000 WTO tanks now include about 1,000 of the newest T−72 model. *Die Welt*, 24 December 1976.

20. Moscow radio, 26 November 1976, gave the text.

the troops and staff training of Warsaw Treaty states." The meeting at Kiev, for example, discussed "current activity of the Joint Armed Forces and adopted some [unspecified] coordinated recommendations."[21] The latest such gathering in Sofia during 10–11 December 1976 must have been related to the Political Consultative Committee session mentioned above.

Apart from positions within their own armed forces, no East European military officer heads any top-level WTO organ or command. Air defense for the entire area has been integrated under a Soviet commander who has been, since 1970, Marshal of the Soviet Union P. F. Batitskiy, the director of the equivalent armed-forces branch in Moscow. The officer in charge of the August 1968 invasion of Czechoslovakia, Soviet General of the Army I. G. Pavlovskiy, probably commands the Warsaw Pact ground forces, as he does those of the Soviet Union. WTO air and naval units are under, respectively, Aviation Marshal P. S. Kutakhov, chief of the USSR's air force, and Fleet Admiral S. G. Gorshkov, who commands the Soviet navy.[22]

Despite the fact that no top WTO position is held by any East European, it is probable that at least the Defense ministers (the great majority of whom have had Soviet training) are given the feeling of participation in decision-making. The situation has changed since the time when thirty-two former Soviet general officers in the Polish army, together with Poland's Defense minister, the former Marshal of the Soviet Union K. K. Rokossovsky, returned to Moscow toward the end of 1956 "with the gratitude of the Polish nation." Several, however, remained in high positions in Poland after that date. They included Lieutenant General J. Bordzilowski, first deputy Defense minister and chief inspector for training; Major General J. Urbanowicz, third deputy Defense minister and chief of political indoctrination; and Vice Admiral Z. Studzinski, ex-navy commander.[23] These three positions were among the more sensitive within the military hierarchy of Poland. They are occupied today by native-born Polish citizens.

Many of the East European officers have attended military schools in the USSR, and this may provide them with a common experience, if nothing else. Integration of command obviously requires a single language. Here the chosen one is Russian, a knowledge of which represents a prerequisite for training in the Soviet Union. Bulgarians, Czechoslovaks, and Poles have found Russian relatively easy to learn because of its similarity to their own tongues. It has proven more difficult for East Germans, Hungarians, and Romanians, since their languages are not related to the Slavic group. Learning has proceeded rapidly, however, since ignorance of Russian presents an obstacle to obtaining higher

---

21. *Ibid.*, 27 May 1976.

22. *Directory* (in note 12 above), pp. 1–2.

23. Studzinski later became deputy chief of staff for the WTO unified command. *Trybuna ludu,* 8 May 1970. His death was announced by Warsaw radio on 8 March 1976.

TABLE 53

WARSAW PACT, POLITICAL CONSULTATIVE COMMITTEE MEETINGS, 1956–1976

Number	Place	Date(s)	Proposals and Decisions
1.	Prague	27–28 January 1956	*Approved:* Statute for Unified Military Command; admitted GDR; established Standing Commission and Secretariat.
2.	Moscow	24 May 1958	*Proposed:* Nonaggression pact with NATO; summit meeting. *Approved:* Withdrawal of USSR troops from Romania.
3.	Moscow	4 February 1960	*Proposed:* Atom-free zone and cessation of nuclear tests.
4.	Moscow	28–29 March 1961	*Proposed:* Universal disarmament.
5.	Moscow	7 June 1962	*Discussed:* Albanian refusal to cooperate with WTO.
6.	Moscow	26 July 1963	*Discussed:* Status of pact armed forces and coordination of training.
7.	Warsaw	19–20 January 1965	*Discussed:* Possible multilateral nuclear force within NATO and "appropriate countermeasures."
8.	Bucharest	4–6 July 1966	*Proposed:* Reduction of tensions through military détente; conference on security in Europe.
9.	Sofia	6–7 March 1968	*Discussed:* Vietnam conflict; nonproliferation of nuclear weapons.
10.	Budapest	17 March 1969	*Approved:* Military Council and Committee of Defense Ministers.

TABLE 53 (Cont.)

Warsaw Pact, Political Consultative Committee Meetings, 1956–1976

Number	Place	Date(s)	Proposals and Decisions
11.	Moscow	20 August 1970	*Approved:* Moscow-Bonn treaty.
12.	East Berlin	2 December 1970	*Discussed:* European security, Vietnam, Middle East, Guinea.
13.	Prague	25–26 January 1972	*Approved:* Agenda for conference on peace, security and cooperation in Europe (CSCE); statement on Vietnam.
14.	Warsaw	17–18 April 1974	*Approved:* Statements on Middle East, Vietnam, mutual force reduction, CSCE.
15.	Bucharest	25–26 November 1976	*Proposed:* Treaty on no first use of nuclear weapons and freeze on current membership in military alliances (NATO and WTO).

Sources: U.S. Senate, Committee on Government Operations, 89th Cong., 2d sess., *The Warsaw Pact: Its Role in Soviet Bloc Affairs* (Washington, D.C., 1966), p. 32, on the first seven meetings; *Krasnaya zvezda*, 8–9 July 1966, 10 March 1968, 18 March 1969, 21 August 1970, and 3 December 1970, for others; Lawrence Caldwell, "The Warsaw Pact: Directions of Change," *Problems of Communism* (September–October 1975), p. 5; Moscow radio, 28 November 1976.

Note: The PCC secretary-general is N. P. Firyubin, who holds the rank of USSR deputy foreign minister. Bucharest radio, 26 November 1976.

command positions within the armed forces of the individual East European military establishments. Russian expressions have penetrated the military vocabularies of most of the countries within the Soviet bloc.

Execution of Decisions. The WTO Unified Command, which has its headquarters in Moscow, theoretically correlates and orders the implementation of decisions reached by the representatives of the deputy commanders (i.e., of the bloc countries' Defense ministers), who make up the staff of this headquarters.

Under the unification program, certain national contingents have been specifically earmarked for WTO service. Although these groups have never been openly identified, it is probable that only elite units are assigned, such as the regiment from the sixth Pomeranian Parachute-Assault Division stationed near Krakow in Poland, which participated in operation October Storm. Its commanding officer, who was at that time thirty-nine-year-old Colonel Edwin Rozlubirski, was the subject of a biographic sketch that appeared, along with his photograph, in the daily newspaper of the Soviet Defense ministry.[24] The twelfth Mechanized Division and a brigade of frontier troops in Poland have also reportedly been assigned specifically to WTO. On the other hand, all East German troops are at the disposal of the Warsaw Pact.

The transfer of Soviet troops from the western parts of the USSR to any place outside its borders by any means other than air might present some difficulty, although surmountable to be sure, owing to the limited number of interchange points between broad-gauge USSR and standard-gauge East European railroad lines. These points reportedly existed several years ago only at Zhelezno-dorozhny, Brest-Terespol, Przemysl-Medyka, Chop-Zahony, Iasi, and Galati.[25] In the meantime the number of these points must have been increased, with a corresponding expansion in machinery for loading and unloading. The construction of secondary railroad links and transmountain lines has been noted. Traffic management is centralized through the Council for Mutual Economic Assistance (CMEA).

The CMEA is building a network of automobile expressways that will link the major cities in Eastern Europe with Moscow and Kiev.[26] The Permanent Commission for Transportation of the CMEA has the task of coordinating this

---

24. Yezhi Lentsut [Jerzy Lencut], "The Commander of Airborne Infantry," *Krasnaya zvezda,* 21 August 1965. Another example might be the Fifth Army Corps of Hungary, which in August 1968 helped to invade Czechoslovakia. The late General Shtemenko had stated in "Combat Fraternity," *Krasnaya zvezda* 24 January 1970 that troop contingents have been allocated by member states for WTO joint armed forces.

25. Hanns von Krannhals, "Leadership Integration in the Warsaw Pact Area," *Military Review* (May 1961), pp. 50−51.

26. Stefan C. Stolte, "Comecon's Nineteenth Conference," *Bulletin of the Institute for Study of the USSR* (May 1965), p. 21.

ambitious scheme. Another project involves the expansion of the nineteen-hundred-mile petroleum pipeline that links the Volga-Ural oil fields with Poland, East Germany, Czechoslovakia, and Hungary. All of the WTO members except Romania are to a great extent dependent on the USSR in this respect, as the next chapter mentions. Oil remains indispensable for moving modern armies, and its delivery from the Soviet Union has facilitated the organization of joint maneuvers.

Credit for the idea of joint maneuvers has been claimed by the communists in Poland:

> Initiated by our [Polish] side, joint field exercises by the armies of Warsaw Pact countries have become permanent. Our troops, staffs, and commands annually train on land, on sea, and in the air with troops, staffs, and commands from brotherly armies: the Soviet Army, the Czechoslovak People's Army, and the GDR National People's Army.[27]

Actually, the first (1961) maneuvers included only Soviet and East German units. During the following spring, the USSR, Romania, and Hungary conducted joint field exercises.

It is noteworthy that until Operation Vltava (1966), the Hungarians had never trained with the Czechoslovaks. This may have been due not only to the events of 1956, but also to the fact that about one million ethnic Hungarians lived in Czechoslovakia between the wars and many still reside there. Nationality differences cause friction that could lead to incidents during joint field exercises. Except for Czechoslovaks and Bulgarians, the East European populations have traditionally been hostile to the Russians, for good historical reasons. Even so, none of the communist sources mentions any Soviet dissatisfaction with the performance of troops from the bloc countries during maneuvers. On the contrary, the Defense minister of Czechoslovakia even applauded the invasion of his own country in August 1968 by "troops from five fraternal states."[28] Such cooperation has extended even to the smuggling of weapons.

The merchant marines of the East European countries have been utilized for the delivery overseas of military equipment. One such instance came to light in which the captain of the Bulgarian vessel *Veliko Tirnovo* was fined 5.4 million Lebanese pounds (about $1.75 million) in Beirut for the attempted smuggling of fifteen hundred automatic rifles. The official Bulgarian news agency argued: "It is a well-known fact that the carrier is not held responsible for the content of the

---

27. Marshal Marian Spychalski, speech at the fourth congress of the Polish communist party, *Trybuna ludu*, 18 June 1964.

28. Colonel General Martin Dzur, "Loyalty to the Immortal Ideas," *Krasnaya zvezda*, 20 February 1970. The Soviet air force scattered aluminum foil along the Czechoslovak-West German border so that movements of its ground and airborne troops would be difficult to detect by NATO electronic devices. *New York Times*, 13 September 1976.

commodities shipped and declared in the bill of lading,"[29] as if the Navibulgare, in owning the ship, were not a state-controlled enterprise.

Although the destination of these rifles (which were possibly intended for Kurds) was not revealed, it is known that Bulgarians had also been selling weapons to royalist forces in Yemen. Some $25 million in Saudi-Arabian gold reportedly had been paid for these weapons, many of which were channeled through the Bulgarian military attaché in Paris. One such shipment was seized by the French when a chartered transport airplane carrying rifles from Belgium landed at Djibouti in French Somaliland (Territories of Afars and Issas).

Czechoslovak weapons have been received clandestinely on Cyprus. Little information can be found about similar arms shipments during the past several years, although in 1976 submachine guns, ammunition, and grenades from bloc countries were found on Marxist terrorists in Iran.[30] Apart from creating a future dependence for spare parts and bringing in foreign exchange, supplying arms to insurgents contributes to instability, and this in turn creates new communist opportunities to advance Soviet influence throughout the underdeveloped countries of the world.

In addition to facilitating the secret sale of arms, military attachés from East European countries also engage in espionage on behalf of the USSR. Two of these men, Monat and Tykocinski, defected to the West and have spoken about their experiences.[31] After reassignment back to Warsaw, Monat handled reports from all Polish military attachés and forwarded them to Moscow via his office. Tykocinski more recently corroborated the existence of this system and disclosed that for a period of time a career Soviet officer had functioned as chief of Polish military intelligence.

Another example of military espionage is provided by the extensive operations of East European agents in the Federal Republic of Germany. During 1975 the number of efforts at the recruitment of informants increased only slightly, but thirty-three persons were still convicted of high treason or treasonable relations by the federal constitutional court at Karlsruhe and the appellate tribunals in that country. Most of the cases involved GDR intelligence, but Poland, Romania, Hungary, Czechoslovakia, and Bulgaria—not to mention the USSR— all actively engage in espionage.[32]

---

29. Sofia radio, 2 February 1966.

30. *Christian Science Monitor*, 21 May 1976. About 200 million marks worth of GDR weapons are exported each year to Arab and African states, according to *Der Spiegel* (30 August 1976), pp. 60–65.

31. Pawel Monat, with John Dille, *Spy in the U.S.* (New York, 1962), especially pp. 104–112; U.S. House of Representatives, Committee on Un-American Activities, 89th Cong., 2d sess., *Testimony of Wladyslaw Tykocinski* (Washington, D.C., 1966).

32. Werner Maihofer, *1975 Verfassungsschutz* (Bonn, Bundesinnenministerium, 1976), pp. 110–122.

Soviet Forces in Eastern Europe. With the exception of Poland and Czechoslovakia, all of the bloc countries have had a so-called Soviet Consultative Group as an element of WTO activity. The rights and privileges of individuals belonging to the Group have allegedly remained concealed in various secret agreements. The effectiveness of this operation in Hungary obviously could be guaranteed by the presence of USSR troops. Group members functioned as military advisors.

Before 1956 this Soviet organization in Hungary reportedly controlled both logistics and the armaments industry, with each headed by a deputy Defense minister who had a Soviet officer with the rank of colonel as an advisor. The Defense minister, his deputies, and these USSR advisors reportedly comprised the "military collegium" in the ministry. The same system applied to the general staff. Each section of the latter (operations, intelligence, organization and mobilization, military installations, service regulations, military geography, communications, technology and transportation, air force, anti-air defense, civil defense, training, and logistics) included at least one Soviet staff officer as advisor. To each Weapons Inspectorate—armored and motorized troops, air force, communications units, artillery, engineers, ABC (atomic, biological, and chemical) weapons—were attached a Soviet colonel or general and two to four other Soviet officers as assistants.

Similar arrangements supposedly prevailed in the military districts and in each regiment. At the corps level, one senior Soviet officer is said to have controlled operations and another logistics. It is reported, further, that each of the eleven frontier-guard district commands had a Soviet officer and several aides assigned to it and that the entire political indoctrination system within the Hungarian armed forces was directed by a high-ranking USSR officer and six other advisors.[33]

In Bulgaria, on the other hand, Soviet advisory activities had been conducted with considerable restraint. Both the main political administration of the armed forces and the military intelligence section may still have Soviet observers. These officers also served as unit advisors, but mostly at the division level, although their network had previously extended into the regiments. Each motorized rifle and armored division reportedly had on its staff a Soviet officer with the rank of lieutenant colonel or major, under whom four or five others functioned as instructors. Certain armored regiments and operational squadrons of the Bulgarian air force (possibly those assigned to WTO) still have Soviet advisors attached to them.

Among the reasons for these differences between Hungary and Bulgaria was the 1956 revolution in Budapest. There has been nothing comparable in Sofia

---

33. Thadaeus Paschta, "Das System der sowjetischen Militaerberater in den Satellitenstaaten," *Wehrkunde* (September 1962), pp. 496–499, is the source for much of the following information. See also F. Rubin, "The Hungarian People's Army," *Journal of the Royal United Services Institute for Defence Studies* (September 1976), pp. 59–66.

because the Bulgarians have been consistently loyal to the USSR. Another reason is probably Bulgarian national pride: the people would resent any openly exercised foreign command. A third reason amounts to a corollary of the others. Key positions in the military hierarchy had been staffed by natives of Bulgaria who were trained as officers in the USSR and resumed their original citizenship upon returning home after the war. These officers have included former

> Defense minister, Army General Ivan Mikhailov;
> chief of the general staff, then first deputy Defense minister, later
>   head of the Administrative Organs Department in the Central
>   Committee, Colonel General Ivan Bachvarov, killed in an airplane
>   crash at Bratislava;
> commander of the Bulgarian navy and ex-Soviet naval officer, currently
>   deputy Defense minister and chief of civil defense, Admiral Branimir
>   Ormanov;
> commandant of the general staff academy, trained as an officer in the
>   USSR and currently deputy Defense minister, Colonel General Slavcho
>   Trunski;
> commander of the Sofia garrison and later head of the Main Political
>   Administration in the armed forces, graduate of both the ''Frunze''
>   and the general staff academy in the USSR, currently member of the
>   ruling party's Central Committee, Lieutenant General Velko I. Palin.[34]

In Czechoslovakia, the Soviet advisors for the most part control industries that produce weapons and war materiel for the armed forces of other bloc countries. The use of Soviet personnel in training Czechoslovak troops produced an extensive organization called the ''Soviet Satellite Coordination Command,''[35] which preceded the 1955 military-system alliance. References have appeared to Soviet general officers as representatives of the Joint Supreme Command of the Warsaw Pact armies in the capital cities of member countries,[36] with the exception of Romania.

In Poland it was not necessary to establish a Soviet military mission at all. Some seventeen thousand Soviet officers directed the Polish armed forces after transferring from the Red Army and accepting citizenship in the country to which they had been detailed.[37] Following the change in communist-party leadership at Warsaw in October 1956 mentioned above, many of these men returned to the USSR. The functions of those who remained consisted of observing, giving advice, and serving as liaison officers, as well as securing

---

34. U.S. Department of State, *Directory of Bulgarian Officials* (Washington, D.C., August 1969), p. 23; *ibid.* (September 1975), pp. 30–31.

35. von Krannhals, *op. cit.* (in note 25 above), p. 44.

36. Names are listed in *Directory* (in note 12 above), p. 28.

37. *Zycie i mysl*, no. 10 (October 1964).

communications with Soviet troops stationed in Lower Silesia (Poland) and East Germany. The situation in the GDR need not be discussed. With approximately twenty Soviet divisions on East German territory, there is no doubt about who remains in control.

By contrast, Romania certainly presents a picture of greater independence from the USSR than any other bloc state does. Military service was reduced to sixteen months in 1964, and during a period of ten years (1966–1976) Bucharest reportedly balked at permitting WTO maneuvers or even meetings of its Political Consultative Committee to be held in its own country. The Soviet military mission is said to number only two or three men today, compared to fifteen or sixteen in the past. However, staff officers from the USSR and Romania did hold a six-day map exercise in Bucharest[38] and the WTO Political Consultative Committee finally did convene its fifteenth session there.

Soviet troops are garrisoned in four of the Warsaw Pact states. In Poland, there is the Northern Group of Forces, with its headquarters at Legnica in Lower Silesia; in Hungary, the Southern Group of Forces, at Tokol near Budapest; in Czechoslovakia, the Central Group of Forces, at Milovice; and in the GDR, the Group of Soviet Forces in [East] Germany, with its headquarters at Zossen-Wuensdorf near East Berlin. The generally accepted figures for these forces outside the borders of the USSR are respectively two, four, five, and twenty divisions.[39] An approximate one-to-one ratio of armored to motorized rifle divisions among these Soviet units shows a considerably heavier concentration of fire-power than prevails in the indigenous East European armed forces. (See table 54.)

In East Germany, Soviet troops outnumber those permitted the GDR regime by a ratio of almost 3½ to one, but in tanks and aircraft the preponderance is somewhat less. However, East German armed forces have been equipped with Frog-7- and Scud-A-type ground-to-ground rockets, with the latter employing a guided missile. They are being supplied by the Soviet Union to GDR forces at division and army levels, respectively, and are allocated to the artillery. These weapons have the capability of delivering nuclear warheads over distances of up to 185 miles. It is doubtful that the USSR would allow the East Germans[40] to assume control over atomic warheads, however.

According to a former commander of the Soviet forces in the GDR, after 1965 his troops underwent a process of regrouping. Missile and armored units were added but other types were withdrawn. Russian anti-aircraft defense SA-2

---

38. Sofia radio, 23 February 1974.

39. International Institute for Strategic Studies, *The Military Balance 1976–1977* (London, September 1976), p. 9. For an order of battle see John Erickson, *Soviet-Warsaw Pact Force Levels* (Washington, D.C., 1976), pp. 65–88.

40. Eric Waldman, "The Military Policy of an Archetypal Soviet Satellite, the German Democratic Republic," *Canadian Defense Quarterly* (Spring 1976), pp. 46–52; see also note 19 above.

TABLE 54

WARSAW PACT ARMED FORCES, 1976

Country	Ground Forces Personnel	Divisions[a]	Tanks	Security Forces Personnel	Navy Personnel	C^b	D^c	S^d	Air and Air Defense Personnel	Aircraft[e]
Bulgaria	125,000	6(5)[f]	2,200	16,000	11,000	—	—	2	4	33,000	320
Czechoslovakia	140,000	10(5)	3,300	20,000	—	—	—	—	—	57,000	760
USSR	70,000	5(2)	1,800	—	—	—	—	—	—	—	—
East Germany	105,000	6(2)	3,115	65,000	16,000	—	—	2	—	34,000	441
USSR	370,000	20(10)	7,500	—	(80,000)[g]	(4)	(25)	(75)	—	—	1,100
Hungary	75,000	6(1)	1,475	70,000	—	—	—	—	—	24,000	220
USSR	60,000	4(2)	1,500	—	—	—	—	—	—	—	350
Poland	210,000	15(5)	3,775	100,000	25,000	—	—	1	4	90,000	1,050
USSR	38,000	(2-3)	700	—	—	—	—	—	—	—	350
Romania	140,000	10(2)	2,070	35,000	11,000	—	—	—	—	34,000	400
					(50,000)[h]	(3)	(20)	(40)		
Total	1,333,000	82(37)	27,435	306,000	193,000	7	50	123	272,000	4,991

SOURCES: John Erickson, *Soviet-Warsaw Pact Force Levels* (Washington, D.C., 1976), p. 88; International Institute for Strategic Studies, *The Military Balance, 1976–1977* (London, September 1976), pp. 8–14.

NOTES: [a]Armored divisions, included in total, are indicated in parentheses. [b]Cruisers. [c]Destroyers. [d]Submarines. [e]Combat aircraft. [f]Figures in parentheses refer to Bulgarian tank brigades, not divisions. [g]Soviet Baltic Sea fleet, estimated allocation. [h]Soviet Black Sea fleet, estimated allocation.

batteries are being phased out, but SA-3 and SA-4 units remain. The main centers of concentration for Soviet troops since the reorganization are in the area around Suhl in Thueringen, the province of Brandenburg, and territories along the GDR's borders with Czechoslovakia and Poland.[41]

Such regroupings have brought these Soviet troops closer to Czechoslovakia, where five Soviet divisions are stationed and where it is important that the uranium mines at Jachymov, Teplice, and Pribram remain protected, as well as those in adjacent East Germany south of Aue. The output of this strategic material goes to the USSR, in amounts that remain secret. The closer disposition of Soviet troops to Poland provides for better contact with the two Soviet divisions in Lower Silesia. This will allow for a rapid linkup between forces in the event of other crises, such as those in 1956 and 1968 in which Polish and Czechoslovak troops, respectively, proved unreliable from the communist point of view.

The redeployment of Soviet forces in East Germany may have been the result of plans for more flexibility in potential countering operations, should hostilities break out in Central Europe. These troops had formerly been concentrated along the frontier between East and West Germany in several parallel lines, from Luebeck in the north to the border with Czechoslovakia at Hof in the south. The new scheme will presumably permit the deployment of Soviet troops in echelons, following an east-west direction, with most of them concentrated along the Oder and Western Neisse rivers.[42]

In Hungary, although indigenous forces are almost 25 percent greater than those of the Soviet Union, the latter maintain a preponderance of two to one in armored divisions and about three to two in aircraft. Besides serving to prevent a repetition of the 1956 rebellion, Soviet troops ensure the delivery of uranium from the Hungarian mines at Pecs. It should be noted, however, that ground-to-ground missiles were displayed at a military parade in Budapest only nine years after the revolution. All of the other Warsaw Pact states have also been equipped with these. In addition, Soviet MIG-21 delta-wing fighter interceptors and Ilyushin medium-range bombers belong to the inventories of all East European alliance members.

According to the first secretary of the Hungarian communist party, Janos

41. Some of these measures will depend upon how much Moscow trusts the GDR. Dale Herspring, "Technology and Political Reliability in the East German Military," *Journal of Political and Military Sociology* (Fall 1975), pp. 153–163.

42. *Soldat und Technik* (June 1975), pp. 279–281. See also Captain Eugene D. Betit, USA, "Soviet Tactical Doctrine and Capabilities and NATO's Strategic Defense," *Strategic Review* (Fall 1976), pp. 95–107.

Over the past decade the USSR has added 130,000 men, increased the number of tanks by 40 percent and conventional artillery by 50 to 100 percent in the GDR, according to an interview that NATO commander General Alexander M. Haig, Jr., gave *U.S. News & World Report* (17 January 1977), pp. 35–37.

Kadar, the presence of Soviet troops is in conformity with domestic as well as international law. Speaking to his parliament, he declared:

> [The USSR armed forces are] an immense help for our people, because if these troops were not here, we would be forced to keep more soldiers under arms at the expense of the living standard, because the fatherland is more important and stronger than the living standard! [Further,] the presence of Soviet troops in Hungary has no internal reason. It depends on the international situation alone. . . . We are not afraid of the withdrawal of Soviet troops, but we do not support any unilateral withdrawal, and this is in the interest of the international political situation.[43]

Almost twelve years later, in reply to a question regarding Soviet troops, Kadar replied that a continued USSR presence depended on "the general situation in world politics" and expressed the hope that all foreign troops would be withdrawn in the future.[44]

CHANGES IN SOVIET CONTROL

Penetration by Soviet nationals into the East European military establishments has definitely decreased over the past two decades. For instance, whereas at one time virtually all of the high positions in Poland's armed forces were held by former Soviet officers "fulfilling the duties of Poles," this rarely occurs today. Although it would be difficult to show where the loyalty of these officers lies, the case of K. K. Rokossovskiy may be illuminating. He came to Warsaw in November 1949 as Defense minister and remained exactly seven years. After that, he returned to Moscow and resumed his rank as Marshal of the Soviet Union. Apparently not having lost any seniority, he was made a USSR deputy Defense minister, perhaps in reward for services rendered while he was on detached duty in Warsaw.

Military Intelligence in Eastern Europe. Only sparse information is available about intelligence operations in the WTO countries. Close cooperation, and perhaps even a superior-subordinate relationship, between the counter-espionage establishments of the Soviet Union and one of its client states became evident with the arrest of British subject Greville Wynne[45] jointly by Soviet and Hungarian security services at Budapest, and his subsequent trial with Soviet Colonel O. V. Penkovskiy in Moscow.

An even more significant and openly admitted role was played by Soviet

---

43. Kossuth radio, 11 February 1965. See also Charles Fenyvesi, "Hungary 20 Years Later," *New York Times Magazine* (17 October 1976), pp. 32–33, 101–109.

44. *New York Times*, 8 December 1976.

45. Oleg Penkovskiy, *The Penkovskiy Papers* (New York, 1965), pp. 373–375.

intelligence during the arrest of plotters against the Bulgarian regime. Communist journalists in Sofia received a briefing on the conspiracy that was "uncovered by Soviet intelligence agents." One of the ten men involved committed suicide. The others, five army officers and four civilians, were sentenced to prison for high treason. In the first announcement of the plot, only three persons were mentioned and all three had belonged to the "Gavril Genov" partisan detachment during World War II. At least one other had also fought in a guerrilla unit.[46] The fact that most of those tried had been high-ranking military officers on active duty would appear to indicate strong army involvement in the plot.

A further case of collaboration between the Soviet and East European intelligence services appeared in connection with the purge of Aleksandar Rankovic in Yugoslavia. His subordinates in the security apparatus, which he had controlled, were accused of having "too close links" with their Soviet counterparts.[47] Nothing regarding these charges was made public at the subsequent plenum of the Central Committee. It should be recalled, however, that Greville Wynne had lost a notebook at a Belgrade hotel. It later turned up in Moscow during the trial of Colonel Penkovskiy.

Military Production.   As a source of war materiel, the most important geographic area in Eastern Europe is the Czechoslovakia-GDR-Poland industrial triangle. All three states encompass a human pool of skilled technicians, have precision equipment, and possess modern scientific-research facilities, especially in nuclear physics. That the USSR hesitates to permit sophisticated military production can be seen from the decision taken at the fourteenth CMEA session, which discontinued the East German manufacture of four-engine turbojet aircraft already in the testing stage.[48]

On the other hand, Eastern Europe is of great value to the Soviet Union as a source of uranium in several countries; bauxite for the production of processed aluminum in Czechoslovakia; basic chemicals, rare metals of particular importance for nuclear energy programs, and bismuth mined in association with uranium in East Germany; metallic sodium from a Silesian plant in Poland for the construction of nuclear-powered reactors; cadmium, which is used in regulating the speed of nuclear reactions, in both Poland and the GDR; molybdenum for the production of crucially important materiel in Bulgaria and Poland; and titanium used in nuclear technology and graphite required for nuclear reactors in Poland. It

---

46. A discussion of this case appears in James F. Brown, *Bulgaria under Communist Rule* (New York, 1970), pp. 173–187.

47. *New York Times,* 22 July 1966.

48. *Pravda,* 5 March 1961. On Soviet control, see Hans Joachim Berg, "Ursachen, Entwicklung und Auswirkungen der sowjetischen Hegemonialstelling in Warschauer Pakt," *Politische Studien* (May–June 1976), pp. 267–280.

should also be mentioned that the CMEA includes a defense-industry commission[49] within its framework.

PARTY CONTROL OVER THE MILITARY

Political controls by local regimes do not appear to have been altered significantly. The primary party organization, however, does comprise a separate hierarchy. Delegates representing the individual military districts attend national party congresses. The criteria for admission to communist-party membership are the same for officers and enlisted men as for civilians. Apparently, it is still a prerequisite for promotion to the rank of colonel that an officer be a member of the ruling party. In all WTO countries, between 80 percent and 90 percent of the regular officers belong to the party or its youth affiliate.[50] This high percentage should not be equated with reliability, which is always difficult to measure.

The only hard figures on defections come from the Federal Republic of Germany, and these involve GDR military personnel who flee across the frontier. For example, some East German battalions of border troops had as many as fifteen successful escape attempts and twenty failures during 1965. A total of 1,850 East German soldiers, including 466 border guards, defected in the first five years after the construction of the Berlin Wall.[51]

The Bulgarian military conspiracy mentioned earlier perhaps indicates dissatisfaction in that country with its subordination to the USSR. Soviet decision makers in a hot war situation probably would not plan to employ jointly Polish and East German, Czechoslovak and Hungarian, or Romanian and Hungarian troops in actual combat, even though combined maneuvers have taken place over the past several years.

CHANGES IN POPULAR SUPPORT

In 1960 researchers at the University of Warsaw polled a representative sample of that city's inhabitants regarding their opinions of the military-officer profession as a career. The prestige of the armed forces has probably risen somewhat since then. Compared with the pre-1939 period, however, when officers in the Polish military stood at or near the top of the career scale, at the time of this poll they ranked fourteenth financially, below lathe operators; sixteenth in job

---

49. Revealed by Prague radio, 17 January 1969. This may be the Weapons and Equipment Standardization Group to coordinate military technology, mentioned by Defense minister Lajos Czinege in *Nepszabadszag*, 10 May 1969.

50. *Krasnaya zvezda*, 11 April 1975.

51. *Soldat und Technik* (April 1966), p. 202. See also *Die Welt* (2 December 1976) on the thirtieth anniversary of GDR border troops.

security, below accountants; and twenty-first in social prestige, below office supervisors.[52]

No similar investigation is known to have been made public by any other East European regime, but apart from this limited indication of changed attitudes, it seems likely that the lack of any tradition in the Soviet bloc has reduced the attractiveness of a military career among officers and enlisted men alike. Communist propaganda classifies the pre-1939 armies in Eastern Europe as either feudal or fascist. The riots in East Germany (1953), the Hungarian revolution (1956) and the events in Poland at the same time, when local units in both states took up defensive positions against the threat of Soviet troop intervention, the complete immobility of Czechoslovak forces (1968), and the refusal of the regular Polish army to fire upon demonstrators (1970 and 1976) all proved that morale has not been high from the communist point of view.[53]

FUTURE DEVELOPMENTS

Trends and goals remain difficult to project, but it is quite clear that the Warsaw Treaty Organization has changed its emphasis radically from a defensive to an offensive posture. This trend most probably will continue, unless Soviet military doctrine itself undergoes a fundamental transformation.

Over the two decades from 1956 through 1976, the military equipment and the training of WTO forces have developed consistently in one direction: toward preparation for a war in which it is conceivable to the Soviet High Command that nuclear weapons may be used. Even the previously avowed intention not to be the first to introduce such arms in a conflict is no longer being repeated. The Soviet military hierarchy certainly would not knowingly allow an opponent endowed with atomic and hydrogen warheads to apply the element of surprise and to initiate hostilities. However, increasing attention has been paid to the conventional option: "While working out methods for waging combat under conditions of nuclear war, Soviet military science does not exclude the possibility of combat operations being waged with only conventional weapons."[54]

Soviet military doctrine probably also anticipates a possible conflict in Central Europe within the next decade involving a confrontation between the main forces of NATO and the Warsaw Treaty Organization. Beginning with Soviet strategic

---

52. A. Sarapata and W. Wesolowski, "Evaluation of Occupation by Warsaw Inhabitants," *American Journal of Sociology* (May 1961), pp. 583–585. See also the more recent article by Sarapata, "Social Mobility," *Polish Perspectives* (January 1966), especially table 1, p. 20, regarding the prestige of occupations, including that of army officer.

53. A posthumously published article by the former WTO chief of staff indicates that Pact troops will be used to suppress "counterrevolutionary activities" throughout Eastern Europe, with the 1968 example of Czechoslovakia specifically listed. S. M. Shtemenko, "Brotherhood Born in Combat," *Za rubezhem* (7–13 May 1976), pp. 6–7; Moscow.

54. Major General I. Ye. Krupchenko et al., *Voennaya istoriya* (Moscow, 1971), p. 345.

nuclear strikes, ground operations would be launched simultaneously by massive armored and motorized rifle divisions in conjunction with airborne units employed on a large scale. These movements, at speeds of up to seventy-five kilometers per day, would be supported by tactical nuclear weapons,[55] unless, of course, the conflict remained at the conventional level.

The role of WTO members in such a war can be seen in broad outline even today. For example, Soviet conflict managers are making a concentrated effort to woo Turkey away from the Western alliance. If Greece, where a parallel diplomatic offensive is being carried on by Bulgaria, and Turkey can both be neutralized so that their membership in NATO will become ineffective, the Warsaw Treaty Organization could then concentrate on the main enemy: the Federal Republic of Germany. Such WTO members as Bulgaria, Hungary, and Romania (which are not powerful and not particularly reliable, except for Bulgaria) could be eliminated from the Kremlin's contingency plans.[56]

The Warsaw Pact would then base its military plans on the GDR and Poland as the main allies of the USSR. The continuous barrage of German propaganda against the Federal Republic of Germany, especially in Poland, has had the obvious purpose of maintaining a war psychosis that is fed by the fear of a Nazi resurgence and a new *Drang nach Osten*. Since the 12 August 1970 Moscow-Bonn treaty on the renunciation of force, this fear has become muted, but it still exists.

Even so, it is doubtful that Polish or East German troops would be allowed to operate independently in any conflict. As part of Soviet fronts (groups of armies), they would fight with Soviet units on both flanks and in the rear. The performance of the Warsaw Treaty Organization will depend ultimately on the specific military situation. Should NATO be dissolved, WTO forces could march to the Atlantic with little or no opposition.[57]

---

55. "Der Warschauer Pakt: militaerische Fakten und Trends," *Soldat und Technik* (October 1976), pp. 503–505. A new 180-millimeter field gun with a 27 mile range supplements the 203.2-millimeter gun-howitzer, both having nuclear capability, according to the *New York Times*, 10 December 1976.

56. One of these contingency plans reportedly involves the crossing of Austria and the military occupation of Yugoslavia. See the two-part interview with the Czechoslovak defector, Major General Jan Sejna, "Moskaus Aufmarschplaene gegen Oesterreich," *Profil* (14 and 21 February 1974), pp. 39–43 and 29–35; Vienna.

57. Major General Robert Close, who commands the Belgian Sixteenth Armored Division in the Cologne area, will publish a book entitled "Defenseless Europe?" during 1977 which states that the USSR has the capability of occupying the Federal Republic of Germany within 48 hours. *Philadelphia Inquirer*, 12 January 1977, based on a Reuters dispatch from Brussels.

Chapter 10

Economic Integration: CMEA

Before the Second World War most of Eastern Europe could be classified as economically underdeveloped. With roughly four-fifths of the population living in rural areas and more than half of the gainfully employed engaged in agriculture, the entire region was almost self-sufficient in food and the small requirement for manufactured goods was met by the limited output. The one exception, Czechoslovakia, did have certain lines of industry that were highly developed. Elsewhere, the growth of a strong industrial working class and of a middle class of private entrepreneurs in the urban centers lagged by comparison.

The military occupation of certain East European states and the transformation of others into Nazi satellites during the war altered the economies in some areas. Under compulsion to turn out materiel for the Wehrmacht and help supply the domestic needs of the Third Reich, the industries of Czechoslovakia, Hungary, and what is today East Germany underwent considerable expansion. Romania served primarily as a producer of agricultural commodities and petroleum. On the other hand, Bulgaria and Poland were allowed to stagnate. All of the countries suffered war damage, but Czechoslovakia emerged with relatively less destruction than the others.[1] All eventually became satellites of the USSR.

For almost a decade after the war the economies of the satellite states remained under the tight control of the Soviet Union. They were even discouraged from developing economic links among themselves. Most major business transactions had to be cleared through Moscow. Following the death of Stalin, however, a change took place. A meeting in March 1954 of the Council for Mutual Economic Assistance (CMEA), also known as Comecon, recommended the coordination of all national economic plans within the bloc. The CMEA, which had been set up by the USSR at the beginning of 1949 as a response to the Marshall Plan, had been dormant until then.

---

1. In 1945, however, Czechoslovak industry was producing at only half its 1937 level. V. I. Morozov, *Sovet Ekonomicheskoi Vzaimopomoshchi* (Moscow, 1964), pp. 80–81.

The founding communiqué from Moscow indicated that the six charter members included the Soviet Union, Bulgaria, Czechoslovakia, Hungary, Poland, and Romania.[2] Subsequently four other countries were admitted: Albania (1949), East Germany (1950), Mongolia (1962), and Cuba (1972). At the CMEA council's fifteenth session, in December 1961, Albania's delegate announced that his government would no longer participate in any of the activities. Since that time Tirana has refused to pay its dues to the council and also has not been represented at any of the meetings.[3] Yugoslavia applied for and received limited-participant status in 1965 at the nineteenth session of the CMEA council.

In addition, Finland (July 1973), Mexico (August 1975), and Iraq (July 1976) all ratified agreements of cooperation with the CMEA. These do not make them even associate members. Nevertheless, such developments do project an image of an open organization. Angola, for example, sent observers to attend the thirtieth CMEA session in July 1976 at East Berlin. Other observers came from the communist-ruled states of Laos, North Korea, and Vietnam.[4]

The date set for beginning the coordination of economic plans by all CMEA members was 1956, but the ensuing revolution in Hungary and related events in Poland during that year disrupted trade and communications over a wide area of the bloc. In the process of reestablishing control and bolstering communist regimes throughout Eastern Europe, the Soviet Union claims to have sent considerable emergency credits into the area.[5] (See table 55.) By the end of 1958 industry had recovered, by and large, in both Hungary and Poland.

Soviet credits to the East European regimes must be repaid. In addition, the USSR seems to have followed a policy of charging higher than world market prices for certain of its exports into the bloc and of underpaying for commodities imported from this area. Information regarding Soviet credits is based on official statistics that are now being published annually by East European governments. It is apparent that these figures are subject to manipulation in ways other than straight numerical falsification. Propaganda images still represent primary motives for the fabrication of reported economic results. Internal misreporting by subordinate officials contributes to unintentional inaccuracies. Statistical inflation at higher levels magnifies the initial error, especially in agriculture.

It is true that the rapid expansion of industry has made possible great increases

---

2. Text in Alexander Uschakow, *Der Rat fuer gegenseitige Wirtschaftshilfe* (Cologne, 1962), p. 86. The 1959 CMEA charter has been translated into English by Michael Kaser, *Comecon* (London, 1967), 2d ed., pp. 235–246. Amended in 1962 and again in 1974, it appears in RFE report (by J. L. Kerr), "A Revised Comecon Charter," 6 August 1975, pp. 15–27.

3. Lucjan Ciamaga, *Od wspolpracy do integracji* (Warsaw, 1965), p. 17, n. 2.

4. Communiqué in *Izvestiya,* 10 July 1976; Moscow.

5. Poland allegedly received the equivalent of $420 million (mainly in rubles) and Hungary about $285 million during the 1956–1957 period. Ciamaga, *op. cit.* (in note 3 above), pp. 39–40.

TABLE 55

USSR Credits to Eastern Europe, 1947–1980
(in millions of U.S. dollars)

Country	Years	Credits
Albania	1957–1960	246.0
Bulgaria	1954–1975	1,993.0
Czechoslovakia	1947–1957	76.0
East Germany	1954–1975	990.0
Hungary	1954–1975	348.0
Poland	1954–1980	2,789.0
Romania	1954–1962	123.0
Yugoslavia	1973–1978	990.0
Grand Total		7,555.0

Sources: Lucjan Ciamaga, *Od wspolpracy do integracji* (Warsaw, 1965), pp. 39–40; Marshall Goldman, *Soviet Foreign Aid* (New York, 1967), pp. 24–25; R. F. Staar (ed.), *1976 Yearbook on International Communist Affairs* (Stanford, Ca., 1976), p. 97; CIA, *Handbook of Economic Statistics* (Washington, D.C., September 1976), p. 71; *New York Times*, 30 December 1976.

Note: The figures do not include credits for defense purposes. Dollar values presumably are derived from official rates of exchange. The USSR claims to have given CMEA members through the end of 1968, "more than 10 billion rubles worth of credits and loans on favorable terms." *Trud*, 14 January 1969; *Narodna Armiya*, 29 January 1970.

in the gross national product (GNP) of Eastern Europe.[6] To a considerable degree, however, the increase has been achieved by deliberately restricting consumption. The rates of gross investment have allegedly reached 25 percent of the total income. Sustained emphasis on heavy industry, especially for defense purposes, and inadequate investments for agriculture have merely accentuated the structural imbalance that had arisen at the expense of the general standard of living.

At the beginning of 1958 indications appeared that the high rate of GNP growth was beginning to decrease. In general, the downward rate of growth for industrial output reflected a similar trend in the Soviet Union. The various five-year plans in most of the East European countries for the years 1961–1965 finally began to include reduced targets in comparison with previous periods. Average increments of national income were now envisaged at 6 percent or 7 percent a year except in Bulgaria and Romania, where growth rates were to be much higher. Apart from Hungary, the average increase before the decline had been 8 percent annually. Even these more limited targets for 1961–1965 were not attained by most of the countries. (See table 56 for projections.)

---

6. Actually GNP, as used here, refers to the growth of the net material product excluding services (government administration, legal, passenger transportation, etc.) that do not directly affect production.

TABLE 56

NATIONAL INCOME FOR EASTERN EUROPE, 1975–1980 (PROJECTED)

Country	Real GNP (annual percent change)			Five-year average growth rate 1976–1980 (percentages)	Current dollar GNP 1975 (billions)	1975 per capita GNP (dollars)
	1975	1976	1977			
Bulgaria	9.0	9.0	8.5	7.7[a]	30.0	3,350
Czechoslovakia	5.4	5.0	5.0	4.9–5.2[b]	60.0	4,000
East Germany	5.5	5.3	5.0	5.7[c]	70.0	4,150
Hungary	5.5	5.0	5.5	5.4–5.7[d]	40.0	3,800
Poland	8.0	8.0	7.0	7.3[e]	105.0	3,100
Rumania	9.8	10.0	7.0	10–11[f]	60.0	2,950
USSR	4.0	5.0	4.5	4.7[g]	680.0	2,700
Yugoslavia	4.0	5.0	6.0	ca. 7[h]	60.0	2,800

SOURCES: [a]Sofia radio, 29 October 1976; [b]*Rude pravo,* 21 April 1976, special supplement; [c]*Neues Deutschland,* 4–5 September 1976; [d]*Nepszabadsag,* 21 December 1975, supplement; [e]*Kurier polski,* 13–14 December 1975, supplement; [f]*Scinteia,* 3 July 1976; [g]Moscow radio, 27 October 1976; [h]*Sluzbeni list SFRJ,* no. 33 (23 July 1976), pp. 789–830. Also, Moscow radio, 7 July 1976, for 1975 and GNP figures.

Although they represent the most industrialized states within the area of Eastern Europe, both the German Democratic Republic and Czechoslovakia suffered from acute economic problems in the first half of the last decade. During the sixth congress of the Socialist (communist) Unity party in January 1963 at East Berlin, a substitute seven-year plan was unveiled for the 1964–1970 period. Index figures showed that the preceding plan had been dropped. The new targets for national income, industrial production, and labor productivity were lower than those of the unfinished 1959–1965 plan.

A similar situation had developed earlier in Czechoslovakia, which announced in the middle of 1962 that its five-year plan would be abandoned. After a twelve-month interim period, a new seven-year plan for the years 1964–1970 was introduced, as in East Germany. It is clear that Czechoslovakia, which experienced a 4 percent decline in national income during 1963 and only a 1 percent increase in 1964, had failed to become the show window of Eastern Europe. The aftermath of the August 1968 invasion involved more debts to bolster a faltering economy, and only 1970 could be proclaimed the year of economic consolidation.

FORCED INDUSTRIALIZATION

A basic CMEA document that was adopted by the sixteenth council session authoritatively laid down the guidelines for the economic integration of industry along the following lines: "Socialist industrialization, with the principal emphasis being placed upon heavy industry and its core, engineering, is the main path toward the elimination of technical and economic backwardness.''[7] This belief is basic to most East European communist thinking. The results could be observed in the establishment, at a heavy cost to the populations involved, of modern industries in areas that more often than not remained short of raw materials. Despite the admission of excesses during the early 1950s, heavy industry still leads in investments and, indeed, absorbs the lion's share of each annual budget.

Thus, relatively underdeveloped Bulgaria allocated 38.5 percent of its capital investments during 1949 to industry. Twenty years later the allocation was 48 percent, amounting to more than 2.5 billion leva.[8] In a classic example, Hungary's determination to pursue ''extended reproduction'' is seen in the fact that 66 percent of that country's output came under the category of producers' goods, with the remainder being consumers' goods and food. Emphasis continues to be placed on iron and steel facilities as well as on the development of engineering projects. Poland plans to triple production at a single Nowa Huta metallurgical complex near Krakow by 1980 to almost nine million tons of steel; this is approximately the amount that was produced in 1965 by the whole country.[9] Still, the country will be forced to rely mainly on the Soviet Union, which provides 76 percent of the iron ore used in Polish industry.

Also importing Russian coal, coke, and iron ore, Romania had planned for 1975 a national output of about ten million tons of steel. The Bulgarians, proclaiming the priority of heavy industry in a country without any substantial raw-materials base, produced some 1.7 million tons of steel during 1969 at their Kremikovtsi complex. From these few examples it can be seen that the development of basic industry in each country has not been molded to any great extent by supranational considerations. All of the bloc members desire steel mills, but they are not endowed with the varied or substantial raw-materials base needed for heavy industry. (See table 57.)

Still lacking an overall plan, and in most cases distrusting the ''international socialist division of labor'' principle, most of the East European states have made only uncertain steps toward commodity specialization despite the CMEA's efforts along these lines over the past decade and a half.[10] Efforts and responses have been less than wholehearted. Even bilateral projects are not developing as had been anticipated. Although the basic form of cooperation still remains the all-member approach, two other methods have evolved in practice.

---

7. Quoted from ''Fundamental Principles of the International Socialist Division of Labor,'' *Pravda,* 17 June 1962; Moscow.

8. Sofia radio, 24 January 1970.

9. [Poland], *Maly rocznik statystyczny 1966* (Warsaw, 1966), table 7, p. 64.

10. It is claimed that about fifty specialization agreements cover more than six thousand machine-building items in the CMEA area. *Pravda,* 29 July 1976; Moscow.

TABLE 57

SELECTED CMEA INDICATORS, 1975

Product	Total CMEA output	USSR output	USSR percent of total	Exported by USSR to East Europe
	million tons			*million tons*
Petroleum	508.6	491.0	96.5	67.70
Iron ore	242.7	233.0	96.0	38.16
Pig iron	132.9	103.0	77.5	4.11
Steel (crude)	192.5	141.2	73.3	0.65
Coal	1,351.0	701.0	51.9	16.20
Grain	212.5	139.9	65.8	2.32
Cement (1974)	170.9	115.1	67.3	1.99
		billion KWH		
Electricity	1,378.0	1,038.0	75.3	n.a.
		billion cubic feet		
Natural gas	n.a.	10,215.0	n.a.	n.a.

SOURCES: Ministerstvo Vneshnei Torgovli, *Vneshnyaya torgovlya SSSR v 1975 g.* (Moscow, 1976), pp. 68–69, 71, 73, 79–80, 85; Moscow radio, 4 July 1976; *Petroleum Economist* (July 1976), p. 206; CIA, *Handbook of Economic Statistics* (Washington, D.C., September 1976), pp. 19, 26–27.

JOINT PROJECTS

The first of the new cooperative techniques theoretically involves participation by almost all CMEA members. Such activities as the "Friendship" oil pipeline, the "Peace" electric-power distribution system, the "Brotherhood" natural-gas pipeline, the pooling of railroad freight cars, the contemplated network of expressways, two CMEA banks, and the "Intermetal" steel community are good examples. The very fact that not all East European countries have availed themselves of the opportunity to join these organizations remains noteworthy in itself. A hard core of six members (the USSR, East Germany, Czechoslovakia, Poland, Hungary, and Bulgaria) appears to be developing within the CMEA that leaves Romania voluntarily on the periphery and Yugoslavia maintaining only affiliated status.

Much publicity has been given to certain ambitious schemes sponsored by the CMEA. By the end of 1975 the "Druzhba I" pipeline had supplied about 337 million tons of petroleum from the Volga-Ural oil fields[11] to the several East European petrochemical industries. The pipeline extends some nineteen hundred miles from Kuibyshev through Mozyr in the western part of the USSR and Plock, Poland to the city of Schwedt, East Germany. A branch runs southwest through Brody and Uzhgorod, USSR and ends at Bratislava, Czechoslovakia, with a spur going south to Szaszhalombatta, Hungary; it has an annual capacity of 105

---

11. *Krasnaya zvezda*, 16 July 1976; Moscow.

million tons.[12] Romania also imports petroleum, but neither it nor adjacent Bulgaria contributed toward the cost of the pipeline's construction. The headquarters for the organization are at Moscow, with a Soviet diretor in charge. More limited in nature is the "Bratstvo" natural-gas pipeline that, during 1970, delivered approximately 4.5 billion cubic meters of this fuel to Czechoslovakia and Austria from the USSR. By 1978 this source will be expanded through the addition of a new line from Orenburg to Uzhgorod and will be able to supply all of the other East European states except Yugoslavia.

Romania and Bulgaria participate in the CMEA electric-power project "Mir," which connects with the western Ukraine and specifically the city of Kiev. The first leg of a 750-kilovolt line is under construction as part of this "peace" grid. The coordinating authority is located at Prague. About eighty billion kilowatt hours of electricity were exchanged during the 1971–1975 five-year planning period.[13] The so-called Iron Gates project, which involves the construction of a hydroelectric power dam and navigation system along sixty miles of the Danube River at a cost of about four hundred million dollars, will supply Romania and CMEA-affiliate Yugoslavia with about ten billion kilowatt hours of electricity when completed.

The pooling of railroad freight cars is yet another project, one that was established in 1964 with its main offices at Prague. In 1976 it had some 250,000 units, which transported most of the commodities exchanged within the CMEA area.[14] Joint use of containers for shipping by rail is being established. A network of high-speed expressways, still on paper, will ultimately connect Moscow, Warsaw, and East Berlin; Warsaw and Prague; Warsaw, Krakow, and Budapest; Krakow and Brno; Moscow, Kiev, Bucharest, and Sofia; Kiev and Brno; East Berlin, Prague, Brno, Budapest, and Bucharest. The CMEA council's Permanent Commission for Transportation is coordinating this ambitious highway project.

A joint operation that is attempting at least in part to emulate Western Europe's highly successful Coal and Steel Community is "Intermetal," which was established by a 1965 agreement. Although the signing took place at Moscow, the Soviet Union did not become a charter member; the original signatories were Czechoslovakia, Poland, and Hungary. Subsequently the USSR, East Germany, and Bulgaria joined. With its head offices at Budapest, this organization has the task of modernizing CMEA steel industries and reducing the time required for production and delivery. A noteworthy provision is that "Intermetal" can pass resolutions that are binding on all members.[15] Perhaps that is why Romania has

---

12. By the end of 1976 a new 290-kilometer pipeline called "Druzhba II" will have connected Uzhgorod with Szaszhalombatta and will give Hungary ten million tons of oil a year. *Ibid.*

13. Moscow radio, 20 September 1976. Nuclear power generating capacity exceeded 7,500 megawatts in CMEA countries according to a TASS communiqué, 6 January 1977.

14. *Krasnaya zvezda*, 16 July 1976.

15. N. V. Faddeev in *Izvestiya*, 27 March 1970.

not become a member officially, although it does participate in and benefit from the organization. Neither does the Bucharest regime belong to the CMEA unit formed earlier that directs the production of ball bearings and is administered from Warsaw, or to "Interkhim," which coordinates chemical production from headquarters at Halle, East Germany.

Finally, a so-called International Bank for Economic Cooperation is in operation, headed by Konstantin Nazarkin, the former deputy chairman of the USSR State Bank. The eight participating CMEA governments contributed a total of three hundred million rubles to start banking. (See table 58.) This capital is in the form of "transferable" rubles. This CMEA bank settles commercial accounts among member states, largely on a bilateral basis, and also grants credits to member states at 1.5 percent or 2 percent annual interest. It reported a profit of only five hundred thousand rubles during the first year of operation, presumably from loans, but it claimed to have had its turnover almost triple from twenty-three billion rubles during 1964–1965 to sixty-seven billion rubles only twelve years later.[16]

TABLE 58

CONTRIBUTIONS TO THE INTERNATIONAL BANK
FOR ECONOMIC COOPERATIONS

Country	Capital	Percent of total
	millions of rubles	
Mongolia	3	1.0
Romania	16	5.4
Bulgaria	17	5.7
Hungary	21	7.0
Poland	27	9.0
Czechoslovakia	45	15.0
East Germany	55	18.2
Soviet Union	116	38.7
Total	300	100.0

SOURCE: Lucjan Ciamaga, *Od wspolpracy do integracji* (Warsaw, 1965), p. 93.
NOTE: Contribution quotas were based on the volume of exports within the CMEA.

One of the bank's problems has to do with making the "transferable" ruble convertible, instead of using it merely as an accounting unit to settle payments among member countries. Although a decision was reached to transform 10 percent of the bank's capital into gold and hard currency, its impact has not affected East-West trade to any noticeable degree. Multiple exchange rates actually exist

16. *Ekonomicheskaya gazeta*, 2 August 1976; Moscow.

within the CMEA trading area itself.[17] An International Investment Bank also exists for all CMEA members. Established in 1971, it gave 2.9 billion transferable rubles in loans during the ensuing five-year period for the construction of some forty projects. Disposing of more than one billion rubles, with 30 percent in convertible currency, this bank charges between 3 percent and 5 percent interest on credits over a five to fifteen-year period.[18]

BILATERALISM AND FUNCTIONALISM

The other method of CMEA collaboration is for one member to finance projects on the territory of another. As is the case in bloc ventures overseas, medium-term credits are repayable at a low rate of 2 percent interest. The project is owned by the government on whose territory it has been constructed. Repayment follows usually in the form of deliveries from the project itself or from other sources. There has been some recognition of the need to distribute the burden of new bilateral investments among more parties than the two that are immediately involved.

Romanian reed cellulose and Bulgarian copper represent examples of raw materials that are extracted and processed with the aid of loans from other CMEA members. Poland has developed its natural resources, coal and sulphur, for bloc needs. Czechoslovakia gave credits to help Polish mining and also for the expansion of iron-ore output from Krivoi Rog, USSR. The reason for this, of course, is that Czechoslovakia's economy remains sensitive to and dependent upon "outside relations." This euphemism stands for the importing of practically all its necessary raw materials.

An extension of the bilateral arrangements involves the so-called interested party or functional approach, which centers on projects that are of immediate concern to several CMEA members. Joint agreements among Czechoslovakia, Hungary, and Poland have dealt with the ferrous metallurgical industry. Other programs, in which more than two states have participated, include cooperative production of fertilizer and the development of basic fuels. In addition, intergovernmental commissions have been organized for economic and scientific-technical cooperation on a bilateral basis.

Bilateralism can also be illustrated by Polish-Czechoslovak cooperation in manufacturing farm tractors, East German and Polish joint production of high-pressure steam boilers as well as cotton textiles, and the Polish-Hungarian joint stock company called "Haldex," which extracts coal from what was formerly scrapped as waste in Poland's mines. Hungary and Bulgaria have also established

---

17. RFE report (by Harry Trend), "The Labyrinth of Intra-Comecon Exchange Rates," 30 August 1976.

18. East Berlin radio, 7 July 1976; Moscow radio, 4 October 1976.

mixed companies, such as "Agromash," for the production of agricultural machinery, as have Czechoslovakia and Bulgaria.

CMEA RELAUNCHED

Soviet leaders belatedly recognized the gathering momentum of West European economic integration and probably decided to give CMEA a new impetus. (See chart 2.) After the twenty-second congress of the Soviet communist party in October 1961, the perspective shifted forward to 1980, or a time-span of twenty years. This date was to represent the beginning of a promised transition to communism. As early as March 1961, the CMEA council noted at its fourteenth session in East Berlin that member countries had begun to draw up plans that would reach two decades into the future.

Assuming that the CMEA does increasingly adopt the character of a general staff for bloc plan coordination, its work is likely to be more effective insofar as it refrains from attempts at drastic interference with national economic goals and concentrates on selected areas such as fuel and power. Local approaches to industrial development that have already been laid down no longer seem to be challenged. Bulgaria and Romania, for example, are no longer being asked to remain predominantly agricultural. Bulgarian production of some 120,000 automobiles per year after 1980 has been forecast.[19]

The Soviet leaders finally must have come to realize that they cannot simply order all of the East European countries to do their bidding. The fact seems to have been recognized that not all CMEA members will "fully exploit the possibilities offered by the international socialist division of labor." Poland has proposed that certain CMEA organs should function above the authority of national sovereignty. Bulgaria and East Germany support this view. Hungary and Czechoslovakia favor reorganization but are against (guardedly, to be sure) any supranational character for the CMEA. Romania sharply opposes any kind of external economic authority. Perhaps the greatest obstacles are the unwieldy bureaucracies that would have to be integrated.[20]

It was only in the middle of 1964 that delegates to the CMEA executive committee, meeting at Moscow, for the first time exchanged data concerning their broad intentions for the 1966–1970 planning period. At the 1970 session in Warsaw, the coordination of national economic plans was agreed upon. The communiqué[21] spoke about the adoption of concrete measures for the most important branches and types of production during 1971–1975. Subsequent coordination agreements were signed between the Soviet Union and other CMEA

---

19. [Bulgarian Communist Party], *Directives of the Eighth Congress of the People's Republic of Bulgaria in the Period of 1961–1980* (Sofia, 1963), p. 36.

20. *The Economist*, 24 July 1976; London.

21. *Pravda*, 15 May 1970.

CHART 2

CMEA Organization, 1976

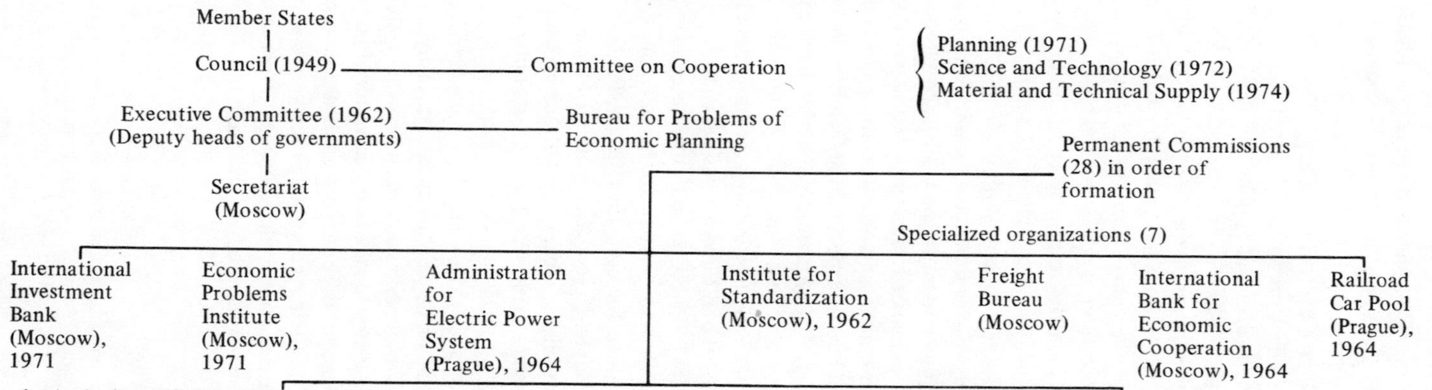

Member States

Council (1949) ——— Committee on Cooperation

Executive Committee (1962) (Deputy heads of governments) ——— Bureau for Problems of Economic Planning

Secretariat (Moscow)

Permanent Commissions (28) in order of formation

- Planning (1971)
- Science and Technology (1972)
- Material and Technical Supply (1974)

Specialized organizations (7)

- International Investment Bank (Moscow), 1971
- Economic Problems Institute (Moscow), 1971
- Administration for Electric Power System (Prague), 1964
- Institute for Standardization (Moscow), 1962
- Freight Bureau (Moscow)
- International Bank for Economic Cooperation (Moscow), 1964
- Railroad Car Pool (Prague), 1964

1. Agriculture (Sofia), 1956
2. Forestry (Bucharest)
3. Foreign Trade (Moscow), 1956
4. Coal Industry (Warsaw), 1956
5. Mechanical Engineering (Prague), 1956
6. Petroleum and Natural Gas Industry (Bucharest), 1956
7. Ferrous Metallurgy (Moscow), 1956
8. Nonferrous Metallurgy (Budapest), 1956
9. Chemical Industry (East Berlin), 1956
10. Timber, Cellulose, and Paper Industry (Budapest)
11. Transportation (Warsaw), 1958
12. Building Industry (East Berlin), 1958
13. Electrical Energy (Moscow), 1958
14. Peaceful Uses of Atomic Energy (Moscow), 1960
15. Economic Problems (Moscow)
16. Standardization (East Berlin), 1962
17. Scientific and Technological Development (Moscow), 1962
18. Statistics (Moscow), 1962
19. Machine Construction (Moscow), 1962
20. Monetary-Financial Problems (Moscow), 1962
21. Food Industry (Sofia), 1963
22. Light Industry (Prague), 1963
23. Radio, Engineering, and Electronics (Budapest), 1963
24. Geology (Ulan Bator), 1963
25. Telecommunications and Post (Moscow), 1971
26. Environmental Protection (East Berlin), 1973
27. Health Affairs (Moscow), 1975
28. Civil Aviation (Moscow), 1975

Sources: N. V. Faddeev, *SEV: 1949–1974* (Moscow, 1974), p. 67; RFE report (by Harry Trend), "Comecon's Organizational Structure," Part I, 3 July 1975; *Ibid.,* "An Assessment of the Comecon 30th Session," 23 August 1976.

member states before the end of the year. The continued primacy of planning and the subordinate role of market relations would appear to indicate Soviet resistance to economic reform; if this is true, it might result in the further strengthening of the USSR's control over Eastern Europe.

One country that is affiliated with CMEA presumably has not gone so far as to reveal its planning to the others. Yugoslavia had applied for affiliation in September 1964, and at that time a preliminary agreement was initialed. Ratification did not take place until early the following year, at the nineteenth council session. This limited status allows Yugoslavia to participate in a number of the permanent commissions and to attend council sessions with an advisory vote. The commissions it originally joined were foreign trade, monetary-financial problems, ferrous industry, nonferrous industry, machine construction, chemical industry, and scientific and technological development. It later joined three additional commissions,[22] and by now belongs to almost all of them.

The affiliated status granted to Yugoslavia may have established a precedent leading to the possible admission of other states to the CMEA. What the Soviet leader had in mind may never be known, since Khrushchev was deposed approximately four weeks after the preliminary agreement with Yugoslavia was reached. In the other direction, he had been responsible in October 1961 for the suspension of Albania from the CMEA. At any rate, it is doubtful that the CMEA will become "an open organization" and that "adequate forms exist for the participation in its work of any country which would join the basic principles of its activity," as its secretary-general Nikolai Faddeev has declared.[23]

The current Kremlin leadership team probably believes that the economic facts of life are sufficient to keep the CMEA viable. After all, between one-fifth and more than one-half of all intrabloc trade for each East European state (except Yugoslavia and Albania) is with the Soviet Union. (See table 59.) Intrabloc trade during 1975 totaled more than seventy billion rubles. Most of these countries also rely on Soviet deliveries of iron ore and coking coal for their steel plants, which are basic to industrial development.

To achieve industrial growth, all of the CMEA members have been adopting rational techniques to a larger or smaller degree, even though many obstacles exist to economic change within the bloc. Slowdowns in growth, warehouses filled with unsold goods of inferior quality, and waste that results from central planning have contributed to a barrage of criticism against the command economy with its regimentation and inefficiency. Although the vested interest of the plant managers often may involve maintaining the status quo, inter-enterprise cooperative arrangements of various types have begun and probably will expand in the future.

---

22. Belgrade radio, 11 August 1969.

23. Interview in *Journal Export* (Belgrade), quoted by Zagreb radio, 26 December 1965. A few years later, however, the CMEA was called the first "socialist" collective organization by this same man. *Izvestiya*, 27 March 1970. See also his book, *SEV: 1949–1974* (Moscow, 1974), p. 375.

TABLE 59

BLOC EXPORTS (IMPORTS), 1975–1980 (PLAN)

Country	annual percent change				Level 1975 (millions of dollars)
	1975	1976	1977	Average 1976–1980	
Bulgaria	20.0 (24.0)	—	—	—	4,600 (5,600)
Czechoslovakia	6.7 (7.6)	7.0 (8.0)	7.5 (7.6)	7.5 (7.5)	8,350 (9,200)
East Germany	9.2 (9.0)	10.0 (15.0)	—	—	9,620 (11,000)
Hungary	11.1 (20.6)	11.5 (15.0)	15.0 (12.0)	15.0 (14.0)	6,083 (7,175)
Poland	23.4 (20.0)	20.0 (20.0)	15.0 (15.0)	15.5 (15.0)	11,700 (13,900)
Rumania	19.0 (25.0)	—	—	14.0 (12.0)	5,800 (6,940)
USSR	12.7 (35.0)	15.0 (20.0)	15.0	15.0	30,890 (35,600)
Yugoslavia	4.6 (0.0)	12.5 (7.9)	12.0 (6.1)	12.0 (6.5)	3,980 (7,533)
Totals					81,023 (96,948)

SOURCES: Sovet Ekonomicheskoi Vzaimopomoshchi, *Statisticheski ezhegodnik stran-chlenov SEV 1975* (Moscow, 1976), p. 325; Budapest radio, 24 January 1975; Prague radio, 30 March and 1 June 1976; *Rynki zagraniczne*, no. 88–89 (22–24 July 1976), special insert; *ibid.* (26 February 1976); *Neues Deutschland*, 15 January 1976.

Other obstacles to reform include (1) the lack of stability regarding the economic plans themselves; (2) the contradiction between the slow growth of agriculture and the promises of a higher living standard; and (3) the problems involved in actually drafting specific multiyear economic plans. Many of these problems came out into the open at a meeting of the CMEA council held in July 1976 at East Berlin.[24] (See table 60 for a listing of all the sessions.)

This thirtieth session ended with agreement on five major sectors that were to be treated as problem areas: fuel, energy, and raw materials; machine building; agriculture and food production; light industry; and transportation. It was also agreed that targets would be established through 1990 and even longer. Joint investments call for nine to ten billion rubles during 1976–1980, with most of the projects located on Soviet territory. They include the construction of a natural-gas pipeline from Orenburg, a pulp factory at Ust-Ilimsk, an asbestos mining and enrichment combine at Kiyembayevskiy, a 750-kilowatt line from Vinnitsa to Albertirsa in Hungary that will become the first leg of a 750-kilovolt network, nickel production in Cuba, and an isoprene rubber plant for Romania.[25] Also mentioned in the communiqué, and probably discussed in great detail, was the topic of East-West trade.

The basic reason for the drive toward the expansion of trade with Western Europe and the United States is that all bloc countries require high-grade materials, quality equipment, and technological expertise that remain available only from the outside. Since the CMEA has proven ineffectual for the most part as a device for obtaining these from the USSR, it is probable that the member states will continue along their separate paths in attempting to satisfy their requirements. Romania signed the first 51:49 percent joint-enterprise production agreement with the Federal Republic of Germany.

Even the deep-rooted psychological antipathy of the Poles toward West Germans, for example, has not inhibited the Warsaw regime from negotiating with such companies as Krupp and Grundig. About a dozen joint manufacturing projects already exist. Trade agreements were signed between West Germany and six of the East European countries as far back as 1969, but the Soviet Union still dominates bloc trade with the Common Market as a whole.

The method used by the West Germans is to provide the technological expertise, engineering skills, and capital to begin a project; the partner contributes the site, factory buildings, labor, and raw materials. Machine tools are being produced jointly with Hungary in this manner. Ownership always remains in the hands of the government on whose territory the plant is situated. This is the case with an automobile factory in Poland, estimated to have cost about $40 million,

---

24. *Izvestiya*, 10 July 1976, gave the communiqué.

25. *Ekonomicheskaya gazeta*, 2 August 1976: *Pravda*, 20 November 1976. Note also that East Germany allocated 8 billion marks for construction projects during 1977 in other CMEA member states, according to *ibid.*, 7 January 1977.

that was established jointly with Fiat of Italy. The coordinating committee in charge of NATO's trade with the bloc countries has indicated that it would even be legal to sell nuclear reactors for peaceful purposes to communist-ruled states.

The main problem in the relations of the bloc countries with the West is the increasing amount of foreign debts because of a chronically adverse balance of payments and the necessity to service interest as well as repay credits. At the end of 1975, Eastern Europe alone owed almost twenty-five billion dollars and had available only somewhat more than three billion dollars in foreign-exchange reserves. (See table 61.) Almost two-thirds of the total indebtedness is owed to private banks in the West.

Should these bankers begin to question CMEA members' credit-worthiness, the East European regimes may attempt to lease equipment and fall back on "compensation" contracts, that is, to repay loans with raw materials. Poland has done just that with a $150 million credit from Italy (1974) that was repayable in coal, and a $100 million credit from West Germany (May 1976) that was to be repaid with copper concentrate. The Soviet Union, of course, remains in a strong position with respect to raw materials, and the joint projects mentioned above in effect will be financed by credits and labor from Eastern Europe.[26]

PROBLEMS IN AGRICULTURE

The dogmatic Marxist belief that farming must involve collective activity, controlled through bureaucratic-industrial methods, has led to the elimination of most of the private-entrepreneur farms throughout Eastern Europe. A communiqué issued by the CMEA at its June 1962 meeting in Moscow spoke of the "historic victory" in agriculture by communist-ruled member states (except for Poland and Yugoslavia, which was not then affiliated). The statement, which meant complete collectivization, remains true in ideology and organization only. In production, the collective farm system has been and continues to be for the most part a failure. Its destruction of personal responsibility and incentive has to a large extent alienated the rural population.

For the millions of collectivized farmers and their families, earnings had been until recently related mainly to the number of labor-days accumulated. This figure was used to calculate each worker's share of the net earnings. It is evident that little incentive existed. Nor was there until recently in the majority of countries any minimum level of earnings on the collective, such as the state farms had provided under their quasi-industrial wage systems. Bulgaria was the first to introduce a scheme for guaranteed labor-day remuneration, providing collective farm workers with a daily minimum of 1.8 leva. Hungary has the "Nadudvar" system of monthly payments in cash plus remuneration in kind. Czechoslovakia also makes monthly payments, but without any guaranteed minimum. Romania

---

26. *The Economist,* 24 July 1976; Moscow radio, 20 November 1976.

TABLE 60

CMEA Sessions, 1949–1976

Session	Date	Place	Principal discussion or action
1.	26–28 April 1949	Moscow	Organization and plans for 1949
2.	25–27 August 1949	Sofia	Multiyear trade agreements
3.	24–25 November 1950	Moscow	Reports on commercial expansion
4.	26–27 March 1954	Moscow	Coordination with USSR economic plans
5.	24–25 June 1954	Moscow	Priorities for coordination
6.	7–11 December 1955	Budapest	Economic plans, 1956–1960
7.	18–25 May 1956	East Berlin	Coordination for 1956–1960
8.	18–22 June 1957	Warsaw	Permanent commissions
9.	26–30 June 1958	Bucharest	"Socialist division of labor"
10.	11–13 December 1958	Prague	Chemical industry
11.	13–16 May 1959	Tirana	Steel production in 1961–1965
12.	10–13 December 1959	Sofia	Charter approval
13.	26–29 July 1960	Budapest	Agriculture and 1961–1980 plans
14.	28 February–3 March 1961	East Berlin	Cooperation in chemical industry
15.	12–15 December 1961	Warsaw	"Socialist division of labor"
16.	7 June 1962	Moscow	Executive Committee established
17.	14–20 December 1962	Bucharest	Freight-car pool organized
18.	25–26 July 1963	Moscow	Plan coordination, 1966–1970

TABLE 60 (Cont.)

CMEA Sessions, 1949–1976

Session	Date	Place	Principal discussion or action
19.	28 January–2 February 1965	Prague	Yugoslav associate status approved
20.	8–10 December 1966	Sofia	Coordination in 1971–1975
21.	12–14 December 1967	Budapest	Mutual-interest projects
22.	21–23 January 1969	East Berlin	Scientific and technical cooperation
23.	23–26 April 1969	Moscow	CMEA infrastructure
24.	12–14 May 1970	Warsaw	International Investment Bank
25.	25–29 July 1971	Bucharest	Comprehensive program
26.	10–12 July 1972	Moscow	Cuba accepted as member
27.	5–8 June 1973	Prague	Cooperation with Finland approved
28.	18–21 June 1974	Sofia	Twenty-fifth anniversary report
29.	24–26 June 1975	Budapest	Joint five-year development projects
30.	7–9 July 1976	East Berlin	Fifteen-year economic goals

SOURCES: Lucjan Ciamaga, *Od wspolpracy do integracji* (Warsaw, 1965), pp. 209–237; Warsaw radio, 2 February 1965; *Życie Warszawy*, 18–19 December 1966; *Pravda*, 16 December 1967; *ibid.*, 24 January 1969; *Ekonomicheskaya gazeta*, 28 April 1969; *Krasnaya zvezda*, 15 May 1970; RFE report (by Harry Trend), "Comecon's Organizational Structure," 7 October 1975; *Izvestiya*, 10 July 1976; N. V. Faddeev, *SEV: 1949–1974* (Moscow, 1974), pp. 266–273, for a discussion of sessions 1–27.

TABLE 61

FOREIGN EXCHANGE HOLDINGS AND EXTERNAL DEBTS, 1974–1976
(in U.S. dollars)

Country	Official foreign reserves level in millions		Official external debt (1976 est.)
CMEA Banks			3.5
Bulgaria	December 1974	360	2.8
Czechoslovakia		350	2.9
East Germany		400	6.0[a]
Hungary		500	3.3
Poland		410	10.8
Romania		110	2.8
USSR	December 1975	11,000	16.0
Yugoslavia	February 1976	1,098	6.0
Total		14,228	53.3

SOURCES: *Financial Times,* 29 July 1975; and *East West Markets,* 20 September 1976; cited by RFE report (by Harry Trend), "A Suggested Framework for Analyzing East European Indebtedness," 28 September 1976. See also *Washington Post,* 17 October 1976, which states that the total may reach $42 billion by the end of that year; *Business Week* (7 March 1977), p. 40, citing the Chase Manhattan Bank.

NOTES: [a]Includes one-billion-dollar GDR debt in "clearing account units," which represents largely interest-free financing by the Federal Republic of Germany.

adheres to a rigid labor-day system but offers private-plot privileges. In Poland minimum earnings could not make much difference because of the small degree of collectivization, and the labor-day remains the rule.

Apart from Poland and Yugoslavia, more than 90 percent of all agricultural land in the bloc countries has been brought into the so-called socialist (collective and state) farm sector. Private plots, although limited in size, retain a disproportionate importance in the economy. This is because of the concentration on intensive-labor, high-value agricultural products. A high percentage of livestock remains in private hands, more than four-fifths of the total in Poland and more than two-thirds in Romania; nowhere is the proportion less than one-fifth. An East European who traveled throughout the CMEA area more than a decade ago[27] reported that the 4 percent of Hungarian land in garden plots supported 34 percent of all pigs, 36 percent of all cattle, and 88 percent of all domestic fowl. In Czechoslovakia, the 6.8 percent of farmland that was in private use accounted for 21 percent of all agricultural production. Bulgaria's 8.7 percent of farmland under private ownership produced 31.7 percent of the meat, about 20 percent of all vegetables and potatoes, approximately 32 percent of the fruit, and 19.4 percent of the total crop production.

---

27. *Polityka,* 3 July 1965; Warsaw.

Even the level of mechanization, which was heralded as the great panacea that would solve most problems, remains far below that of Western Europe. For example, in 1939 Czechoslovakia and France had the same ratio of 1.5 tractors per one thousand hectares of arable land. More than two decades later, the respective figures were six and twenty-six. It is claimed that the CMEA member states during the year 1969 alone received a total of 550,000 new tractors and one hundred thousand grain-harvesting combines.[28] Problems include a lack of spare parts and even a deficiency in technological culture—the general attitude that if a piece of machinery belongs to the government it belongs to everybody, with the result that no particular care is taken of it. In addition, not enough equipment is available to cope with above-average production periods.

Most of this equipment had been owned by the government in Machine Tractor Stations (MTS). Once the Soviet Union began to transform its agricultural system by selling machinery to collective farms, most of Eastern Europe began to do the same. By the end of 1965 all MTSs in Hungary had been converted into Tractor Repair Stations, which kept only the heavy tractors and special combines. By 1966 Bulgaria had almost completely phased out the MTSs except in hilly areas. On the other hand, Czechoslovakia adopted a dual system: collective farms purchase most of the machinery, but MTSs are still operated. Poland abolished the MTSs, converting them into repair stations and selling the machinery to collectives. Romania alone has expanded the system, adding to the number of MTSs and selling no equipment to farms.

General stagnation continued in agriculture despite these measures. The area could no longer support itself in food, as it had been able to do before the war, and the overall production deficit remained at about 6 to 7 percent. After poor harvests, the deficit became greater and more grain had to be imported. This problem was approached in several different ways.

Czechoslovakia and East Germany initially took a harsh line, whittling down the size of private plots as well as the number of livestock allowed and imposing tighter party/state controls over agriculture. The various changes introduced in the organization of Soviet collective and state farms were emulated by these two regimes. Romania announced a proposal for the establishment of cooperative farm unions that would be organized at local, district, and national levels, with congresses meeting every five years and suggesting basic agricultural policy. During 1929–1932 a similar system had existed in the USSR. The Bulgarian communists deliberately strengthened the farmers' incentives, at the expense of the consumers, by raising both government-paid and retail prices for livestock products. Poland announced a shift toward larger state investments in agriculture.

However, because of a deteriorating economic situation in general, the Warsaw regime announced on 24 June 1976 its intention to raise the cost of food

---

28. *Ekonomicheskaya gazeta,* 16 March 1970.

by 70 percent. Spontaneous demonstrations[29] throughout the country forced the government to rescind the proposed measure and to promise that price changes would be introduced only after consultation with workers. At the same time, the Polish regime applied for two hundred million dollars in credits with which to purchase agricultural products from the United States.

Consumer subsidies, which amount to approximately 30 percent on retail food sales in Poland, have also been used by other East European states. In Hungary the average government subsidy for one kilogram (2.2 pounds) of pork is eighteen forints or almost one dollar and for one kilogram of beef is twenty-six forints, so that the annual consumption of meat rose to seventy kilograms per person.[30] However, the regime in Budapest raised meat prices as of July 1976 by an average of 30 percent without precipitating the food riots that had occurred in Poland just ten days earlier.

TRADE BETWEEN CMEA STATES

CMEA members do not belong to a common market in actual practice, since the organization maintains no uniform external tariff and apparently does not aspire to one. Therefore the area cannot be regarded as a single market. Nevertheless, orthodox East European economists insist that the CMEA states strive to increase trade among themselves in preference to commerce with the "capitalist world." This represents an ideological imperative. However, in actual practice, the percentage of trade with nonbloc countries has been expanding for most CMEA members.

Up to now, trade within the CMEA area has been conducted almost entirely within the framework of bilateral agreements. Khrushchev had emphasized the need for measures to enhance mutual responsibility within a truly multilateral framework. This has not been achieved, although a communiqué issued following the seventeenth CMEA council session indicated that price adjustments would be made on the basis of average world levels during the preceding five-year period. This system continued until the USSR raised the price of oil in 1974 by 131 percent (Eastern Europe had to pay an additional three billion dollars) and in 1976 by another 8 percent. The previous static five-year average pricing system was replaced as of 1 January 1975 by a movable three-year average, with prices recalculated annually.[31]

---

29. Seven workers at the Ursus tractor plant went on trial in Warsaw under article 220 of the penal code, which envisages sentences from five years in prison to death. *The Observer*, 18 July 1976; London.

30. Budapest radio, 4 July 1976. CMEA meat production during 1975 totaled twenty-five million tons, or 28 percent above 1970, according to Moscow radio, 10 December 1976.

31. Romanian dissatisfaction with the CMEA pricing system was reported by *Politika*, 10 August 1976; Belgrade. The USSR apparently will not discuss oil prices beyond 1977 deliveries. *New York Times*, 14 December 1976.

Progress toward effective coordination in trade, however, has been brought about by the USSR. Within the CMEA area commercial exchange almost tripled between 1971 and 1975. (See table 62.) Between 16 percent and roughly half of the foreign trade of each East European state is with the Soviet Union, and the USSR in turn, conducts 70 percent of its foreign trade within the bloc.

With regard to the specialization of production, the East European communist regimes hesitate to surrender their right to engage in particular branches of industry. Nor are the industrially more advanced states necessarily keen to see competitive production established by their more backward neighbors. The Soviet Union has proclaimed its prerogative of strengthening all branches of the economy because of an international duty to build communism. Thus, efforts to achieve a more rational division of labor among the bloc states have been countered by more or less concealed resistance from the threatened producers and by the determination of the USSR to proceed along its own path.

TABLE 62

TRADE WITHIN THE CMEA AREA, 1971–1975
(In millions of dollars)

Country	1971	1972	1973	1974	1975	1975 total trade
Bulgaria	2,120	2,567	3,266	4,326	7,266	9,980
Czechoslovakia	4,010	4,662	6,137	7,532	11,326	17,449
East Germany	4,981	5,905	7,854	9,646	13,852	21,700
Hungary	2,990	3,154	3,919	5,576	8,584	13,222
Poland	4,038	5,335	7,814	10,482	11,277	22,834
Romania	2,103	2,616	3,468	5,144	4,320	10,664
USSR	12,480	16,047	21,112	24,890	31,882	70,228
Total	32,722	40,286	53,570	67,596	88,507	166,077

SOURCES: United Nations, *Statistical Yearbook 1975* (New York, 1976), p. 432; CIA, *Handbook of Economic Statistics* (Washington, D.C., September 1976), pp. 63–64.

The nature of the organization also militates against effective supranational planning. The CMEA council, an advisory body that issues recommendations to member governments, had to wait until the middle of 1962 to acquire an executive committee. Six months later Khrushchev spoke out plainly on the need to establish a joint body that was "empowered to formulate common plans." Developments since that time suggest that the USSR has not yet managed to advance this politically delicate matter beyond some joint planning in limited areas, for example, international economic enterprises and associations. The CMEA committees for cooperation in planning, science and technology, and material and technical supply were all established during the first half of the 1970s (see chart 2) and represent moves in that same direction.

The communiqué[32] issued after the July 1976 CMEA session mentioned that concrete proposals for improvement in the style and method of work would be drafted by the executive committee and submitted to the thirty-first CMEA council meeting in 1977, but no details were released. Romania's delegate cautioned that "any measures taken in this area will have to be based on full respect for the fundamental principles of relations among our states, on the provisions of the CMEA charter and of the Comprehensive Program."[33]

Regardless of whether these future proposals are implemented, it may not be possible to solve the many economic problems of Eastern Europe unless closer relations are developed with Western Europe and the United States. Regional integration may have become obsolete, as recent trends toward an international monetary system and a world economy indicate. Finally, it behooves the East European members of the CMEA to become postindustrial societies as rapidly as possible, or they will continue to remain far behind their West European counterparts.[34]

32. *Izvestiya*, 10 July 1976.

33. Cited in RFE report (by Harry Trend), "An Assessment of the Comecon Council 30th Session," 23 August 1976.

34. A proposal by the CMEA requesting most-favored nation treatment by the European Economic Community was rejected. The EEC prefers the continuation of trade links with individual Soviet bloc states. *New York Times*, 16 November 1976. See also the Radio Liberty report (by Allan Kroncher), "Hard Times for Comecon," 8 December 1976.

Chapter 11

Intrabloc Party Relations: Unity in Diversity

The experiment of maintaining a single organization, the Communist Information Bureau, or Cominform, to control Eastern Europe politically from Moscow
existed less than nine years. It is doubtful that this instrument could have been
used at all after the death of Stalin. The only eyewitness account of the Cominform's establishment tells how Andrei Zhdanov proposed that its weekly newspaper be called *For a Lasting Peace, For a People's Democracy*. This political
slogan was treated as a joke, especially by the Italians and the French. Only after
Zhdanov had explained that he was voicing Stalin's suggestion did the laughter
cease.[1]

This organizational meeting took place during 22–27 September 1947 at
Szklarska Poreba (the former Bad Schreiberhau) in the part of Silesia that Poland
had annexed with Soviet support at the end of the Second World War. Representing the host country's communist party was Wladyslaw Gomulka, who also
signed the original Cominform manifesto denouncing the Marshall Plan and condemning the United States as "an arsenal of counterrevolutionary tactical
weapons."[2] The other delegates came from the other East European parties
(except for the Albanian party) as well as from those in Italy and France, where it
was assumed that the communists would be in power shortly.

The second meeting took place at the beginning of 1948 in Belgrade, where
Cominform headquarters functioned for a brief period. The third, which was held
at Bucharest on 28 June 1948, issued the communiqué excluding the Yugoslav
communist party from the organization. A fourth meeting, held at Budapest

---

1. Eugenio Reale, *Nascita del Cominform* (Rome, 1958), p. 51. For the predecessor organization
see the research guide by Witold S. Sworakowski, *The Communist International and Its Front
Organizations* (Stanford, Ca., 1965).

2. Guenther Nollau, *Die Internationale* (Cologne, 1959), pp. 193–196.

toward the end of 1949, devoted its time to planning a world drive for signatures to a so-called peace manifesto.[3] After that, little could be accomplished and the Cominform had been all but forgotten until April 1956, when it was dissolved, apparently as part of the price for reconciliation between Belgrade and Moscow.

The abolition of the Cominform, the existence of which had manifested itself during the last few years only by publication of the weekly newspaper, left a vacuum in the Soviet bloc. Coinciding with what has become known as destalinization, this act seems to have had a further purpose, that of helping to transform the image of East European leaders so that they would appear not as Moscow agents but as respectable "national communists." (It should be noted that this term has never been used in official Soviet or East European terminology.) Khrushchev had launched the destalinization process with his secret speech in February 1956 to the twentieth CPSU congress.[4] After hearing about Stalin's crimes vis-a-vis domestic as well as foreign party members, this elite gathering could surmise that future relations with member states in the East European "commonwealth of nations" would follow a new course.

Whatever may have motivated Khrushchev to repeat his denunciation of Stalin publicly at the twenty-second CPSU congress in October 1961,[5] sweeping changes in Eastern Europe did not materialize. The simple fact of the matter was that many regimes would have fallen if full-fledged destalinization had been implemented. The same has continued to be true since then. Most of the leaders in power as of January 1977 had been at one time or another ardent supporters of Stalinist techniques, and some might even yet like to revert to them. Hence, by and large, destalinization was restricted to changing the names of streets and cities, taking down statues of Stalin, including the five-ton monument in Prague that had been made from a solid piece of marble, and removing the mummies of Stalin and Gottwald from their mausoleums. Nothing has come, however, of Khrushchev's proposal to "erect a monument in Moscow to perpetuate the memory of comrades who fell victims to arbitrary rule."[6]

EAST EUROPE'S LEADERS

The men controlling the communist regimes within the Soviet bloc, even those in Albania and Yugoslavia, share many characteristics. They are all hard-core

---

3. *For a Lasting Peace, For a People's Democracy,* 1 July 1948, and 29 November 1949.

4. U.S. Senate, Committee on the Judiciary, 85th Cong., 1st sess., *Speech of Nikita Khrushchev before a Closed Session of the XXth Congress of the Communist Party of the Soviet Union on February 25, 1956* (Washington, D.C. 1957), 66 pp.

5. Translation in Charlotte Saikowski and Leo Gruliow (eds.), *Current Soviet Policies IV* (New York, 1962).

6. *Pravda,* 29 October 1961.

apparatus workers, professional revolutionaries who reached the top posts after having served in less responsible positions when their parties were banned by the prewar or World War II governments. They have all proven themselves to be dedicated communists, some of them in "capitalist" prisons and even in their own postwar jails. (See table 63.)

Enver Hoxha[7] is one of the best educated among these eight communist leaders in Eastern Europe. Definitely of "bourgeois" origin, he attended the French secondary school of Korce and after graduation studied one year at the University of Montpellier in France. Back in Albania after working in Paris and Brussels over a period of five years, he taught the French language at a secondary school until the Italian occupation. Hoxha became first secretary of the Albanian communist party when it was founded and has directed the movement ever since. After his Yugoslav mentors were expelled from the Cominform in 1948, he took advantage of this development to become a favored protégé of the USSR. Another turn in his fortunes came at the twenty-second CPSU congress, when the Albanian communists were read out of the world movement loyal to the Soviet Union. Hoxha had already shifted his allegiance to Peking, which was much further away geographically.

Bulgaria's leader, Todor Zhivkov,[8] spent the war years in his own country, like Hoxha, as one of the communist partisans. Here, however, the resemblance ends. Born into a peasant family, Zhivkov completed only a few years of elementary school. Between 1936 and 1941 he may have been in Moscow undergoing training; there is a gap in his biography for this period. In 1952 Zhivkov succeeded the notorious "little Stalin," Vulko Chervenkov, as a member of the new collective leadership in Bulgaria. He has followed consistently the Moscow line and rivals his East German colleague in this respect.

The leader in Czechoslovakia is Gustav Husak,[9] who became a member of the communist youth movement at age sixteen and joined the party four years later. He worked in a factory to finance a law-school education at Bratislava. During these years he was arrested several times for illegal communist activities. In 1943 he entered the leadership of the party in Slovakia. After the war Husak spent nearly a decade in prison and was not rehabilitated until 1963. During the next five years he held employment in the State and Law Institute at the Slovak Academy of Sciences. His political comeback dates from April 1968 when he received a deputy premiership; the following August he became the Slovak party's first secretary, and in April 1969 he attained the top position for the entire

---

7. U.S. House of Representatives, Committee on Un-American Activities, *Who Are They?* (Washington, D.C., 1958), part 9, pp. 3–7.

8. RFE, *Eastern Europe's Communist Leaders: Bulgaria* (Munich, 1966), vol. IV, pp. 34–37.

9. Biography appeared in *Krasnaya zvezda*, 19 April 1969; Lenin Order in the *New York Times*, 28 August 1969.

TABLE 63

East Europe's Communist Leaders, 1977

Country	Leader's name and party position	Year of Birth	Father's occupation	Joined communist party	Profession	Years in jail	Spent Second World War	Years in Russia	Government Post	Became member of party Politburo
Albania	Hoxha, Enver First Secretary, 1941–	1908	Small landholder	1941	Teacher	1939 (briefly)	Albania	None	None	1941
Bulgaria	Zhivkov, Todor First Secretary, 1954–	1911	Peasant	1932	Printer	None	Bulgaria	1936–41?	Chairman, State Council	1951
Czechoslovakia	Husak, Gustav First Secretary, 1969–	1913	Poor peasant	1933	Lawyer's assistant	1951–60	Czechoslovakia	None	President	1968
East Germany	Honecker, Erich, First Secretary, 1971–	1912	Coal miner	1929	Roof tiler	1935–45	Germany	1930–31; 1956–57.	Chairman, State Council	1950
Hungary	Kadar, Janos First Secretary, 1956–	1914	Peasant	1932	None	1933–35; 1951–54	Hungary	None	Member Presidential Council	1956

TABLE 63 (Cont.)

East Europe's Communist Leaders, 1977

Country	Leader's name and party position	Year of Birth	Father's occupation	Joined communist party	Profession	Years in jail	Spent Second World War	Years in Russia	Government Post	Became member of party Politburo
Poland	Gierek, Edward First Secretary, 1970–	1913	Coal miner	1931	Coal miner	1934 (briefly)	Belgium	None	Member Council of State	1956
Romania	Ceausescu, Nicolae Secretary-General, 1965–	1918	Poor peasant	1936	None	1936–39; 1940–44	Romania	None	Chairman, Council of State; President	1954
Yugoslavia	Tito, Josip Broz, Secretary-general, 1937–1966; President, 1966–	1892	Peasant	1920	Metal-worker	1915–17; 1928–34	Yugoslavia	1915–20; 1934–36	President	1934

SOURCES: RFE, *Eastern Europe's Communist Leaders*, 5 vols. (Munich, 1966), with 1976 identifications from the press; *Krasnaya zvezda*, 19 April 1969; *Figyelo*, 14 October 1970; *Pravda*, 3 November 1970; Sofia radio, 4 November 1970; Prague radio, 5 November 1970; *Trybuna ludu*, 1 December 1970; Guenther Buch (comp.), *Namen und Daten* (Berlin, 1973), p. 120; RFE, *Communist Party-Government Line-Up* (Munich, 7 January 1977), p. 32.

communist party of Czechoslovakia. He was awarded the Order of Lenin the following August by the Soviet Union.

Among all East European leaders, Erich Honecker[10] of the German Democratic Republic has no choice but to remain the most submissive in his relations with the Soviet Union. Born of communist parents in the Saar, he joined the party's youth organization as a ten-year-old and later received training at Moscow's international school. Honecker spent a full decade in a Nazi prison for illegal activities but survived to become the chairman of the East German communist youth movement and in 1948 a member of the SED Central Committee. After training in the USSR, he took over defense and security affairs for the party in February 1958 when he was appointed to the Secretariat. His elevation to first secretary came in May 1971, and in October 1976 he was elected State Council chairman or chief of state.

Another man who has also spent almost his entire life in the service of communism is Janos Kadar[11] in Hungary. Although he remained in his native country during the war (and thus did not receive training in Moscow), by 1948 he had become deputy secretary-general of the party. There are indications that in the following year Kadar may have betrayed his best friend, Interior minister Laszlo Rajk, who was executed. Regardless of what really happened, Kadar too became swept up in the purge of suspected Titoists and spent thirty-two months in a communist prison. He next betrayed the Imre Nagy government, in which he had been a member without portfolio, by clandestinely establishing a counter-regime at Uzhgorod in Soviet-annexed Sub-Carpathian Ruthenia and calling on the USSR in early November 1956 to suppress the Hungarian freedom fighters. Two years later Nagy was hanged. Since the Hungarian rebellion, Kadar has always been sensitive to Moscow's advice.

Unlike his counterpart in Budapest, Edward Gierek[12] spent nine years abroad in Belgium and did not return to Poland until 1948. A coal miner and a resident of France for over a decade before the war, he was deported back to his native country in 1934 because of communist strike activities. Gierek's prominence began in 1951 after his appointment as first secretary for Katowice province. Three years later he joined the central apparatus in Warsaw and subsequently, in March 1956, he became a national secretary. He served as chairman of the commission to investigate the Poznan Uprising and returned to Katowice in March 1957 as first secretary. He briefly served on the Politburo in 1956 and has been on that body continuously since March 1959. The fact that he resided outside Warsaw and headed the Silesian party organization may have contributed

10. Guenther Buch (comp.) *Namen und Daten* (Berlin, 1973), p. 120. See also Branko Lazitch and Milorad M. Drachkovitch, *Biographical Dictionary of the Comintern* (Stanford, Ca., 1973), p. 155.

11. RFE, *op. cit.: Hungary* (in note 8 above), vol. I, pp. 27–33.

12. R. F. Staar, *Poland* (Westport, Conn., 1975), pp. 183–184, gives a biographic sketch.

to his selection on 20 December 1970 as a replacement for Gomulka, since he had not been directly involved with the latter's policies.

The youngest leader in the bloc is Nicolae Ceausescu[13] of Romania. Like several others, he experienced imprisonment under the precommunist government of his country. Always advancing to more important party positions, Ceausescu spent the war in Romania and most of this time in prison. His contacts with the Soviet Union have included repeated visits ever since 1957, when he attended the fortieth anniversary celebrations of the Bolshevik Revolution. Even so, no delegation from Bucharest went to Moscow for the 1−5 March 1965 meeting of communist parties that was intended as a preliminary to a world conference. The Albanians and the Chinese also refused to attend. On the other hand, Ceausescu was host to the Warsaw Pact and CMEA sessions during July 1966 in Romania. He also attended the June 1969 world communist conference in Moscow and the June 1976 meeting of European party chiefs in East Berlin. Ceausescu hosted a Warsaw Pact session the end of November 1976 at Bucharest.

Finally, a man unique in Eastern Europe is Josip Broz-Tito,[14] whose relationship with the Soviet Union goes back to 1917, when he served in a Red Guards unit at Omsk, Siberia. He subsequently returned to Yugoslavia but left again for Moscow, where he taught in the mid-1930s at the International Lenin School of political warfare, where Gomulka was one of the students. In 1937 the Comintern appointed Tito secretary-general of his party and sent him back to Yugoslavia. He spent the war there and emerged as leader of the country, only to have his party expelled from the Cominform by Stalin. The rapprochement that started with Khrushchev has continued under subsequent leadership, with setbacks from time to time. Despite a personal visit by Brezhnev in late November 1976, Tito has maintained Belgrade as a center independent from Moscow.

Unity in Diversity. As the foregoing sketches show, the backgrounds of these eight communist leaders suggest that they could be difficult for the USSR to manipulate. Interestingly enough, it was a communist from outside the bloc who coined the somewhat misleading term "polycentrism" for a policy that had already been put into practice six years earlier by Tito.[15]

Palmiro Togliatti, the secretary-general of the Italian communist party, is credited with having used the term in 1956. While Stalin was still alive, this man had been among the most obedient among prominent foreign communists. In 1964, however, during a vacation at Yalta, he wrote a memorandum that was

---

13. RFE, *op. cit.: Rumania* (in note 8 above), vol. III, pp. 19−22. See also his biography in the *New York Times,* 15 October 1970.

14. Biography in Lazitch and Drachkovitch, *op. cit.* (in note 10 above), pp. 41−42.

15. Even the Yugoslavs adopted this term, as can be seen from a lecture by Milenko Markovic at the Institute for Study of Workers' Movements, over Belgrade radio, 5 February 1965.

intended to represent the basis for discussions with Khrushchev. These never took place because Togliatti died. His body and the memorandum were taken back to Italy.

Brezhnev, who was at that time the Soviet heir apparent, represented the CPSU at Togliatti's funeral in Rome. He first learned of the memorandum there and attempted to have it suppressed. Although it probably never would have appeared if Togliatti had lived, the new Italian communist leadership under Luigi Longo eventually decided to publish it.[16] *Pravda* carried a translation five days later, but without any comment. Subsequently the press of most other East European communist parties also printed the memorandum. Many of its ideas, of course, had already surfaced prior to that time in one way or another.

Togliatti maintained that the Soviet bloc had been developing a "centrifugal tendency," that is, that the individual parties had been moving away from the centralized control exercised by Moscow. He went on to express opposition to any proposal for again creating organizations like the Comintern (1919–1943) or the Cominform (1947–1956). Togliatti rebuked the USSR and the communist-ruled states in Eastern Europe for their slowness in, and resistance to, "overcoming the regime of restrictions and suppression of democratic and personal freedom introduced by Stalin." Finally, he asserted: " . . . one must consider that the unity one ought to establish and maintain lies in the diversity and full autonomy of the individual countries."[17]

If Khrushchev had permitted the translation and publication of the Togliatti memorandum, this might have meant that his policy toward Eastern Europe included an effort to modify the master-servant relationship existing under Stalin. His goal appeared to be the introduction of more flexible contacts with the various communist parties, whereby common policies might be reached by means of discussion, although the USSR would still maintain the decisive voice because of its power position. A most important aspect of his plan was economic integration, that is, a supranational division of labor through the CMEA. This grand design failed for various reasons, including the half measures that Khrushchev allowed, the unexpected strength of nationalism, the effects of incomplete destalinization, and the impact of the Soviet dispute with China.

Ever since the dissolution of the Cominform, the day-to-day business of handling relations among the various bloc communist parties has been conducted through special units within the Central Committee apparatus of each organization. (See table 64.) Mikhail Suslov, the chief ideologist for the CPSU, indicated early in 1964 that international discipline no longer involved orders "from above" but that it had become voluntary.[18] The most that he and Khrush-

---

16. The memorandum appeared first in *Rinascita* 5 September 1964.

17. *Ibid.*, points 33 and 34.

18. *Pravda*, 3 April 1964.

TABLE 64

RELATIONS WITH OTHER PARTIES IN EASTERN EUROPE, 1976

Country	Individual responsible	Position
Albania	No relations with other East European parties	
Bulgaria	Velchev, Boris	Politburo member and Secretary
Czechoslovakia	Bilak, Vasil	Politburo member and Secretary
East Germany	Axen, Hermann	Politburo member and Secretary
Hungary	Gyenes, Andras	Secretary, Central Committee
Poland	Babiuch, Edward	Politburo member and Secretary
Romania	Andrei, Stefan	Executive Political Committee member and Secretary
Soviet Union	Katushev, Konstantin	Secretary, Central Committee
Yugoslavia	Grlickov, Aleksandar	Secretary, Executive Committee

SOURCE: East Berlin radio, 4 May 1976.

chev seem to have regarded as attainable among the communist-ruled countries was an international system of "democratic centralism" in party relations, wherein the minority would accept the decisions of the majority.

FALL OF KHRUSHCHEV AND AFTER

Togliatti had dealt with deficiencies of intracommunist state relationships, and the manner in which Khrushchev was dismissed enhanced the impact of his memorandum. The nuances of the slogan "unity in diversity" can be observed very well in the various reactions to the *Pravda* editorial explaining the change in leadership at Moscow.[19] Even the most obedient among the East European regimes had finally come to the realization that it should not accept without question what Khrushchev's successors proclaimed.

Thus the fall of Khrushchev at first caused general bewilderment across almost the whole of Eastern Europe. Whereas previous changes of this kind had been accepted without hesitation by all communists, there was now comment that included questioning and, in many cases, even criticism. Demands for more detailed explanations of why Khrushchev had been deposed continued, and the new Soviet leadership found itself compelled to state its case in Moscow to delegations from a number of communist parties. Some of these explanations could be taken care of during the traditional anniversary celebration of the Bolshevik Revolution in November. It is not known from the communiqués issued at various times whether the delegations were satisfied with the results of these talks.

Khrushchev had scheduled a preparatory conference of twenty-six communist

19. Issue of 17 October 1964.

parties from Eastern and Western Europe to be held at Moscow on 15 December 1964. The conference was to draw up an agenda for a world congress of representatives from the international communist movement. A high-level Chinese delegation headed by Chou En-lai attended the anniversary celebrations in the USSR during the preceding month and probably influenced the new Soviet leaders to postpone the preparatory conference until the following spring. Finally, it was scheduled definitely for 1–5 March 1965.

Only eighteen of the parties invited sent delegations, and another one sent an observer, so the gathering became merely a "consultative meeting," which meant that it could make no binding decisions. The Albanians, like the Chinese, refused to attend. Aside from them, the other East European communist parties that decided not to send any representatives were those in Romania and Yugoslavia. The communiqué[20] on the meeting, which was issued five days after it was over, for the time being and for all practical purposes dropped the idea of holding a world congress, but left open the possibility of having one sometime in the future, providing conditions changed.

The USSR under Khrushchev and his successors has been unable to supply Romania's needs in full and, thus, has not been able to respond satisfactorily with economic pressure to that country's occasional defiance. Romania's struggle for economic independence has been closely related to the process of limiting Soviet political influence. For a brief period Bucharest even suspended publication of the *World Marxist Review* in the Romanian language. When publication was resumed, the journal came out with reduced content and the specific deletion of articles that might endanger Bucharest's neutrality in the Sino-Soviet dispute[21] or contradict its position on other political and economic matters.

Certain East European leaders are, to some extent, exploiting feelings of nationalism to obtain some identification with the people. In the case of Romania, this has led to an overtly anti-Soviet attitude. On the other hand, Gierek in Poland has had to discourage the deep feelings of hostility on the part of the Polish people against Russians in general and Soviet communists in particular. His avowed patriotism and independence have become diluted in recent years.[22] Since 1967, and perhaps even before that, Bulgarian communists have been paying lip service to nationalism. The East German regime, of course, is in no position to do even that.

In all the East European countries except Bulgaria and Czechoslovakia, the people (in contrast with their rulers) for good historical reasons have been traditionally antagonistic toward the colossus in the east. The Germans fought

---

20. *Krasnaya zvezda*, 10 March 1965.

21. In an article published by *Pravda*, 19 April 1970, Ceausescu implied that Romania would not support the USSR in a war against China, since the Warsaw Pact applies only to Europe.

22. R. F. Staar, "Poland: The Price of Stability," *Current History* (March 1976), pp. 101–106, 134.

against the Russians in both world wars. The same is true of the Hungarians, even though many of them may have done so reluctantly. During the Second World War the USSR forced Romania to cede Northern Bukovina and Bessarabia under a direct threat of force. The people of Poland, steeped as they are in history, remember that Russia (both tsarist and communist) participated in all six dismemberments of their country: in 1772, 1793, 1795, 1939, and 1945. Neither have they forgotten the suppression of revolts in the nineteenth century, the mass deportations that followed the Hitler-Stalin pact, the massacre of prisoners of war in Katyn Forest, and the failure of the Red Army to assist in the 1944 Warsaw uprising against the Germans.[23] No sweeping generalization could cover isolated Albania and multinational Yugoslavia, but popular feeling in those two countries has hardly ever risen above distrust or indifference toward the Soviet Union.

At the leadership level, opposition surfaced to a limited extent at a meeting of representatives from twenty-nine communist parties from both East and West Europe during 29–30 June 1976. It had taken sixteen preliminary sessions over a period of twenty months to hammer out a document that would be acceptable to all. The final text,[24] entitled *For Peace, Security, Cooperation and Social Progress in Europe,* did not include the term "proletarian internationalism," which is understood to mean CPSU preeminence. This omission was achieved by the West European parties, with support from the Romanians and Yugoslavs. The other East Europeans did not oppose Moscow's supremacy.

Although the communist parties in many of the West European states can safely oppose Soviet domination, this certainly is not true for those in Eastern Europe. For countries like Czechoslovakia, East Germany, Hungary, and Poland, the so-called Brezhnev Doctrine remains in force. Their regimes are fully aware of the prevailing power relationships, that is, that the Soviet Union can intervene with its armed forces anywhere in the bloc if it considers that communist rule is threatened.

CONFLICTS WITHIN EASTERN EUROPE

Whatever may be their unarticulated reservations about the Soviet Union, the East European peoples have many traditional enmities among themselves. The image of East Germany is affected by the painful memories of other countries of Nazi occupation or domination during World War II. Although the communist regimes attempt to divert these feelings westward toward the Federal Republic of Germany, much of the hatred for all Germans still remains, some of it going back to before the war. It has been especially prevalent in Czechoslovakia since the

23. J. K. Zawodny, *Nothing But Honor: The Story of the Warsaw Uprising* (London and Stanford, Ca.), forthcoming in 1977.
24. Moscow radio, 30 June 1976, broadcast the full text.

Munich crisis of September 1938 and in Poland as a result of its occupation by Prussia/Germany from 1796 to 1918.

Minority Problems. The most important potential area of bloc conflict involves the Hungarians in the territory of Transylvania that was acquired by Romania. Discrimination against these people was intensified after the 1956 uprising in Hungary, when the possibility of contagion seemed imminent. Budapest has made no public effort to intercede on behalf of this minority, but behind-the-scenes efforts have been frequent. It is probable, however, that Hungarians even within the communist party feel strongly about the repression of their kinsmen across the border.

Czechoslovakia too has its Hungarian minority and is pursuing a process of integration. For example, a Slovak communist-party weekly stated that the "participation of workers and collective farmers of Hungarian nationality in the country's economic upsurge will depend on the extent to which they can master Czech and Slovak technical literature as well as on expertise in their respective fields."[25] It is noteworthy that bus lines between Czechoslovakia and Hungary were not opened until 1964 and that the bridge over the Danube between the two countries at Esztergom had not been rebuilt almost thirty years after it was destroyed at the end of the Second World War.

The best illustration of minority problems can be found in Yugoslavia, with its many nationalities. Bulgaria has persistently maintained that the majority of inhabitants in the Yugoslav federal republic of Macedonia are of Bulgarian ethnic origin. For their part, the Yugoslavs have protested Bulgaria's recent official policy of denying that there is a sizeable number of Macedonians living within its borders.[26] Officially, formal relations exist between the two countries, but they are not friendly. There are also close to one million Albanians inside Yugoslavia, and Belgrade has been trying since at least 1971 to normalize contacts with Tirana.

Internal Nationality Problems. Two of the East European countries, Czechoslovakia and Yugoslavia, are faced with the question of how to foster and preserve unity among their different ethnic groups without erasing national identities. The two states have not existed long enough to change the fundamental individualism of their minority components. The Slovaks remember their brief separate statehood during the Second World War, and even the communists are proud of the 1944 uprising against the Germans in Slovakia. After the war local autonomy was granted, but resentment flared in 1960 when the Board of Com-

---

25. *Predvoj,* 19 January 1961.

26. Postwar censuses in Bulgaria showed 500,000 Macedonians in 1946, 180,000 in 1956, down to 8,000 in 1965, and none at the end of 1975; the Zagreb *Vjesnik,* 11 January 1976, called this "statistical assimilation."

missioners, which symbolized that self-rule, was dissolved under the new "socialist" constitution.

The dismissal during 1963 of two notorious Stalinists of Slovak extraction only contributed to further demands for the restoration of autonomy. The fact that the new premier, Jozef Lenart,[27] had formerly been president of the Slovak National Council suggests that the government wished to appear to have made a concession. The powers of the National Council were increased, and this culminated in a federation on 1 January 1969. However, there has been a gradual erosion of the federal system, and this process could involve the curtailment of Slovak autonomy.

The problems in Yugoslavia are more complex. The general domestic relaxation of the late 1960s led to a revival of nationalism within the individual republics that Belgrade could not leave unchecked. Thus the latest Yugoslav constitution (1974) reemphasized the federalist nature of the state, while the nationalist-inclined party leadership in Croatia underwent a purge during 1971 – 1972. Official policy centers on the Titoist system of workers' self-management within a decentralized framework; this system allegedly permits each nationality to solve its problems and guarantee its own interests.

Nationality, however, most assuredly will play a part in the leadership succession. The fact that Tito is a Croatian may be insignificant, but this will not be the case with regard to his successor. The fact that the collective presidency includes eight members, with one from each of the federal republics and the autonomous regions,[28] indicates that the ethnic balance is important. The results of the ninth and tenth party congresses (1969 and 1974), and specifically the makeup of the new party authorities, emphasized this point again.

Conflicts Among States. The governmental system that is now in operation throughout Eastern Europe was imposed upon those countries against the wishes of the vast majority of their populations. This basic conflict between the people and their rulers exploded into riots during 1953 in Czechoslovakia and especially East Germany, and into demonstrations three years later in Poland and a simultaneous full-scale revolution in Hungary.[29] Poland again experienced riots at the end of 1970 and again during the summer of 1976 because of food prices. Other conflicts at the intrastate level have involved Yugoslavia twice and Albania once with the USSR since 1948 and 1961, respectively. These two countries broke away completely from the Soviet bloc. However, Yugoslavia has improved its relations significantly with other East European states, maintains

---

27. Lenart subsequently became the first secretary in the Communist Party of Slovakia. RFE, *Communist Party-Government Line-Up* (Munich, 22 April 1976), p. 7.

28. Listed in *ibid.*, p. 30.

29. Ferenc A. Vali, *Rift and Revolt in Hungary* (Cambridge, Mass., 1961), especially pp. 358– 380.

close economic ties within the CMEA, and supports many basic tenets of Soviet foreign policy. The most recent case in which independence is being asserted concerns Romania and dates back in its overt form only about fifteen years. But even in that instance Bucharest has attempted to make an accommodation with Moscow rather than to challenge it openly. However, the attempt to provide a socialist system in Czechoslovakia "with a human face" led to the August 1968 invasion of that country by neighboring Warsaw Pact troops. On the whole, differences in both politics and economics exist among the East European regimes themselves, affecting their relations with the Soviet Union but not threatening Moscow's preeminence.

Although intervention by Soviet armed forces crushed the revolution in Hungary, apart from the initial postrevolt terror in that country, there has been no return to the Stalinist type of government that precipitated the uprising. Kadar soon demonstrated firmly the impossibility of any alternative to the communist regime, and it seems that the population has indeed come to terms with reality.[30] This situation is reinforced by the presence of sixty thousand Soviet troops that are permanently garrisoned in Hungary. Although these forces pose a sensitive problem, Kadar has indicated openly that they will remain as long as they are needed. The same can be said of Czechoslovakia, where Husak has repeatedly thanked the USSR leadership for saving communism in that country.

No Soviet troops have been stationed in Romania since 1958, and it is perhaps because of this situation that the communist regime in Bucharest dares to exploit nationalist sentiments domestically. There has been a deliberate attempt to under-emphasize the role the Red Army played at the end of the war in establishing the present system. Compulsory study of the Russian language was discontinued in secondary school, and the Soviet names of streets in Bucharest were changed in the early 1960s. This trend reached a high point in 1964 with the publication of previously unpublished notes by Karl Marx on Romanian history of the late eighteenth and early nineteenth centuries; these notes indicted tsarist policies and accepted the Romanian claim to Bessarabia. Further, Romanian party leaders and historical journals have criticized Comintern interference in party affairs during the interwar period. Romania's right to independence and sovereignty has been asserted repeatedly.[31]

As these developments have been taking place in various East European countries, bringing some internal relaxation and even some attempts at asserting a certain degree of independence vis-a-vis the Soviet Union, one of the bloc states has remained locked in the vise of Stalinism. East Germany's position will continue to be unique because of the fact that it is part of a divided country. Honecker must counter all independent tendencies and prevent domestic relaxa-

---

30. See editorial, "Twenty Years Ago," in *Nepszabadsag*, 4 November 1976.

31. For a recent example, see *Lumea*, 2 September 1976; cited in RFE, *Situation Report*, 10 September 1976.

tion to avoid ferment and agitation for union with the much larger and wealthier Federal Republic of Germany. This has also been the reason behind his successful drive for diplomatic recognition of the German Democratic Republic as a sovereign state in its own right.

Initial agreements to establish West German trade offices in Poland, Romania, Hungary, Bulgaria, and Czechoslovakia made the East German regime uneasy. Negotiations by the Krupp combine for economic cooperation and joint enterprises in Eastern Europe certainly have political as well as economic overtones. Obviously, a growing trade with Bonn will make the other bloc partners less sensitive to the needs of Pankow. That is why East German propaganda has been stressing the danger of subversive activities by the trade missions and raising the specter of economic blackmail by the West. This campaign continues, despite the fact that the trade missions have become embassies.

On the other hand, Yugoslavia has always supported East Germany and extended de jure recognition to that regime despite the sanctions applied to West Germany under the former Hallstein Doctrine, whereby Bonn claimed to speak for all Germans and until early 1967 would not exchange ambassadors with any government recognizing the GDR. Attitudes by the bloc toward Yugoslavia have varied, depending upon the behavior of Moscow. During two periods, 1948– 1955, and 1958–1962, Tito found himself ostracized. By December 1962, however, when he visited the USSR, Khrushchev personally conceded that Yugoslavia was indeed a socialist country. The following month, a Yugoslav communist delegation traveled to East Berlin to attend another bloc party's congress for the first time since 1948.

All but one of the East European governments now accept Yugoslavia as a member of the "socialist camp," even though it does not belong formally to the Soviet bloc. Albania alone continues to denounce its communist neighbor. The reasons for this continued hostility include the fear of possible annexation and the presence of a sizeable Albanian minority in Yugoslavia whose number equals nearly two-fifths of the total population inside the borders of Albania itself. Toward the end of 1960, at the conference of eighty-one communist parties in Moscow, Enver Hoxha attacked the Soviet Union and accused it of attempting to starve Albania into submission. In the spring of the following year the USSR and Czechoslovakia stopped aid to Tirana, which over the preceding thirteen years had amounted to more than one billion rubles; by the end of the summer all bloc experts and technicians had left Albania.

At the twenty-second CPSU congress, Khrushchev openly attacked the Albanian leadership for "resorting to force and arbitrary repression."[32] Diplomatic relations between the two countries were severed in December at the instigation of Moscow. After that time Albania stopped sending representatives to any CMEA or Warsaw Pact meetings (withdrawing from the latter after the

---

32. Moscow radio, 28 October 1961.

1968 military occupation of Czechoslovakia). The other bloc countries reduced their ranking diplomatic representatives to the levels of chargé d'affaires. Only the Romanians have maintained relatively friendly relations with the Tirana regime.

Sino-Soviet Dispute. Apart from the conflicts between the USSR and individual countries within Eastern Europe, as well as among the latter states themselves, the Sino-Soviet dispute has made an impact on the bloc due to the differing attitudes toward this rift. Ideologically, of course, the communist parties of all these countries except for Albania, Romania, and Yugoslavia never waver from their support to Moscow. Besides proclaiming its neutrality, Romania has attempted to mediate the quarrel by dispatching delegations to Peking and Moscow. Bucharest is definitely against any excommunication of China and remains opposed to a world conference that might precipitate such a move. The leaders of Bulgaria, Czechoslovakia, East Germany, and Poland support the Soviet position as being correct both doctrinally and in the tactics used to handle the differences.[33]

THE LIMITS OF RELAXATION

It would seem logical that the attainment of some freedom from Soviet control throughout Eastern Europe should be connected with a loosening of the totalitarian control exercised by each regime upon the population concerned. That this is not necessarily true can be seen from the example of Albania, which has been de facto outside the bloc since the end of 1961, when the USSR severed diplomatic and party relations with that country. The leadership in Tirana continues its harsh rule and, hence, will not be treated in this section.

Among the other bloc countries, three have long delayed an internal détente for various reasons, including the fact that some of the leaders could not overcome their Stalinist background. In Czechoslovakia, the nationalism of the Slovaks and a general intellectual ferment precipitated disputes within the leadership that led to the ouster of Novotny. His successor, Dubcek, introduced reforms, but these were cut short by the 1968 Soviet-led invasion. East Germany has not experienced any relaxation to speak of and it recently ''celebrated'' the fifteenth anniversary of the Berlin Wall.[34] Domestic policy in Romania has vacillated between strict internal control and limited liberalization, with the

---

33. Speeches given at the 1969 world conference of communist parties in Moscow were broadcast over radio stations in Warsaw, 6 June 1969; East Berlin, 9 June 1969; Sofia, 10 June 1969; and Prague, 12 June 1969.

34. In addition to the Wall, a new nine-hundred-mile barrier is being constructed along the border between the two Germanys. It will have a twelve-foot high fence (extending three feet below ground), an antivehicle ditch five feet deep and fifteen feet across, and a plowed strip of soft dirt to detect footprints. The total cost is esimated at $627 million. *New York Times,* 3 October 1976.

former being the more recent, in sharp contrast to its assertions of independence within the CMEA and the Warsaw Pact.

Major differences can be seen between the two countries that played principal roles in attempts at defiance of the Soviet Union during 1956. Kadar, who was put into power in Hungary by the USSR and served its interest by betraying the government of Imre Nagy, has tried to obtain the support of the population and, by and large, has relaxed domestic conditions. Gierek, conversely, on whom so much hope was placed in Poland after December 1970, has pursued policies that have led the country (after only six years) to political stagnation and economic bankruptcy.[35]

Despite some changes, the communist regimes in Eastern Europe remain more similar than they are different. Not one of them has indicated an intention to abandon one-party rule or the centrally planned economy. Regardless of the speculation engendered by some of its behavior, even Romania will not leave the CMEA or the Warsaw Treaty Organization. It is true that the secret police are less in evidence throughout the bloc, but detailed card files on persons suspected of antiregime feelings are most certainly being maintained. Last but not least, the April 1969 ouster of Dubcek has served to remind the average citizen that change in the top leadership in Eastern Europe may come suddenly and at the instigation of the USSR.

Repressive policies do not seem to have affected the numerical strength of the various communist parties. If anything, membership has increased. Until 1969 Czechoslovakia claimed the highest proportion of party members (11.4 percent) in relation to the total population.[36] East Germany has that distinction today. In other bloc countries this proportion ranges from 5 percent to 10 percent (see table 65). Drives to increase membership alternate with purges, which are conducted periodically in connection with the exchange of party cards, so that the movement can cleanse itself.

Thus a trend has developed, beginning in Hungary and spreading throughout Eastern Europe, toward professional qualifications rather than party service as the basis for determining who shall occupy certain positions in the economy and public administration. The resulting conflict between the young, by and large nonpolitical, cadres and the old party members, who lack any training in management, is becoming intensified. The need for economic reform is closely connected with this trend and with the differing attitudes espoused by the young managerial elite and the party-apparatus workers. Most of the countries in the bloc now realize that progress cannot be achieved without a more realistic pricing system, at least some decentralization, and appropriate incentives for workers. This realization should not be confused with a relaxation of economic control,

---

35. Staar, *op. cit.* (in note 22 above).

36. During 1970, however, an exchange of party identification cards took place that led to a substantial decrease in membership. *Rude pravo,* 23 September 1970.

however, because all measures are to remain within the framework of central planning.

These developments have been accompanied by more contacts with the West, even in the case of regimes that have maintained the tightest control over their own populations. Although tourism is recognized as a major source of foreign exchange, Western visitors are still thought to represent a danger from the ideological point of view. In the opposite direction, Bulgaria, East Germany, and Romania have an almost complete ban on foreign travel by their citizens, and currency restrictions are probably the main reason why it is also difficult for Hungarians and Czechoslovaks to obtain passports.

TABLE 65

EASTERN EUROPE AND USSR, BASIC DATA, 1976

Country	Population	Communist party membership	Elections (percent of vote) (and seats)	Sino-Soviet dispute
Albania	2,469,000	101,500	99.9 (1974); all 250 Democratic front	pro-Chinese
Bulgaria	8,803,000	789,796	99.9 (1976); 272 of 400 Fatherland Front	pro-Soviet
Czechoslovakia	14,928,000	1,382,860	99.9 (1976); all 200 National front	pro-Soviet
East Germany	16,849,000	2,043,697	99.9 (1976); 127 of 500 National front	pro-Soviet
Hungary	10,603,000	754,353	99.6 (1975); all 352 Patriotic People's Front	pro-Soviet
Poland	34,383,000	2,453,000	99.4 (1976); 255 of 460 National Unity Front	pro-Soviet
Romania	21,452,000	2,577,434	99.9 (1975); all 349 Front of Socialist Unity	neutral
USSR	256,885,000	15,900,000	99.9 (1974); all 1,517 CPSU-approved	–
Yugoslavia	21,548,000	1,400,000	? (1974); all 220 Socialist Alliance	independent

SOURCE: R. F. Staar (ed.), "Introduction," *1977 Yearbook on International Communist Affairs* (Stanford, Ca., 1977).

Perhaps the threat of Western ideological "corruption" has caused the reimposition of strict controls on cultural life in Eastern Europe. Throughout the area, it seemed that the early 1960s represented the beginning of greater freedom for writers. This could be observed in Czechoslovakia, Hungary, Poland, and particularly Yugoslavia. Since that time, journals have been closed down, editorial boards have been changed, and some individuals have been indicted. The well-publicized cases of the Polish philosophy professor Leszek Kolakowski and the Yugoslav university instructor Mihajlo Mihajlov are especially pertinent;

Kolakowski has been expelled from the Polish communist party (and is now in Britain), and Mihajlov has been in and out of prison.

Although a certain degree of relaxation has taken place in Eastern Europe during the past several years, it is strictly limited and subject to sudden reversal. If developments in the Soviet Union may serve as a rough model, we should anticipate a struggle for power within the communist parties of the individual countries as soon as, or even before, the current leaders pass from the scene. It is not unlikely that one or more of these key individuals may follow in the footsteps of Khrushchev and be overthrown by a palace coup.

What Will the USSR Do? The future of intrabloc relations will depend primarily upon the new Soviet leadership after Brezhnev has been removed or retires. The present decision-making group remains essentially hard-line and even retrogressive. The invasion of Czechoslovakia carried a warning to all other East European regimes against close bilateral dealings with the Federal Republic of Germany. It is not inconceivable, however, that a new group of Soviet leaders might decide in the future to purchase a West German exit from NATO by agreeing to the same status for East Germany, that is, withdrawal from the Warsaw Pact and some form of neutralization.

If these moves materialize during the 1980s as part of a new overall European settlement, relations within the Warsaw Treaty Organization will undergo modification. A decision may be reached to separate the WTO's political functions from its military ones. The reported appointment of a civilian Soviet government official as Warsaw Pact secretary-general, a post always held before by the chief of staff (a career military officer), could represent a move in this direction. The new Foreign Ministers' Council may indeed provide the East European representatives with a greater feeling of participation in the decision-making process.

On the other hand, eventual Soviet military withdrawal from East Germany would probably necessitate strengthening the Soviet garrisons in Poland, Czechoslovakia, and Hungary. As compensation, the USSR might allow the rotation of WTO ground, air, navy, and air-defense commands among qualified senior officers from these three countries. Candidates could be selected from the graduates of the war college in Moscow. Their first deputies, however, would certainly be Soviet officers functioning as control agents. None of this will happen, however, if the new Soviet leadership consists of hard-liners.

The economies of the East European countries will probably also remain dependent to a considerable degree upon Soviet raw materials, especialy petroleum, iron ore, and cotton. Some problems within the CMEA can be solved if and when an intrabloc convertibility of currencies is implemented. The long-range viability of the CMEA, however, will require closer relations with Western Europe. Czechoslovakia, Poland, and Romania, not to mention CMEA-affiliated Yugoslavia, are already members of the General Agreement on Tariffs and Trade

(GATT). Such moves have paved the way for receiving hard-currency loans from the West. Apparently the Soviet Union has no objection to such commercial transactions and conceivably might even welcome credits for Eastern Europe if these should also bring the latest Western technology to the Soviet bloc.

Any true détente must be limited, however, due to domestic as well as external considerations. The common desire on the part of all communist regimes is to remain in power, and they do not now and never have held this position by the will of the people they rule. This, then, is the broad framework within which the communist systems operate: they cannot permit freedom of expression, and their choice of policies is limited by the ideological straitjacket of Marxism-Leninism. Perhaps the only hope for Eastern Europe must be sought in the long-range process governing the development of human society, which in fact represents communism's invincible enemy.

Selected Bibliography

Agerpres communiqué. *Statement on the Stand of the Rumanian Workers' Party.* Bucharest: Rumanian News Agency, 1964. Pp. 51.

[Albania]. *Twenty Years of Socialism in Albania.* Tirana: Naim Frasheri, 1964. Pp. 127.

―――. *Vjetari Statistikor i Republika Popullore te Shqiperise 1965−1972.* Tirana: Drejtoria e Statistikes, 1966−1973.

Albanian Party of Labor. *Geschichte der Partei der Arbeit Albaniens.* Tirana: M. L. Studien Institut, 1971. Pp. 746.

Allen, Richard V. (ed.). *1968 Yearbook on International Communist Affairs.* Stanford, Ca.: Hoover Institution Press, 1969. Pp. 1,165.

Apro, Antal. *Sotrudnichestvo stran-chlenov SEV v ekonomicheskikh organizatsii sotsialisticheskikh stran.* Moscow: Ekonomika, 1969. Pp. 110.

Balogh, Sandor. *Parlamenti es Partharcok Magyarorszagon, 1945−1947.* Budapest: Kossuth Konyvkiado, 1975. Pp. 631.

Bardhoschi, Besim, and Theodor Kareco. *The Economic and Social Development of the People's Republic of Albania during Thirty Years of People's Power.* Tirana: 8. Nentori, 1974. Pp. 247.

Bass, Robert, and Elizabeth Marbury (eds.). *The Soviet-Yugoslav Controversy, 1948−1958: A Documentary Record.* New York: Prospect Books, 1959. Pp. 225.

Benes, Edward. *Memoirs of Dr. Edward Benes.* London: Allen & Unwin, 1954. Pp. 364.

Benes, Vaclav, Robert F. Byrnes, and Nicolas Spulber. *The Second Soviet-Yugoslav Dispute: Full Text of Main Documents, April−June, 1958.* Bloomington, Indiana: University Publications, 1959. Pp. 272.

Bernov, Yu. V., and G. A. Cherneiko. *Narodnaya Respublika Bolgariya (spravochnik).* Moscow: Politizdat, 1974. Pp. 127.

Bertsch, Gary K. *Values and Community in Multinational Yugoslavia*. New York: Columbia University Press, 1976. Pp. 160.

Bidinskaya, L. (ed.). *Istoriya Bolgarskoi Kommunisticheskoi Partii*. Moscow: Gospolitizdat, 1960. Pp. 392.

Boskovic, Mirko. *Drustveno-politicki sistem Jugoslavije*. Zagreb: Naprijed, 1963. Pp. 365.

Braham, Randolph L. *Education in the Rumanian People's Republic*. Washington, D.C.: U.S. Department of Health, Education and Welfare, 1963. Pp. 229.

Brown, James F. *Bulgaria under Communist Rule*. New York: Praeger, 1970. Pp. 339.

Brzezinski, Zbigniew K. *The Soviet Bloc*. Cambridge, Mass.: Harvard University Press, 1960; rev. ed., New York: Praeger, 1961. Pp. 467.

Buch, Guenther (comp.). *Namen und Daten: Biographien wichtiger Personen der DDR*. Berlin: Dietz, 1973. Pp. 332.

[Bulgaria]. *Constitution of the People's Republic of Bulgaria*. Sofia: Foreign Languages Press, 1964. Pp. 33.

————. *Konstitutsiya na Narodna Republika Bolgariya*. Sofia: Nauka i Izkustvo, 1971. Pp. 64.

————. *Statistichesky ezhegodnik 1969*. Sofia: Gosudarstvennoe Upravlenie Informatsii, 1969. Pp. 279.

————. *Statistichesky godishnik na Narodna Republika Bolgariya, 1964–1975*. Sofia: Ministerstvo na Informatsiyata, 1965–1976.

Bulgarian Communist Party. *Directives of the Eighth Congress of the Bulgarian Communist Party for the Development of the People's Republic of Bulgaria in the Period of 1961–1980. Sofia: Foreign Languages Press, 1963. Pp. 72.*

————. *Osmi Kongres na Bulgarskata Komunisticheska Partiya (5–14 Noemuri 1962); stenografski protokol*. Sofia: Izdatelstvo na BKP, 1963. Pp. 1,064.

Bulgarska Akademia na Naukite, Institut za Istoria. *Problems of the Transition from Capitalism to Socialism in Bulgaria*. Sofia: Bulgarian Academy of Sciences, 1975. Pp. 365.

Byrnes, Robert F. (ed.). *Yugoslavia*. New York: Praeger, 1957. Pp. 488.

Bystrzhina, Ivan. *Narodnaya demokratiya v Chekhoslovakii*. Moscow: Gosyurizdat, 1961. Pp. 265.

Cerny, Jan, and Vaclav Cervenka (comps.). *Statni obcanstvi CSSR*. Prague: Orbis, 1963. Pp. 196.

Cherneiko, G. A., et al. (eds.), *Narodnaya Respublika Bolgariya*. Moscow: Nauka, 1974. Pp. 175.

Chung, Il Yung. *Legal Problems Involved in the Corfu Channel Incident*. Geneva: Droz, 1959. Pp. 287.

Ciamaga, Lucjan. *Od wspolpracy do integracji: zarys organizacji i dzialalnosci RWPG w latach 1949–1964.* Warsaw: Ksiazka i Wiedza, 1965. Pp. 250.

Clissold, Stephen (ed.). *Yugoslavia and the Soviet Union, 1939–1973: A Documentary Record.* New York: Oxford University Press, 1975. Pp. 318.

Colakovic, Rodoljub (ed.). *Pregled istorije Saveza Komunista Jugoslavije.* Belgrade: Institut za Izucavanje Radnickog Pokreta, 1963. Pp. 571.

Cretzianu, Alexandre (ed.). *Captive Rumania: A Decade of Soviet Rule.* New York: Praeger, 1956. Pp. 424.

[Czechoslovakia]. *Ceskoslovensky voensky atlas.* Prague: Nase Vojsko, 1965. Pp. 375.

———. *The Constitution of the Czechoslovak Socialist Republic.* Prague: Orbis, 1964. Pp. 70.

———. *Statisticka Rocenka CSSR, 1969–1975.* Prague: Statni Nakladatelstvi Technicke Literatury, 1969–1975.

Czimas, Michael. *Der Warschauer Pakt.* Bern: Schweizerisches Ost-Institut, 1972. Pp. 152.

Dedijer, Vladimir. *The Battle Stalin Lost: Memoirs of Yugoslavia, 1948–1953.* New York: Viking, 1971. Pp. 341.

———. *Jugoslovensko-Albanski odnosi, 1939–1948.* Belgrade: Borba, 1949. Pp. 227.

Delaney, Robert F. (ed.). *This Is Communist Hungary.* Chicago: Regnery, 1958. Pp. 260.

Dellin, L. A. D. (ed.). *Bulgaria.* New York: Praeger, 1957. Pp. 457.

Dellin, L. A. D., and Hermann Gross (eds.). *Reforms in the Soviet and East European Economies.* Lexington, Mass.: Lexington Books, 1972. Pp. 175.

Denitch, Bogdan Denis. *The Legitimation of a Revolution: the Yugoslav Case.* New Haven: Yale University Press, 1976. Pp. 254.

Devedjiev, Hristo H. *Stalinization of the Bulgarian Society, 1949–1953.* Philadelphia: Dorrance, 1975. Pp. 216.

Dilo, Jani I. *The Communist Party Leadership in Albania.* Washington, D.C.: Institute of Ethnic Studies at Georgetown University, 1961. Pp. 20.

Dimitrov, Georgi. *Georgi Dimitrov: An Outstanding Militant of the Comintern.* Sofia: Sofia-Press, 1972. Pp. 369.

Djilas, Milovan. *Conversations with Stalin.* New York: Harcourt, Brace & World, 1962. Pp. 211.

———. *The New Class.* New York: Praeger, 1957. Pp. 214.

———. *Parts of a Lifetime.* New York: Harcourt, Brace & Jovanovich, 1975. Pp. 442.

Dobrin, Bogoslav. *Bulgarian Economic Development since World War II.* New York: Praeger, 1973. Pp. 185.

Dodic, Lazar. *Historischer Rueckblick auf die Stellung Albaniens im Weltkommunismus.* Trittau/Holstein: Juergen Scherbarth, 1970. Pp. 142.

Domes, Alfred (ed.). *Ost-West Kontakte: Gefahren und Moeglichkeiten.* Bonn: Atlantic Forum, 1975. Pp. 235.

——. *Reformen und Dogmen in Osteuropa.* Cologne: Wissenschaft & Politik, 1971. Pp. 269.

Dornberg, Stefan, *Kurze Geschichte der DDR.* East Berlin: Dietz, 1964. Pp. 558.

Drachkovitch, Milorad M. *United States Aid to Yugoslavia and Poland: Analysis of a Controversy.* Washington, D.C.: American Enterprise Institute, 1963. Pp. 124.

——. (ed.). *1966 Yearbook on International Communist Affairs.* Stanford, Ca.: Hoover Institution Press, 1967. Pp. 766.

Drachkovitch, Milorad M., and Branko Lazitch (eds.). *The Comintern—Historical Highlights.* New York: Praeger, 1966. Pp. 430.

Dragnich, Alex N. *Tito's Promised Land, Yugoslavia.* New Brunswick, N.J.: Rutgers University Press, 1954. Pp. 337.

Dulles, Eleanor Lansing. *The Wall: A Tragedy in Three Acts.* Columbia: University of South Carolina Press, 1972. Pp. 105.

Durdenevskii, V. N. (ed.). *Konstitutsii evropeiskikh stran narodnoi demokratii.* Moscow: Gosyurizdat, 1954. Pp. 183.

——. *Konstitutsii zarubezhnykh sotsialisticheskikh gosudarstv.* Moscow: Gosyurizdat, 1956. Pp. 460.

Durovic, Bozidar (ed.). *Social Plan of Yugoslavia, 1976—1980.* Belgrade, Kultura, 1976. Pp. 146.

Durovic, Dragoljub (ed.). *Narodna vlast i socijalisticka demokratija, 1943—1963.* Belgrade: Mladost, 1964. Pp. 212.

Duzevic, Stipe (ed.). *Tenth Congress of the League of Communists of Yugoslavia.* Belgrade: Komunist, 1975. Pp. 210.

Dziewanowski, Marian K. *The Communist Party of Poland: An Outline of History.* 2nd ed. Cambridge, Mass.: Harvard University Press, 1976. Pp. 419.

Egorov, Yu. (ed.). *Kadar, Yanosh; Izbrannye statii i rechi (1957—1960 gody).* Moscow: Gospolitizdat, 1960. Pp. 643.

Ehlermann, Claus-Dieter, et al. *Handelspartner DDR: Innerdeutsche Wirtschaftsbeziehungen.* Baden-Baden: Nomos, 1975. Pp. 336.

Epifanov, M. P. (ed.). *15 let svobodnoi Chekhoslovakii.* Moscow: IMO, 1960. Pp. 191.

Evans, Stanley George. *A Short History of Bulgaria.* London: Lawrence & Wishart, 1960. Pp. 254.

Faddeev, N. V. *Sovet Ekonomicheskoi Vzaimopomoshchi.* 2nd ed. Moscow: Ekonomika, 1969. Pp. 263.

Farrell, R. Barry (ed.). *Political Leadership in Eastern Europe and the Soviet Union.* Chicago: Aldine, 1970. Pp. 359.

Fejto, Francois. *A History of the People's Democracies: Eastern Europe Since Stalin.* New York: Praeger, 1971. Pp. 374.

Flavien, Jean, and André Lajoinie. *L'Agriculture dans les Pays Socialistes d'Europe.* Paris: Editions Sociales, 1976. Pp. 288.

Fournial, Georges (preface). *Le proces des espions parachutes en Albanie.* Paris: Editions Sociales, 1950. Pp. 201.

Free Europe Committee, Inc. *A Chronology of Events in Albania, 1944–1952.* New York: Free Europe Press, 1955. Pp. 150.

Gabor, Robert. *Organization and Strategy of the Hungarian Workers' (Communist) Party.* New York: Free Europe Press, 1952. Pp. 84.

Galinski, Tadeusz (ed.). *Rocznik polityczny i gospodarczy 1963.* Warsaw: Panstwowe Wydawnictwo Ekonomiczne, 1963. Pp. 735.

[German Democratic Republic]. *The Constitution of the German Democratic Republic of 1968 as modified in 1974.* East Berlin: Staatsverlag der DDR, 1974. Pp. 56.

———. *Der Grundvertrag.* East Berlin: Staatsverlag der DDR, 1973. Pp. 224.

———. *Statistical Pocket Book of the German Democratic Republic, 1969–1975.* East Berlin: Central Administration for Statistics, 1969–1975.

———. *Statistisches Jahrbuch der Deutschen Demokratischen Republik, 1970–1975.* East Berlin: Staatsverlag der DDR, 1970–1975.

[Germany (Federal Republic of)]. Bundesministerium fuer gesamtdeutsche Fragen. *A bis Z.* 11th ed. Bonn: 1969. Pp. 832.

———. ———. *Der Staats-und Parteiapparat der Deutschen Demokratischen Republik.* Bonn: Bundesanstalt fuer gesamtdeutsche Aufgaben, 15 August 1976. Pp. 52.

———. ———. *SBZ von 1945 bis 1954.* 3d ed. Bonn: 1961. Pp. 324.

———. ———. *SBZ von 1955 bis 1958.* Bonn: 1961. Pp. 594.

———. ———. *SBZ von 1959–1960.* Bonn: 1964. Pp. 317.

Golan, Galia. *Reform Rule in Czechoslovakia: The Dubcek Era, 1968–1969.* Cambridge, England: Cambridge University Press, 1975. Pp. 349.

Goldman, Marshall I. *Soviet Foreign Aid.* New York: Praeger, 1967. Pp. 265.

Gomulka-Wieslaw, Wladyslaw. *Ku nowej Polsce.* Katowice: Literatura Polska, 1945. Pp. 109.

————. *Przemowienia*. 11 vols. Warsaw: Ksiazka i Wiedza, 1957–1969.

Gosciniak, Kazimierz. *Czym jest, a czym nie jest konstytucja PRL*. Warsaw: Wiedza Powszechna, 1969. Pp. 126.

Gosztony, Peter (ed.). *Zur Geschichte der europaeischen Volksarmeen*. Bonn - Bad Godesberg: Hochwacht, 1976. Pp. 270.

Gotsche, Otto. *Wahlen in der DDR*. East Berlin: Staatsrat der DDR, 1963. Pp. 59.

Gottwald, Klement. *Vojenska politika KSC*. Prague: Nase Vojsko, 1972. Pp. 428.

————. *Vybor z dila*. 2 vols. Prague: Svoboda, 1971.

Griffith, William E. (ed.). *The Soviet Empire: Expansion and Détente*. Lexington, Mass.: Heath, 1976. Pp. 417.

Groth, Alexander J. *People's Poland: Government and Politics*. San Francisco: Chandler, 1972. Pp. 155.

Grzybowski, Kazimierz. *The Socialist Commonwealth of Nations*. New Haven, Conn.: Yale University Press, 1964. Pp. 300.

Gyorgy, Andrew (ed.). *Issues of World Communism*. Princeton, N.J.: Van Nostrand, 1966. Pp. 264.

Hacker, Jens. *Deutsche unter sich: Politik mit dem Grundvertrag*. Stuttgart: Seewald, 1977. Pp. 192.

Hamm, Harry. *Albania: China's Beachhead in Europe*. London: Weidenfeld & Nicolson, 1963. Pp. 176.

Hammond, Thomas T. (ed.). *The Anatomy of Communist Takeovers*. New Haven, Conn.: Yale University Press, 1975. Pp. 664.

Heidenheimer, Arnold J. *The Governments of Germany*. 2d ed. New York: Crowell, 1966. Pp. 254.

Helmreich, Ernest C. (ed.). *Hungary*. New York: Praeger, 1957. Pp. 466.

Herrmann, Friedrich-Georg. *Der Kampf gegen Religion und Kirche in der Sowjetischen Besatzungszone Deutschlands*. Stuttgart: Quell, 1966. Pp. 142.

Herspring, Dale R. *East German Civil-Military Relations*. New York: Praeger, 1973. Pp. 256.

Hindrichs, Armin. *Die Buergerkriegsarmee: Die militanten Kampfgruppen des deutschen Kommunismus*. 2d ed. West Berlin: Arani, 1964. Pp. 174.

Hoehmann, Hans-Hermann, Michael C. Kaser, and Karl C. Thalheim (eds.). *The New Economic Systems of Eastern Europe*. Berkeley: University of California Press, 1976. Pp. 423.

Holzman, Franklyn D. *International Trade Under Communism—Politics and Economics*. New York: Basic Books, 1976. Pp. 239.

Honecker, Erich. *Reden und Aufsaetze*. East Berlin: Dietz, 1975. Pp. 552.

Horsky, Vladimir. *Prag 1968: Systemveraendervung und Systemverterteidigung*. Munich: Koesel, 1975. Pp. 534.

Hoxha, Enver. *Selected Works*. 12 vols. Tirana: 8 Nentori, 1974–1976.

Hungarian Socialist Workers' Party. *A Magyar Szocialista Munkaspart XI. Kongresszusa 1975. Marcius 17–22*. Budapest: Kossuth Konyvkiado, 1975. Pp. 247.

[Hungary]. *The Constitution of the Hungarian People's Republic*. Budapest: Office of the Parliament, 1972. Pp. 63.

————. *Statistical Pocket Book of Hungary 1969–1975*. Budapest: Statistical Publishing House, 1969–1975.

————. *Statisztikai Evkonyv 1975*. Budapest: Kozponti Statisztikai Hivatel, 1976. Pp. 493.

Ilinskii, I. P., and B. A. Strashun. *Germanskaya Demokraticheskaya Respublika: gosudarstvennyi stroi*. Moscow: IMO, 1961. Pp. 205.

Institut za Vunshna Politika. *Sotsialisticheskata vunshna politika na Narodna Republika Bolgaria, 1944–1974*. Sofia: Partizdat, 1974. Pp. 253.

Instituti i Studimeve Marksiste-Leniniste. *History of the Party of Labor of Albania*. Tirana: Naim Frasheri, 1971. Pp. 691.

International Institute for Strategic Studies. *The Military Balance 1976–1977*. London: September 1976. Pp. 111.

Ionescu, Ghita. *Communism in Rumania, 1944–1962*. London: Oxford University Press, 1964. Pp. 378.

Isusov, Mito et al. (eds.). *Problems of Transition from Capitalism to Socialism in Bulgaria*. Sofia: Academy of Sciences, 1975. Pp. 365.

Italiaander, Rolf. *Albanien: Vorposten Chinas*. Munich: Delp, 1970. Pp. 282.

Janicki, Lech. *Ustroj polityczny Niemieckiej Republiki Demokratycznej*. Poznan: Instytut Zachodni, 1964. Pp. 361.

Jowitt, Kenneth. *Revolutionary Breakthroughs and National Development: The Case of Romania, 1944–1965*. Berkeley: University of California Press, 1972. Pp. 325.

Kadar, Janos. *For a Socialist Hungary: Speeches, Articles, Interviews, 1968–1972*. Budapest: Corvina, 1974. Pp. 404.

Kaser, Michael. *Comecon: Integration Problems of the Planned Economies*. 2d ed. London: Oxford University Press, 1967. Pp. 279.

Kazantsev, N. D. (ed.). *Osnovnye zakonodatelnye akty po agrarnym preobrazovaniyam v zarubezhnykh sotsialisticheskikh stranakh*. 4th ed. Moscow: Gosyurizdat, 1958. Pp. 239.

Keefe, Eugene K. et al. *Area Handbook for Bulgaria*. Washington, D.C.: U.S. Government Printing Office, 1974. Pp. 330.

Kertesz, Stephen P. (ed.). *East-Central Europe and the World: Developments in the Post-Stalin Era*. Notre Dame, Ind.: University of Notre Dame Press, 1962. Pp. 386.

———. *The Fate of East Central Europe*. Notre Dame, Ind.: University of Notre Dame Press, 1956. Pp. 463.

Kessel, Patrick. *Les communistes albanais contre le revisionnisme: de Tito a Krouchtchev, 1942–1961: Textes et documents*. Paris: Union Generale d'editions, 1974. Pp. 426.

King, Robert R. *Minorities under Communism: Nationalities as a Source of Tension among Balkan Communist States*. Cambridge, Mass.: Harvard University Press, 1973. Pp. 351.

King, Robert R., and Robert W. Dean (eds.). *East European Perspectives on European Security and Cooperation*. New York: Praeger, 1974. Pp. 254.

Kleinheyer, Gerd, and Bernard Stasiewski (eds.). *Rechts-und Sozialstrukturen im Europaeischen Osten*. Cologne: Boehlau, 1975. Pp. 100.

Korbel, Josef. *The Communist Subversion of Czechoslovakia: 1938–1948*. Princeton, N.J.: Princeton University Press, 1959. Pp. 258.

———. *Tito's Communism*. Denver, Colo.: University of Denver Press, 1951. Pp. 368.

Kostov, Pavel, Minka Trifonova, and Mircho St. Dimitrov (eds.). *Materiali po istoriya na Bulgarskata Komunisticheska Partiya (1944–1960 g)*. Sofia: Izdatelstvo na BKP, 1961. Pp. 195.

Kovaly, Heda, and Erazim Kohak. *The Victors and the Vanquished*. New York: Horizon, 1973. Pp. 274.

Kovrig, Bennett. *The Hungarian People's Republic*. Baltimore, Md.: Johns Hopkins University Press, 1970. Pp. 206.

———. *The Myth of Liberation: East Central Europe in U.S. Diplomacy and Politics since 1941*. Baltimore, Md.: Johns Hopkins University Press, 1973. Pp. 360.

Krannhals, Hanns von. *Der Warschauer Aufstand 1944*. Frankfurt/Main: Bernard & Graefe, 1962. Pp. 445.

Krechler, Vladimir (ed.). *Prirucni slovnik k dejinam KSC*. 2 vols. Prague: Nakladatelstvi Politicke Literatury, 1964.

Krupchenko, Major General T. Ye et al. *Voennaya istoriya*. Moscow: Voenizdat, 1971. Pp. 351.

Kuhn, Heinrich (comp.). *Biographisches Handbuch der Tschechoslowakei*. Munich: Robert Lerche, 1969. No pagination.

———. *Der Kommunismus in der Tschechoslowakei*. Cologne: Wissenschaft & Politik, 1965. Pp. 304.

Kulbakin, V. D. et al. (eds.). *Istoriya Germanskoi Demokraticheskoi Respubliki.* Moscow: Nauka, 1975. Pp. 487.

Kusin, Vladimir V. *Political Grouping in the Czechoslovak Reform Movement.* New York: Columbia University Press, 1972. Pp. 224.

Lange, Klaus. *Grundzuege der albanischen Politik: Versuch einer Theorie politischer Kontinuitaet von den Anfaengen der albanischen Nationalbewegung bis heute.* Munich: Rudolf Trofenik, 1973. Pp. 129.

Lauen, Harald, *Polen nach dem Sturz Gomulkas.* Stuttgart: Seewald, 1972. Pp. 260.

Lazitch, Branko, and Milorad M. Drachkovitch. *Biographical Dictionary of the Comintern.* Stanford, Ca.: Hoover Institution Press, 1973. Pp. 458.

League of Communists of Yugoslavia. *Osmi Kongres SKJ: 7—13 Decembra 1964.* Belgrade: Kultura, 1964. Pp. 286.

————. *Yugoslavia's Way: The Program of the League of the Communists of Yugoslavia.* New York: All Nations Press, 1958. Pp. 263.

Leonhard, Wolfgang. *Child of the Revolution.* Chicago: Regnery, 1958. Pp. 447.

Lippmann, Heinz. *Honecker: Portraet eines Nachfolgers.* Cologne: Wissenschaft & Politik, 1971. Pp. 272.

Loebl, Eugen. *My Mind on Trial.* New York: Harcourt, Brace & Jovanovich, 1976. Pp. 235.

Lorenz, Lothar. *Volksrepublik Albanien.* Giessen: Aschenbach, 1974. Pp. 204.

Ludz, Peter Christian, and Johannes Kuppe. *DDR Handbuch.* Cologne: Wissenschaft & Politik, 1975. Pp. 992.

Lukovets, A. (ed.). *Narodnaya Rumyniya segodnya, 1944—1964.* Moscow: Pravda, 1964. Pp. 231.

Maihofer, Werner. *1975 Verfassungsschutz.* Bonn: Bundesinnenministerium, 1976. Pp. 155.

Maiorov, S. M. (ed.). *Vneshnyaya politika Sovetskogo Soyuza v period Otechestvennoi Voiny.* 6 vols. Moscow: Gospolitizdat, 1947—1950.

Mamatey, Victor S., and Radomir Luza. *A History of the Czechoslovak Republic, 1918—1948.* Princeton, N.J.: Princeton University Press, 1973. Pp. 534.

Mampel, Siegfried. *Die volksdemokratische Ordnung im Mitteldeutschland: Text zur verfassungsrechtlichen Situation mit einer Einleitung.* Frankfurt/Main: A. Metzner, 1963. Pp. 155.

Marmullaku, Ramadan. *Albania and the Albanians.* London: Hurst, 1975. Pp. 178.

Maziarski, Jacek et al. *The Polish Upswing 1971—75.* Warsaw: Interpress, 1975. Pp. 151.

Meier, Jens, and Johann Hawlowitsch (eds.). *Die Aussenwirtschaft Suedosteuropas.* Cologne: Wissenschaft & Politik, 1970. Pp. 181.

Meissner, Boris (ed.). *Der Warschauer Pakt: Dokumentensammlung*. Cologne: Wissenschaft & Politik, 1962. Pp. 204.

Mensonides, Louis J., and James A. Kuhlman (eds.). *American and European Security*. Leiden: Sijthoff, 1976. Pp. 190.

———. *The Future of Inter-Bloc Relations in Europe*. New York: Praeger, 1974. Pp. 214.

Mesa-Lago, Carmelo, and Carl Beck (eds.). *Comparative Socialist Systems: Essays on Politics and Economics*. Pittsburgh, Pa: University of Pittsburgh Center for International Studies, 1975. Pp. 450.

Mihajlov, Mihajlo. *Underground Notes*. Kansas City: Sheed, Andrews & McMeel, 1976. Pp. 204.

Mikolajczyk, Stanislaw. *The Rape of Poland: Pattern of Soviet Aggression*. New York: McGraw-Hill, 1948. Pp. 309.

Mineev, P. D., and V. A. Tokarev. *Yugoslaviya*. Moscow: Znanie, 1963. Pp. 48.

Mitskevich, A. V. *Gosudarstvennyi stroi Rumynskoi Narodnoi Respubliki*. Moscow: Gosyurizdat, 1957. Pp. 94.

Monat, Pawel, with John Dille. *Spy in the U.S.* New York: Harper & Row, 1962. Pp. 208.

Morozov, V. I. *Sovet Ekonomicheskoi Vzaimopomoshchi: soyuz ravnykh*. Moscow: IMO, 1964. Pp. 128.

Mueller-Roemer, Dietrich (ed.). *Die neue Verfassung der DDR*. Cologne: Wissenschaft & Politik, 1974. Pp. 112.

Mury, Gilbert. *Albanie, terre de l'homme nouveau*. Paris: Maspero, 1970. Pp. 175.

Myrdal, Jan, and Gun Kessle. *Albania Defiant*. New York: Monthly Review Press, 1976. Pp. 185.

Nikiforov, L. A. et al. (eds.). *Sotsialisticheskaya Federativnaya Respublika Yugoslaviya*. Moscow: Nauka, 1975. Pp. 180.

Nollau, Guenther. *Die Internationale: Wurzeln und Erscheinungsformen des proletarischen Internationalismus*. Cologne: Wirtshaft & Politik, 1959. Pp. 344.

Oren, Nissan. *Bulgarian Communism, 1934–1944*. New York: Columbia University Press, 1971. Pp. 293.

———. *Revolution Administered: Agrarianism and Communism in Bulgaria*. Baltimore, Md.: Johns Hopkins University Press, 1973. Pp. 204.

Orlik, I. I. *Vengerskaya Narodnaya Respublika: vneshnyaya politika i mezhdunarodnye otnosheniya*. Moscow: IMO, 1962. Pp. 87.

Orlik, I. I. et al. *Sotsialisticheskaya Respublika Rumyniia*. Moscow: Nauka, 1974. Pp. 190.

Oshavkov, Zhivko et al. (eds.). *Izgrazhdane i razvitie na sotsialisticheskoto obshchestvo v Bulgariya*. Sofia: Akademiya na Naukite, 1962. Pp. 488.

Owen, J. I. H. (ed.). *Warsaw Pact Infantry and Its Weapons*. Boulder, Colo.: Westview Press, 1976. Pp. 112.

Oxley, Andrew, Alex Pravda, and Andrew Ritchie. *Czechoslovakia: The Party and the People*. London: Penguin, 1973. Pp. 303.

Padev, Michael. *Dimitrov Wastes No Bullets*. London: Eyre & Spottiswoode, 1948. Pp. 212.

Palmer, Stephen E., and Robert R. King. *Yugoslav Communism and the Macedonian Question*. Hamden, Conn.: Archon Books, 1971. Pp. 247.

Paloczi-Horvath, George. *The Undefeated*. Boston: Little Brown, 1959. Pp. 305.

Pano, Nicholas C. *The People's Republic of Albania*. Baltimore, Md.: Johns Hopkins University Press, 1968. Pp. 185.

Peaslee, Amos J. (ed.). *Constitutions of Nations*. 4 vols.; 3d ed. The Hague: Nijhoff, 1968.

Pech, Stanley Z. *The Czech Revolution of 1948*. Chapel Hill: University of North Carolina Press, 1969. Pp. 386.

Pelikan, Jiri. *S'ils me tuent*. Paris: Grasset, 1975. Pp. 293.

Penkovskiy, Oleg. *The Penkovskiy Papers*. New York: Doubleday, 1965. Pp. 411.

Piekalkiewicz, Jaroslaw A. *Public Opinion Polling in Czechoslovakia, 1968–1969: Results and Analysis of Surveys Conducted During the Dubcek Era*. New York: Praeger, 1972. Pp. 330.

Plischke, Elmer. *Contemporary Government of Germany*. 2d ed. Boston: Houghton Mifflin, 1969. Pp. 248.

[Poland]. *Concise Statistical Yearbook of Poland 1969–1975*. Warsaw: Central Statistical Office, 1969–1975.

———. *Maly rocznik statystyczyny 1966–1970*. Warsaw: Glowny Urzad Statystyczny, 1966–1970.

———. *Organizacja Ukladu Warszawskiego, 1955–1975: Dokumenty i materialy*. Warsaw: Ksiazka i Wiedza, 1975. Pp. 288.

———. *Rocznik statystyczny 1975*. Warsaw: GUS, 1975. Pp. 642.

Polish United Workers' Party. *III Zjazd PZPR*. Warsaw: Ksiazka i Wiedza, 1959. Pp. 1,268.

———. *IV Zjazd PZPR*. Warsaw, 1964. Pp. 989.

———. *V Zjazd PZPR*. Warsaw, 1969. Pp. 1,015.

————. *VI Zjazd PZPR*. Warsaw, 1972. Pp. 318.

————. *VII s'ezd Polskoi ob'edinennoi rabochei partii, 8–12 dekabrya 1975 g*. Moscow: Politizdat, 1976. Pp. 256.

Prifti, Peter. *Albania since the Fall of Khrushchev*. Cambridge, Mass.: MIT Center for International Studies, 1970. Pp. 35.

Radio Free Europe. *Communist Party-Government Line-Up*. Munich: 7 December 1976. Pp. 32.

————. *Eastern Europe's Communist Leaders*. 5 vols. Munich, 1966.

Radvanyi, Janos. *Hungary and the Superpowers: The 1956 Revolution and Realpolitik*. Stanford, Ca.: Hoover Institution Press, 1972. Pp. 197.

Rajovic, Radosin (chief ed.). *Jugoslovenski savremenici: Ko je ko u Jugoslaviji*. Belgrade: Hronometar, 1970. Pp. 1,208.

Ratiu, Ion. *Contemporary Romania: Her Place in World Affairs*. Richmond, England: Foreign Affairs Publ. Co., 1975. Pp. 138.

Reale, Eugenio. *Nascita del Cominform*. Rome: Mondadori, 1958. Pp. 175.

Reiman, Pavel (ed.). *Dejiny Komunisticke Strany Ceskoslovenska*. Prague: Statni Nakladatelstvi Politicke Literatury, 1961. Pp. 710.

Remington, Robin A. *The Warsaw Pact: Case Studies in Conflict Resolution*. Cambridge, Mass.: MIT Press, 1973. Pp. 268.

Richert, Ernst. *Das zweite Deutschland: Ein Staat, der nicht sein darf*. Gutersloh: Mohn, 1964. Pp. 341.

Ripka, Hubert. *Eastern Europe in the Post-War World*. New York: Praeger, 1961. Pp. 266.

Roberts, Walter R. *Tito, Mihailovic and the Allies, 1941–1945*. New Brunswick, N.J.: Rutgers University Press, 1973. Pp. 406.

Robinson, William F. *The Pattern of Reform in Hungary: A Political, Economic and Cultural Analysis*. New York: Praeger, 1973. Pp. 467.

Rodionov, N. N. et al. (eds.). *Organizatsiya Varshavskago dogovora, 1955–1975*. Moscow: Politizdat, 1975. Pp. 192.

[Romania]. *Anuarul Statistic al Republicii Socialiste Romania, 1969–1976*. Bucharest: Directia Centrala de Statistica, 1969–1976.

————. *Constitution of the Socialist Republic of Rumania*. Bucharest: Meridiane, 1965. Pp. 35.

Rothschild, Joseph. *The Communist Party of Bulgaria: Origins and Development*. New York: Columbia University Press, 1959. Pp. 354.

Saikowski, Charlotte, and Leo Gruliow (eds.). *Current Soviet Policies IV: The Docu-*

mentary Record of the 22nd Congress of the Communist Party of the Soviet Union. New York: Columbia University Press, 1962. Pp. 248.

Schaefer, Henry W. *Comecon and the Politics of Integration.* New York: Praeger, 1972. Pp. 218.

Schechtman, Joseph B. *Postwar Population Transfers in Europe, 1945–1955.* Philadelphia: University of Pennsylvania Press, 1962. Pp. 417.

Sergeev, S. D., and A. F. Dobrokhotov. *Narodnaya Respublika Bolgariya: ekonomika i vneshnyaya torgovlya.* Moscow: Vneshtorgizdat, 1962. Pp. 272.

Seton-Watson, Hugh. *The East European Revolution.* New York: Praeger, 1956. Pp. 406.

Shawcross, William. *Dubcek.* New York: Simon & Schuster, 1971. Pp. 317.

Siegert, Heinz. *Bulgarian Heute: Rotes Land am Schwarzen Meer.* Vienna: Econ-Verlag, 1964. Pp. 269.

Sik, Ota. *Das kommunistische Machtsystem.* Hamburg: Hoffmann & Campe, 1976. Pp. 357.

Skendi, Stavro (ed.). *Albania.* New York: Praeger, 1956. Pp. 389.

Skilling, H. Gordon. *Czechoslovakia's Interrupted Revolution.* Princeton, N.J.: Princeton University Press, 1976. Pp. 924.

Solberg, Richard W. *God and Caesar in East Germany: The Conflicts of Church and State in East Germany Since 1945.* New York: Macmillan, 1961. Pp. 294.

Sovet Ekonomicheskoi Vzaimopomoshchi. *Statisticheskii yezhegodnik stran-chlenov SEV, 1975.* Moscow: Sekretariat SEV, 1975. Pp. 480.

Spasov, Boris, and A. Angelov. *Gosudarstvennoe pravo Narodnoi Respubliki Bolgarii.* Moscow: Inostrannaya Literatura, 1962. Pp. 607.

Staar, Richard F. *Poland, 1944–1962: The Sovietization of a Captive People.* Westport, Conn.: Greenwood Press, 1975. Pp. 318.

————— (ed.). *Aspects of Modern Communism.* Columbia: University of South Carolina Press, 1968. Pp. 416.

————— (ed.). *1969–1977 Yearbook on International Communist Affairs.* Stanford, Ca.: Hoover Institution Press, 1969–1977.

Starrels, John M., and Anita M. Mallinckrodt. *Politics in the German Democratic Republic.* New York: Praeger, 1975. Pp. 350.

Stefanov, I., and T. Lyubikov (eds.). *Natsionalnoto bogatstvo na N. R. Bolgariya.* Sofia: Nauka i Izkustvo, 1975. Pp. 293.

Stehle, Hansjakob. *Die Ostpolitik des Vatikans, 1917–1975.* Munich: Piper, 1975. Pp. 487.

Swearingen, Rodger (ed.). *Leaders of the Communist World.* New York: Free Press, 1971. Pp. 632.

Swiatkowski, Henryk (ed.). *Stosunek panstwa do kosciola w roznych krajach.* Warsaw: Ksiazka i Wiedza, 1952. Pp. 177.

Sworakowski, Witold S. *The Communist International and Its Front Organizations.* Stanford, Ca.: Hoover Institution Press, 1965. Pp. 493.

————— (ed.). *World Communism: A Handbook, 1918–1965.* Stanford, Ca.: Hoover Institution Press, 1971. Pp. 576.

Szawlowski, Richard. *The System of the International Organizations of the Communist Countries.* Leyden: Sijthoff, 1976. Pp. 322.

Taborsky, Edward. *Communism in Czechoslovakia, 1948–1960.* Princeton, N.J.: Princeton University Press, 1961. Pp. 628.

Tanev, S. *Internatsionalnata misiia na Suvetskata armiia v Bulgariia (1944–1947).* Sofia: DVI, 1971. Pp. 250.

Tang, Peter S. H. *The Twenty-second Congress of the Communist Party of the Soviet Union and Moscow-Tirana-Peking Relations.* Washington, D.C.: Research Institute on the Sino-Soviet Bloc, 1962. Pp. 141.

Thomas, John I. *Education for Communism: School and State in the People's Republic of Albania.* Stanford, Ca.: Hoover Institution Press, 1969. Pp. 131.

Thomas, Stephan. *Das Programm der SED.* Cologne: Wissenschaft & Politik, 1963. Pp. 160.

Tito, Josip Broz. *Selected Speeches and Articles, 1941–1961.* Zagreb: Naprijed, 1963. Pp. 460.

Tolkunov, L. N. (ed.). *Sotsialisticheskii lager: kratkii illyustrirovannyi politiko-ekonomicheskii spravochnik.* Moscow: Gospolitizdat, 1962. Pp. 430.

Tomala, Mieczyslaw. *Polen nach 1945.* Stuttgart: Kohlhammer, 1973. Pp. 133.

Tyagunenko, L. V. *Development of the Albanian Economy.* Washington, D.C.: U.S. Joint Publications Research Service, 1961. Pp. 75.

Unger, Peter. *Die Ursachen der politischen Unruhen in Polen im Winter 1970/71.* Berne: Herbert Lang, 1975. Pp. 287.

United Nations. *Statistical Yearbook 1975.* New York: Department of Economics and Social Affairs, 1976. Pp. 914.

[United States]. Central Intelligence Agency. *Directory of Officials of the People's Republic of Albania.* Washington, D.C., June 1974. Pp. 127.

—————. *Directory of Officials of the Bulgarian People's Republic.* Washington, D.C., September 1975. Pp. 240.

————. *Directory of Officials of the Socialist Federal Republic of Yugoslavia*. Washington, D.C., February 1976. Pp. 240.

————. *Directory of Officials of the Socialist Republic of Romania*. Washington, D.C., July 1976. Pp. 226.

————. *Directory of USSR Ministry of Defense and Armed Forces Officials*. Washington, D.C., September 1976. Pp. 82.

————. *Handbook of Economic Statistics 1976*. Washington, D.C., September 1976. Pp. 165.

————. *National Basic Intelligence Factbook*. Washington, D.C., July 1976. Pp. 230.

————. *The Soviet Economy: Performance in 1975 and Prospects for 1976*. Washington, D.C., May 1976. Pp. 30.

[United States]. Congress, House Committee on Foreign Affairs, 87th Cong., 2d sess. *Captive European Nations: Hearings*. Washington, D.C., 1962. Pp. 377.

————, House Committee on Un-American Activities, 87th Cong., 1st sess. *Who Are They?* Washington, D.C., 1957−1958. 9 parts.

————, Senate Committee on Foreign Relations, 81st Cong., 1st sess. *A Decade of American Foreign Policy*. Senate Document 123. Washington, D.C., 1950. Pp. 1,381.

————, Senate Committee on the Judiciary, 85th Cong., 1st sess. *The Church and State Under Communism*. Washington, D.C., 1964−1966. 9 vols.

————, Senate Committee on the Judiciary, 89th Cong., 2d sess. *A Study of the Anatomy of Communist Takeovers*. Washington, D.C., 1966. Pp. 70.

————, Senate Committee on the Judiciary, 85th Cong., 1st sess. *Speech of Nikita Khrushchev before a Closed Session of the XXth Congress of the Communist Party of the Soviet Union*. Washington, D.C., 1957. Pp. 66.

————, Senate Committee on the Judiciary, 87th Cong., 1st sess. *Yugoslav Communism: A Critical Study*. Washington, D.C., 1961. Pp. 387.

————, Department of Agriculture, Economic Research Service. *Eastern Europe's Agricultural Development and Trade*. Washington, D.C., 1970. Pp. 62.

————, Department of Commerce, Bureau of the Census. *Projections of the Population of the Communist Countries of Eastern Europe: 1975−2000*. Washington, D.C., 1976. Pp. 51.

————, Department of State, Bureau of Intelligence and Research. *World Strength of the Communist Party Organizations*. Washington, D.C., 1973. Pp. 182.

————, Department of State, Division of Biographic Information. *The Central Leadership of the Union of Communists of Yugoslavia, Elected at the Seventh Congress, April 22−26, 1958*. Washington, D.C., 1958. Pp. 67.

————, Department of State. *Moscow's European Satellites: A Handbook*. Washington, D.C., 1955. Pp. 52.

U.S. Office of the High Commissioner for Germany. *Soviet Zone Constitution and Electoral Law*. Washington, D.C., 1951. Pp. 107.

Uschakow, Alexander. *Der Ostmarkt im Comecon*. Baden-Baden: Nomos, 1972. Pp. 486.

————. *Der Rat fuer gegenseitige Wirtschaftshilfe*. Cologne: Wissenschaft & Politik, 1962. Pp. 199.

[USSR]. *Narodnoe khoziaistvo SSSR v 1974 g*. Moscow: Statistika, 1975. Pp. 862.

————. *Vneshnyaya torgovlya SSSR v 1975 g*. Moscow: Statistika, 1976. Pp. 316.

Vali, Ferenc A. *Rift and Revolt in Hungary: Nationalism versus Communism*. Cambridge, Mass.: Harvard University Press, 1961. Pp. 590.

Volgyes, Ivan. *The Hungarian Soviet Republic 1919: An Evaluation and a Bibliography*. Stanford, Ca.: Hoover Institution Press, 1970. Pp. 90.

Vucinich, Wayne S. (ed.). *Contemporary Yugoslavia*. Berkeley: University of California Press, 1969. Pp. 441.

Waterston, Albert. *Planning in Yugoslavia: Organization and Implementation*. Baltimore, Md.: Johns Hopkins Press, 1962. Pp. 109.

Weber, Hermann (ed.). *Die SED nach Ulbricht*. Hannover: Fackeltraeger, 1974. Pp. 135.

Weber, Hermann, and Fred Oldenburg. *25 Jahre SED: Chronik einer Partei*. Cologne: Wissenschaft & Politik, 1971. Pp. 160.

Wettig, Gerhard. *Frieden und Sicherheit in Europa*. Stuttgart: Seewald, 1975. Pp. 264.

Wiener, Friedrich. *Soldaten im Ostblock*. Munich: Lehmanns Verlag, 1972. Pp. 208.

Yugoslav Communist Party. See League of Communists of Yugoslavia.

[Yugoslavia]. *The Constitution of the Socialist Federal Republic of Yugoslavia*. Belgrade: Federal Assembly Information Service, 1974. Pp. 311.

————. *Statisticki godisnjak Jugoslavije, 1970—1975*. Belgrade: Savezni zavod za Statistiku, 1970—1975.

————. *Ustav Sotsijalisticke Federativne Republike Jugoslavije*. Belgrade: Sluzhbeni List SFRJ, 1974. Pp. 200.

Zaninovich, M. George. *The Development of Socialist Yugoslavia*. Baltimore, Md.: Johns Hopkins University Press, 1968. Pp. 182.

Zhivkov, Todor. *Selected Articles and Speeches, 1965—1975*. Moscow: Politizdat, 1975. Pp. 580..

Zinner, Paul E. *Communist Strategy and Tactics in Czechoslovakia.* New York: Praeger, 1962. Pp. 264.

Zolotarev, V. I. *Vneshnyaya torgovlya sotsialisticheskikh stran.* Moscow: Vneshtorgizdat, 1964. Pp. 390.

Index of Names